THE BEST AMERICAN COMICS CRITICISM

Fantagraphics Books

7563 Lake City Way NE
Seattle, Washington 98115

Editor Ben Schwartz
Editorial Associate Kristy Valenti
Designer Alexa Koenings
Dutch Uncle Kim Thompson
Production Paul Baresh
Interns Ian Burns, Claire Burrows, Brittany
Kusa, Jessica Lona
Associate Publisher Eric Reynolds
Publishers Gary Groth and Kim Thompson

THE BEST AMERICAN COMICS CITICISM

To receive a free full-color catalog of comics,
graphic novels, prose novels, and other fine works
of artistry, call 1-800-657-1100, or visit www.
fantagraphics.com. You may order books at our
web site or by phone.

Distributed in the U.S. by W.W. Norton and
Company, Inc. (212-354-5500)

Distributed in Canada by the Canadian Manda
Group (416-516-0911)

Distributed in the United Kingdom by
Turnaround Distribution (108-829-3009)

ISBN: 978-1-60699-148-0

First Fantagraphics Books printing: March,
2010

Printed in China

the

BEST AMERICAN COMICS CRITICISM

edited by Ben Schwartz

Table of Contents

COVER

"The Comics Critics of America" by DREW FRIEDMAN

Drew Friedman's comics and illustrations have appeared in many publications, including *Time*, *The New Yorker* and *Sluts & Slobs*. His books include *Warts and All*, *The Fun Never Stops!* and the *Old Jewish Comedians Trilogy* (which will be completed in late 2010 with *Yet Even MORE Old Jewish Comedians*). A comprehensive collection of his celebrity portraits, *Too Soon?*, will be released this year as well.

⋆ APPRAISALS ⋆

★ REVIEWS ★

★ INTERVIEWS ★

Ben Schwartz

Introduction

A year or so ago at The Grove, a mall in Los Angeles, I rode down the escalators of its three-story Barnes and Noble bookstore. Two teenage girls, 13 or 14, stood in front of me, discussing a key issue of the day:

Girl #1   Then what's a graphic novel?
Girl #2   I can't believe you don't know what a graphic novel is. A graphic
             novel is *serious*. Comics are *funny*.

Now, I by no means regard that exchange as definitive. That mall tweens debate what to call comics at all, now that is a definitive moment. How comics got to be a hot topic—to the Hot Topic crowd, and Oscar voters, Guggenheim committees, public librarians stocking comics sections, major book-review outlets, and on their own *New York Times* best-seller list—is what this book is about.

And if I may, I can't believe I don't know what to call "graphic novels." Or at least, I wish I knew a term that covered cartoon fiction, graphic non-fiction, picto-novellas, tone poetry funnies, autobiographical comics, or doodles with words. Funny or not, I just call them comics. As far as the type discussed most in this book goes, I call it literary, or "lit" comics.

This anthology covers critical writing, thinking, and a little cartooning from the years 2000–2008: specifically, September 12th, 2000 through 2008. September 12th, that's the day Pantheon released Chris Ware's *Jimmy Corrigan* and Daniel Clowes' *David Boring*. From that point on, literary comics expanded in distribution, access, and public interest to their current status.

2000-2008: I suppose there's an obvious joke to make about comics arriving as serious reading in the George W. Bush Era. Then again, President Barack Obama is a known collector of *Conan* and *Spider-Man* comics. One of our contributors, John Hodgman, attained heroic status in comics criticism circles (well, everywhere, actually) by personally challenging the President's nerd credentials at the 2009 Washington, D.C. Radio and Television Correspondents' Association dinner. The President may have most of the Washington press corps whipped, but not us.

2000-2008: If you jump from Brian Doherty's opening piece from 2001, "Comics Tragedy," to the 2008 HeroesCon New Art Comics panel moderated by "blogger" (a word we didn't have in 2000) Tom Spurgeon, and publishers Sammy Harkham and Dan Nadel, you'll see what happened. Doherty extols Ware and Clowes, but doubts that lit comics could ever supplant the superhero in the public's mind as what comics are. By 2008, Harkham and Nadel explain their decision to self-publish their non-literary art comics because, in the wake of Ware and Clowes and the lit era, publishers simply saw no market for non-lit comics.

To clarify, September 12th 2000 is a "tipping point" (another popular phrase from this era). Certainly, Clowes and Ware didn't invent the literary comic. Just as certainly, cartooning post-September 12, 2000 is not dominated by Clowes-Ware imitators. But, as another one of our contributors, the novelist Rick Moody, points out, "… it's with the advent of Chris Ware's *Jimmy Corrigan: The Smartest Kid on Earth* (2000) that comics and comic artists became unavoidable in literary circles."

True, but it wasn't obvious to everyone. The month following *Jimmy Corrigan*'s release, on October 17th, 2000, Alan Moore told Blather.net's Barry Kavanagh what he hoped to accomplish with his *League of Extraordinary Gentlemen*:

> …if you do stuff out on the margins it actually makes no difference whatsoever to the broad sweep of comic book culture. Like, *Maus* is never going to make any impact at all upon mainstream comics, because it was done outside the mainstream, it was in the margins. I just thought I'd like to do some cool stuff in the mainstream that is still progressive and forward-looking enough to actually be valid and worthwhile material but do it in the mainstream so that it can have an impact and hopefully can in some small measure go towards regenerating the currently dismal medium.

Moore wasn't putting Art Spiegelman's *Maus* down. It's a book he admires. He simply noted that it had no effect on the mainstream comics of 2000—i.e., superhero comics. And he was right. What no one, including Moore and Doherty, saw coming was a) that lit comics, once on the "margins," and profoundly shaped by *Maus*, rapidly expanded their audience and b) that what was then "mainstream," superhero comics sold in comic-book shops, was irrelevant to that expansion. That is, in 2000, lit comics looked like a luxury to the direct-sales world (i.e. comic stores), bundled along each month to the superhero shops as a speciality-within-a-speciality. Post-2000, they found their way to the rest of the world, benefiting from new distribution (D&Q via Farrar, Straus, and Giroux; Fantagraphics via W. W. Norton; and Pantheon Books, a division of Random House), and attention everywhere from *The New York Review of Books* to the Whitney Museum.

To lit comics of this era, *Maus* is everything: a model of creative ambition, length, serious of purpose, marketing, critical perception, design, and publication strategy. In *Maus*'s day, and indeed until recently, cartoonists rarely received the large advances that allow prose authors the time to complete their books. A Will Eisner, independently wealthy by the 1980s, could treat his late-career cartooning the way other retirees chose to travel or perfect a golf game. But few cartoonists had this luxury. Spiegelman's solution, publishing *Maus* serially in *RAW*, was embraced by the majority of lit cartoonists who pre-serialized their novel-length comics, usually in their own solo comics.

Today, with publishers offering sizable advances in the wake of so many mainstream lit comics successes, cartoonists are able to create major new books directly without going through serialization—although many others still find pay-as-you-go serialization a necessary (or convenient) way to work.

The first volume of the *Maus* collection debuted in 1986, the same year that DC Comics began releasing, in serialized form, Alan Moore and Dave Gibbons's *Watchmen* and Frank Miller's *Batman: The Dark Knight Returns*. Both books were huge crossover successes, especially once they were collected into book form the following year. Unlike *Maus*, which opened up the lit comics genre to general audiences, their long-term effect was to further seal off the direct-sales stores from the mainstream world.

Indeed, as of this writing, in a Comicbookresources.com interview dated September 9, 2009, Marvel editor-in-chief Joe Quesada dismisses the idea of a lit comics, or "original graphic novel," approach for Marvel at all, as a bad business model. He's right, too. Superhero fans get what they want in serialized long-running continuity. It's taken movies and animation, the true home of the superhero today, with a new talent pool's take on the genre, to creatively reconnect superheroes to mainstream audiences. Have superheroes ever looked better than in *Spider-Man 2, The Dark Knight, Iron Man, Hancock,* or *The Incredibles*?

Since 2000, lit comics have entered the real mainstream of American culture. *The New Yorker*—whose weekly circulation tops any best-selling superhero comic's monthly sales—has embraced the lit aesthetic, with frequent covers and interior illustrations by Clowes, Ware, Adrian Tomine, Seth, and Ivan Brunetti, and occasional narrative comics by Ware, Robert Crumb, and Spiegelman. Charles Burns has illustrated every cover to date for the literary magazine *The Believer*, and the libertarian magazine *Reason* has run dozens of opinion and journalism pieces by Peter Bagge in comics form. In *The New York Times*, Marjane Satrapi writes op-eds, Alison Bechdel writes reviews in comics form, and yes, Ware, Seth, and Jaime Hernandez appeared as Sunday cartoonists—a rarity in that newspaper's history. The Whitney Museum, Guggenheim Fellowships, the 2005 Masters of Comic Art show that toured nationally—as the ladies on the escalator could tell you, it's the clumsily named "graphic novel," the idea of the self-contained literary work of cartooning, that's changed the game.

September 12, 2000 reminds one of several pop-culture pivots. In 1967, *Bonnie and Clyde* validated a decade of subculture and New Wave filmmaking from the U.S. and Europe to a mass audience. In 1953, Saul Bellow's *The Adventures of Augie March* arrived, mainstreaming a generation of heated postwar New York intellectualism and *Partisan Review* café debate into one of the great novels of the 20th Century (according to James Atlas' *Bellow: A Biography*). Jackson Pollock's 1940s abstracts, the 1914 Armory Show, 1986 hip-hop crossover hits like the Beastie Boys' *Licensed to Ill* and Run-DMC's *Raising Hell*—aesthetically, they have little, no, nothing in common. Commercially, critically, they rewrote the *public perception* of what was, until that time, subculture. In the case of Ware and Clowes, 25 years of lit comics—from *American Splendor* and *Love and Rockets*—went mainstream "overnight," as well as the work of 1920s American lit comics pioneers Frank King and Harold Gray.

Since 2000, comics recall the cinema of the 1960s and '70s. New and vital works appear with surprising regularity, accompanied by a rediscovery of the medium's history, and classic works. Publishers invest money in serious biographies and histories and critical works. In the '70s, you could go into a bookstore and buy a volume of essays on genre directors like Howard Hawks or art-house masters like Federico Fellini, histories of the Marx Brothers, or a book-length interview between Alfred Hitchcock and François Truffaut (the inspiration for *Eisner/Miller*, excerpted here).

After September 12th, 2000, the greater publishing industry took notice. The appearance of Michael Chabon's best-selling, Pulitzer Prize-winning *The Amazing Adventures of Kavalier & Clay* that same September helped, too. Works by Will Eisner, Seth, Chester Brown, Lynda Barry, Satrapi, Phoebe Gloeckner, Tomine, Kim Deitch, David B., and Bechdel received hardcover releases via major publishing houses or their distributors. New audiences found comics they had never read by King, Gray, Yoshihiro Tatsumi, Milton Caniff, and E.C. Segar. Nor were they read as nostalgia. They were marketed and sold as F. Scott Fitzgerald and Ernest Hemingway are today, as classic reading. Even Charles Schulz, the most famous cartoonist of the century, has been reinvented, transformed from mass-market pop icon to his current status as postwar intellectual, on par with J. D. Salinger, Joseph Heller, Bellow, or John Updike.

Histories and biographies and critical writings of comics found a golden age of their own: David Michaelis' *Schulz and Peanuts*, R.C. Harvey's *Meanwhile…*, Gerard Jones' *Men of Tomorrow*, David Hajdu's *The 10-Cent Plague*, Bob Levin's *The Pirates and the Mouse: Disney's War Against the Counterculture*, Blake Bell's *Strange and Stranger: The Worlds of Steve Ditko*, Mark Evanier's *Kirby: King of Comics* (precursor to his long-in-the-works full biography of Kirby), Donald Phelps' *Reading the Funnies*, Douglas Wolk's *Reading Comics*, Dan Nadel's *Art Out of Time*, David Kunzle's *Rodolphe Töpffer: The Complete Comic Strips*, and the University Press of Mississippi's *Conversations With Comic Artists* series. A small industry of critical and historical journals found readers, from *The Comics Journal*'s continuing 33-year run to *Comic Art*, *The Imp*, and

TwoMorrows Publishing's line of monographs, book-length interviews, and historical magazines. Blogs like Tom Spurgeon's *The Comics Reporter* and Heidi MacDonald's *The Beat* for *Publishers Weekly* review and report on the industry, as well as sites like *Comics Comics*, *Jog the Blog*, and *Newsarama*. Bob Andelman's ongoing *A Spirited Life* blog allows him to continue researching Will Eisner after publishing his biography of the cartoonist.

The book you're about to read hopes to serve as a primer for this renaissance. If that's what it tries for, there's a few things it doesn't do. It is not a guide to the Top 10, 20, or 100 cartoon masterpieces You Need to Read. Houghton Mifflin's annual *Best American Comics* anthology and Ivan Brunetti's two-volume anthology of graphic fiction for Yale do that quite nicely.

Indeed, while the reviews reprinted here were originally intended as consumer guides, I chose them for the insight their authors bring to the medium via specific books. If some of the great works of cartooning done in the last few years aren't represented here—Joe Sacco, Burns, the Hernandez Brothers, Gary Panter, Lewis Trondheim, Ben Katchor, Brunetti, the *Kramers Ergot* scene all come to mind—it's because this editor couldn't find a great piece about them, not because they and others lack merit.

There is also the misleading title of this book to consider—*Best American Comics Criticism*. I owe the reader an apology, as several of our authors are not American. Immigration being the hot button political issue it is, I realize I risk angry protests over space that should have gone to American critics. Like so many employers with low-paying, unrewarding work, I've simply found that not many Americans actually want the job.

Context

As to the sections, three pieces set the table for us circa 2000. First is Brian Doherty's spot-on summation of the state of the art at a time when lit comics still found themselves chained to their large dumb friend, the superhero. Paul Gravett follows, explaining the mysterious gap of lit comics between 1987, the year of *Maus*, *Watchmen*, *The Dark Knight Returns*, and 2000—a key piece in understanding why comics didn't find mainstream access after 1987 and why Ware and Clowes did. Then, R. Fiore offers two essays and a reflective note for this collection from his three-decades-long running *Comics Journal* column, *Funnybook Roulette*. Fiore's "Moment of Noise" and "Make Me a Liar" look at the comics of 9/11, and how cartooning dealt with that seminal event— or didn't. Fiore's three points of view here evolve with the incredible pace of post-9/11 events, and explain perhaps why comics fared no better in clearly defining that day for us than movies, television, fiction, or theater have. As Harold Ross once said, "These are not Ho-Hum times."

History

If that's where we are, a selection of historical books follows, with a focus on something new in comics history—the impact of fans. In comics, the line between fan and professional (cartoonist, critic, publisher, archivist) is etched in sand. Compare that to movies, sports, or any other going concern dependent on fans—comics fans cross the line into professional ranks regularly. Gerard Jones' *Men of Tomorrow* excerpt, "American Boys," describes the first-wave fan base that created Superman. Specifically, Jones focuses on those tragically unsophisticated American boys from Cleveland, Jerry Siegel and Joe Shuster, who lost control of their creation in 1938 and immediately tried to redress that mistake.

Seven decades later, that redress is the subject of our excerpt from U.S. District Judge Stephen G. Larson's 2008 ruling in the Siegel v. Time-Warner copyright case, a landmark legal and historical ruling for the comics world. David Hajdu's *Ten-Cent Plague* reveals another side of fandom, a generation later, when 1950s anti-comics crusades turned fans into easily manipulated book-burners for culture-warring adults. As Hajdu's book came out, riots around the world over Danish cartoons depicting the prophet Muhammed actually caused more instant mayhem and fatalities than photos of Abu Ghraib prison torture, revealing Hajdu's history as relevant as today's headlines.

This section on fans concludes with "High Standards," excerpted from the cartoonist Seth's 2005 novella, *Wimbledon Green*. Seth's study of a classic comics collector is fiction, not academic criticism. But this excerpt, featuring the fictional comics critic Art Stern, perfectly depicts a critical epiphany, if you will, a moment that a generation of us raised on superhero comics went through upon realizing just how much this medium had to offer and how little we knew.

Appraisals

As this literary generation has come to co-opt the public perception of comics, so has its aesthetic. A reevaluation of comics as a whole goes on, and the Appraisals section captures that, starting with Will Eisner. Eisner's career stretches back to an era where he could truthfully introduce himself as the publisher who passed on Superman. His is also the name most closely associated with the term "graphic novel," mostly because he himself so closely associated himself with the term "graphic novel." Since his death in 2005, Eisner's career has been assessed and reassessed. One reason for that is Eisner no longer stands alone as our only "graphic novelist." The company he's in includes many of the artists discussed herein, from Ware and Burns to King and Satrapi. Offered here are three points of view: First, Eisner and his most accomplished student, Frank Miller discuss the impact of *A Contract With God* from their book-length interview *Eisner/Miller*, conducted by Charles Brownstein. Douglas Wolk's astute critical assessment of Eisner and Miller's creative bond follows, excerpted from his canon-challenging *Reading Comics*. Finally, Eisner's biographer Bob Andelman interviews cartoonist Howard Chaykin, an admirer of Eisner to a point, but one with a less idealized take on Eisner's self-promotion and place in comics history.

Conversely, cartoonist Steve Ditko received more widespread discussion in this period than anytime his long career, which began in 1953. British talk show host Jonathan

Ross produced and hosted *In Search of Steve Ditko* (2007), which debuted on national television in the United Kingdom. In 2008, Fantagraphics published Blake Bell's widely reviewed *Strange and Stranger: The Worlds of Steve Ditko*. Yet, in 2009, the public knows Ditko's creations better than his name, perhaps due to his refusal to be a public figure. He won't be interviewed, photographed, nor, in his ninth decade, does he work with traditional publishers or their distribution networks. Still, Ditko's imagination fuels the billion-dollar multi-media *Spider-Man* franchise, and his philosophical embrace of Ayn Rand and Objectivist philosophy give voice to his greatest post-Marvel creation, Mr. A—the basis for Rorschach in Alan Moore and Dave Gibbons' *Watchmen*. A full transcript of Alan Moore's interview with Ross opens the Ditko section. Indeed, given Rorschach's central role in *Watchmen*, the book can be fairly read as a referendum on Ditko's absolutist worldview, which Moore discusses at length. An opposite view of Ditko comes from indie comics founding father Peter Bagge, who immersed himself in Ditko's work for a rare venture of his own into the Marvel Universe. A magazine editor commissioned Bagge to write a hoped-for glowing essay on his Spider-Man experience. Instead, Bagge gave them "Spider-Man Sucks," and the editor politely asked him to air his views elsewhere. This essay eventually appeared in the 2006 print edition of *Comics Comics #2*.

The final word on Ditko, at least here, is given to critic Donald Phelps. Phelps has written on comics since the 1950s, in national magazines and in his own collections *Covering Ground* and *Reading the Funnies*, and most recently in *The Comics Journal* and *Comic Art*. Phelps' 2004 Ditko piece presents a brilliant cataloging of Ditko's expressive formal innovations, so much so you wonder if Ditko has an equal in this area outside of George Herriman.

In 2008, publisher Idea and Design Works (IDW) began the second attempt at reprinting the complete *Little Orphan Annie* by Harold Gray (the 1980s attempt faded from weak sales). Its current success could only have come in the lit era, when computer technology brought reproduction costs down so drastically and Gray can be reintroduced as actual reading, not as nostalgia or merchandise for the *Annie* musical. For my own contribution, I reprint my 2008 piece on Gray from *Bookforum*. The "graphic novel" is often sold as a modern invention. From *Little Orphan Annie*'s 1924 debut, Gray offered complex narratives, and controversial ones to be sure, which he then repackaged as hardcover books. If the ladies on the escalator debated just what "graphic novels" and "comics" are, Gray's dire tales challenged his 1920s audience's insistence on calling comics "the funnies."

Jeet Heer follows with "Drawn From Life," his groundbreaking biographical piece on Frank King, easily the most dramatically revived cartoonist of the period in the *Walt & Skeezix* series from Drawn & Quarterly. Alongside Gray, King was a central figure in the development of narrative comics. Yet, in recent years, his body of work wasn't even known to his own family, much less the reading public. In this single piece, Heer reintroduces King to a greater degree than the very private King ever allowed at the height of his own celebrity.

An equally dramatic piece of history comes from critic and cartoonist Sarah Boxer.

She presents the first serious reading of *Krazy Kat* creator George Herriman's work in light of the (relatively) recent discovery that he was Creole, not Caucasian. Why is his race so important? If only one could find an aspect of American life where race doesn't matter. The discovery has launched comics on its own "birther"-style dispute, with those who argue the 1880 census report is false and that Herriman was Caucasian. For comics history, discovering that the 20th Century's greatest prewar cartoonist—arguably the greatest—is Creole, equals Jackie Robinson's arrival in major league baseball or the final proof of Thomas Jefferson's African-American family. Boxer takes this fact and revisits Herriman with a close reading—a rarity in itself in Herriman studies—of the strip Gilbert Seldes famously called "the greatest living work of American art yet produced." With Boxer's reading, we begin to see the only non-white vision in the golden age of the comic strips.

The late John Updike, and it's still unsettling to write those words, approved our use of "Thurber's Art" a few months before his death in January 2009. In 1929, James Thurber's anti-illustration, modernist "scrawl" — "doodles," he called them — challenged the finely crafted drawings championed by his fellow *New Yorker* artists and editors working down the hall from him. At that time, *The New Yorker* staff saw itself as the rebels of the cartooning world for their sleek, sophisticated, single-panel, single-dialogue-line format.

Then Thurber's doodles came along and upped the ante on them in a way that no one's matched since. Thurber proved that a visual premise and raw emotion are all you need. That, as Ivan Brunetti has written, "The very genesis of the cartoon, paradoxically, is its own end goal." Thurber's revelation, and the critical imprimatur publishing in *The New Yorker* gave it, paved the way for a generation of Blechmans, Feiffers and Schulzes to follow and the Gary Panters and Jeffrey Browns of today. Eighty years later, his aesthetic dominates both the *New Yorker*'s single-panel artists and the most compelling of today's cutting-edge, art-comics anthologies, *Kramers Ergot*. If his writing has slipped from sight, Thurber's cartooning remains a vital force.

Updike's fellow *New Yorker* contributor, frequent cover artist Seth, flips the Thurber paradigm for us in his assessment of cult favorite John Stanley. If Thurber offered a deceptively crude line and emotionally rattling humor, Stanley—best known for his *Little Lulu* comics—offers a polished style in the deceptively simple-minded genre of kids comics. Thurber's genius was obvious from the start: Stanley...not so much. Seth excavates Stanley from the dime bins of Toronto comics shops in his *Comics Journal* piece "John Stanley's Teen Trilogy" (updated for this volume), and currently designs the *John Stanley Library* for his publisher,   Drawn & Quarterly.

Looking back, Jonathan Franzen's 2005 introduction to *The Complete Peanuts: 1957-1958* stakes out a safe high ground in the growing debate over Charles Schulz's expansive legacy. Schulz' death was a generational watershed. Not only in one of the great entertainers of the World War II generation leaving us, but also for those lit cartoonists whose work is so much more profoundly shaped by him today than that of previous generations. Schulz's minimalist art dominates newspaper gag strips out of necessity—how else could they survive today's market? Lit cartoonists embrace

Schulz out of choice. To them, he's as an artist offering an inspiring philosophical and intellectual example, unprecedented, and (for the most part) unmatched, in cartooning.

Thus, publication of David Michaelis' 2006 biography, *Schulz and Peanuts*, was understandably a highly anticipated event. Michaelis' scholarship was championed by John Updike, Bill Watterson, Chris Ware, and in the interests of full disclosure, myself. Still, the book's portrait of Schulz generated an unprecedented level of public debate over a cartoonist. Schulz' oldest son, Monte, answered *Schulz and Peanuts* with a 35,000-word rebuttal in *The Comics Journal* (joined by several critics appearing here, R.C. Harvey, R. Fiore, and Jeet Heer). *Who* Schulz was is the crux of that debate. *What* Schulz was, an artist first and foremost, is the subject of Jonathan Franzen's essay. Franzen makes an assessment he is uniquely qualified to give on Charles M. Schulz—as artist to artist.

Daniel Clowes discusses another of our key humorists, Will Elder. *MAD* magazine publisher Bill Gaines considered Elder *MAD*'s defining voice long after Elder left. He remains a primary influence on Crumb and the baby-boomer underground, and the man J. Hoberman called our "most acute chronicler of mid-20th-century American pop culture." Like Eisner and Schulz, a reassessment of Elder reveals him a full partner to Harvey Kurtzman in their work, not simply executing Kurtzman's ideas as other artists did. Between Clowes' nuanced appreciation and Gary Groth's interview with Elder later in this volume, one hopes this view will take hold.

One of the lucky breaks of this period was the founding of the only magazine to rival *The Comics Journal*, Todd Hignite's *Comic Art*. Ken Parille's extensive study of *David Boring* appeared in 2005's *Comic Art #7*. It's offered here as an example of just how many layers of thought exist in a great work of cartooning, an explication of Clowes that nearly goes panel-to-panel in showing the multiple layers of his storytelling.

Donald Phelps follows with essays, first on Lynda Barry, still strong after three decades of cartooning, and Phoebe Gloeckner, winner of a Guggenheim Fellowship and currently teaching at the prestigious University of Michigan at Ann Arbor.

When recounting that conversation I witnessed between the tweens on the escalator, I've been asked more than once, "Really? That happened?" Yes, it did, and hopefully, Phelps' look at how these two artists dealt with their teen years will make clear that, yes, the comics audience is changing drastically.

Closing out this section is Dan Nadel's "What Went Wrong With The Masters Show." Most of us who attended the show debated *who* should be in it. Nadel took a step back and asked much more. In *Art Out of Time*, his collection of overlooked, idiosyncratic cartooning talents, Nadel offers the first formal redress of the established cartooning canon in a generation. In his piece on the "Masters" show, Nadel asks "Why? Why? Why? Why?" like a toddler on his first trip to the zoo. Nadel's is an assessment of the assessment process, what we're valuing in comics, even where we should value them. His questions get to the heart of the show, its mistakes in how to use cultural institutions in pursuit of cultural respect, and the built-in biases of both the public and the show's curators.

Reviews

A happy by-product of serious literary quarters taking notice of comics is that they hire serious literary types to review them. *Bookforum* alone published David Hajdu, Timothy Hodler, Jeet Heer, and Chris Ware. Ware offers a unique perspective on David Kunzle's *Rodolphe Töpffer: The Complete Comic Strips*. Töpffer invented the form we call comics, or what he called "*histoires en estampes*," which Kunzle translates as "engraved novels," or "graphic novels." Ware is the artist most closely identified by the public with the current lit renaissance, but also one who has nearly equaled his cartooning accomplishments by editing, designing, and curating vital historical projects such as *McSweeney's* Vol. 13, *Krazy & Ignatz* series, the *Walt & Skeexiz* series, and museum shows like *Uninked*. Who better to discuss the man who invented comics than the man so often cited as reinventing them?

The New York Times also made a point of hiring important writers to review comics, including Rick Moody, Dave Eggers, John Hodgman, and in a turnaround, cartoonist Alison Bechdel, who reviewed a prose novel for them in comics form. Moody's review of David B.'s *Epileptic* for the *Times* is an excellent example of the way lit comics entered the literary world's conversation. Moody also presents French cartoonist David B.'s achievement in a specific light, as the artist who brought cartooning its first autobiographical intellectual history, or *bildungsroman*. That is, European literary tradition presented in a uniquely American medium.

Frequent *Times* contributor John Hodgman is perhaps most familiar to readers for his almanacs, as a "resident expert" on *The Daily Show*, and a series of popular television commercials. All of this, sad to say, is the type of day job needed to support his career as a comics critic. The essay that appears here concerns the seminal Jack Kirby and his Fourth World books. Inspired by the popularity of J.R.R. Tolkien's *Lord of the Rings* trilogy on 1960s college campuses, Kirby intended his Fourth World to expand comics narrative with multiple monthly titles telling one epic tale from several angles. After weak sales, DC Comics unceremoniously cancelled the line before Kirby could finish. A few years later, Eisner issued *A Contract With God*, proving Kirby correct in suspecting readers wanted more out of comics. Here, Hodgman considers Kirby's Fourth World and its lasting impact on two current epics, Eric Shanower's *Age of Bronze* and Brian K. Vaughan and Pia Guerra's *Y: The Last Man*.

R.C. Harvey's *Meanwhile...: A Biography of Milton Caniff*, remains his major contribution since 2000, but hardly his only one. Here, he discusses a subject as far removed from *Steve Canyon* as one can get, Alison Bechdel's remarkable *Fun Home*, her memoir of coming out as a lesbian and her father coming out to her about his own past. Harvey looks at Bechdel's work, but he also uses it as a case study in reviewing comics itself and the specifics of reviewing stories told in words and pictures.

In Rick Moody's review of David B., he writes "It's not at all uncommon now for readers of literature to admire Chris Ware or Julie Doucet or Joe Sacco or Joe Matt with a partisan vigor formerly reserved for renegades like Kurt Vonnegut or Richard Brautigan." By 2008, the king of partisan vigor remains Joe Matt, the comical memoirist who inspires more debate than any cartoonist not currently drawing the prophet Muhammed.

What divides readers? ? Matt barely touches the usual laundry list of culture war flashpoints (politics, religion, violence, sex). He leads an incredibly dull existence spent in rented rooms collecting rare comic strips, Pez dispensers, and pornography —masturbating (although that is never shown, thankfully). Detractors deride Matt as pointless and depressing. Supporters champion him as a brutally honest comedian (I've come around to the latter opinion, for the record). But no single critic holds all these views, which is why I'm handing Joe Matt over to the Customer Reviews department of Amazon.com. The posted reviews of Matt's *Spent* (seven, as of this writing) represent exactly the ongoing partisan vigor Moody describes, with a passion few cartoonists inspire.

This section concludes with a study of C. Spinoza's *Pacho Clokey* by the critic Nate Gruenwald. In 2001 or so, I found this booklet stuffed into a back spinner full of minicomics and Xeroxed 'zines at Los Angeles' Meltdown Comics (it's still available online from Robot Publishing). When I first saw it, I thought I had stumbled on a self-published mini-monograph by this Gruenwald, discussing a lost masterpiece, *Pacho Clokey*.

Ho, ho, ho. Instead, I found myself the victim of what I now believe a cruel hoax, a satire of the ponderous overreaching comics criticism that has come to be somewhat common in this period. If *Wimbledon Green* deflates the modern comics fan, *Pacho Clokey* does the same for us critics. I have never met the author, who chooses to remain anonymous, nor am I so inclined to meet him. I present it to you now as evidence of what the comics critic endures.

Interviews

A selection of interviews closes this volume. David Hajdu's *Bookforum* profile of Marjane Satrapi captures a cartoonist beleaguered by the racial, gender, and cultural biases only an Iranian female cartoonist would face post-9/11. As much as Frank King's revival, Satrapi's success could only come in this period. Had her books been thrown to the pre-2000 direct-sales shops, she would be nearly anonymous in the States. Instead, in a post-lit-comics world, Hajdu finds Satrapi struggling with international literary fame after presenting a welcome, non-hateful image of Iran and the Islamic world.

Darrell Epp's 12,000-word interview with Chester Brown, which runs online at his site *The Two-Fisted Man*, is excerpted here to focus on Brown's non-fiction epic, *Louis Riel* (2003). Epp brings out not only the historical sources of Riel, a 19th Century Canadian revolutionary, but the vital themes that dominate Brown's writing: politics, psychiatry, and religion. Epp offers one of the more complete discussions of not only this book, but any comics masterwork yet done.

At 55, Gary Groth still manages to hold the title of *enfant terrible* of American critics. The founding editor of *The Comics Journal* in 1976, he brought high standards and an unforgiving critical voice to a medium that before him had known mostly fanzine coverage. As a critic, Groth's style is pugnacious, to say the least. When this book was first pitched to him, he asked me if I really thought I could fill a whole book with good writing on comics (and sent me a copy of his own essay, "The Death of Criticism").   Hopefully I've convinced him…if not, I'm sure I'll read about it.

That said, no one writing on comics history researches long without going to a Groth interview. Schulz, Spiegelman, Crumb, to recent conversations with Ivan Brunetti and Frank Thorne, his interviews remain the bedrock of comics history for the last 30 years. Herein, examples of his range: Yoshihiro Tatsumi, Will Elder, and Kim Deitch. In each, Groth discusses their breakthrough moments, where these artists became the artists we know: Tatsumi's championing of *gekiga*, Elder's seminal *MAD* work, and Deitch on the works that have given him one of the great third acts in comics history.

Finally, we end on two conversations. First, at the 2005 Museum of Comic and Cartoon Art Festival (MoCCA), author Jonathan Lethem interviewed Daniel Clowes. Two remarkable contemporaries, in this meeting they realize they were also neighbors with mutual friends, managing to nearly cross paths several times in Berkeley and New York. Fortunately, a video camera was available when they finally did meet. Here then, for this literary era of cartooning, a conversation between a cartoonist fundamentally influenced by the novel and a novelist fundamentally influenced by cartooning.

And last, the New Art Comics panel from HeroesCon 2008, a public discussion moderated by blogger Tom Spurgeon of *The Comics Reporter*, featuring publisher/ cartoonists Sammy Harkham (*Kramers Ergot*) and publisher/editor/writer Dan Nadel (PictureBox, *The Ganzfeld, Art Out of Time*). Nadel and Harkham discuss a constant of the comics universe, one that perhaps brings us full circle to the era Brian Doherty describes, the futility of selling art comics to superhero fans. The unique problem they face, however, is selling *non-literary* art comics in a market dominated by the breakthrough of September 12th, 2000. I include it as a reminder that this evolving period isn't over, and the ladies on the escalator aren't finished with this topic yet. Nadel and Harkham are publishing the latest wave of American art-comics, and as far as that genre goes, it feels like 2000 again. ★

History

Brian Doherty

Comics Tragedy: Is the Superhero Invulnerable?

In the climactic moment of Michael Chabon's recent novel, *The Amazing Adventures of Kavalier & Clay*, a character dressed as a comic book superhero called The Escapist shuts down the Empire State Building by threatening to leap from its 86th floor observation deck. In Chris Ware's new graphic novel, *Jimmy Corrigan, The Smartest Kid on Earth*, a character in a generic superhero costume leaps to his death from a tall building before the shocked eyes of the eponymous protagonist.

In both works, the superhero—that absurdly evocative, ridiculously outfitted icon of Truth, Justice, and the American Way—takes a fall. Although the superhero defines the comic book form for many readers, imagining the death of the colorful avenger in tights warms the hearts of more than a few authors and fans who love comic books but hate the general disrepute in which they are held. The superhero and his fans are routinely figured as hopelessly puerile and possibly dangerous. But though those who would upgrade comics to Art or Literature may hate him, it could be that the super-

---

"Comics Tragedy" first appeared in the May 2001 print edition of *Reason* magazine.
[©2001 *Reason* magazine]

hero has given the form the energy to survive at all in a crowded and changing pop entertainment market. The superhero's decades-long dominance of the comic book—and the backlash against that fact—is a fascinating study in cultural path dependence. It also suggests how something that meets an audience need can flourish despite the contempt of the taste-making class.

Chabon's novel, which has rightly garnered much critical and commercial success, is a valentine to the struggling comic book artist, a romantic figure well known to every serious comics fan. In the 1940s, when the novel is mostly set, comic book creators were anonymous, thought of as hacks not artists, and condemned as purveyors of junk for the barely literate at best and grotesque seducers of the innocent at worst. Chabon's sweeping saga relates the life and times of two fictive superhero creators who are very loosely based on Joe Siegel and Jerry Shuster, the pair that birthed Superman, the first great comics superhero, in 1938.

Chabon portrays Josef Kavalier and Sam Clay (né Klayman) with love, respect, and a careful attention to period detail. Kavalier is an escapee from Prague who struggles to free the rest of his Jewish family from the Nazis; Clay is his American cousin. They team up to create a superhero, The Escapist, through whose stories Kavalier dreams of bringing freedom to his family and crushing the supervillainy of Hitler. They fast-talk a reluctant novelty salesman, Sheldon Anapol, into becoming a comics mogul. Anapol strikes it rich. The creators do OK for a while, too, until Anapol screws them over in a radio and movie deal, and they end up legally and artistically separated from their own creation.

Greedy corporations systematically cheating superhero artists out of their own creations is a recurring motif in every history of the comics industry. From the very beginning of the comics trade, artists and writers labored under "work for hire" contracts that gave publishers ownership of the characters and trademarks and full control over any ancillary uses and income derived from them. (This model broke down somewhat in the 1980s, when some companies finally made room for creator-owned properties.) In a representative instance of the relationship between artists and publishers, it was only in 1978 that DC Comics, the owners of the Superman copyright, finally coughed up small stipends to Siegel and Shuster—and even then only as an act of largess, not an acknowledgment of the creators' rights. (There has been a rash of recent lawsuits by comic creators trying to win back ownership of everyone from Captain America to Green Lantern to Josie and the Pussycats, though none has yet succeeded.)

One effect of that longstanding arrangement was that comics were thought of as essentially creatorless, the brainchildren not of artists with something meaningful to say but of cash-conscious companies trying to squeeze one more dime out of a child's sweaty palm. Hence, critics, when they deigned to notice comics at all, dismissed them as junk, an unlikely place for anything approaching serious artistic effort. Although plenty of fascinating and valuable work—both with superheroes and without—has appeared in comic book form, the larger critical attitude has barely changed. In percentage terms, the vast quantity of comics are certainly nonsense (though nonsense of unique vitality, because of the strangely resonant power of combined words and pictures). But unlike the novel—another form overstocked with meretricious garbage—comics as a form tend to be judged by its worst examples, not its best.

Chabon's novel is a deep and touching exploration of how such a situation alienates and demeans a creator, even of something as seemingly silly (though massively popular) as Kavalier & Clay's Escapist. By his sophisticated and detailed explorations of the inner lives of Kavalier & Clay and how they translated their experiences and obsessions into their characters, Chabon, while not writing a comic book per se, offers a large measure of dignity to the makers of that much-derided art.

It is not surprising then, that in his "Author's Note," the acclaimed writer of such highly literary novels as *The Mysteries of Pittsburgh* and *Wonder Boys* writes, "I want to acknowledge the deep debt I owe in this and everything else I've ever written to the work of the late Jack Kirby, the King of Comics." Even more than Siegel and Shuster—who at least got credit lines and a stipend—Kirby is the poster boy for the mistreated comic book genius. The co-creator of Captain America, the Fantastic Four, the X-Men, and the Hulk (and possibly many more, depending on the source), Kirby, who died in 1994, was never given full credit—much less what most would consider fair compensation—for his contribution to the field. His mythic imagination and the sheer power of his linework and composition remain unparalleled in comics.

Adult Books?

Both Chabon and Chris Ware, a cutting-edge comics *wunderkind* whose work is published by the hip independent comics company Fantagraphics, play with the superhero motif while not themselves writing "superhero" stories. That is, their stories are not set in a world of superpowered beings who wear costumes and fight crime. Rather, they are about the people who imagine such worlds. This metafictional remove may be precisely why their works can be widely accepted as artistic, as a step above comic books.

Very occasionally, comic books do connect with a more respectable audience, but usually as a one-shot phenomenon that says nothing about more general acceptance of the medium. *Maus*, the graphic novel by Art Spiegelman that won him a Pulitzer Prize in 1992, is the most successful example. An autobiographical tale of the artist's relationship with his Holocaust-survivor father, all of *Maus'* characters are drawn as animals. Spiegelman avoided the silly superhero, but embraced the second-most-popular comic art trope: the anthropomorphized animal. He seems to recognize, as other serious comic artists have, that perhaps it is the seemingly childish, but unique, iconographies of comics that give them power. (Spiegelman can't escape superheroes either: His latest project is an off-Broadway musical about a superhero creator victimized by a ruthless comics company.)

To aficionados serious about the possibilities for artistic greatness within the comic form, both the general cultural condescension toward them and the loss of 50 percent of the industry's yearly revenue during the '90s are too much to bear. (In the early '90s, some individual titles sold 1 million copies an issue—now selling 100,000 is considered a great success.) A revolution against both popular and highbrow prejudices is

The few popular titles *read* by *girls* were created primarily by *men* --

-- and if ever there was a genre *tailor-made* for *adolescent boys,* the market-winning *Superheroes* were *it.*

At that time, the *spinner rack* at my local convenience store represented the *whole world* of *comics* to me, and it was a *male-dominated world.*

HEY, KIDS COMICS

in order. Scott McCloud, the formerly obscure creator of the '80s superhero comic *Zot!*, is the firebrand of this revolution. He's garnered an audience outside comic fandom with two clever books about the history, grammar, and possibilities of comics. He writes passionately and convincingly of the uniquely evocative power of cartoon images mixed with words and placed in sequence. His books are literal demonstrations of his point: Rather than writing traditional essays on the history, theory, and practice of joining words and pictures, McCloud makes his case mostly by using cartoon images of himself speaking.

Understanding Comics (1993) became a cult-intellectual hit and put McCloud on the academic lecture circuit. In a new sequel, *Reinventing Comics*, McCloud cheerleads for a comics universe bigger and more varied than we see now. He wants more women and minorities in the field, more formal innovations, and a greater reliance on digital distribution. But first, comics creators and fans must dethrone the superhero comic, "a genre tailor-made for adolescent boys," says McCloud.

But in discussing the possibilities of a glorious, cornucopian future for comics, McCloud must address the obvious question: If comics have such unlimited potential as a serious art form, why are so damned many of them dominated by heavily muscled men (and the occasional woman) in tights engaging in fisticuffs? The standard history posits that superheroes began dominating the form because greedy businessmen saw Superman's success in the late '30s and fell over one another in the rush to cash in. After World War II, the superhero no longer conquered all opposition. Many overarching sociological reasons have been proffered by comics historians—that the need for stories of conquering heroes faded with Hitler's villainy vanquished, for instance—though none is completely convincing. Whatever the reasons, crime, Western, jungle, horror, funny animal, and teen comedy comic books did in fact become increasingly popular after the war. A thousand four-colored flowers were a-bloom, and comics had the genre diversity, if not the aesthetic maturity, that McCloud craves.

Then, in the mid-1950s, the increasing gruesomeness of the crime and horror comics raised the hackles of censors both within the government and without. Sen. Estes Kefauver, head of the Senate Judiciary Subcommittee on Juvenile Delinquency, held hearings on the "threat" posed by comics to decent society, most memorably grilling William Gaines, the head of EC Comics, whose horror line was particularly lurid. Famously, Gaines was reduced to defending a cover depicting someone brandishing a decapitated head by effectively saying, Hey, it didn't show that much dripping blood.

After those hearings, the comics industry adopted the Comics Code, an act of "self-regulation" designed to stave off actual government censorship. But the price, goes the standard history, was a high one: Comics were doomed to perpetual childishness.

In fact, mass-market comics were not, by any real evidence, on a path toward Shakespearean grandeur before the banal Code stopped such progress. See, for examples, William W. Savage Jr.'s entertaining *Commies, Cowboys and Jungle Queens*, which reprints representative examples of pre-Code comics and analyzes what they reveal of the post-war American psyche. In Savage's reading, they mostly exude anxiety about the Bomb, Soviet subversives, outsiders of various sorts, racism, and drugs. The war, spy, and jungle stories he reprints don't seem like an art form on the verge of greatness. If anything, they're just *fershlugginer* pop silliness that proves non-superhero comics can be as inane as men in tights at their dumbest. Still, for all that, these crude works have a power that fascinates middle-aged academics as much as wide-eyed kids in the candy store decades ago.

The Submerged Superhero

In the wake of the Code's adoption, goes the standard history, mainstream comics publishers played it safe by sanitizing their superheroes (Batman was rarely left alone with Robin anymore) and rarely wandering into topics and genres that might cause controversy. By the early 1970s, after Marvel comics had revamped and repopularized the superhero for a decade, that genre had established a virtual monopoly on mainstream comic books (though a lively "underground" of often drug-inspired counterculture humor existed). The superhero rules to this day, at least among comics publishers with titles that regularly sell in the tens of thousands of issues. So McCloud and others who hope for an expanded range of possibilities seem to have ample reason to gripe.

Yet in many ways, McCloud has already gotten what he wants. There are, and have been for at least 15 or 20 years, many non-superhero comics around, mostly from smaller independent presses. The problem is, hardly anyone wants to buy them. The creators and their champions tend to blame the association of comics with superheroes for that relative market failure. Certainly it doesn't help that, over the past two decades and for a variety of reasons, comics have mostly been sold only in specialty stores. Not only does such a situation tend to reinforce the idea of comic books as marginal and slightly perverse, but the shops help create a subcultural insularity among comics fans, and, as important, limits the means by which new readers once entered the world of comics. The old spinner racks that announced "Hey, Kids! Comics!" have largely disappeared from convenience stores, drug stores, and the like.

The superhero's dominance of the form goes even deeper than one might expect. Even Chris Ware's *Jimmy Corrigan* and Daniel Clowes' *David Boring*, two recent comic book "novels" published by reputable New York literary house Pantheon and intended for mature audiences, are heavily indebted to men in tights. These are serious works about enduring human concerns; they're not mere blood-and-thunder adventure tales of square-jawed, Never-Never Landers slugging it out with poorly motivated cardboard villains. Yet neither breaks entirely free of the superhero trope. If anything, they are consciously energized by it.

Jimmy Corrigan is a multi-leveled tale of four generations of American losers (three of them named Jimmy Corrigan), trapped in emotional prisons of their own making. The youngest Jimmy's life, and those of his father, grandfather, and great-grandfather, are chronicled in 380 densely designed and marvelously depressing pages, most of which appeared originally in the Chicago alternative weekly *New City* and the Fantagraphics comic book *The Acme Novelty Library*.

In a mordant four-page opening sequence, the last Jimmy Corrigan is taken by his mother to a car show where he watches the actor who stars as "Super-Man" on TV. (His costume is not the same as Clark Kent's alter ego.) The actor ends up coming home with Jimmy and his mother, and sleeping with the latter. He gives Jimmy his mask as he slips out early the next morning, before the mother wakes up. She stumbles into the kitchen, to see her young son wearing her lover's mask. "Mom!" Jimmy announces, "He said to tell you he had a real good time!" With this weird parody of the primal scene, the "Super-Man" character casts a shadow over the work, both as a symbol of Jimmy's hopeless quest for an honorable, admirable, loving, and powerful father figure, and as a source of cruel humor.

David Boring is a mysterious yet strangely funny meditation on the nature of narrative, explored through an affectless young man's obsessive search for a woman to be obsessed with. Like *Jimmy Corrigan*, *David Boring* concerns sons, lost fathers, and superheroes. Themes of the nature of narrative vs. real life unfold underneath *Boring*'s phantasmagoric events, which include murder, incest, and an offstage apocalyptic war. Yet the narrative is strangely calm, and the characters often make telling references to seeing life as a movie or story. Within the context of what the reader knows is a comic book, this could be seen as slyly welcoming the comic book within the canon of acceptable storytelling forms, as valid as a novel or movie.

The mixed figure of the father/superhero is central here, too. David Boring's father, whom he never knew, was a comic book artist. David totemically carries around a copy of the one comic by his father he owns, a *Yellow Streak Annual*. (The Yellow Streak is a costumed crime-buster.) Disconnected images from that comic-within-a-comic hint obliquely at themes in David's own story. It's as if Clowes is saying one can't read any comic book narrative without the ever-present undercurrent of the superhero concept in the reader's mind.

The superhero as a replacement for an absent or failed father also makes an appearance in Chabon's *Kavalier & Clay*. Sam Clay is brought before the Kefauver Commission to discuss the supposed link between comic books and juvenile delinquency. He is confronted with accusations that the superhero's young sidekick represents a homosexual fantasy. (The charge comes from comic books' greatest arch-enemy, psychiatrist Fredric Wertham, whose 1954 book, *Seduction of the Innocent*, is an unintentionally hilarious and lamentably long-out-of-print screed against the form.) Clay, himself gay and troubled by that fact, thinks to himself that it isn't a gay love relationship that the hero-sidekick dad represents to young comic book readers in the '40s. It is the fantasy of a healthy, loving, dedicated father-son relationship in a time—during World War II and afterwards—when American children were largely apt to lack it.

The father/superhero figure may well be part of the superhero's enduring appeal, especially among adolescent boys—an image of a heroic father figure who is not only able to leap tall buildings in a single bound, but someone to pal around with between adventures. Such a fantasy may seem unbearably childish; it is, in fact, merely human and underwrites any number of universally acclaimed novels. Literature mavens may groan, but doubtless more people worldwide have been moved by Bruce Wayne's relationship with the orphaned Dick Grayson than have been touched by Holden Caulfield's search for a responsive father figure.

Heroes Unlimited

Superheroes infect the imagination of more than just comic book artists. It's a cultural conceit that can be found in all manner of creative expression—from rock videos (such as 3 Doors Down's recent song "Kryptonite," which features aged superheroes on one last mission) to literary short stories in *The Atlantic*. ("Superassassin" by Lysley A. Tenorio, from the October 2000 issue, is about a comic-book-obsessed kid who starts to injure people in the name of justice.) The superhero motif regularly fuels big-money Hollywood summer extravaganzas, from 1978's *Superman* to 1989's *Batman* (both of which gave rise to a series of increasingly absurd and shoddy sequels) to 2000's *X-Men* to this summer's *Spider-Man*.

Last December, M. Night Shyamalan, a film director known both as a box office God and an accomplished auteur after the commercial and critical success of *The Sixth Sense*, essayed the superhero trope in a quieter way—so quiet that the movie's ad campaign sloughed over the film's main idea entirely. Shyamalan's *Unbreakable* tells a classic comic book superhero origin story: What happens to a real man when he discovers, through the intersection of a horrible accident and the intrusions of a mysterious stranger who happens to be a comic book fanatic, that he might have powers far beyond those of mortal men?

Bruce Willis, under the unwanted prodding of Samuel Jackson as the comics fan, gradually becomes a vigilante. Both the futility and glory of such acts in a brutally real world are played out in a straightforward and intelligent way. Shyamalan, like others before him, suggests there is something about obsession with comic books that can lead to twisted behavior, especially if the fan tries to apply comic book scenarios of heroism and justice to the real world.

Shyamalan uses more realistic storytelling than is typical in comic books to relate his superhero tale. There is more focus on the hero's relationship with his family, more concern for the real-world legal and ethical implications of a vigilante beating up criminals. Playing with how the superhero idea might work in something more closely resembling our real world has been common even in comic books since the mid-'80s, when it was done to spectacular effect by Alan Moore and Dave Gibbons in the DC series *Watchmen*. Even Scott McCloud praised *Watchmen* for "breaking nearly every one of the tried and true rules." But however sophisticated an adventure story *Watchmen* was, in terms of audience expansion it was a dead-end. "Sophisticated" superhero comics remain insular works whose resonance relies greatly on a previous understanding and interest in the comic book medium. One most enjoys seeing conventions subverted when one understands the conventions. Indeed, this may help explain why *Unbreakable* didn't match the popular success of *The Sixth Sense*. *The Sixth Sense* played with the conventions of horror and psychological thrillers and was hence far more accessible to moviegoers.

This doesn't mean work dedicated to playing with aesthetic convention is necessarily aesthetically inferior—great novels from *Don Quixote* to *Madame Bovary*, for instance, do precisely this. Different communities of readers always understand things differently; comic book fans will appreciate *Kavalier & Clay* and *Unbreakable* (and *Jimmy Corrigan* and *David Boring*) in ways that non-fans won't. Those acquainted with or obsessive about details of a form's history will always see things others won't. And artists of serious comic book stories, like Ware and Clowes, are probably inspired to use the superhero as a postmodernist metacommentary on their own form—and also because, as comic artists, they doubtless have that idea infecting their imagination.

Which suggests the real reason comics haven't yet escaped the artistic ghetto that McCloud decries: Anyone who even aspires to being a comics artist in an American context will by necessity have been steeped in the superhero motif. Ultimately, McCloud's argument about superhero dominance is similar to what economists call a path-dependence argument, by which "inferior" products are believed to sometimes wrongly rise to dominance in a given market. McCloud grants that the dominance of comics by a single genre might have been inevitable, but stresses that it didn't have to be the superhero genre. That, he contends, is simply a lamentable historical accident. This line of thinking suggests that the triumph of the superhero over, say, the funny animal comic, is not so different from the way QWERTY keyboards or VHS videotapes won out over superior alternatives.

But there is something suspicious about using path-dependence arguments to say that things ought to be different than they are, and are only that way because of a circumstantial lock-in of a supposedly inferior product. As economists Stan Liebowitz and Stephen E. Margolis have shown, claims that a dominant product does not deserve its market position are often self-interested and fail to appreciate the ways in which a castigated product serves consumers. For instance, the source of the idea that the QWERTY keyboard is inefficient was the creator of a rival keyboard (who used spurious studies to bolster his case); QWERTY critics also routinely fail to ask whether the relative benefits of switching to a new keyboard are worth the effort.

So it is with the superhero comic. Indeed, in this case, one might add something more to the mix: Far from choking off the vitality of the comic book, superheroes may be precisely that which has kept the form alive, albeit on a smaller scale than decades ago. Look at the fate of another form of pop entertainment that, along with comics, had a huge following in the 1940s: radio drama. There was no one unique thing that it provided better than any other art form, and it died.

Though McCloud tries to deny it, the serialized superhero comic provides something unique, something that other art forms can't quite match, even when they try to. (Few familiar with both the comic book and film *Batman* would disagree that the former is more dramatically satisfying.) As one of the publishers in *Kavalier & Clay* puts it while looking at Kavalier's crazily eye-catching art, "Half bad is maybe better than beauteeful." Such an inexacting but heartfelt standard may be key to superhero comics' unique value and long-lasting appeal: They are attractive and inspire passion because they provide a structurally different kind of aesthetic/storytelling experience than other, more respected storytelling forms.

The sort of non-superhero comics for which McCloud cheerleads do exist, and can be found in most comic shops (and even in many megabookstores). The market has made room for them. It's just that no one seems to want them on the same scale they want *Spider-Man* or *Superman*. Despite a solid audience, no huge popular fan base is crying, "Make Mine McCloud!"

The Enduring Superman

Both Michael Chabon and Chris Ware showcase the image of the superhero falling to his death. Are they wishing for the death of the icon that so dominates the form they clearly love? Or are they infusing the superhero with a new power, to move adult readers' hearts and minds? At the very least, Chabon has proven that comic books can inspire what virtually anyone would grant is true art, an imaginative reflection of deep human concerns and experiences.

Since its birth, the superhero has been seen as a symbol of America's innocent vitality, of its barely repressed sexual confusion, and of its incipient fascism. It has been the vehicle for *sui generis* American geniuses such as Jack "King" Kirby and for numerous anonymous hacks. The superhero comic can be incandescently great and grimily idiotic, but even at its worst, it playfully evokes a wonder-inducing sense of fantastic human invention, of a fertile reworking of eternally appealing myths of beings with powers far beyond those of mortal men.

Chabon's novel and other works discussed here show that there is a rich vein of pathos and insight to be mined from the gold first discovered by Siegel and Shuster. As an American icon, the comic book superhero shares some of the legendary values of the nation of its birth—he is brash, energetic, wildly imaginative, unbound by Old World standards of propriety and gentility.

It will probably turn out, to the consternation of McCloud, that comics, even if they are freed from the shackles of superherodom, will remain a niche market, a weird little sub-eddy in the ocean of popular entertainment. As the very necessity of a book called *Understanding Comics* admits, many perfectly literate adults just can't grasp comics storytelling—they literally don't know how to read them, aren't versed in the grammar. There may be no explosive renaissance ahead for comics; they are unlikely to dominate cultural production the way the novel did in the 19th century or film did in the 20th. But artists like Ware and Clowes will continue to do fascinating work, and their audiences will find it, even if it doesn't conquer all. And the caped shadow of the superhero will doubtless, in various ways, continue hanging over comics for a long time to come. ★

Brian Doherty is a senior editor at *Reason* magazine and author of the books *This is Burning Man*, *Radicals for Capitalism: A Freewheeling History of the Modern American Libertarian Movement*, and *Gun Control on Trial*. He lives in Los Angeles and has been a devoted Friend of Comics since 1975.

Paul Gravett

Graphic Novels: Can You Hear The Trucks?

Do you ever get a sense of déjà vu? Recently I've been getting the eerie feeling that I've gone back through the Time Tunnel and it's the late Eighties all over again. Some of you will remember the buzz starting in 1987 surrounding the so-called "Big Three" breakout comics: Miller's *Batman: The Dark Knight Returns*, Moore and Gibbons' *Watchmen* and Spiegelman's *Maus*. From style mags to Sunday papers, from 'yoof' TV to highbrow arts programs, it seemed the media couldn't get enough of these alien artefacts, "graphic novels." Here supposedly was proof that comics "had finally grown up." Big-time publishers led by Penguin Books lurched into the market and major bookchains devoted shelf space and window displays to the flurry of titles.

I remember the mood of optimism that comics were poised to cross over and finally enjoy critical acclaim and commercial success. Sound familiar? Currently, we're witnessing another promising period for graphic novels, so to avoid the boom-bust cycle repeating, I thought it might be instructive to look back and examine why all those hopes in 1987 seemed to go pear-shaped by the early Nineties.

There were a great many contributing factors to the backlash and collapse. A glut of mediocre product drowned all but a few of the strong, original works that came on the heels of the "Big Three." A hasty cobbling together of a few serialized comic books does not necessarily make a worthwhile graphic novel. For every *Spiral Cage*, *Love and Rockets* or *Sandman* there came a horde of embarrassments. How many more grim, psychotic remakes of superheroes could anyone stomach?

Then there was the disappointment when some of Moore and Miller's much-anticipated, over-hyped follow-ups, like *Batman: The Killing Joke* or *Give Me Liberty*, came nowhere near the lofty standards they had set for themselves. And why did any publisher think that Lenny Henry, Doris Lessing or Ramsey Campbell were bound to write brilliant graphic novel bestsellers? On top of these errors in judgement, the tragic finality of Moore and Sienkiewicz's *Big Numbers* collapsing after only two published issues in 1990 could be seen as a symbolic final nail. Was it too ambitious even for two such towering talents to realise the rich potential of this medium?

Another problem was pretension, either way too much of it or not nearly enough. In an attempt to be taken more seriously, some writers and artists tried too hard and became preachy, overearnest or dull. That only served to reinforce the view of some cultural critics who insisted that comics should stick to being "rock'n'roll," and stay wild, rebellious and permanently pubescent. As one commented, "Do comics rot your brain? Only if they're done properly."

Plenty of industry pros, old and young, agreed. They poo-pooed their peers' poncey aspirations and simply pumped out more of the same, only nastier. Pretension and underachievement together bred disenchantment among the new buying public and the media. Only a few years after singing their praises, in 1991 fickle *Time Out* whined "If adult comics are the wave of the future, how come nobody's reading them?"

More factors conspired, from the chilling effects of the economic downturn and customs seizures and shop raids of adult comics to the saturating presence of Tim Burton's Batman movies and high levels of theft of overpriced graphic novels from bookstores. It's also worth remembering that of the "Big Three," two featured superheroes, an instant turn-off to many non-comics readers, while *Maus* came to be hailed for its treatment of the Holocaust almost in spite of it being in comics form.

Perhaps the most fundamental problems were the exaggerated expectations of everyone involved. The seismic scale of this cultural shift could never happen overnight. People tend to have a rather rose-tinted view of comics in France or Japan, forgetting that *bande dessinée* and *manga* took many years, at least since the Sixties, before they gained an adult audience and a measure of respect.

But maybe here this change in attitude might start to take hold within a generation. Now that it's fifteen years later, almost a generation, some truly formidable graphic novels have been completed: *Palestine*, *Preacher*, *Cerebus*, *Bone*, *From Hell*, *Locas*, *Palomar*, *Jimmy Corrigan*, *Epileptic*, *Cages*, for starters. A library of undeniable quality is amassing. Patience is a virtue, because great graphic novels need time to come to fruition and more are slowly ripening. Chris Ware is laboring on two epics serialized in weekly pages. Crumb is illuminating the Book of Genesis. We've entered an era of large, doorstop compilations like *Lost Girls*, *Black Hole*, *Buddy Does Seattle*, *La Perdida* and more meaty reads you can't whiz through on the toilet.

It's different from 1987 in other ways now. There may be yet another Bat-film looming, but the public is starting to discriminate between movies from superhero comics and movies from graphic novels like *American Splendor*, *Road to Perdition*, *Ghost World* or *Sin City*. It is also discovering that the originals these come from are frequently far superior. Then there's manga, a whole culture hooking new readers. And the internet, bypassing journos to spread info and opinions as never before.

I'm sure mistakes will be made, bad books published, great books stupidly slammed or ignored, and anti-comics prejudices will rear up (manga have already been the targets). But it's not 1987 and we won't get fooled again, because lots of people, writers, artists, editors and readers, are in this for the long haul, for however long it takes for the graphic novel to achieve its possibilities. About that vision, pioneer of the form Will Eisner once remarked, "I put up a tollbooth out in a field and I've been waiting for a highway to come through. And now I can hear the trucks."

Actually, Will, there's a massive, never-ending, unstoppable convoy of trucks roaring along that route you trailblazed. And maybe this time round, we might just get there. ★

Nicknamed "The Man at the Crossroads" by Eddie Campbell, **Paul Gravett** is an English writer, lecturer, curator and reviewer for *The Times Literary Supplement*, *Art Review*, *The Independent*, and others (www.paulgravett.com). He curates comic art exhibitions and directs Comica, the London International Comics Festival. www.comicafestival.com With Peter Stanbury he co-edited *Escape*, the seminal British comics magazine (1983–89) and graphic-novel label, relaunched as (www.escape-books.com in 2009. His books include *Manga: 60 Years of Japanese Comics* (2004), *Graphic Novels: Stories to Change Your Life* (2005), *Great British Comics* (2006), *The Mammoth Book of Best Crime Comics* (2008) and *Holy Sh*t!: The World's Weirdest Comic Books* (2008).

R. Fiore

9/11 Comics

A Moment of Noise

The Sept. 11 attacks on the World Trade Center and the Pentagon hit the United States in a vulnerable spot—right in the fantasies. Hit particularly hard was the religion of safety, the idea that having eliminated 90 percent of the dangers of life it ought to be possible to eliminate the other ten. Paradoxes abound. The safety obsession results not in a feeling of security but an irrational fear of minuscule risks. In a population as large as ours, even terrorism on this scale doesn't greatly increase the danger to any given individual, but it destroys the illusion. You have to wonder how much blood and treasure is going to be expended trying to recapture what was illusory to begin with. Paradoxically, al Qaeda's great successes (the barracks in Saudi Arabia, the U.S.S. Cole, Sept. 11) all exploited our assumption that no one would dare attack us.

The second casualty was the belief that the whole world saw us as we saw ourselves; as the heroes of history. The national reaction was—how does one put this

"Moment of Noise" and "Make Me a Liar" first appeared as *Funnybook Roulette* columns in *The Comics Journal* #247 (October 2002) and *The Comics Journal* #259 (April 2004) respectively.

politely?—not exactly a display of the spirit of the Blitz. A wave of these-colors-don't-run jingoism, however distasteful, would have at least been understandable. Instead, the whole country seemed to melt into a puddle of warm, sticky goo. America was like a child whose mother told him he couldn't live in the house anymore—hurt, confused and insecure. You would have thought the flag was a talisman against evil. You wanted to ask people why, if they thought they had no enemies, they were paying $330 billion a year on defense. (On the other hand, when the Usurper announced the formation of his Office of Homeland Security, the first question in my mind was, "So what is the Department of Defense for now?") A nation taught by media culture that the only place to keep your heart is on your sleeve was faced with a situation that demanded stoicism and acceptance of risk, and didn't know where to find them. The Ray Charles version of "America the Beautiful" became a ballad of national self-pity. The point is not that America deserved to be bombed because it bombs others. The point is that any country that dishes out the ordnance as freely as ours should have been better prepared to take it if that was what fate decreed.

Fortunately, among our many blessings we can count a wide margin for error. Though difficult, the problems presented by terrorism are simple, which, given the state of our leadership, is all to the good. (In other news, the president reiterated his respect for Islam and desire for good relations with the Arab world, and expressed the hope that he might one day have a chance to eat at this "Allahu Snackbar" they're always talking about.) The terrorists are gambling that they can strike the United States without the United States effectively striking back, and the United States has to demonstrate that this is an error. Unlike the war against fascism or the Cold War, terrorism presents no substantive ideological challenge. It's like getting bitten by a rat out of the dustbin of history. There is no dissent worth mentioning because nobody is in favor of having buildings dropped on top of them. Appeasement is out of the question because you can't appease an enemy that neither identifies itself nor makes demands. The politics of oil dictate that finesse, relatively speaking, must be the order of the day. The main concern at the beginning was whether the enemy could sustain the offensive, and so far they haven't been able to. Put it this way: If Andrew Golota came up to you once a day and gave you a punch in the nuts, you'd have a very serious problem. If he does it once a year, you still have a problem, but it's not going to change your life.

So speaketh the armchair general. You're here to read about comics. God knows why. This was an event that belonged to the camera and the camcorder. In order to represent something on paper an artist has to be able to comprehend it, and the destruction was incomprehensible. All a camera has to do is expose the film. Watching the collision from across the country (and never have I been so glad to live in a city without landmarks), I was reminded of the Challenger explosion: First you looked for some reason to think it wasn't as bad as it looked, and then you realized it was exactly as bad as it looked. The initial collision brought to mind a couple of lines from an E.E. Cummings poem about a suicide: "A finger pulls a trigger/A bird flies into a mirror." But the tapes said it better.

I have before me a copy of the Sept. 24, 2001 issue of *The New Yorker* that illustrates the point beautifully. First we have a suite of photos of the towers as they were before the attack, which remind us once again how thoroughly they ruined the proportions of the Manhattan skyline. While I want to emphasize that this has no bearing on the calamity whatsoever, and is in no way a consolation, I note for the record that the World Trade Center was the second biggest mistake New York City ever made (number one being the destruction of Penn Station). Then we have a half a dozen photos that tell you more about the horror and chaos of that day in Manhattan than all the comics under discussion here, and for that matter all the verbiage that surrounds them in the magazine. Where the cartoonist in his depiction of the police and firemen attempts to convey his own gratitude and admiration—not an unworthy goal but doomed to cliché—the photographs show what inspires that admiration: skilled people in extremis, falling back on their training and experience to cope with an overwhelming situation.[1]

All this notwithstanding, all of comicdom—mainstream, alternative and polemical—decided that the best response to the situation was to throw comics at it. The critic is well aware that if anything ought to be review-proof, it's a benefit for widows and orphans. All concerned seem to have put out their best efforts; there's almost none of the offhand or slapdash one expects in benefit comics. In a way, repeating the commonplace in a situation where cleverness would be tantamount to tastelessness is an aesthetic sacrifice.

No one threw comics at the situation as prolifically as DC, with its anthology *9-11: September 11, 2001* Vols. 1-2 and the mini-major consortium of Chaos, Image and Dark Horse with theirs, *9-11: Artists Respond* Vol. 1. These two are so similar in format, length, style and tone that it seems pointless to differentiate between them, and between them they define the parameters of their short-lived genre.

Most of the comics therein can be divided into allegories and earthquake stories. I suppose the East-Coast equivalent would be blackout stories, but the difference is that in a blackout the same thing happens to everyone, whereas in an earthquake, as in the 9/11 attacks, the same thing appears to be happening to everybody but the brunt of the disaster is borne only by a few. The main reason for listening to an earthquake story is to find out when the other fellow's mouth stops moving, so you can tell your own. Having forsworn negative aesthetic judgments, I merely relate what I learned from 300+ pages of comics:

---

[1] Incidentally, since when did anyone have anything against firemen? ("Them and their goddamned helmets, saving children from burning buildings—who the hell do they think they are?") As for police, it would be well to remember that this society in effect sends them into collapsing buildings every day of the year. The police department is the only institution in society that doesn't have the option of defaulting on its obligations. Whatever trash society fills to clean up, whatever social pathology it fails to resolve, the police have to deal with, on some level, often using tools utterly unsuited to the job. So long as the people think that all they have to do to absolve themselves of social responsibility is to put a political boundary between themselves and trouble, then all this love and admiration for the police is a lot of bushwa.

★ Children of martyred police and firemen have eyes about a third the size of their heads. The knowledge that their fathers died as heroes will be a powerful consolation for their catastrophic loss.

★ Superman thinks police and firemen are the real heroes. Also, Superman's dog Krypto thinks that police and fire dogs are the real heroes.

★ I'll bet Superman's dog Krypto gets to be the alpha dog in any pack he joins.

Sikhs are the nice Muslims.

★ Jerry Falwell is a real asshole.

★ New York, New York, it's a hell of a town.

★ All our petty little pursuits and complaints look pretty gosh-darn trivial in the light of an event like this.

★ Having 3,000 people crushed to death not far from where you are really gets on your nerves.

★ There is nothing particularly funny about peace, love and understanding.

★ Any group of ordinary New Yorkers, after a brief intemperate venting of their personal anger, will arrive at the proper rational and tolerant view of things.

★ The vicinity of any great national tragedy will soon become infested with eagles.

★ The sadness and dismay of homeless people over the incident is the most poignant sadness and dismay of all.

★ This is the greatest country in the world, except it's kind of shitty what we did to the Indians.

★ The teepee Indians, that is, not the dot-head Indians.

★ If you have absolutely no ideas whatsoever, you can always invoke the raising of the flag on Iwo Jima.

★ I ♥ NY gets a workout, too.

★ Many people of different nationalities live side-by-side in New York City without feeling the need to drop buildings on one another.

★ The recovery from this tragedy may best be symbolized by (a) flowers; (b) apples; (c) restoration of a ruined Ferris wheel; (d) all of the above.

(I realize that some will object to the application of humor to this event. The way I see it is: What more appropriate place is there for gallows humor than on the gallows?)

So are there any standouts? One way to stand out is to draw well, and Sergio Aragonés does some truly beautiful work in service of an unfortunately pedestrian script. Another is to be really screwy, and invoking historical personages really seems to bring out the screwiness in these folks. Alex Simmons and Angelo Torres' "Spirit" starts out with Winston Churchill and Dr. Martin Luther King and soon mixes in an incoherent mélange of historical icons including Chief Joseph, Abraham Lincoln, Douglas MacArthur, Shaka Zulu, Golda Meir…and on and on until it looks like the statesmen version of the stateroom scene in *A Night at the Opera*. But leave it to Stan Lee to really take the fruitcake. He considers his story "an undiscovered Aesop's fable," apparently under the impression that Aesop was a deranged bigot. Once upon a time there was this happy land ruled by this perfectly benevolent elephant who let all the other animals live there in peace and plenty even though it was really an elephants' kingdom. He even let in some dirty, rotten ingrate mice who made common cause with dirtier and rottener turban-wearing mice from overseas and attacked the elephants' realm while the elephant was sleeping. But the attack wakes the elephant, and just as the mice were breaking out the good cheese to celebrate, here he comes to stomp every dirty stinking rotten towel-headed mother's son of them into mouse paste. When he revealed that it was the mice who burned down the Reichstag the elephant was granted the title of Fuehrer as well as Chancellor and then he annexed the Sudetenland and then—oops, wrong elephant.

But, you ask, you persistent devil you, is there anything that rises above the commonplace and says something original and trenchant about the event? Two things, I think. In a project where nearly everyone seems to be straining to express the right feelings in the right way, Frank Miller's direct, honest and well-placed anger is like a faceful of ice water. But it's Steve Guaracci's modest parody of René Magritte's *La Trahison des Images* that approaches eloquence. Beneath the diagram of a passenger plane from one of those seatback cards is written in the familiar Magritte script, "This is not a bomb." There's a helpless sanity about it that captures the feeling of the day about as well as anything I've seen.

Alternative Comics' *9-11: Emergency Relief* anthology is only distinguishable from its mainstream cohorts in that the drawing is crappier, there's a whole lot more verbiage and it's in black and white. In keeping with the self-absorption of alternative cartoonists, it's also much heavier on earthquake stories, but it does feature the best of them; Ted Rall's "The Day My Train Stood Still." Caught out of town on a business trip, Rall is desperate to return before the dust settles. Rall is the king of the contrarians, but in this he's expressing the sentiments of many New Yorkers who watched the events unfold from afar. A city is a story; a story its citizens seek to be a part of and to be absent for something like this, horrible as it is, is to fall out of your place in the story. (Me, I wouldn't have missed the Rodney King riots for the world, but I got a VCR and a pair of Air Jordans out of it.) Rall isn't a native, but he's certainly got the attitude; when

The scope of it was too much to take in; the tragedy too unbearable -- I was shaken to the core. It was as if my whole world was threatening to collapse.

And then it did.

security measures are stepped up in Philadelphia, his reaction is "How cute—this little town wants to share the crisis!" Rall succeeded in getting home in time to capture some telling detail that you wouldn't have seen elsewhere. And it wouldn't be a Ted Rall story without a charge of a cover-up; it ends with a near-miss survivor claiming "It was worse than they're reporting... why aren't they saying how bad it really was?" Number one, as all these comics show, it's not so easy. Number two, as I recall, the initial casualty guesses were in the five-figure range, which came down to 6,000 once some actual information was available, and stayed there for about a week until it came down to less than 3,000, so it was actually being reported as worse than it was.

One thing that struck me in the aftermath was the strange symmetry between the trial lawyers and the remnants of the radical left. Both factions could be divided into two factions we might call the Stupids and the Savvys. Among the lawyers, while the Stupids could only smell money and salivate, the Savvys understood that (a) the potential liability far outstripped the pool of available cash and (b) the political cost of going for all the potential gelt far outstripped any excess gain that was to be got. On the left, while the Stupids were dusting off all the old Vietnam-era rhetoric, the Savvys—represented most notably by Christopher Hitchens and Marc Cooper—understood that the standard reflexive sanctification of political violence would extinguish the left's last few smoldering embers of public support completely.

World War 3 Illustrated's September 11 issue could be classed as Semi-Stupid. While being careful not to endorse the attackers' goals or actions, they are still unwilling to abandon their homely faith that all evil in the world is ultimately the responsibility of the United States. Their general theme seems to be "Isn't it awful what Ronald Reagan did to New York." Specifically, the consensus appears to be that the attacks are the end result of the Reagan administration's arming and training of the Moujahadin in the Soviet-Afghan war, presumably based on the assumption that if they hadn't been given box cutters to open the crate of Stinger missiles they never would have had the weapons to carry out the hijackings.

There is a common coin in American political discourse. One side of it says that if the United States were strong enough then everyone in the world would do exactly what we want, and the other says that if the United States were nice enough then everyone in the world would do exactly what we want. The fallacy behind both beliefs is the notion that the United States has the power to control events. This kind of thinking ignores the possibility that other people might have agendas of their own, and might be independently susceptible to malice. In any case, the greater issue here is one of tactics.

Terrorism is an illegitimate tactic because it has no practical military value. The reason is simple. A nation—any nation, regardless of political system—puts its autonomy first and the well-being of its people, well...second would be well over the international average. Therefore, the moment when terrorism begins to become effective is the moment terrorism loses its effectiveness, because that's the moment the target nation quits giving a damn about how many civilians die. The foregoing

principles are confirmed in an oblique way in the case of Osama bin Laden. So long as his organization confined itself to pin-pricks, or even the occasional kick in the shins, the United States was apparently willing to let him play holy warrior as long as he wanted. Then he landed a body blow and before he knew it he was on a tour of the caves of provincial Afghanistan, to the tune of the United States Air Force rhythm section.[2] Furthermore, errorism makes the assumption that the wretched of the Earth have a higher capacity for violence than the ruling classes. It's hard to know where to begin to explain what's wrong with that one. Terrorism serves no purpose except to give the perpetrator the satisfaction of inflicting pain. Thus, even if the United States has committed crimes against the Islamic world to which the Islamic world is bound to respond, resorting to terrorism is at best a waste of energy that could better be used elsewhere.

Comics, General Sofacushion, comics is what we're talking about here. Aside from political twaddle and the sort of "research" we've become accustomed to from *WW3*, we have the usual earthquake stories and ill-drawn expressions of anguish. As usual, it's salvaged by Peter Kuper, who makes some mordant observations about what it was like to see the real thing after having drawn imaginary calamities for so long, and provides not just one but two bits of "life goes on" reassurance.

Our insurance policy requires that you not read the following unless you are sitting down: The most tasteful and appropriate 9/11 comic was published by Marvel. *A Moment of Silence* stands out from the pack through simple modesty. Its wordless documentation

2 It also dovetails nicely with George Bush's ultimatum to the Taliban, which amounted to making them an offer they couldn't accept. Essentially the United States told Afghanistan, "You are a make-believe country. A genuine country now wishes to send troops into your territory for an unspecified amount of time and capture or kill anybody or anything it wishes. While it is a matter of supreme indifference to us whether you agree or not, should you acquiesce we may allow you to go back to pretending you're a country again once we're finished." Of course, it couldn't have happened to a nicer bunch of guys.

of the event comes off as an acknowledgment that under these circumstances a comic book can be little more than a gesture. If the imagery is clichéd, the absence of bombast is certainly refreshing — at least until the last page, where the Incredible Hulk stands tall among the ruins, orphaned urchin with fire helmet on his shoulder, as the Blue Angels stunt flying team performs overhead. Of course, if there's one thing Marvel isn't going to take to excess it's good taste; the balance is redressed in the companion volume to *Heroes*, subtitled "The World's Greatest Superhero Creators out from Honor the World's Greatest Heroes." Where *A Moment of Silence* is a dignified commemoration, *Heroes* is more like the Police, Fireman and Grieving Superhero Coloring Book, except someone's already colored it in. Like

said, this kind of thing ought to be review-proof, but you have to wonder at how a segment of the medium entirely dedicated to the concept of heroism can have such a limited visual vocabulary for portraying it.

Editorially, Marvel takes the glass-half-full view of the catastrophe. "In the midst of the horror," *Heroes* concludes, "something wonderful happened"— meaning people joined together and became more patriotic and foreigners were sorry for us and suchlike. Similar sentiments are expressed in *A Moment of Silence* and *Spider-Man's* 9/11 issue. And to think all it took was unimaginable death and destruction. It's oblique, but this brings to mind a story I once heard about Sigmund Freud when he was stuck in Vienna during the German annexation. After his house had been ransacked, he was offered the opportunity to leave the country with as much as he could carry provided he signed a statement, thoughtfully prepared for him in advance, declaring that his rights had not been violated in any way. The father of psychoanalysis acquiesced, and added his own handwritten note: "I would recommend the Gestapo to anyone."

The way people talked about it last fall, you would have thought that all that was required to perpetrate a devastating terrorist attack was the will to do it. The administration seems to expend more energy trying to convince people that it shouldn't be blamed if another attack occurs than preventing it. I'm sure there are people who know things I don't, but common sense would seem to indicate that if our enemies had the capacity to attack at will, they would have done so by now. It surprises me that no on ever notes the silver lining in the stories of intelligence failure: That if we had had all our ducks in a row we could have prevented even these attacks. On the other hand, we are saddled with weak leaders whose weakness is expressed in their demands for dictatorial powers.

In Dashiell Hammett's *The Maltese Falcon* Sam Spade tells a story about Flitcraft, an ordinary man of settled habits, who suddenly disappears. Five years later, his wife sees a man who looks like him in a nearby town and engages Spade to track him down. Sure enough, it's Flitcraft, and he explains that one day he was walking past a construction site when a steel beam fell eight stories and landed inches from where he was standing. As Spade describes it, "[Flitcraft] felt like somebody had taken the lid off life and let him look at the works." For the next couple of years, he goes drifting from place to place, finally remarrying under a different name to a woman much like his first wife and assuming a life much like his old one in a town not far away. "But that's the part of it I always liked," Spade concludes, "He adjusted to beams falling, and then no more of them fell, and he adjusted himself to them not falling."

Chance would be a fine thing.

Make Me a Liar

Here's a nice little howdy-do for a critic: A work that refutes not only one position he's staked out, but several. About a year and a half ago in these pages there appeared a review of comics about the 9/11 atrocities in which I held forth that not only had no significant statement been made about those events in the comics medium, but that none would because the medium was unsuited to the subject. As for Art Spiegelman, well, I wouldn't say I *never* expected to see another major work from him, but I would say that I couldn't imagine what form that work would take. The problem, as I opined in these pages, was that the work that won him his fame was not really characteristic of the bulk of his work, and that if he did follow it with a more characteristic work, the audience he had established would be apt to be disappointed. The post-*Maus* material reprinted in the exhibition catalog *From Maus to Now* doesn't show much of an appetite for a major statement. With its book reviews, profiles of libraries and provocative but glib magazine covers, it might just as well have been entitled *Ten Years of Futzing Around*. The quotation on the back of the first Fantagraphics *Krazy Kat* book did not inspire confidence. ("Osama bin Ignatz, Offissa Bush, us poor Krazy New Yorkers," *puh-leeze!*)

Apparently, there was nothing wrong with Spiegelman's work that another incomprehensible humanitarian disaster couldn't cure. Not only is *In the Shadow of No Towers* (which scores points on title alone) likely to be one of the most significant artistic responses to the attack and its aftermath, but it succeeds precisely because of those aspects of Spiegelman's methods—his fascination with form and the history of comics—that one would have thought were least suited for the subject. The form it takes is that of the full-page Sunday comic. This is no conceit because in doing so he taps into something deep in the DNA of the city. It is as if the trauma were so deep that it shook the ghosts of Manhattan's past out of their graves, like Henry Hudson's men in *Rip Van Winkle*. Spiegelman's personal involvement plays no small part. In last year's article I used the term "earthquake story" to describe the accounts of those who feel they've participated in a disaster but did not truly feel the brunt of it. Spiegelman's encounter was far too close to be called an earthquake story: His daughter was attending a high school within shrapnel distance of the towers, and he arrived to pick her up just as a disaster that was already staggering became a thousand times worse. What *No*

Towers captures most vividly in its documentary sections are those moments when the witnesses began to comprehend the magnitude of the catastrophe, when that almost holiday atmosphere of a normal evacuation turned into horror. It is Spiegelman's ability to recapture the feelings of the moment before that will make *No Towers* an important document in times to come.

One dimension *No Towers* does not add to is the political; in this respect, it is actually rather less sophisticated than that issue of *World War 3: Illustrated* I gave such a hard time in my round-up. Spiegelman's self-characterization as "equally terrorized by Al-Qaeda and his government" might have led one to expect an exercise in moral equivalence. Such fears were unjustified: Osama bin Laden drops off Spiegelman's radar almost immediately, except perhaps as the vector through which the Bush Administration's perfidy will blow back at New York. (At one point he seems to be saying he grew a beard in sympathy with the deposed Taliban.) In truth, it would be impossible to infer from the episodes I've seen what Spiegelman believes an appropriate response would be. All one can glean is that he sees terrorism as an irrational and unstoppable force of nature, like locusts, and believes that in trying to fight it the president is in effect pointing out Manhattan to the locusts and saying, "Good eating over here!" He is a patriot, but he's a Manhattan patriot, and all his views are reflected through that prism. He is stopped short in a condemnation of the administration's cover-up of the health consequences of the debris because he realizes that to have evacuated lower Manhattan until the dust settled would have exponentially increased the economic damage to the city. His perspective leads to a certain tunnel vision: He imagines that half the populace is outraged at the disputed election of George Bush. The reality is that support for Al Gore was lukewarm at best, and the only people who were most outraged over the Florida debacle were the nimrods who threw the election to Bush by voting for Ralph Nader. Regardless of how dubiously elected he was, in the wake of the attacks Bush got what amounted to a vote of confidence. That vote of confidence entailed a free hand to conduct the "War on Terror" as he saw fit, and we'll have a referendum on it in November of 2004. Like many in the anti-war faction, Spiegelman has a weakness for the premature harangue that might tend to alienate middlebrow voters he'll want on his side later.

Ultimately, though, politics and persuasion are beside the point. What *No Towers* speaks most eloquently to, albeit between the lines, is the quandary of the left-liberal intelligentsia. Even if one doesn't agree with Spiegelman's particular politics, one suspects he's boarding early on the same boat a lot of people are going to be in before too long. It is often said that the intelligentsia is out of touch with the values of the mainstream. It would be just as accurate to say that the mainstream is out of touch with the values of the intelligentsia. In reality, the former is no more bound to respect the values of the latter than vice versa. The difference is that the mainstream has much greater resources to express its alienation than the intelligentsia. They elected Richard Nixon, they elected Reagan, they almost elected George W. Bush—and if they can find a dumber millionaire, they'll probably elect him too. Spiegelman finds himself in a looking-glass world. Since 1918, Western nations (not least of them the United

States) have attempted to establish a code of behavior regarding war. In fomenting the Iraq war George Bush trampled this code so thoroughly that it's the diplomatic equivalent of defecating in the front parlor. Now, let's say he had a really good reason: He had it on good authority that the carpet would cure cancer if fertilized by president shit. You'd still think it would behoove him to acknowledge that this behavior is out of the ordinary, and explain why normal etiquette should be suspended in this instance. Instead, he doggedly maintains that his behavior is the most ordinary thing in the world, and his stalwart people cannot see why these silly foreigners don't see the transparent truth of this assertion. Spiegelman can see that, on the other side of the looking glass, the mainstream view is much closer to his own. He does not relish the thought of carrying the stigma of the looking-glass toilet habits when he encounters the intelligentsia of other countries. Yet in spite of all temptations to belong to other nations, Spiegelman is trapped because the United States has custody of New York City in the same way that Saudi Arabia has custody of Mecca. (An eyeball kick in a later installment proclaims, "USA out of NYC!") If the intelligentsia wants to live in an America more to its liking, it's going to have to create it, and this is going to be difficult because traditionally the intelligentsia does not recruit; it's something that you're supposed to aspire to. Moreover, it's going to have to go more than half way, to engage the mainstream on the mainstream's terms, because the mainstream isn't going to budge an inch toward it.

A Note Circa 2009
"Yes, I know. I'm in the future, also." — Mike Birbiglia

"Moment of Noise" was written in mid-2002, between the invasion of Afghanistan and the invasion of Iraq, and "Make Me a Liar" was written in February of 2004, after the capture of Saddam Hussein and before the release of the Abu Ghraib photos. My feelings about the Iraq War in 2002 were that what I wanted was for there to be no war, but as the administration was absolutely determined to have a war and nobody was going to stop them, I wanted them to get it over with as quickly as possible. You can

imagine my disappointment. Two errors in my thinking stick out in retrospect. First, I did not in my wildest dreams imagine how utterly incompetent the conduct of the war was going to be. Second, I had no idea how fucking evil these people were. What the paleoradicals who I treat with such condescension in these reviews would say is, "Well, we did." I don't think that was the case. It seems to me more a case of a president living up to the most deranged charges his most extreme opponents made against him. The paleoradical strategy was to drive George W. Bush out of office with a mass antiwar movement. My strategy was to vote for Al Gore in 2000. Back then, for all their insight into the true character of George Bush, paleoradicals thought it was more important to keep the Green Party on the ballot. Like me, they assumed that Bill Clinton had established a new political norm and that from then on we'd just have Democratic and Republican versions of it. Little did we know what was actually at stake.

Of course George Bush won the 2004 referendum I referred to in the *No Towers* review, which was like Lincoln reappointing George B. McClellan to lead the Army of the Potomac and worked out about as well. The end result was that the mainstream did indeed get in step with the intelligentsia, at least as far as getting Republicans out of office was concerned. It looks to me now that by 2012 paleoradicals will have the same attitude to Barack Obama that they had to Al Gore in 2000, but that the Republicans will have marginalized themselves too much by then for it to make any difference. I've been wrong before. ★

R. Fiore has written the *Funnybook Roulette* column for *The Comics Journal* since sometime during the Carter administration. This is the only thing of consequence R. Fiore has ever done. If this is of no consequence, then R. Fiore has never done anything of consequence. Like a lot of people, he lives in Los Angeles.

Fans

Gerard Jones

American Boys

At the end of his iconographic history of midcentury America, *The Glory and the Dream*, William Manchester conjures a snap-shot of average people at the bottom of the Depression: "It is summer, yet the adults look very formal. The men are wearing stiff collars, the women vast hats and shapeless cotton dresses. But it is the children who seem oddest. Like their parents they are quaintly dressed. There is something else, though. It takes a moment to realize why they look so peculiar. Then you see it. There is an intensity to their expressions. They are leaning slightly forward, as though trying to see into the future. And they are smiling."

That Depression Smile is hard to understand across the intervening generations, but it's impossible to deny. For all the stories of growing up in hard times, the voices that tell those stories crackle with a humor and optimism that somehow never buckled. The generation born around 1915—those kids who spent their childhoods in times of

---

wild promise and entered the workforce just after it fell apart—attacked the hustle and shuffle of the Thirties with an astonishing lack of self-pity and despair. The texture of American life after the World War may hold part of the answer. They were raised in an atmosphere of daily revolution and constant novelty, led to believe that their own futures must coincide with the great Future of mankind. They were the first generation raised in the age of popular psychology, their childhoods examined and designed for the furtherance of their happiness. They were sheltered from hard work and adult knowledge like no generation before, allowed to play past an age when their parents would have already slipped on the yokes of realism. They were given the inexhaustible fantasies of a juvenile culture industry such as the world had never known. Whatever the reasons, in the worst of times, they proved themselves capable of the most acrid pragmatism, the biggest dreams, the most exuberant resiliency, and the grittiest laughs.

The dreams, laughs, wisecracks, and schemes came loudest from the throats of Jewish kids. It was a breathtaking moment for Jewish possibilities. Frankin Delano Roosevelt had Jews in his Brain Trust and cabinet. Every intellectual and pseudointellectual in the world was citing Karl Marx, Sigmund Freud, and Albert Einstein. The Jew haters were getting noisy again, but no one thought they could stand against the rising tide. Irving Thalberg of MGM, after visiting Germany in 1934, said, "A lot of Jews will lose their lives… [but] Hitler and Hitlerism will pass, and the Jews will still be there." There was even something faintly ridiculous about crazy Adolf. Jewish teenagers hooted at him in the newsreels. Anti-fascist movements were growing quickly, becoming downright fashionable over the war in Spain. The Nazis would probably come crashing gloriously down before they did any real harm.

Nowhere was Jewish influence greater than in American popular culture. Jews ran the movie studios and wrote the songs—and not the pampered children of rich German families but old *shtetl* fur peddlers and Delancy Street spielers. Benny Goodman was the sound of sex. There were Jewish movie stars, not only clowns like Eddie Cantor but Paul Muni, Sylvia Sydney, even Ricardo Cortez. Jewish dads made sure their gangster-crazy kids knew who Edward G. Robinson and John Garfield were behind their goyish screen names. "Did you read Walter Winchell today?" they'd say. "He's Jewish, you know." Those dads had grown up viewing American culture through the eyes of outsiders, but the kids knew it was their culture, theirs to take and theirs to remake.

These pop culture kids were mostly an urban, middle-class generation. The garment trade, still the Jewish community's greatest source of income, muscled through the Depression, while such Twenties bonanzas as cars and construction collapsed. The immigrants and their kids kept moving out of the Lower East Side, Williamsburg, and Greenpoint, out to the newly built comforts of Bayside, Bensonhurst, and the Bronx. Critics called the Bronx sterile and mechanistic, built too quickly with too little thought, but the kids who lived in its intellectual and cultural life, its edgy insolence and electric competitiveness, knew they were in the middle of something that mattered. Queens was quiet. Brooklyn was Brooklyn. The Bronx was a cheer, a clanking elevated train, the arrogance of Yankee fans. It was a bedroom community, emptied of men every morning and given over to schoolboys who ran the streets. Compared to the

Lower East side, it was spacious and peaceful. The buildings were new regular, the parks large, the sidewalks free of whores and hustlers. It was also an abrasive, hastily settled ethnic patchwork. Alex Singer, a movie director who grew up in the Bronx during the Depression, has said that when he wasn't reading violent pulp magazines he was "working out routes to get to school and back every day with the lowest likelihood of getting beaten up." "The Italian and Irish kids hated Jewish kids," he said. "Our only saving grace was that they hated each other more."

A lot of families moved to the Bronx just to get their sons into DeWitt Clinton High, an all-boys school, overwhelmingly Jewish, with tough entrance requirements. It was the most competitive school in the city, and it had turned out a staggering number of successful intellectuals and artists: the reputations of Mortimer Adler, Edward Bernays, Lionel Trillling, Richard Rodgers, and even Fats Waller loomed over the kids who climbed its wide steps. Bronx kids came of age with armor on their feeling and razors in their brains. They rode the trains south to Manhattan hot with expectations. When the comic book burst suddenly upon New York, they were ready to make it their own.

Most Weisinger, Julie Schwartz, Bob Kahn, Will Eisner, and Bill Finger were only five of the hundreds of Bronx kids who loved comic strips and pulp magazines and wanted to make their futures somehow in the worlds of writing and art. They were all born between 1914 and early 1917, within about two years of Jerry Siegel and Joe Shuster. Like Jerry and Joe they all grew up speaking English in the home, none had much use for religion or tradition, and all defined themselves clearly as Americans. "I knew I was Jewish in the same sense that any American knows he's Irish-American or Italian-American," Eisner has said. "It influenced me in that the stories I grew up hearing were the stories told in Jewish families, but I never thought about being Jewish when I did my work." Like Jerry and Joe, these kids believed in their power and right to create their own futures. Some of them would go on to attain the very futures those boys in Cleveland reached for but couldn't hold.

Mort Weisinger was a great slab of a kid. Early descriptions call him genial, later ones domineering. He loved to laugh and greet his friends loudly, and he loved controlling conversations with his booming voice and big waving hands and forward-thrusting torso. Mostly he used laughter, wild anecdotes, and chest-swelling confidence to dominate a room, but he had anger in him, too, and he knew how to use it. His father was a successful footwear manufacturer who wanted his son to be a doctor. Mort didn't want to be a doctor. He loved magazines. He was another of those isolated, frustrated twelve-year-olds who fell in love with Hugo Gernsback's *Amazing Stories* in the late Twenties. He quickly moved to the fore of New York fandom, offering a room in his parents' big house as the monthly meeting place of the club that called themselves the Scienceers, launching *The Time Traveller* with his friends Julius Schwartz, Alan Glasser, and Forrest Ackerman.

Mort felt a power in the science fiction world that he never found in academic competition or under his father's roof. As he entered his teens, he fought bitterly with the old man over his refusal to throw out his cheap magazines and concentrate on his grades and over his stubborn insistence that he wasn't going to medical school. His father told him he'd never amount to anything. For the rest of his life, Mort would fight angrily, bitterly, to prove his father was wrong. He even attempted a fan club *putsch*, resulting in a two-year schism that left two groups calling themselves Scienceers. Commanding loyalty mattered a great deal to Mort.

His most loyal follower was Julie Schwartz, an epically homely boy with a great convex nose, buck teeth, a soaring dome of a forehead, and bottomless watery eyeglasses. He and Mort formed a sort of Mutt and Jeff team, Mort always pouncing first on a conversation, Julie's disarming baritone drawling dreadful puns and calming the nerves of those who found Mort unnerving. They'd ride down to Manhattan together to the rare audiences that Hugo Gernsback and other mavens allowed their most loyal fans. They served as gossip columnists for *The Time Traveller*, a sort of Walter Winchell and Ed Sullivan of fandom. They even supplied gossip to Jerry Siegel's *Science Fiction*.

While Julie seemed content to be a funny kid having a good time, Mort was hungry to get somewhere. He saw writing as his route. He'd write anything: essay contests in newspapers, brain twisters for puzzle books, phony inspirational stories, hobby hints, detective stories. He lived according to *Writer's Digest* and *Author and Journalist*. When the writing itself wasn't enough, he found other ways of building his reputation. He'd point to a piece in magazine with a phony-sounding byline and claim he'd written it under a pseudonym. Then he'd use that to talk an editor into assigning him a short piece, retype something from another magazine, and submit it as his own. Once he had a track record, he started telling friends he'd split the money with them if they'd let him sell their stories under his name. Once those were in print, he'd tell anyone but the authors that he'd written them himself. His buddy Julie used to say his headstone should read "Here Lies Mort Weisinger—As Usual."

When Mort was only eighteen, he pulled off a dazzling gambit. Few writers allowed themselves the luxury of literary agents in the depressed pulp market, and no science fiction writers did. There were three magazines in the genre, everyone knew everyone's name, and the established writers, more fans than businessmen, mostly felt grateful to be doing as well as they were. But Mort saw money and influence to be won and talked Julie into joining him in the "Solar Sales Service." They'd already corresponded with writers who lived far from New York: Edmond Hamilton in Ohio, Stanley Weinbaum in Wisconsin, the team of Earl and Otto Binder in Michigan. Now they offered their services, promising they'd take no commission until they proved their value. The Mort went to T. O'Connor Sloane, the elderly retired scientist who had been placed in charge of *Amazing Stories* by an uncomprehending publisher, and convinced him that he represented the cream of science fiction writers and could get them to deliver whatever the market wanted. Next he told Charles Hornig, Hugo Gernsback's new teenaged editor of *Wonder Stories*, that he was going to take his who stable of writers to *Amazing* unless *Wonder* bough just as much from them. Then he told F. Orlin Tremaine at *Astounding* that he had the other two magazines in his pocket. Finally he went back to his writers with story suggestions and promised sales. Mort and Julie had made themselves the first literary agents in a field that didn't even know it needed agents.

When a better deal presented itself, though, Mort didn't hesitate to dump the agency and run. He heard that Gernsback had run into money trouble and decided to sell *Wonder Stories* to Ned Pines's publishing company, and immediately he called Pines's chief editor to ask who the editor of the new *Wonder* would be. The editor said he wanted to keep Charles Hornig in the job. Mort snorted. What did that milquetoast know about running a magazine? Hornig was just a fan who lucked into a job. His heart was still in the fanzines—that's why *Wonder* went broke. But Mort was a pro. So Charlie Hornig was out of the job; Mort Weisinger was in. It wouldn't be the last time Mort showed that he wasn't intimidated by more established men or scrupulous about other people's careers; Jerry Siegel would come to know those qualities well. He left Solar Sales to Julie Schwartz. Mort, at twenty years of age, was editing the most respected magazine in his field.

Not that it would be so well respected by the time he was done with it. His fellow fans were thrilled at first that one of their own had taken the torch that Gernsback could no longer carry, but they would learn quickly that Mort no longer had any use for being one of them. Ned Pines published *Thrilling Mystery*, *Thrilling Love*, *Thrilling Adventure*, and other energetic schlock, and from the moment he walked in the door, Mort Weisinger made himself Ned's kind of guy. He let his writers know that he wanted less science, less futurism, less thought, and more hideous creatures, beautiful girls, and blazing ray guns. There could be no more gracious Frank R. Paul cityscapes on his covers. Mort knew what scared little boys and agitated their older brothers; he gave the world the "bug-eyes monster" and the space opera damsel in bustier and shorts. The motto of the new *Thrilling Wonder Stories* was "Stranger Than Truth," and every cover-featured story came with an ad line: "A Novelette of Mad Catastrophe," "A Novelette of Universal Destruction," "A Story of Throttled Life Forces." The titles of the stories in the first few issues left little doubt of the new tone: "The Brain Stealers of Mars," "The Revenge of the Robot," and from Earl and Otto Binder, "The Hormone Menace." Mort even added comic strips to the pages.

Older fans screamed, but sales climbed. In 1938, Mort was asked to launch a second magazine, *Startling Stories*. He was climbing toward the top of the pulp heap, when comic books struck.

Robert Kahn was born in the Bronx in 1916, a year after Mort and Julie. He was famous at DeWitt Clinton as a mama's boy. His mother would sometimes walk him to school or show up to walk him home. If he had the sniffles, at least so his classmates said, his mother would keep him home. Rumors ran wild that he was a bed wetter, but maybe that was just an easy slur to slap on a slight, sensitive, big-eyes boy who liked girls better than the fellas. His father was an engraver and printer with the *New York Daily News* and encouraged Bob's love of drawing. As an artist, Bob was a talented mimic, better at pleasing adults than depicting any inner reality; at fifteen he won a prize for his imitation of the newspaper strip *Just Kids*, an event he took as a sign that he was meant to be a comic strip star. His father would bring him home the Sunday funnies still smelling of ink, before any other kids in the neighborhood saw them, and Bob would sit down and copy them. "I could copy them exactly," he said. "I impressed everybody."

As he grew up, Bob realized he had another way to attract attention: He was handsome. Skinny as a hose but with a long, fine nose, a dimpled smirk, brushstroke brows, and eyes that crinkled when he smiled. He compared himself to Robert Young, that favored young male of MGM who always played the insouciant son of the stuffy plutocrat, and he cultivated the style. If girls giggled when he crinkled his eyes, then he'd polish his crinkling in the mirror. Word spread quickly at that all-boys school that Kahn was the fellow to know if you wanted to meet girls, assuming you could endure his boasting and preening and flagrant lies. "We were supposedly friends because we were both artists," said one classmate, Will Eisner. "But really, it was so we could double-date and he could set me up with the most beautiful girls. Then it started to dawn on me that I wasn't getting anywhere with these girls—and neither was Bob. You couldn't get all the way with the beautiful girls. I decided I'd rather date the average girls who'd actually let you get somewhere." So it would always be with them: Eisner wanted action, Kahn the appearance of action.

Their families help pay their ways to art school in Manhattan, Bob to the Commercial Art Studio in the Flatiron Building, Will to the Art Students League at the top of the Times Square triangle. Like Bob's, Will's father was an artisan working below his aspirations, a Viennese painter who had apprenticed to masters working in Catholic churches, who'd come to America to work in theater painting, only to be forced by the Depression to make his living in furniture decoration. He took little Willie to the Metropolitan Museum, encouraged his love of H. Rider Haggard and O. Henry, threw away his pulp magazines to save him from the debasement of junk. He loved Willie's experiments in woodcut and drypoint and bought him expensive books illustrated by Rockwell Kent.

Willie's mother, though, was a peddler's daughter from Romania who spent her life concealing the fact that she was illiterate. "She had peasant smarts," said her son, "but no sophistication, no understanding of culture." Her complaints about her husband's trouble keeping a job pushed Willie to work. Sixty years later, in an autobiographical graphic novel, *To the Heart of the Storm*, he had her saying to his father, "Sam, why don't you go into house painting! It's a good living. But no! He wants to be a big shot." How they had come to marry Will never quite understood, but he carried the duality of art and money inside him all his life.

The Art Students League crackled with artistic fire: A battle raged between the faculty's leftists, who wanted to hire the acidic German caricaturist George Grosz, and the old guard, who found him too dangerous; and the students chose sides. Will Eisner, though, stuck to the business of learning to draw cartoons. That was part honest passion—he loved the adventure comics of Hal Foster and Alex Raymond—but it was part hard pragmatism too. Rough-edged Jewish kids knew they had a steep hill to climb if they wanted to become "high-class" illustrators, not only because of editors' prejudices but also because of the costs of the training, studio lighting, and live models needed for that perfect sheen. "The comics were still viewed as trash," Eisner said, "so they were an easier business to enter, the way peddling or the rag trade had been."

Bob Kahn saw things similarly. He loved the gag cartoonists of *Judge* and *College Humor* but felt he couldn't sell his work with an obviously Jewish name, so he took the name "Bob Kane," not only in print but in his private life as well. He worked hard on a signature that couldn't be missed, a big box holding the bold letters of his new name with a voluptuous "O" riding high. Sometimes he and Will would run into each other on the cartoonists' track, carrying their portfolios to editors' and art directors' offices, Will picking his way through crowds of tourists and touts, Bob hiking up Fifth Avenue past the men in suits to the magazine publishers, syndicates, and ad agencies that littered Midtown. They'd sit in offices for hours waiting to have their stuff looked at, passing portfolios around to the other kids waiting with them, discreetly studying the older cartoonists who came in after them and were shown in first. They must have been a striking pair: Will, broad-shouldered and straight-backed, hair rolling in waves back from a high brow above an aquiline nose; Bob dimpled and grinning, flirting with the receptionists. Neither got much but rejection.

Bob had to take a job in his uncle's garment factory. "It's difficult to put into words the loathing I felt for this type of operation," he said, "for I knew in my heart that it was not meant to be my destiny." Finally he picked up some work at Max Fleischer's animation studio, cleaning up drawings and "in-betweening" the cell-by-cell movement.

Will found a job cleaning presses at a printer's in the far south of Manhattan. He grabbed every drawing gig he could find—almost. One of the printer's sidelines turned out to be "eight pagers," cheap comic books showing celebrities and comic strip characters making whoopee in pornographic, and illegal, detail. The mobster who distributed them offered to pay Will to draw a few. "It was one of the toughest moral conflicts of my youth," Will said. But he passed.

Then one day when they were both nineteen, Will and Bob ran into each other on a Midtown street. Bob announced he was organizing a cartoonist's union and invited Will to the meeting. Will scoffed at the idea of freelance cartoonists ever unionizing; more than likely Bob just wanted himself known to editors as a potential troublemaker so they'd raise him from five to six bucks per cartoon to keep him quiet. What Will wanted was work, any work, drawing. Bob said he'd sold a few "Hiram Hick" cartoons to something called *Wow, What a Magazine!* Will hiked straight down Fourth Avenue to show his stuff.

The garment industry was still the source of much of the investment capital that launched Jewish publishing enterprises in the 1930s, and the piecework and sweatshop models of the trade were employed by many small publishers. Nothing, however, blurred the line between *shmattes* and magazines quite so literally as *Wow*. It was made in a shirt factory. A failed cartoonist named Samuel "Jerry" Iger had talked a shirtmaker into bankrolling a boys' magazine and giving up some space at the front of his factory for the editorial office. One artist who worked for Iger called him "a promoter and operator." He was another of those would-be syndicators like Major Malcolm Wheeler-Nicholson who thought if he could just connect the right cheap talent to the right hungry publisher, he's strike it rich. He was short, cigar-stinking, in his thirties and still hustling for his break, talking like a big-shot and a ladies man.

Will Eisner did not have high hopes when he rode the elevator through the shirt factory to *Wow*'s offices, but as he put it, "I was hungry. I was real hungry." He walked in the door with his portfolio. Iger immediately brushed him off. He had to go solve a problem at his engraver's. Will wouldn't be brushed. He walked out of the office with Iger, stuck to him along Fourth Avenue, saying, "Why don't you just look at my portfolio while we walk?" He ended up walking into the engraver's with him. The engraving company must have been cheap, a fly-by-night, because the problem that was stumping them was one Will had already learned to solve at his printing job. "Does anyone have a burnishing tool?" he asked. The engravers stood around stunned while this teenager burnished down the plates that had been tearing up the mattes. "Who is this kid?" one asked. "He's my new production man," said Iger.

In fact Will got only a few comics jobs out of *Wow*. One was a story about a two-fisted treasure hunter inspired by H. Rider Haggard, another a swashbuckling adventure aspiring to the romance of Rafael Sabatini and the illustrative sweep of N. C. Wyeth. It was elegant work for a kid, more mature in its use of page design and the multipage format than anything coming simultaneously from Major Wheeler-Nicholson's *More Fun* or *New Adventure*. Will thought he was on his way—until the shirtmaker decided he'd lost enough money on *Wow* and turned off the spigot. He and Iger were both out of work again.

That's when the businessman in Will Eisner stirred. He knew the comic book business was growing, and he knew that comic strips were becoming increasingly popular as cheap filler in magazines but that publishers couldn't afford the staff to find the talent or do the production work. Will called Jerry Iger. "I'd like to meet with you," he said. "I've got an idea."

They had lunch across from the *Daily News*, where Bob Kane's father worked. Will pitched. Surely publishers would appreciate the partnership of a cartoonist and a salesman-editor who could deliver camera-ready comics pages of reliable quality. It was simple piecework, the lifeblood of the New York garment industry. Iger said it would cost money to start up, and that's what he didn't have. "My second wife's divorcing me and she's taking me for everything I've got." Then Will played the big shot. He had $15 to his name, money he's just earned off a one-shot advertising job. He still lived with his parents and didn't have to pay rent. Midtown was full of half-vacant office buildings, erected on Twenties expectations and emptied by Thirties realities. Will found one on 41st Street and Madison that rented small offices for $5 a month, no questions asked, and so they moved in among the bookies and con men. Iger began to peddle their services to publishers, calling himself "S. M. Iger" in the manner of W. R. Hearst. He claimed to have a five-man art staff, but it was all Will under pseudonyms. Will insisted they call the company "Eisner & Iger," because the money man's name should always come first, even for $15.

Iger came in with one major contract in his pocket. Through that invisible network of barterers and favor-traders that spread through New York in the 1930s, he'd hooked up with a man named Joshua Powers who claimed to be a former secret agent now making his fortune from the contacts he'd made overseas. Powers bought up the foreign rights of comic strips ranging from *Mutt and Jeff* to *Dick Tracy* and packaged them for export to Britain, Australia, and South America. But in that global depression, foreign newspapers couldn't pay for comics, so Powers traded them for column inches in the papers, which he then resold to American advertisers. It worked well until one of Powers's partners broke with him and made off with the British rights to his comics. Powers had to scramble to come up with cheap original comic strips—and that's where the Eisner and Iger shop suddenly came in handy.

With cash coming in, Eisner and Iger jury rigged their own variation. They hired a couple of salesmen—"fast-talking hotshots," in Eisner's words—who visited small-town newspapers all over the Northeast and sold them a page of comics with a blank space for ads at the bottom; then they'd go personally to local merchants and find someone to buy that ad space from the same price as the comics page. The newspapers got comics for nothing and Eisner and Iger got the money minus sales commission.

Now they put an ad in the paper calling for young artists who were willing to sit in a studio drawing comic strips for $15 a week. Sixty a month was just barely enough for a young man to survive on if he lived at home or with other young guys; in a good month, Jerry Siegel and Joe Shuster split five times that. The number of responses showed just how many young artists were out there, inspired to draw by the comics, yearning to be the next Hal Foster or Milton Caniff, desperate for an open door. Eisner was able to pick only the best of them, kids who'd gone to Pratt Institute or the School of Industrial Art. When Siegel and Shuster sent him a couple of strips called *Spy* and *Superman*, he sent them back with the note, "You're not ready yet." (So Eisner joined the club of men who could look back on that great missed opportunity and laugh at themselves.)

The names of the young men he hired over the next two years read like the roll call in one of those war movies celebrating the melting pot: Klaus Nordling, Stanley Pulowski, Chuck Cuidera, Chuck Mazoujian, Reed Crandall, Nick Viscardi, Bob Fujitani, "Tex" Blaisdell. There were no women among the artists. Like science fiction fandom, the world of adventure comics was a boy's club in which women figured only as mothers and girlfriends. It was a bit more blue-collar and socially normal, though: At least these guys actually *had* girlfriends.

In the early going, Eisner would develop the ideas, design the characters, sometimes do a few pages, then turn them over to the studio hands. Often one artist would draw in pencil, then hand it over to other to finish it in ink, rule the panel borders, do the hand lettering. The boys would work all day and deep into the night if the jobs were there, cheek by jowl at their drawing boards, kibitzing and wise-assing, sharing brushes, pooling the change for beer and smokes. From one another they learned how to draw and how to work with people. They learned that Mort Meskin would stare at his drawing board for hours in blank-page anxiety until somebody else walked up and scribbled random lines on it. With lines to connect, Meskin's hands could start moving, could start carving those square, craggy, expressive figures of his. They learned to put up with Stan Pulowski's griping about "kikes," telling each other a Polack didn't know any better (and it was Pulowski, no Meskin or Fine, who signed his work "Bob Powell"). And they gathered around Lou Fine just to watch him draw, to watch those wonderfully liquid lines flow from his brush and bring to life men of a sinuous grace and weightless agility that his polio-crippled body would never know.

At twenty Eisner was younger than half the boys he hired but was already the picture of the shop boss: demanding and decisive, pushing his young workers hard but able to inspire their loyalty. They called the studio a "sweatshop," not always in jest, but usually. They did nice work too, in almost every genre: cops, spies, spacemen, buccaneers, magicians, and a female version of Tarzan they called Sheena, Queen of the Jungle. And Eisner was making money off them. He moved out of his parents' house and rented an apartment in Tudor City, a modern middle-class development within walking distance of the studio.

By early 1983 comic books were still a modest but obviously growing field. Harry Donenfeld was giving the big push to his comics, and sales were rising past 100,000 copies a month, up there with reasonably successful pulps. The publishers of *The Comics Magazine* and *Detective Picture Stories* were expanding their line. Now Jerry Iger cut a deal with Fiction House, one of the smaller pulp publishers, to produce *Jumbo Comics*. It was tabloid-sized, black and white, featuring mostly material Eisner and his studio had already created. Sheena and her leopard skin swimsuit got no more space on the cover than Peter Pupp; the comic book makers didn't know their market yet, but they knew a market was there.

The creator of Peter Pupp, and a provider of regular humor pages to Eisner, was Bob Kane. But Kane didn't work in the studio with the rest of the artists. He wasn't a man to play on a team, especially if he weren't the captain. By now he was telling his friends that he reminded himself of Tyrone Power: less jollity, more dash. He'd had just enough success getting his name in print and just enough failure lining up a regular berth that he was hungry for a high-profile strip of his own. He started selling humorous private-eye fillers to Vin Sullivan at Major Wheeler-Nicholson's comics, and he wanted to develop ideas for stories longer than a page or two. But stories were Bob's weak spot. As Eisner would say, "Bob wasn't an intellectual."

Then he met Bill Finger. Bob said it was at a "cocktail party"; one imagines a kid's parents gone to the Catskills and his pals showing up with beer and gin. Whatever the case, Bill was a drinker. He was another DeWitt Clinton graduate, a couple of years ahead of Bob, smart, articulate, well-read, depressive. He wanted to be a writer, a real one, known for his short fiction and novels, although he enjoyed the better pulps too and was willing to write potboilers if that's what it took to make a living by writing. But he'd gotten married early, and at twenty-four he already had a son to support. When he met Bob, he was selling shoes. When Bob said he was a successful cartoonist who needed help with the writing end of things and was willing to pay for it, Bill jumped at the chance. Bob was likable, the work sounded like fun, and it was money for writing. Finger agreed to help brainstorm the ideas and do the writing for a portion of the income while Kane dealt with the editors and took all the credit. Bill was agreeable, and for the rest of his life, he would suffer terribly for it.

With Finger doing his writing, Kane began to sell regularly to Vin Sullivan. *Rusty and His Pals* and *Clip Carson* were pastiches of *Terry and the Pirates* for *New Adventure* and *Action Comics*. A partnership was born—although everything the partnership produced was still signed just "Bob Kane."

In the spring of 1938, these five Bronx kids were between twenty-one and twenty-four years old. They were making decent livings in the comics and magazine trades. They were building a community too, a geek's community: some geeks handsomer or better at business than others, but all deeply invested in the wild, printed fantasies, all snugly uninterested in the things that occupied most boys in high school and the years right after. Already they'd all climbed a rung above their fathers on the American ladders, in self-satisfaction and glamour if not necessarily in money.

Then the man in the blue tights changed everything.

The consignment system prevented publishers from knowing how well their magazine had sold until months after they'd been shipped. When Vin Sullivan put Superman on the covers of the first and seventh issues of *Action Comics* and gave the others to elegant renderings of parachutists, Mounties, and jungle explorers, he was only guessing at what would attract kids' attention. What publishers did have was word of mouth from local dealers. By the time the fourth and fifth issues hit the stands, in the late summer of 1938, word was coming in that *Action* was selling through quicker than the other comics. Harry Donenfeld sent his sales staff out to run an informal survey of news dealers and their customers, and they came back with word that kids were asking for "the comics with Superman in it."

This was just about the time Superman first truly emerged as a character on the printed page. The cut-and-paste quality of his adventures continued after his first appearance. *Action #2* featured a story strangely similar to one used in *Detective Comics* the year before; some panels seem to have been pasted in from another source, and in some of them Superman's cape has obviously been drawn onto a different character. The next month brought a story about a crooked mine owner, starring not Superman but Clark Kent in disguise, as if a strip about a crusading newspaper reporter had been cobbled together with another effort in order to buy time for Superman. The fourth story was more polished, but it also contained few glimpses of Superman in costume; its centerpiece was a football sequence that echoed a chapter of Philip Wylie's *Gladiator* and may have been a survivor of some earlier version of "the Superman."

AHEAD OF THE RAGING, RUSHING TORRENT, HE SPRINGS TO A HIGH PINNACLE . . . .

Then, suddenly, in the fifth issue, Superman appears. "Telegraph lines broadcast to the world news of a terrible disaster! The Valleyho Dam is cracking under the strain of a huge downpour!" "Kent! Get me Clark Kent!" "He isn't in his office!" "Well, look for him, Lois!"

"But why not have *me* handle the assignment?" "Can't! It's too important! This is no job for a girl!" "No job for a woman, eh? I've half a mind to..." "Clark Kent! Just the man I'm looking for!" "You mean you're actually *glad* to see me?" "I should say I am! Would you do me a favor and cover an assignment for me?...Go to the city hospital's maternity ward. A Mrs. Mahoney is expecting septuplets!" "What a story! Thanks, Lois! You're a peach to let me handle this!" "Somebody's been spoofing you, pal! There's no Mrs. Mahoney registered here." "That's strange! Say! I wonder if Lois is by any chance pulling a double-cross?" "You brainless idiot! The greatest news story in month on the fire, and you waste your time at a hospital! Kent! Report to the cashier! *You're fired!*" "But Kent has other plans! When alone, he strips off his outer garments and stands revealed in the Superman costume!" "Now, to *get that story!*"

He leaps into the night, bounding over the city, outracing the train on which Lois rides. "If Lois thinks she's going to outscoop me, she's badly mistaken!" But he finds the trestle about to give out, so he drops to the base and holds it up as the train hammers across it. Arriving in Valleyho, Lois takes over an abandoned taxi and drives it to the dam, where Superman is holding the concrete together by sheer strength. "Suddenly, with a great roar, the huge dam collapses...Superman leaps above the water's turbulent fury...but Lois finds herself directly in the path of the great, irresistible flood of onrushing water." He plunges in, tears the car open, and bears Lois's limp form back to the air. Now he outraces the flood on its rush to the town, "springs to a high pinnacle...

then pits his tremendous strength against a great projection of rock!…The avalanche of rock crams shut the mountain-gap below—cutting off, diverting the flood to another direction, away from Valleyho Town!"

"You did it! You saved all those people! Oh, I could kiss you! As a matter of fact, I *will!*" "Lady! PLEASE!" "WOW! What a kiss!" "A super-kiss for a Super-man!" "Enough of that! I've got to bring you back to safety—where I'll be safe from you!" Lois tells him she loves him, but he's off with a wave. Then he calls the chief and scoops her. "Lois! That wasn't a nice stunt you pulled on me! But I still like you." "Who cares! (The spineless worm! I can hardly bear looking at him, after having been in the arms of a *real* he man—)."

Shuster's Superman is suddenly exploding through space, his cape flowing behind him as he leaps and races over cities, over water, across the moon in a desert sky. His figures are simple but alive, their faces rich with cartooned expression. The sly Lois, the gibbering Clark, and the arrogant Superman come to life. Shuster's trains and dams and bridges are bold icons of Thirties modernism. He defines vast spaces with sweeping curves and open fields, then places his tiny people against them. His Superman is thrilling not because he's a monumental hero out of *Flash Gordon* or *Tarzan* but because he's as small and colorful and cute as a little boy's drawing, yet by some miracle of unglimpsable power he's able to hold up the trestle and save the train.

This is still not quite the Superman we would come to know. He can't fly, only jump, he has no X-ray vision, and he can hold a dam together only by "battling like mad." But the cataclysmic drama, élan, and winking humor of Superman at his apex are in place. This was something new in entertainment. Whatever antecedents for Superman's powers, costume, or origin we can find in Edgar Rice Burroughs or Doc Savage or the Phantom or Zorro or Philip Wylie or Popeye, nothing had ever read like this before. The racy mix of slapstick, caricature, and danger is familiar from Roy Crane's *Wash Tubbs*, but Crane never leapt into such pure fantasy. Hollywood has made breathtaking moments out of natural disaster, and Douglas Fairbanks had let us feel the same joy in physical liberation, but they had nothing to equal the immediate pleasure of these bright, flat colors and fiercely simplified forms. This was a distillation of the highest thrills in the purest junk.

It's surprising, then, to realize that even this was built up from panels photostated from an earlier version. The letters and line thickness grow and shrink from panel to panel; connective sentences have been written in a different hand; the dam sequence, at least, seems to come from samples for a proposed Sunday comic strip, although the Lois and Clark material may be new. We may be looking here at that "humor-adventure character" Jerry and Joe scribbled notes about in the high hopes of late 1935. This may be the "rugged, narrative drive" that they dreamed would sweep the nation. Belatedly, it seemed to be happening.

The great missing piece in any archaeology of kid culture is what the kids themselves were saying. Were the ten- and eleven-year-olds who discovered Superman in the summer of 1938 and ran to tell their friend, "You gotta read this"? Did the word spread through school playgrounds in the fall? Or was it still mostly isolated kids, each discovering it on his own? All we have now are sales figures and editorial decisions. Over a nine-month period *Action* more than doubled its monthly sales. But other comics started selling better, too. It seems that Superman was selling comic books to kids who didn't normally buy them, and then those kids were trying other comics. Somewhere in the 1938-1939 school year a comic book fad was born.

It was a good time for Superman to arrive. The kids born in the late Twenties and early Thirties had never known the thrill of taking a new medium or genre for their own: The kids a decade older had been pioneer audiences for radio, talkies, adventure comic strips, hard-boiled pulps, and science fiction, but a depressed economy had supported little that was new. Now something had some along that adults and older siblings didn't know about, something cheap and colorful and exotic. This was a skeptical generation, too, raised on lower expectations and hard realities. The comics, cartoons, and radio shows had increased the American appetite for fantastic heroes, but at the same time, plenty of adolescents and precocious kids found Flash Gordon and his ilk fairly ludicrous. The humor and excess of *Superman* made it possible to laugh along with the creators while still thrilling to the fantasy of power. That had always been Jerry and Joe's special insight: You could want the invulnerability and the power, but you had to laugh to keep people from knowing how badly you wanted it. The hero who dressed like a Bernarr Macfadden bodybuilder and bounced bullets off his chest contained that laugh almost by nature.

In their sixth published *Superman* story, perhaps their first conceived for comic books, Jerry and Joe showed that they shared their readers' conflicting cynicism and dreams. They threw their hero up against a would-be manager who sells Superman's name to a car company, has a nightclub singer wail a Superman torch song, and sponsors a Superman radio show. "Why I've even made provisions for him to appear in the comics." They were parodying the genre before the genre existed. The comic book superhero first sold himself to a suspicious public through humor, then dared them to follow him into earnest power fantasies. After all the gags, it was satisfying to see the manager's hired stand-in for Superman break his fist on the real hero's steely chest.

In September 1938 Jerry and Joe took the train to New York, this time not to hustle samples but to be feted by Vin Sullivan. Even Jack Liebowitz and Harry Donenfeld greeted "the boys" who were selling so many comics (although they didn't take them to the Stork Club). Jerry hooked up with some of his pen pals from science fiction fandom, Mort Weisinger and Julie Schwartz among them, finally able to play the role of a fellow success story.

The big news, though, was from Charlie Gaines. He was thrilled by Superman's success. For one thing, he got a cut from everything printed by the McClure Syndicate, and McClure had the printing contract for *Action Comics*. For another, he was still selling McClure items for syndication. He'd failed repeatedly to set Superman up with the syndicate, but now he had evidence that kids liked the thing. He told Jerry and Joe to prepare new samples, insisting that these be more polished than anything they'd sent him before. Presumably, too, he planned to link it with Buck Rogers and Flash Gordon, because the first two weeks of the version finally accepted by McClure were taken up by a grand space opera of Krypton's destruction and baby Superman's exodus. Harry Donenfeld held the rights, of course, but he was eager to make it happen and cut Jerry and Joe a generous deal to do the strip themselves: 50 percent of the take. Harry hadn't made so much money so easily since the Hearst printing deal in 1923. He was in an expansive mood.

Jerry and Joe rode back to Cleveland knowing they were at the brink of hitting the big time. A newspaper strip is what they'd wanted all along. They knew they'd need help. Back in June they'd already hired a couple of young artists to drop by Joe's apartment sometimes and help them handle the growing workload. They'd need more to do this. They'd need to create a studio. Jerry apparently didn't trust his skills as a science fiction writer, because he hired a friend from fandom, Harold Gold, to write the initial origin sequence for the comic strips. He began asking other friends to sell him ideas for stories and help him script.

McClure placed *Superman* with *The Houston Chronicle*, then the *Milwaukee Journal*, then the *San Antonio Express*. The first strip, a stunning sequence of a man racing at superspeed through a futuristic city beneath an alien sky to see his newborn son, would appear in newspapers scattered across America in January 1939. Jerry and Joe celebrated in the final panel of the tenth issue of *Action* with an evocation of dreams once deferred: "Superman, the Strip Sensation of 1939."

But Jerry had already begun to wonder if he'd cut a smart enough deal with his publisher. He looked at the cost of a studio and thought about the $10 a page he and Joe were being paid. In the moment he saw his dreams about to be realized, he began to feel them being stolen. He'd hardly come home from that triumphal trip to New York when he began his first angry letter to Jack Liebowitz. ★

Gerard Jones, who lives in San Francisco, CA, is the author of the Eisner-Award-winning *Men Of Tomorrow: Geeks, Gangsters and the Birth of the Comic Book*, as well as *Killing Monsters, The Comic-Book Heroes*, and *Honey I'm Home*. Jones has also written comics and screenplays, and his work has been adapted for videogames and cartoons. At press time, he is writing his next book, to be published by Farrar, Straus, and Giroux: *The Undressing of America - How a Bodybuilder, a Swimming Queen and a Magician Created Reality Media*.

**Excerpt from the Decision of
U.S. District Judge Stephen G. Larson in
Case No. CV-04-8400-SGL**

UNITED STATES DISTRICT COURT CENTRAL DISTRICT OF CALIFORNIA

JOANNE SIEGEL and LAURA SIEGEL
LARSON, Plaintiffs, v.

WARNER BROS. ENTERTAINMENT
INC.; TIME WARNER INC.; and DC
COMICS, Defendants.

CASE NO. CV-04-8400-SGL (RZx)
[Consolidated for pre-trial and discovery
purposes with CV-04-8776-SGL (RZx)]
ORDER GRANTING IN PART AND
DENYING IN PART PLAINTIFFS'
MOTION FOR PARTIAL SUMMARY
JUDGMENT; ORDER GRANTING IN
PART AND DENYING IN PART
DEFENDANTS' MOTION FOR PARTIAL
SUMMARY JUDGMENT

The termination provisions contained in the Copyright Act of 1976 have
aptly been characterized as formalistic and complex, such that authors, or
their heirs, successfully terminating the grant to the copyright in their
original work of authorship is a feat accomplished "against all odds." 2
WILLIAM F. PATRY, PATRY ON COPYRIGHT 7:52 (2007).

In the present case, Joanne Siegel and Laura Siegel Larson, the widow
and the daughter of Jerome Siegel, seek a declaration from the Court
that they have overcome these odds and have successfully terminated the
1938 grant by Jerome Siegel and his creative partner, Joseph Shuster,
of the copyright in their creation of the iconic comic book superhero
"Superman," thereby recapturing Jerome Siegel's half of the copyright
in the same. No small feat indeed. It requires traversing the many
impediments – many requiring a detailed historical understanding both
factually and legally of the events that occurred between the parties
over the past seventy years – to achieving that goal and, just as
importantly, reckoning with the limits of what can be gained through the
termination of that grant.

Any discussion about the termination of the initial grant to the
copyright in a work begins, as the Court does here, with the story of the
creation of the work itself . . .

CONCLUSION

After seventy years, Jerome Siegel's heirs regain what he granted so
long ago – the copyright in the Superman material that was published
in Action Comics, Vol. 1. What remains is an apportionment of profits,
guided in some measure by the rulings contained in this Order, and a
trial on whether to include the profits generated by DC Comics' corporate
sibling's exploitation of the Superman copyright.

DATE: March 26, 2008
STEPHEN G. LARSON
UNITED STATES DISTRICT JUDGE

David Hajdu

"Then Let Us Commit Them"

The panic over comic books falls somewhere between the Red Scare and the frenzy over UFO sightings among the pathologies of postwar America. Like Communism, as it looked to much of America during the late 1940s, comics were an old problem that seemed changed, darkened, growing out of control. Like flying saucers, at the same time, comics were wild stuff with the garish aura of pulp fantasy. Comic books were a peril from within, however, rather than one from a foreign country or another planet. The line dividing the comics advocates and opponents was generational, rather than geographic. While many of the actions to curtail comics were attempts to protect the young, they were also efforts to protect the culture at large from the young. Encoded in much of the ranting about comic books and juvenile delinquency were fears not only of what comics readers might become, but of what they already were—that is, a generation of people developing their own interests and tastes, along with a determination to

Excerpted from *The Ten-Cent Plague: The Great Comic Book Scare and How it Changed America* by David Hajdu: reprinted by permission of Farrar, Straus and Giroux, LLC.
[©2008 David Hajdu]

indulge them. Young readers argued persuasively for comics through their dimes. In 1948, the 80 million to 100 million comic books purchased in America every month generated annual revenue for the industry of at least $72 million. (The usual cover price was ten cents, although some digest-format books sold for five cents apiece.) Hardcover book publishing, by comparison, brought in about *$285* million—about seven times more, through books priced more than twenty times higher.

In the same year, a few comics readers began to speak out in protest of the crackdown on the books. The most vocal among them was David Pace Wigransky, who was a fourteen-year-old sophomore at Calvin Coolidge Senior High School in Washington, D.C., when he read Fredric Wertham's essay "The Comics... Very Funny" in the May 29, 1948, issue of *The Saturday Review of Literature*. Something of an authority on the subject himself, Wigransky then owned 5,212 comic books. He was a sharp boy and strong-willed; when he was four years old, *The Washington Post* reported how Wigransky, "imbued with something of the pioneer spirit," had climbed up the stairs of his family home in the northwest district and locked himself in his parents' bedroom until police came and forced the door open. Offended by Wertham's article, he countered with a long letter to *The Saturday Review*—one so eloquent that editor Norman Cousins contacted the principal of Wigransky's school to make sure the language of the letter was consistent with the student's usual writing. The July 24 issue of the magazine devoted a page and a third to the letter, and it included a posed studio photograph of Wigransky a skinny gravely serious kid with a dark crew cut, wearing a pressed white shirt, poring over an issue of *Funnyman*. A preface from the editor noted, "Although sections of Mr. Wigransky's letter have been omitted for considerations of space, his copy has not been edited." Wigransky wrote, in part:

> It is high time that we who are on the defensive become as serious as our attackers. We didn't ask for this fight, but we are in it to the finish. The fate of millions of children hangs in the balance. We owe it to them to continue to give them the reading matter which they have come to know and love.
>
> Dr. Wertham seems to believe that adults should have the perfect right to read anything they please, no matter how vulgar, how vicious, or how depraving, simply because they are adults. Children, on the other hand, should be kept in utter and complete ignorance of anything and everything except the innocuous and sterile world that the Dr. Werthams of the world prefer to keep them prisoner within from birth to maturity. The net result of all this, however, is that when they have to someday grow up, they will be thrust into an entirely different kind of world, a world of violence and cruelty; a world of force and competition, an impersonal world in which they will have to fight their own battles, afraid, insecure, helpless.
>
> The kids know what they want. They are individuals with minds of their own, and very definite tastes in everything. Just because they happen to disagree with him, Dr. Wertham says that they do not know how to discriminate. It is time that society woke up to the fact that children are human beings with opinions of their own, instead of brainless robots to be ordered hither and yon without even so much as asking them their ideas about anything.

The Saturday Review ran pages of responses in issues published through the end of September 1948. Several of the letters discounted Wigransky on the grounds that, as an obviously intelligent boy, he could not be representative of comic-book readers, or that, as a comic-book reader, he could not be intelligent enough to write such a letter by himself. Either way, they tended to support Wigransky's claim that adults did not seem prepared to accept the average young person's capacity for independent thought and discrimination. It was a view that ran deep at the time, even among some parties in the comics-reading generation.

When the town of Spencer, West Virginia, incorporated in 1858, it took the first name of a beloved county judge, Spencer Roane. It was a neighborly place with an acute regard for justice. In the late 1940s, Spencer had about 2,500 residents, most of them farmers or coal miners and their families, and, each Friday, almost everyone would go to the livestock market, the hub of the community's commerce and social life. Sheep and cattle overran the crossroads in the center of the village, an intersection called New California because an enterprising local named Raleigh Butcher once announced that he was heading for the West Coast but got no farther than that spot. "You could almost go from house to house, go into anybody's house without knocking on the door, and if they were having lunch or dinner, whatever it was, you could walk right in, sit right down, and you'd be welcome to eat with them," recalled David Mace, the only son of a couple who ran a small family-style restaurant called the Glass Door (specialty: the one-dollar "plate-lunch dinner"). They lived in a red-shingle house about half a mile from New California, toward Oregon.

"My mother and father worked probably sixteen, eighteen hours a day, and they made sure you were fed and you were clothed," said Mace. "But other than that, I can't honestly say what they thought about anything. They expected you to do the right thing, and it was your responsibility to know good from bad. You were on your own. Of course, most everyone in town agreed with everything that went on in Spencer in those days. It wasn't like things got later on, where you'd have so many different public opinions about everything. We had a nice little tight-knit community. I doubt there was a TV in our community at that time." Television, after all, was just beginning to find an audience. Nine years after RCA brought the technology to the American public, there were only twenty-seven broadcast stations in eighteen cities, most of them on the East Coast and half of them in and around New York City. TV sets—hardwood boxes the size of refrigerators with tiny, roundish, gray screens—were extravagances to be found in only one of every ten American homes, where families could watch rudimentary but high-minded broadcasts of civics debates, lectures, and chamber-music performances for a few hours each day.

Several stores in downtown Spencer sold comic books, and David Mace, like every child he knew, bought them. He thought of them as "thrills and fun," until early in his eighth-grade year at Spencer Elementary School, in the fall of 1948, when one of his teachers, Mabel Riddel, asked him to stay after class, sat down next to him in a child's desk, and told him that comics had "an evil effect on the minds of young children." Riddel, acting with the support of the PTA, asked Mace to lead his fellow students in an uprising against comics. "She was extremely dedicated—that's the way our school was and the way our teachers were," Mace remembered. "She explained to me about the [harm of] comic books, which I didn't know about. I read 'em, and I never even noticed. The things she had to say made a lot of sense, I could see that, and she told me we could do something about it, and I said, 'Well, let's go!'" Smallish and good-looking, with dark hair (almost black) and blue eyes, Mace was popular and a talker. With Riddel's encouragement and counsel, Mace hit the schoolyard and rallied the upper-class students to join him in a mission to remove all comic books from the homes and stores of Spencer—an elaborate group activity not unlike the games Mace sometimes organized, a scavenger hunt taken out of the playground and into the adult world, ideal for young adolescents beginning to confront the end of childhood and their grade-school years.

For almost a month, Mace led several dozen students in a door-to-door campaign through Spencer. With milk crates in hand or wagons in tow, they urged children and parents to relinquish all the comics in their houses, and implored retailers to stop selling the books. By the last week of October, Mace's brigade had collected more than two thousand comic books of all sorts, from reprints of the *Dick Tracy* strip to crime comics. The kids brought them into school on Tuesday, October 26, a cool, dry, sunny day, and they piled them on the grounds behind the building. The books made a small mountain about six feet high. At the end of the day, the six hundred children who attended the school emptied into the yard and assembled in a semicircle facing the comics. David Mace walked to the far side of the pile and stood before the crowd in his best clothes, a white shirt and black wool pants his mother had ironed fresh that morning for the occasion. He put his left hand on his hip, and, in his right hand, he held a sheet of lined paper with some words he had written, with considerable help from Mrs. Riddel.

"We are met here today to take a step which we believe will benefit ourselves, our community, and our country," Mace said. "Believing that comic books are mentally, physically and morally injurious to boys and girls, we propose to burn those in our possession. We also pledge ourselves to try not to read any more.

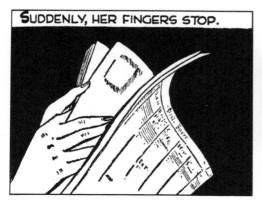

"Do you, fellow students, believe that comic books have caused the downfall of many youthful readers?"

The students answered, in unison, "We do."

"Do you believe that you will benefit by refusing to indulge in comic-book reading?" Mace continued.

"We do."

"Then let us commit them," Mace said. He walked a few steps to the pile, took a matchbook from a pants pocket, and lit the cover of a *Superman* comic.

The flames rose to a height of more than twenty-five feet as the children, their teachers, the principal, and a couple of reporters and photographers from the area papers watched for more than an hour. Mrs. Riddel stared with her arms crossed. Several children wept—a signal to those who noticed that not everyone in town agreed with everything that went on in Spencer that day.

When the Associated Press picked up the story from local accounts, readers of *The Washington Post*, the *Chicago Tribune,* and dozens of other papers around the country learned how, just three years after the Second World War, American citizens were burning books. Mace would remember receiving letters of support from around the country, which his mother kept in a cigar box in the kitchen. "She was really impressed when we got all that mail," Mace recalled. "What we did was a pretty important thing at that time, and it put our little town in central West Virginia on the map." Indeed, the Spencer paper, *The Times Record*, covered the national coverage of the burning: "Spencer Graded School Is Famous." Not all the commentary on the event was so prideful, however; as the *Charleston Daily Mail* noted in an editorial:

> The burning of books is too recent in our memories. The Nazis burned them. They went on from there and, in one way or another, burned the authors too. It was the purge by fire of those elements which the Nazi party could not tolerate.
>
> This purge has no place in a democratic educational system. It is not that books as books are sacred. It is just that the idea of burning them is profane. It is a resort to witchcraft when the need is for education, the use of fire when enlightment *[sic]* is called for. Perhaps the point can be clarified by asking how many of the boys and

girls who burned 2,000 "bad" books have read 2,000 good ones? Of the two possible tasks, the second deserves priority.

Images of Third Reich soldiers in black uniforms emptying military trucks full of books onto bonfires endured in American memory. Yet most of the German book-burning had been done by students, young people stirred to act against literature that they had been led to think of as corruptive to members of their own generation. Worked up to a nationalist frenzy just three months after Hitler assumed the chancellorship, the German Student Association mobilized university students to burn more than 25,000 books advancing "un-German ideas" in Berlin and other cities throughout Germany in May 1933. In the days and months to follow, the student association organized thirty-four more burnings in university towns across the country and young people chanted, sang, and gave speeches before the fires. Who better to inspire contempt for the books than members of their intended audience?

In the United States after the war, the incident in Spencer was not singular. A couple of Catholic schools had staged little-noted comic-book protests with ceremonial fires as early as 1945. In November of that year, during Catholic Book Week, nuns teaching at Saints Peter and Paul elementary school in Wisconsin Rapids, Wisconsin, held a competition among students to gather the highest number of "objectionable" comics, as categorized in lists made by the Rev. Robert E. Southard. The boy and girl who brought in the most books were named the king and queen of a bonfire that consumed 1,567 comic books. (King Wayne Provost collected 109; Queen Donna Jean Walloch, 100.) The event was selective, in its way targeting only comics that Southard listed as Condemned (*Batman, Wonder Woman, The Spirit, Crime Does Not Pay*) or Questionable

(*Superman, Captain Marvel, Archie*). Spared from the pyre were those Southard rated as Harmless (*Mickey Mouse, Donald Duck,* and compilations of the *Popeye* and *Katzenjammer Kids* newspaper strips, comics that had been condemned in their own day). Two years later, in December 1947, students of St. Gall's School in Chicago collected and burned 3,000 comics (including, again, *Superman, Batman, The Spirit,* and *Archie)* in a campaign reported to have been suggested by a ten-year-old fourth-grade girl, Marlene Marrello.

Once the Associated Press spread the news from Spencer, the idea of fighting comic books with fire began to catch on in schools and communities across the country, particularly in Catholic parishes already primed to act on the issue. There were two sizable comic-book burnings in the sixty days after David Mace set *Superman* in flames, both at parochial schools: St. Patrick's Academy in Binghamton, New York, and Saints Peter and Paul elementary in Auburn, New York. Many more would be organized at public and parochial schools in the months and years to follow. Easy to mistake from the distance of time as the puppetmastery of reactionary adults exploiting children too sheepish to defend their own enthusiasms, the comic-book burnings of the late 1940s were multilayered demonstrations of the emerging generation's divided loyalties and developing sense of cultural identity. The events exposed the compliance of some young people in the face of adult authority at the same time the incidents fueled the defiance of others.

In Binghamton, the campaign against comics was almost solely the work of a charismatic student named John Farrell. A sixteen-year-old junior at St. Patrick's in the 1948-49 school year, Farrell was the president of his class, as he had been, on and off, since the fifth grade. He was a chunky boy neither athletic nor conventionally handsome, but a jokester, grand company. He had a broad, toothy grin and a slight underbite that gave him a disarming, comical appearance. In a blue-collar, Irish-Catholic area, where many students' parents (both of them, often) worked in the local factories that manufactured shoes and chemical products, John Farrell was considered well off and cultured; his father was an executive in charge of production at the *Binghamton Press* newspaper, and John dressed and spoke with flair. "He was so damned funny," recalled Paul Plocinski, a classmate who was deeply involved in the comics burning. Tall and sturdy, Plocinski looked like a grown man in his junior year and itched for the freedom of adulthood. "He could imitate every one of those nuns. He was very dignified in his attire, and he knew all about politics, but he used to keep us laughing."

Farrell worked after school as a soda jerk at Crone's pharmacy, a busy, well-regarded store appointed with milled woodwork and a sixteen-foot marble-topped fountain counter. It was a nice environment for good kids to congregate, and it had a magazine rack around the corner from the soda fountain. Part of Farrell's job was to watch the rack to ensure that kids paid for their comics before sitting down at the counter to read them. One of Farrell's friends, Joseph Canny, whose family lived a block away from the Farrells, would sometimes keep John company at Crone's, and even he was granted no free reading privileges. "John was a well-read fellow, and he knew that comic books were controversial," said Canny. A year younger and a grade behind Farrell in school, Canny was a bookish kid, one of three second-generation Irish brothers whose father had died in an odd accident, run over by a driver at his own trucking company when Joseph Canny was nine. "It started to bother John that Crone's was making every kind of comic book available, with no discrimination, and John was in a position to watch the reading habits of his clientele. He started to notice that the more troublesome kind of kids were more inclined to read comic books, and some of [the books] were pretty rough stuff."

Farrell took up the matter with his boss, Ken Crone, but found him unmoved. "That's when John decided to take the initiative, on his own," said Canny. "He was sincere. John was a religious guy and he was irritated by all these comic books and the content in a lot of them. The thing was all John's idea, and he had the support at the school to make it happen."

St. Patrick's Academy was a spartan Catholic institution housed in a boxy, three-story redbrick building dressed up with a pair of Gothic spires jutting high above the turreted front roof, and an opulent, arched entrance for faculty and guests. Students used the side doors, the left for boys, the right for girls. The cafeteria provided tables and a drinking fountain, but no food, and the basketball team, which was often good, played outdoors, because it had no gym. All the teachers were sisters of the order of St. Joseph. Each class of about thirty students spent thirteen years, from ages five to eighteen, together. Like other smallish private schools of all sorts, St. Patrick's fostered mighty feelings of loyalty, pride, exceptionalism, paranoia, and restiveness. At the end of the school day so many students lingered together in the halls of St. Patrick's or stayed in classrooms, talking to the nuns, that the Mother Superior, Anna Frances, had to shoo them away.

"It was very intimate—we knew one another personally and everyone seemed to be involved in whatever was going on, because of the size of the school," recalled James D. Kane, who was a classmate of John Farrell's, took part in the Binghamton comics burning, and went on to enter the priesthood. "It gave us a *good* education," said Kane, emphasizing the word "good" to distinguish it from both "poor" and "excellent." "The others were no better, though the kids in the public schools treated us like second-class citizens. I don't think they liked what we did, most of the time. But we did what we thought was right, regardless of what they thought."

St. Patrick's, the largest of Binghamton's ten Catholic churches in 1948, served about 2,500 residents of the west side, a working-class community of Irish and Slovak families. One neighborhood in the area was essentially owned by Endicott Johnson, the shoe manufacturer, which built solid little A-frame houses for hundreds of its employees and deducted low-interest mortgage payments from their weekly paychecks. (Paul Plocinski grew up in an "Endicott house" and recalled it as "wonderful and beautiful.") Early in the twentieth century, Binghamton had served as the New York State headquarters for the Ku Klux Klan. By 1948, the Klan's legacy was spectral, although the climate of Binghamton remained "fairly judgmental," in the view of Monsignor Kane. "We Catholics were sometimes the target of that," Kane said. "That's one of the reasons we stuck together."

The first phase of Farrell's campaign was a coercion strategy to purge Binghamton stores of objectionable comics. Working under Farrell, students in the four high-school grades of St. Patrick's set out to visit every Binghamton store and newsstand that carried magazines—Murphy's cigar store, Grant's ice-cream shop, Smith's pharmacy— and to urge each of the owners they met to sign a four-by-six index card carrying this pledge: "I will support the drive to end indecent and objectionable literature, comic books and the like, by withdrawing them from my newsstand, and will do all in my power to stop their sale." Dealers who declined were told their stores would be boycotted by the students.

The tactic challenged students as well as the business people they were charged to confront. "We had to go around to all the stores—dime stores, any place they sold magazines—and make sure that they didn't sell comic books anymore, and it was unbearable," said Plocinski. "The storekeepers were shocked—they never heard of such a thing. It was a very difficult thing, but we did it because we were expected to, and we thought we were doing a good thing. But, to tell you the truth, I wasn't completely sure about that." Once, Plocinski picked up a comic to show a dealer an example of the kind of books the students were protesting, and he purchased it, thereby removing it from the shelf. He then took it home and tried to hide it, only to find that the spot under the living-room sofa cushions was already taken: His father was keeping his detective magazines there.

News vendors, riled and unsure how to handle this unusual pressure from youthful ranks, complained to their local magazine distributor, Abraham M. Pierson, who reported their distress to the *Binghamton Sun*, the competition to Farrell's father's paper. "I know a lot of dealers around here were getting worried about the kids asking them to sign cards [and] one fellow told me that he was really sore about the thing," said Pierson. "One fellow was going to throw the boys out." (There were as many teenage girls as boys involved in the campaign.) Still, Farrell and his troops elicited pledges from thirty-five Binghamton retailers.

St. Patrick's students boycotted the rest, including the students' favorite after-school hangout, Smith's, which was across the street from the school on Oak Street. "We were very serious," explained Vincent Hawley, a freshman at the time. A quiet, earnest boy, Hawley entered St. Patrick's in the fourth grade, when his family moved eighteen miles north from rural Silver Lake Township, Pennsylvania, where he had attended a one-room schoolhouse. "We were determined to boycott all these places that were selling these things until they took the comic books off the shelves, and one of the places was the most popular place where we used to go. We were so serious we even made periodic checks to make sure our own students were upholding the boycott, and one day after school, we went over to Smith's—we just stood outside to remind the owner of all the business he was losing, and while we were there, one of our students walked out of the place. Three hundred ninety-nine of us were boycotting the place, and only one kid defied the boycott. When he came out, one of the kids jumped him, and it turned into a huge, big fistfight. We were serious."

For several weeks, St. Patrick's students barnstormed the sidewalks of Binghamton's west side, collecting the materials for the climax of their campaign, a public burning. "We were crusaders," said Hawley "We all read the comics—the comics were huge! But I separated the good ones and the bad ones in my mind. The hero comics were good, and then there were the other ones. The ones that we were trying to eliminate were the bad ones. We weren't against comics per se, but how some of them were being used." Hawley and his fellow crusaders so embraced superhero comics' ethos of eradicating evil that they employed it against other comics.

To Paul Plocinski and some others he knew, however, the distinctions between differing comics or between the comics' form and content were vexing to parse. "I had been trading comics for years," said Plocinski. "I had stacks of them. The drawings were really artful, very much so—the artwork was wonderful. We thought we were doing a good thing by collecting the comics and conducting this protest, but it gave me a pain in my stomach. I was torn up inside, and I wasn't the only one."

The day of the burning, Friday December 10, was cold and gray. Mother Anna Frances ended classes early at 11:00 a.m., and released the entire student body of about 560 onto the playground behind the school. To document the occasion, someone set up a stepladder and took a photograph from the top, moments before the fire was set. Published in the 1949 St. Patrick's yearbook, the picture shows a group of eight students—Plocinski, in the center, dressed nattily in a dark wool coat and a white scarf, flanked by three other boys and four girls (none of them Farrell, who was standing on the photographer's side of the scene). The kids have shipping cartons for Rice Krispies and Ivory Snow full of comic books, and they are emptying them into a deep stone kiln meant for the school trash. Behind them, we see a mass of children, many of them early grade-schoolers bundled in coats with hoods, zippered tight, or wool caps, in gloves or mittens. One boy on the far right is shoving another to make sure he gets in the picture. A small fellow in the front row, wearing a one-piece snowsuit, has his legs spread wide apart, planted to hold his position. In the second row, a boy too short for his face to be photographed waves a cross in the air with his right hand. Most of the faces are smiling; a few brows are furrowed; only two or three young children look afraid.

With a few hundred comics in the kiln, a Sister Lucia, Farrell's chief ally among the nuns, lit the books. Then, as the fire began to rage, she led the students in singing the St. Patrick's alma mater and "The Catholic Action Song":

> *An army of youth flying the standards of truth*
> *We're fighting for Christ, the Lord*
> *Heads lifted high, Catholic Action our cry*
> *And the Cross our only sword.*
> *On earth's battlefield, never a vantage we'll yield*
> *As dauntlessly on we swing*
> *Comrades true, dare and do, 'neath the Queen's white and blue*
> *For our flag, for our faith, for Christ the King*

Farrell and his compatriots kept the fire stoked for four hours, tossing in more boxes of comics while the students of St. Patrick's watched. The flames stretched as high as thirty feet. By three o'clock, when the children were released, the group of onlookers had multiplied to include many parents, neighbors, reporters, and members of the parish command.

"I remember it very vividly," said Joseph Canny. "I watched them burn it all up, and I thought, This is really something! I thought it was good—I thought it was a good thing, and I was impressed that John had been able to pull it off." Through the Associated Press, again, news of the comics burning at St. Patrick's made newspapers around the country. "I had no idea at the beginning that it would turn out to be such a big thing," said Canny. "I was really proud of John."

The *Catholic Sun*, a daily Church paper published in Syracuse, commended the St. Patrick's students for bringing their song of "Catholic action" to life:

The action of the St. Patrick's pupils earned deserved national recognition. It was a public protest. It was a dramatization of a very present problem. It does call for a sincere and sustained response from responsible leaders in the publication business. It does declare that the menace of the comics is not mere theory...The students of St. Patrick's are to be congratulated for they have earned the respect and regard of every good American.

The only public dissent came from magazine sellers watching the dime bins of their cash registers. As the *Binghamton Sun* paraphrased distributor Abraham Pierson, "Banning books should not be left up to a group of high school students," because authority on the matter "should be given only to those acquainted with the problem." In essence, the complaint was consistent with much of the criticism of young comic-book readers, faulting the St. Patrick's students not for their views, but for daring to have any one way or the other. Pierson made no claim that John Farrell and his group acted unfairly illegally or unethically; he never challenged them for being wrong, but only for being young.

The Sunday after the St. Patrick's bonfire, the bishop of Albany, Edmund F. Gibbons, called for a diocese-wide boycott much like the one the students had imposed in Binghamton, dispensing with the gesture of first calling for pledges by the businesses involved. Bishop Gibbons issued a letter to be read at all masses that day which said, in part:

Another evil of our times is found in the pictorial magazine and comic book which portray indecent pictures and sensational details of crime. This evil is particularly devastating to the young, and I call upon our people to boycott establishments which sell such literature.

Less than two weeks later, three days before Christmas, *The Citizen Advertiser* of Auburn, New York, a small city about sixty miles north-west of Binghamton, reported that the students of a local Catholic school, Saints Peter and Paul, took "quick action" and made a "huge bonfire" of comic books collected by students acting under the direction of the principal, Sister Boniface. Praising the action in an editorial, the paper noted, "This action follows that taken elsewhere in many parts of the country by other irritated parents and authorities," reinforcing that the event was not necessarily an expression of all the students' points of view.

"The holidays came, and everything was wonderful," said Paul Plocinski, "except every time I saw a fireplace burning with the Christmas stockings hung, I thought about that bonfire and all those comic books, and it made me sick. I started to get angry and really wished we hadn't done that. Burning things! I said to myself, I'm never going to do that again, and went out and bought myself some comic books." Plocinski would always remember the day during Christmas vacation when he walked alone to Smith's shop, ventured tentatively back into the forbidden place, and picked out a comic from the rack. (The title would escape him with time.) "I put my dime on the counter," Plocinski said, "and I don't know what I said—probably 'Thank you very much, sir.' But I know what I was thinking—Take that, John Farrell!" Plocinski walked home with the comic book rolled tight in his back pocket and tucked under his coat, so no one would see if he bumped into anyone from school. ★

David Hajdu is a professor at the Columbia University Graduate School of Journalism. He is a staff critic for *The New Republic* and the author of four books, including *The Ten-Cent Plague: The Great Comic-Book Scare and How It Changed America* and *Heroes and Villains: Essays on Music, Movies, Comics, and Culture*. He has written about comics for *The New York Review of Books*, *The New York Times Magazine*, *Bookforum*, and other publications. As a teenage cartoonist in the 1970s, he drew a duly forgotten underground strip, *The Endless Odyssey of Skip Toomaloo*.

Seth

High Standards

"High Standards" excerpted from Seth's *Wimbledon Green*.

HIGH STANDARDS

ART STERN
COMICS CRITIC

 I WAS ONLY 18, A MERE LAD, WHEN I FIRST MET WIMBLEDON GREEN.

 I WAS WORKING AT COMIC-ARK THAT SUMMER-- MY FIRST REAL EXPOSURE TO THE WORLD OF COMICS.

 HE WAS A GENUINE ECCENTRIC. I WAS IMPRESSED. A BIT STARRY-EYED ACTUALLY.

 WE HAD WIDE-RANGING CONVERSATIONS AND I LEARNED A LOT.
THE WORKS OF LESTER MOORE REWARD REPEATED READINGS MY BOY.

 HE SEEMED TO BE A SUPERIOR PERSON.
THERE IS A GREAT CLEVERNESS IN THE CONSTRUCTION OF THOSE STRIPS.

 SOMEONE WITH A REAL FORCE OF WILL.
HIS EVOCATION OF PLACE IS QUITE ASTOUNDING.

 AND STANDARDS!
I CANNOT RECOMMEND THE 4th ISSUE OF "MRS. MOP" STRONGLY ENOUGH!

 I MUST ADMIT, FOR A KID LIKE ME, HE WAS A STRONG ROLE MODEL.
I'LL CHECK IT OUT RIGHT AWAY-HONEST.

 THE OTHER CUSTOMERS OF THE STORE SEEMED SHALLOW AND CRASS.
YOU GOT THE NEW "BARN OWL" MINI-SERIES IN YET?

 MEN OF POOR TASTE SEEKING OUT OLD COMICS IN A VAIN ATTEMPT TO BUY BACK THEIR CHILDHOODS.
I HEAR THAT PULVERIZER COMES BACK FROM THE DEAD IN THE NEW ISSUE.

 OR EMPTY SPECULATORS HOPING TO CASH IN ON SOME COLLECTING TREND.
NEW PRICE GUIDES IN YET KID?   AISLE SEVEN

 MOST OF THEM WERE QUITE LACKING IN KNOWLEDGE.
IS THIS GOLDEN AGE OR BRONZE?

 ALL OF THEM WALLOWING IN THE ADOLESCENT KICKS OF GENRE FORMULAS.
WOW

 NOT WIMBLEDON GREEN. HE SAW THROUGH THESE INANITIES.
HOW SAD THAT OUR NOBLE MEDIUM MUST ENDURE THESE FOOLS.

 HE COLLECTED AS A CONNOISSEUR. LOOKING BENEATH THE SURFACE OF THESE CHILDRENS PAMPHLETS FOR THE HIDDEN MESSAGES THEY CONTAINED.
A POWERFUL METAPHOR FOR THE GRACELESSNESS OF HUMAN LIFE.

HE REALLY SEEMED TO <u>KNOW</u> THINGS.

YOU HAVE TO LOOK CLOSELY AT THINGS.

TO UNDERSTAND!

NOTHING IS EVER JUST ON THE SURFACE.

THAT'S WHY I WAS SO SHAKEN THAT DAY.

I WAS ON MY LUNCH BREAK HEADING OVER TO A NEARBY DINER.

NO!

WALKING DOWN QUEEN STREET I SPIED WIMBLEDON THROUGH A PLATEGLASS WINDOW.

THERE HE WAS, SITTING IN THE LOCAL OUTLET OF NORTHERN FRIED CHICKEN.

A LARGE BUCKET OF GREASY CHICKEN IN FRONT OF HIM.

NORTHERN FRIED

AND NEXT TO IT--A STACK OF THE LATEST CRUMMY SUPERHERO COMICS.

CAPT. GRIM

HE DIDN'T SEE ME. HE WAS IMMERSED IN THE CURRENT ISSUE OF "MR. MASK".

I WATCHED HIM GNAW AT THE CHICKEN-- HIS MOUSTACHE SLICK WITH OIL.

THE COMIC BOOK WAS CLUTCHED IN HIS SHINY HAND.

THE LOOK ON HIS FACE WAS THAT OF A PIG IN SHIT!

I STAGGERED BACK-WARD--DISORIENTED.

IT MIGHT SEEM A LITTLE THING TO YOU-- BUT FOR ME IT WAS A SHATTERING EXPERIENCE.

IT HAD ALL BEEN A PITIABLE FACADE.

RIGHT THEN, I SAW HIM FOR WHO HE REALLY WAS...AND WITH GREAT SCORN I PASSED SENTENCE.

WIMBLEDON GREEN WAS JUST ANOTHER FANBOY!

END

Appraisals

Charles Brownstein

The Walk Through the Rain:
Excerpt from *Eisner/Miller*

Will Eisner Black-and-white books demand content because they are *read*. As opposed to color, which is really absorbed porously *[laughs]*. It's not by accident that *A Contract With God* was sepia. I had a choice between doing it in one color, two colors.

Frank Miller That was a dramatic decision. I remember when the book came out, it was almost a physical shock.

EISNER That's exactly what I was trying to say. People say that you dream

in brown, did you ever hear that? Psychologists will tell you that you dream in brown. But it was the only way of introducing color in a way that gave the book a tone. I felt it developed an intimacy between me and the reader, as if we were talking in hushed tones.

MILLER I'd like to dwell on *A Contract With God*. It really is a seminal piece of work. From the walk-in-the-rain opening, part of what really made that an affecting piece of work was that you lettered it big. It drew the reader in. Just a few words, very large lettering, almost the look of a children's book, even though the content was clearly not childlike. And as it got more complex, you were already in the door, so you had to deal with it as you read it. But it very much drew you in. You're walking with somebody in the rain.

EISNER Oh, yeah, the walk through the rain.

MILLER Not just the walk through the rain, but the mounting tension was really something.

EISNER It's a pure theatrical device, which is not of my invention. You may have used it in some of your work.

MILLER I did, in the first *Sin City* [*The Hard Goodbye*]. There's a scene that goes for about ten pages where I wanted to build as much tension as possible with the atmosphere of the rain. That was me saying, "This is where I'm going. I've been away from comics for two years, and I'm back." I sat down and did exactly what I wanted to do without thinking about it. That was my walk in the rain.

EISNER I think I have a copy of that one on the shelf. *[Examines the book.]* This is great. There's real power here. I can hear the wind whistling. Without reading the text... as a [purely] visual thing you're evoking a feeling on the part of the reader. I can feel this rain, and I can hear the roar of the wind and the rain splashing in the gutter. And then suddenly the appearance of a face. All of a sudden it's beginning to take shape. I congratulate you.

MILLER I did a lot of white paint on those pages, too.

EISNER Did you? It looks like you did it on scratchboard.

MILLER No, I did it on white board in layers. I ruled the brush lines in black, and then I came in with white.

EISNER Did you draw the figure in first and then do the rest?

MILLER Yes.

EISNER That's the way I would do it. I'd draw the figure in full and then add the white.

MILLER I tend to work from a pretty specific image and then degrade it.

EISNER Okay, you say "degrade"— you convert it. This book I'm working on [*Fagin the Jew*] has a snow scene. I finished the scene completely and then threw the splashes of snow on it.

MILLER Did you ever use liquid frisket?

EISNER What is it, a kind of rubber cement?

MILLER It's essentially the same as rubber cement, but it's a little more fluid so you can really snap it from a brush. I used a lot of it in *Family Values*. The fun thing about that is that it's really got the art of accident, because you ink on top of the frisket and then pull off the ink, and you have no idea what it's gonna look like when it comes off.

EISNER Oh, yeah! I've done that. In one of the books, I did the title with rubber cement, painted in the letters, and then blacked over it and pulled off the rubber cement. You get some very interesting effects.

MILLER Yeah. I bought an old Johnny Craig EC job once that was on auction,

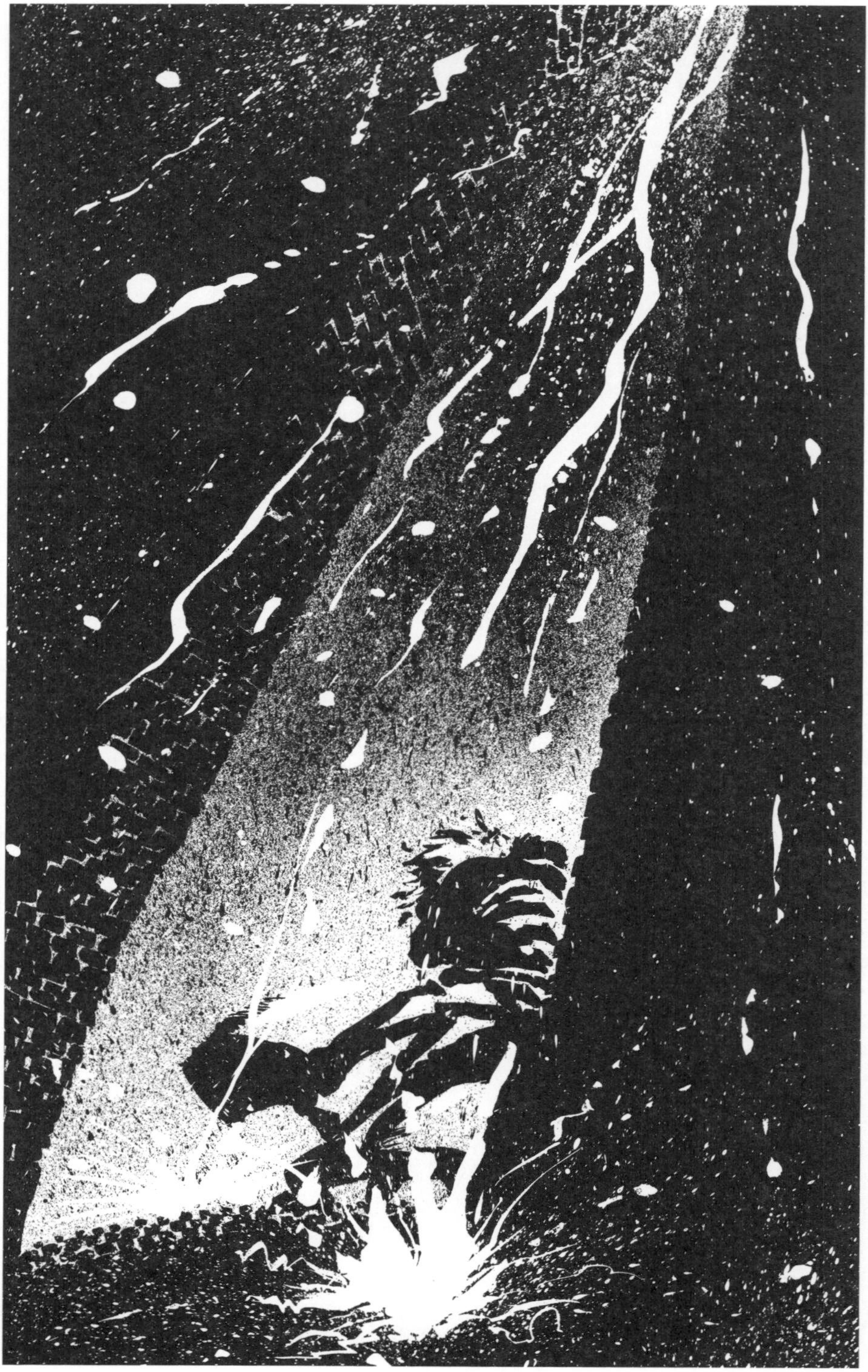

and it was all set in the snow, and I went crazy trying to figure out how he did the snow without any Wite-out. I had no idea you could do that. It leaves a frighteningly clean board *[Eisner laughs]*.

EISNER I was always surprised to find, when I saw Milton Caniff's originals, that he used a lot of white paint. The thing that intrigued me when I first saw Milton Caniff's work was his handling of snow. He did a house in the snow with just a few black shadows and a window, and you knew it was a house in the snow.

MILLER He also had a way of implying texture that was pretty shocking. When I was putting together *300*, I was trying to figure out how to imply the texture of the helmets. I didn't want to do ornate detail, but I wanted them to feel like they were metal and they'd been on blocks the entire time. I was wondering what to do, and I looked at a Caniff *Terry and the Pirates* daily [newspaper strip] from the war [World War II], and there was a helmet there. I swear he must have inked the thing in about ten seconds, and it was perfect. A little stipple and it was there.

EISNER He was good.

MILLER The whole thing about the first *Sin City* is that I was rediscovering the love of drawing on that job. I had absolutely no boss, and it was the first thing I completely did from head to toe by myself.

EISNER That is pure Caniff: good basic drawing with an unlimited amount of black. It's courageous. As a matter of fact, that's what students used to refer to as courage. They used to ask, "Where did you get the courage to do all that black?" It's because you have a good, strong underlying drawing. It's good draftsmanship here.

MILLER The rain scene was one of two scenes where I first got the idea of simply not thinking about the number of pages. For me it was like I'd just stepped out of the cave into the morning.

EISNER I know how you feel. *A Contract With God* was the one where I finally came back and said, "To hell with this! It'll be 200 pages." But the problem that you set for yourself creates the innovation. *The Spirit* splash pages were the result of a problem. I didn't wake up one morning and say, "I'm going to

THE NAME IS **POWDER**, LIKE IN **GUN** POWDER... I BLOW UP JUST AS QUICK, AND I'M TWICE AS **DEADLY**...

THE **SPIRIT**

BY Will Eisner

take four pages for a rain scene leading me up to the character that you want me to see coming out of the rain. Motion is another thing we have a problem with. We have to imply motion.

MILLER When it comes to motion, one of the things I love about comics is that you're free to exaggerate motion.

EISNER You do that very well. Your cars really move *[Miller chuckles]*.

MILLER But we got sidetracked. I want to get back to the point about your lettering in *A Contract With God*. It was quite powerful.

do a splash page." It was a problem. I had a cover that was dropped into a newspaper, and I had to compete with everything else for the reader's attention. And I had another problem: I only had seven pages to tell the story, and I had to get the reader quickly into it. So the splash page came from that.

But the question of time...dealing with time in this medium is one of the key problems. There are several things that this medium is basically unable to deal with. One is sound, so we use balloons. The other is time. We can't deal with time.

MILLER Well, that's where all the fun tricks come in.

EISNER That's where all these things happen. That's where you can afford to

EISNER It was interesting, lettering that book. I threw away about thirteen pages of that book. I had originally set it in type, and I looked at it and looked at it, and thought, "The hell with it—I'm going back to balloons!"

That brings up a very interesting bit of comics history, which may be worth injecting here. Somewhere around the middle Thirties the newspaper syndicates decided they wanted to improve the quality of comics, and so they hired good illustrators like Alex Raymond. The idea was to bring in good people. Then just before the war, there was a newspaper in town, the *New York Compass*, that started a strip called *Barnaby*, and all the balloons were done in typeset. Because suddenly the struggle was about what to do about balloons—this terribly impossible device that we've stuck with—and they had to do something. This was an effort to add "quality."

MILLER I'm signing my death warrant here, but I've gotta say that Hal Foster was wrong.[1]

EISNER Well, Hal Foster was Hal Foster. He was not wrong, he was just Hal Foster *[laughter]*. I'll discuss balloons with you. The syndicates brought in great illustrators. Hal Foster was one, Alex Raymond was another, and there were a few other great pen-and-ink illustrators who were brought in to do comic strips. The idea was, let's get quality. Their idea of quality was better artwork. But the lettering in the balloons was something else again. Some said, "The hell with you, I'm doing my own balloons." Like Al Capp, whose letters were very, very large and really shouted. Just like Al. When Al Capp laughed, the whole building shook. When he talked, he talked *loud*.

MILLER I've always heard he was a handful.

EISNER Oh, he was. The point is, there was an effort to do something about the balloons. The balloons have always been a problem, and they still are today. It's something I've been thinking about and struggling with myself. It seems that one of the great inhibitions in this business, the thing that's keeping adult readers away from us, is the balloon. When readers open a book and they see balloons, they then close it because it's a comic book. If there are no balloons, they'll buy the book.

1 Miller is referring to Foster's lack of dialogue balloons in *Prince Valiant*.

MILLER I think that might be changing.

EISNER I hope so.

MILLER The balloons are so precious—I mean that in a good way.

EISNER Well, it's the only way to deal with a spoken word.

MILLER It's interesting that you mention there was a move to do that, because from time to time comics have employed type. Almost exclusively type and almost always to disastrous effect.

EISNER Harvey Kurtzman did it for years.

MILLER Kurtzman got rid of it.

EISNER No, he didn't. He used type in all of his balloons. He also used the umbilical balloons, which I hate. I used to argue for hours with Harvey. I said, "Harvey, you're going to ruin this business." He couldn't see it that way.

MILLER It's almost like either you decide or you don't that there's an article of faith that there's not more than one exchange per panel.

EISNER A balloon is supposed to be an integral part of the action. When you have type strung across, with umbilicals strung all back and forth, that has no connection with the action at all. But that was a phenomenon. One of the phenomena with this business was an attempt to lift the level of *quality* of the comics by introducing typesetting.

MILLER Remember when Gil Kane did it? Boy, did it not work.

EISNER No, it didn't. Type has a sterility.

MILLER It's cold, and there's

something about it being type that causes a person to overwrite. There aren't enough words here—I'll put some more in!

EISNER Typesetting is a problem with me. I have to do something with it to soften it up.

MILLER I have a real problem with it, too. The only place where I think I might play with it is in sound effects, because there's something so artificial about it that I *want* it to be wrong.

EISNER What I'm doing with it now... in *The Name of the Game* I really went all out trying to develop a combination with typesetting that may work. Really, it may attract the adult reader who's grown up with type and regards comics as a cheesy thing but illustrations as a legitimate thing. I'm trying to integrate them. So I'm using typesetting in that book to deal with time-changes and historical background and so forth. I don't know how well it'll work. I haven't seen the sales figures on that book, and I have no way of knowing how well the book has done so far. I got good reviews in France, however.

Well, so much for balloons. I think balloons are still a continuing problem. ★

Charles Brownstein is the Executive Director of the Comic Book Legal Defense Fund, a not-for-profit organization that defends the First Amendment rights of the comic book field. His publications about comics include *The Oddly Compelling Art of Denis Kitchen* and *Eisner/ Miller*. For more information on Brownstein and the CBLDF, please visit www.cbldf.org.

Douglas Wolk

Will Eisner and Frank Miller: The Raconteurs

I. The Eisnershpritz

There's a certain kind of rain that only falls in comics, a thick, persistent drizzle, much heavier than normal water, that bounces off whatever it hits, dripping from fedoras, running slowly down windowpanes and reflecting the doom in bad men's hearts. It's called an "Eisnershpritz," and it's named after the late Will Eisner, one of the preeminent stylists of 20th-century comics, who never drew a foreboding scene that couldn't be made a little more foreboding with a nice big downpour.

Eisner deserves his veneration in the comics world. He was one of the most gifted, innovative storytellers American comics have produced, and his work has had a lasting impact on the aesthetics and the economics of the medium. The comics industry's annual awards are named after Eisner; until his death in 2005, its honorees had the

"The Eisnershpritz" excerpted from *Reading Comics: How Graphic Novels Work and What They Mean* by Douglas Wolk: reprinted by permission of Douglas Wolk and Perseus Books Group/Da Capo Press. [©2007 Douglas Wolk]

thrill of being handed an Eisner Award by Eisner himself. (I was one of the awards' judges in 2001, and have never been starstruck as badly as I was meeting him.) Nobody's above criticism, though, and as much as I admire Eisner and treasure his work, it's hard for me to enjoy most of it without some severe reservations.

Eisner's '40s series *The Spirit* was the high-water mark of superhero comics for decades. The lead feature in a weekly comic book inserted into newspapers (in lieu of a Sunday comics section), it starred a hero whose mask was fairly incidental: the rest of the Spirit's costume was a crisp blue suit and hat with a red tie. *The Spirit* hit its stride in the half-dozen years after World War II, when Eisner (and his assistant and frequent ghostwriter, a very young Jules Feiffer) started using it as a springboard for an impressive variety of storytelling techniques and kinds of stories.

"*Spirit* sections" had a few hallmarks: exquisitely designed title pages, on which the words "The Spirit" appeared a different way every week (as an ad on the side of a building seen through a roof window, scraps of paper blown in the wind, a headline on a newspaper); beautiful *femmes fatales* with campy, punning names (P'Gell, Sand Saref, Sparrow Fallon); situations in which the Spirit would get badly beaten up (and, perhaps, cuddled afterwards by the *femme* of the week). Other than that, anything went. A Spirit story could be a straightforward detective adventure, a satirical take on the new trends of postwar culture, a ghost story, a little Ring Lardner-style sketch. Readers never knew exactly what to expect.

The real attraction of *The Spirit* was Eisner's visual showmanship. There's something formally dumbfounding on almost every page of prime-period *Spirit*. He knocks out panel borders to let the page's negative space do extra work, aims his picture plane so it cuts through walls and ceilings and the ground, makes panels look like movie frames or file cards or pages from a children's book, and interrupts stories for fake "commercial breaks," all in the interest of keeping the story moving as smoothly and entertainingly as possible. His characters are rumpled and rubbery, emoting like ham actors; Eisner captures every gesture at its most scenery-chewing moment.

The best *Spirit* stories have been reprinted over and over (sometimes in versions Eisner redrew decades after their first appearance), and they're still a delight to read: the brutal showdown with the Spirit's nemesis the Octopus, the introduction of vamp-among-vamps P'gell, the bitter little morality tale "Ten Minutes," the tale of how Gerhard Shnobble discovered too late that he could fly. A few years ago, DC Comics started reprinting all the original *Spirit* stories in handsome-looking hardcovers—the same "Archives" format they use for other old comics they own the rights to—and the cartooning in the Eisner's 1946-1950 *Spirit* books is at least twenty years ahead of its time. Parts of them are more like seventy years ahead of their time.

But open up almost any volume, and you're going to run smack into the most embarrassing stumbling block of the series: the Spirit's thick-lipped, bellboy-attired sidekick Ebony White, sometimes accompanied by his pal Bucken Wing. Yes, those were the sorts of caricatures that were common currency at that time; yes, Ebony makes a few stabs at greater dignity in *The Spirit*'s later years (and is also briefly replaced by an Eskimo sidekick named Blubber—not really an improvement—and then by a stereotype-free and personality-free white kid named Sammy). There's no getting away from the awfulness of the stereotype anyway. If readers have to actively historicize every page Ebony appears on to keep from cringing too hard to see the rest of what Eisner's doing, there's a big problem. That's probably why the *Best of the Spirit* volume published in 2005 is more properly the Just-About-Ebony-Free Best-Of.

It's an unimpeachable introduction to Eisner anyway. The 1949 story "Visitor" isn't one of his most famous stories, but it's a seven-page textbook in how a comics story's formal tricks can serve its plot. The first page, unusually for *The Spirit*, doesn't start the story—it's a symbolic "splash" image, a huge picture of the moon with a profile of the Spirit's head superimposed within it, and a mysterious woman standing on some kind of planetoid in front of it. We don't see the woman, Miss Cosmek, again in person until page four; instead, the story proper begins with a police report (on a black column running down the left side of the page) about a mysterious explosion during a bank robbery (shown as ripped gray-tone drawings that look like burned photographs), and the Spirit investigating on-site. One panel shows the scene of the crime surrounded by white space, as if it's a prop on the page's stage, and the next shows us the Spirit and a pair of cops, in shadow, through a hole blown through the wall—but all we see of the "wall" itself is more white space.

The next page is mostly exposition, but you wouldn't suspect that from its abundance of visual spectacle. It begins with a dramatic overhead long-shot of the Spirit walking along a skinny alleyway (echoing the column-on-the-left composition of the previous page), and goes on to encompass three consecutive images of a conversation with a heavily accented Italian landlady ("Mrs. Pizza") that are respectively from a slightly tilted perspective, looking up a winding staircase, and peeking in through a keyhole in a ramshackle apartment, then a broad comedy routine involving Mrs. Pizza's toddlers crawling all over the Spirit while he's trying to use the phone, then some establishing shots of Miss Cosmek's house—on top of a cliff, by a lighthouse, breakers like upside-down Eisnershpritz crashing against a lookout marker, with dozens of gulls flapping overhead. That's all on *one page*, mind you, and there's a staggering amount of plot and playfulness crammed into the remaining four, too, including a charming, silent nine-panel sequence to end the story.

Eisner drifted away from *The Spirit* in its last few years (and the leaden, run-of-the-mill artwork by other members of his studio suggests that his adventurous techniques didn't rub off), but the science fiction theme of "Visitor" showed up again briefly in some odd strips at the end of the weekly strip's run in 1952, in which the previously street-bound Spirit led an expedition to the moon. After its awkward final weeks, in which *The Spirit* shrank to four pages and incorporated some gorgeous artwork by SF artist Wally Wood (as well as garbled last-minute fill-ins when Wood couldn't meet his deadlines), Eisner spent most of the next few decades working on instructional comics for the U.S. Armed Forces.

His next great leap came in 1978. *A Contract With God and Other Tenement Stories* was a standalone book of four broad, melodramatic comics stories about the residents of an old Jewish tenement in the Bronx. It wasn't serialized, it didn't belong to any particular genre, it didn't look like either mainstream comics or "underground comix," and the cover of the paperback edition (a man walking up tenement steps in a driving Eisnershpritz) was captioned "a graphic novel by Will Eisner." It wasn't the first book-length visual narrative (Eisner mentioned Lynd Ward's novels-in-woodcuts from the '30s as an inspiration), and he wasn't quite the first person to come up with the phrase "graphic novel," but that's the name that stuck.

A Contract With God also introduced Eisner's mature drawing style—a looser, more idiomatic, more fiery version of his *Spirit*-era technique. Freed from a limited page-count, he let his images grow as big as they needed to, and only used panel borders as occasional graphic elements; as often as not, backgrounds would dissolve into a patch of thin vertical or horizontal slashes, fading from consciousness like the borders of the reader's visual field. His characters' body language became rubberier and more stagily expressive than ever before. The whole thing looked exquisite, and for the first time, cartoonists had a model for what long-form art-comics could be. The problem was that it was a badly flawed model, because the stories themselves are club-footed and mawkish. They flow along frictionlessly—Eisner knew how to suck readers into a narrative—but his ironies are cheap, and his attempts at profundity aren't very deep at all.

Over the next 27 years, Eisner wrote and drew about a dozen more graphic novels, with increasing seriousness of purpose. They're all drawn with ferocious, assured verve, and frustrating to try to read: leaden fables populated by oafish Everymen, chops-licking businessmen, women who are almost inevitably either inscrutable erotic temptresses or hen-pecking harridans, and the occasional autobiographical stand-in. He also drew several books of shorter sketches of his beloved New York street scenes, and two of the earliest books to analyze how comics work: his groundbreaking 1985 how-to treatise *Comics and Sequential Art* and its sequel, 1996's *Graphic Storytelling and Visual Narrative*. And he settled into his role as the universally loved elder statesman of comics.

Eisner's importance—and the gift for soulful, essence-capturing drawing that never left him—let him get away with a lot, though. His final graphic novel was the posthumously published *The Plot: The Secret Story of the Protocols of the Elders of Zion*, hailed as an important testament in the way that good artists' posthumous work tends to be whether it deserves it or not. As always, the artwork is splendid: a crew of scraggly characters with grand body language, perfectly idiosyncratic layouts and design, and a range of techniques from woodcut-inspired linework to impressionistic ink-wash. There's even some Eisnershpritz. The subject matter is potentially fascinating, too: the most persistent anti-Semitic libel, "The Protocols of the Elders of Zion," a plagiarized, repeatedly discredited batch of murderous lies that's still reprinted all over the world.

Regrettably, *The Plot* is a trainwreck of a book. Despite the title, there's no plot to speak of, just a pile of undigested factoids about the *Protocols*, stagily arranged into scenes in which all the dialogue is exposition. In the middle of it, there's an unfinishable seventeen-page scene in which prose passages from the *Protocols* are pasted in side-by-side with the sections of Maurice Joly's 1864 *Dialogues in Hell Between Machiavelli and Montesquieu* that they paraphrase. (The story of the *Protocols* is more complicated than that, actually, and Umberto Eco's introduction to *The Plot* mentions some sources

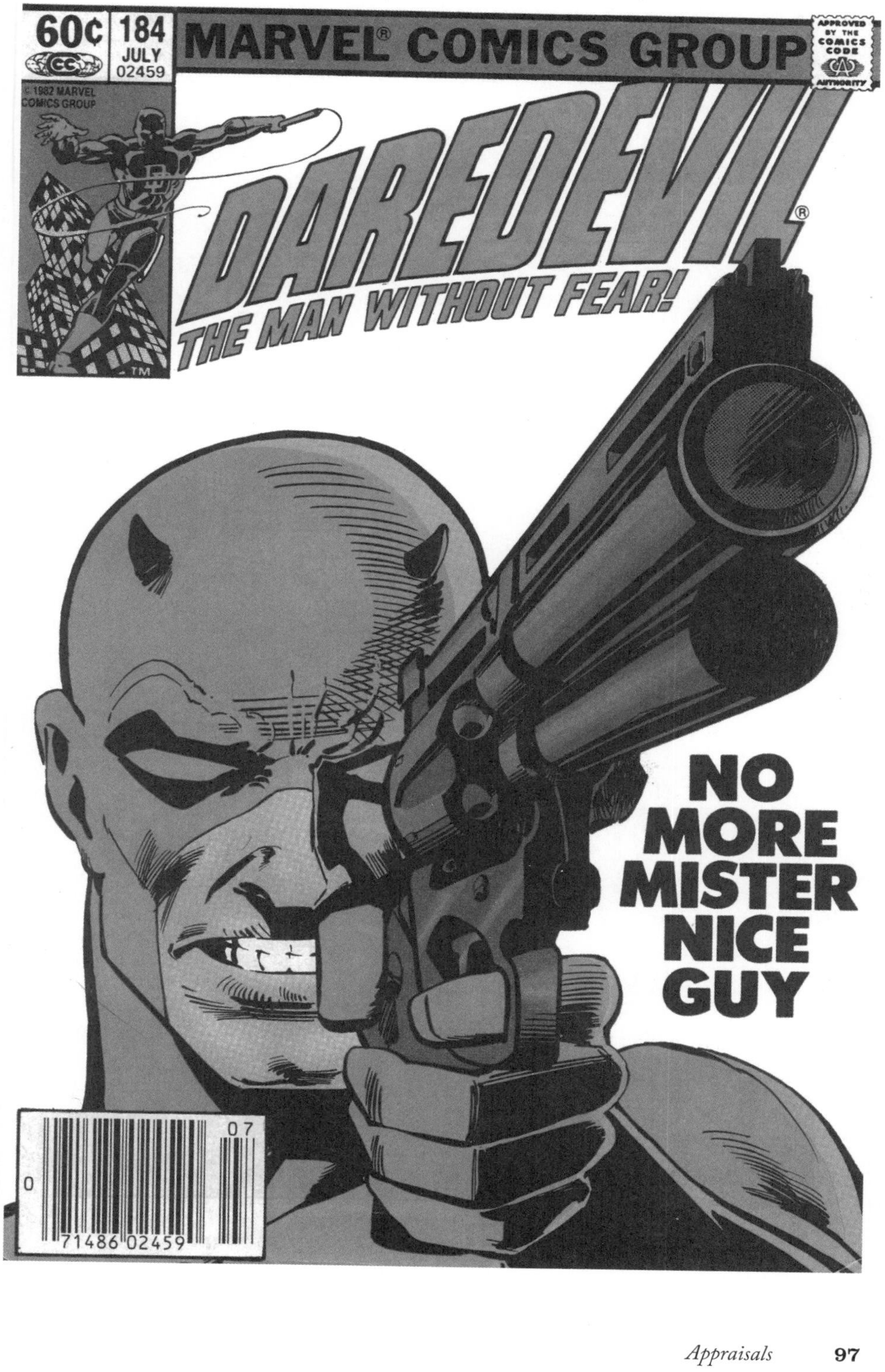
60¢
184
JULY
02459
MARVEL COMICS GROUP
APPROVED BY THE COMICS CODE AUTHORITY
© 1982 MARVEL COMICS GROUP
DAREDEVIL
THE MAN WITHOUT FEAR!
NO MORE MISTER NICE GUY

for them that Eisner doesn't.) Eisner-the-writer, it turned out, stuck Eisner-the-artist with a nearly impossible task: turning a story with virtually no visual elements and no narrative drive into a sequence of images. More than any other cartoonist of his era, Eisner attempted to leap from light entertainment to art. But there wasn't a leap to make, and *The Plot* suggests he didn't realize that what was most valuable about his art was his mastery as an entertainer.

II. Sinners And Saints

Eisner's most prominent disciple is Frank Miller, the writer/artist of *Batman: The Dark Knight Returns* and *Sin City* projects, and probably comic books' biggest marquee name right now. There's a book of conversations between them, *Eisner/Miller*, that's modeled on *Hitchcock/Truffaut*, and in 2006, Miller announced that he would be writing and directing a movie of *The Spirit*. The film will probably give Eisner's work the widest circulation it's had since at least the '40s, which is some kind of karmic payback: when the young Miller made his initial mark with his early-'80s work on the superhero series *Daredevil* (in collaboration with inker Klaus Janson), the *Spirit*-era Eisner was his biggest and most obvious influence.

What Miller brought to *Daredevil* was an almost outlandishly bold sensibility. The New York of its setting became an Eisneresque urban landscape of steam and bricks and shadows, updated for the electric '80s; the narrative tone became savage *noir*, with bracing outbursts of consequential violence; the characters became crisp, grotesque caricatures, talking in clipped and stylized patterns. Miller's drawing proceeded from his striking design sense, and his covers for *Daredevil* practically leaped off the stands and punched readers in the face. Also, there were ninjas—lots of ninjas, including Daredevil's ex-lover, an assassin named Elektra. (The terrible *Daredevil* and *Elektra* movies were both mash notes to Miller's run on the series.)

After *Daredevil*, Miller essentially had carte blanche within the mainstream comics world. The next big project he took on was *Ronin*, an incoherent but spectacular story about a samurai warrior and a future city. It wore its artistic influences on its sleeve: the French cartoonist Moebius and the *Lone Wolf and Cub* comics by the Japanese team of Kazuo Koike and Goseki Kojima. (At the time, almost nobody in America had heard of manga.) It made a splash when it was published in 1983 and 1984, partly because Miller dictated that it had to be printed beautifully on high-grade paper stock, which was unheard of for an American comic at that time.

After that came Miller's greatest hit: *The Dark Knight Returns*, a four-issue miniseries published in 1986, for which he reunited with Janson. (Reportedly, they fell out during the project, but agreed to finish it together.) It was a Batman story, set a few decades in the future, in which the battered old hero comes out of retirement for one final stab at cleaning up his corrupted city, accompanied by a spunky young girl who's the new Robin.

The Dark Knight Returns tipped over most of the superhero clichés within kicking distance, and extrapolated adult psychological complexity from forty-five years' worth of Batman stories in which it had mostly been lacking. Miller treated Batman as a sort of benign psychopath: a man driven by his parents' murder to dress up like a bat and fight crime with his fists, who repeatedly enlisted children into his private war. The standard phrase used to describe *TDKR* and the comics that followed its example was "grim and gritty," which wasn't entirely fair. The book's mood is dark and brutal, and Batman's interior-monologue narration couldn't get any grimmer: "Something explodes in my midsection—sunlight behind my eyes as the pain rises—a moment of blackness—too soon for that... ribs intact—no internal bleeding..." (Dave Sim parodied its tone expertly in *Cerebus*: "Cardiac arrest. Acute uremic failure. Leakage in the left ventricle. Mustn't. Black. Out.") Still, *TDKR* is larded with comedy, if rather black and sour comedy: any character who isn't either a hero or a bastard is an object of ridicule.

TDKR was a huge hit, and its collected edition has never stopped selling (although it's been redesigned a few times). Curiously, a lot of its initial buzz seemed to be about what it *wasn't*—a typical Batman-and-Joker story, unstylish and lily-livered—rather than what it was. Still, a lot of superhero comics suddenly aspired to be just like it, or as much like it as they could manage. Across the board, fight scenes got more brutal than they'd ever been before; ichor flowed everywhere; heroes and villains quickly acquired dark psychological motivations for their actions; a sense of eschatology crept into superhero stories, as their battles became battles for the soul of modernity. The rough-riding, macho pronouncements of Miller's Batman ("Tonight, *I* am the law. Let's ride") became disconcertingly common. And the "prestige format" of nicely printed, squarebound forty-eight page stories about future or past or alternate-world versions of familiar characters spent the next fifteen years being flogged to death.

What ought to have made more of an impact on mainstream comics, though, was Miller and Janson's stylistic distinctiveness and sense of design. Miller had finally found a technique of his own that didn't owe much to Eisner or anyone else: hard-angled vectors crashing into each other, thick and thin, jerking everything into crinkly forms, decorated with tiny, eccentric lines that earlier comics printing techniques wouldn't have been able to reproduce. (*TDKR*, like *Ronin*, was given the deluxe-paper treatment, and its individual installments were squarebound: the message was that this was no floppy little ordinary monthly funnybook.)

And Miller's design for *TDKR* brilliantly allowed him to pack it densely with plot and details. Almost every page is based on a sixteen-panel grid, although most pages combine a cluster of those sixteen spaces for a larger panel, or substitute television shapes with caption above them for a couple of spaces (TV commentators act as a sort of idiot Greek chorus for the story). Some panels bleed out to the margins of the page beyond the confines of the grid itself—the four-by-four checkerboard is a pulse underlying Miller's storytelling, not an unvarying rhythm. He's absolutely in control of the book's pacing and dynamics, from its quiet, wry moments of character interplay to the triple-fortissimo climax. When he gives us a full-page shot of Batman riding a rearing horse straight toward us with his gang of followers behind him against a roiling night sky, it's corny and over-the-top, but it's as huge a moment as he wants it to be anyway.

...BUT HE'S HARDLY AS DANGEROUS AS HIS ENEMIES, IS HE? TAKE HARVEY DENT, JUST TO PICK A NAME...

THAT'S CUTE, LANA, BUT HARDLY APROPOS. AND HARDLY FAIR TO AS TROUBLED A SOUL AS HARVEY DENT'S.

HE CERTAINLY IS TROUBLE FOR HIS VICTIMS.

WAS, LANA. WAS. IF HARVEY DENT IS RETURNING TO CRIME -- AND PLEASE NOTE THAT I SAID IF -- IT GOES WITHOUT SAYING THAT HE'S NOT IN CONTROL OF HIMSELF.

AND BATMAN IS?

CERTAINLY. HE KNOWS EXACTLY WHAT HE'S DOING. HIS KIND OF SOCIAL FASCIST ALWAYS DOES.

THEN WHY DO YOU CALL HIM PSYCHOTIC? BECAUSE YOU LIKE TO USE THAT WORD FOR ANY MOTIVE THAT'S TOO BIG FOR YOUR LITTLE MIND? BECAUSE HE FIGHTS CRIME INSTEAD OF PERPETRATING IT?

YOU DON'T CALL EXCESSIVE FORCE A CRIME? HOW ABOUT ASSAULT, FAT LADY? OR BREAKING AND ENTERING? HUH? TRY RECKLESS EN

SORRY, MORRIE, BUT WE'RE OUT OF TIME -- THOUGH I'M SURE THIS DEBATE IS FAR FROM OVER FOR THOSE OF YOU WHO CAME IN LATE, TODAY'S POINT VERSUS POINT...

...WAS CONCERNED WITH LAST NIGHT'S ATTACK ON DOZENS OF INDIVIDUALS WHO MAY HAVE BEEN CRIMINALS BY A PARTY OR PARTIES WHO MAY HAVE BEEN THE BATMAN.

ALSO OF CONCERN IS THIS MORNING'S ANNOUNCEMENT BY POLICE MEDIA RELATIONS DIRECTOR LOUIS GALLAGHER THAT A DEFACED DOLLAR COIN WAS FOUND ON ONE OF THE SUSPECTS...

...IN LAST NIGHT'S PAYROLL ROBBERY. THOSE WHO REMEMBER THE CRIMES OF HARVEY DENT WILL RECOGNIZE THIS AS HIS TRADEMARK.

POLICE COMMISSIONER GORDON HAS REFUSED TO CONFIRM THAT HE HAS ISSUED AN ARREST ORDER...

SCREW THE PRESS!

STILL HOT ON THE HEELS OF BATMAN'S APPARENT RETURN...

NO MORE LEAKS, GALLAGHER -- OR I'LL HAVE YOUR HEAD ON A STICK!

SON OF A...

...THIS DOES GIVE ONE A SENSE OF DEJA VU...

TURN THAT GOD DAMNED THING OFF, MERKEL.

A SAD, STRANGE CRIMINAL WAS HARVEY

COMMISSIONER, IF YOU PLEASE...

Following a handful of late-'80s one-off projects and collaborations with artists including Geof Darrow and Dave Gibbons, Miller spent most of the '90s writing and drawing *Sin City*, a loosely linked series of stories—or "yarns," as he calls them, which sums up the problem with them concisely. They're all about being hard-boiled. Really hard-boiled. Tough. Manly. Not wimpy. And hard-boiled. And dark. The women are dames. Real dames. The men are real men. Some of them need killing. Some of them are just the kind of men to do it. The hero of the first one, having gotten his first dose of the electric chair, declares "Is that all you got, you pansies?" I mentioned the hard-boiled thing, yes? Also, there are ninjas. One of them is a dame ninja on roller-blades (which, okay, is kind of cool). And there are very tough men with guns. And dames, real dames, with red dresses and lipstick. And so on. Miller has written and drawn seven volumes of this stuff, not to mention co-directing a successful and excruciatingly faithful movie adaptation, with two more to come.

Obviously, *film noir* is a big, big touchpoint for *Sin City*—and that also goes for the new art style Miller developed for it, which cranks up the chiaroscuro effects he's always favored as high as they can go, light and dark exploding against each other and sending shrapnel everywhere. (When it rains in Sin City, we get the Miller version of an Eisnershpritz: cruel, freezing splinters of ink and light.) His drawing is violently powerful, solid, passionate. But there's also something off-putting about the whole affair, which is that the same stark black-and-white contrast extends to *everything* in the *Sin City* books. What kept a lot of classic *film noir* intriguing was the deep, murky gray morality beneath the sharp contrast of its appearance, and *Sin City*'s morality is anything but gray. There's something monotonous and almost infantile about the way the series' characters are all either supermen, patsies or demons; the bad guys aren't just evil, but snorting, cackling, puppy-crushing evil.

Fortunately, he broke away from the clichés of *Sin City* with his ridiculous 2001 sequel to *The Dark Knight Returns*, variously known as *DK2* or *The Dark Knight Strikes Again*. It's much less controlled than the first *Dark Knight*—actually, it's pretty much off the rails, and its tone rarely dips below a full-throttle attack-yodel. It's longer than the first book, too, although it reads a lot faster; instead of reusing the sixteen panel grid, Miller just makes everything huge and spectacular (although he throws in a thirty-three-panel page for the hell of it).

TDKR wasn't exactly crying out for a sequel, and the odd thing about *DK2* is that Miller doesn't seem to have anything more to say about Batman. The "Dark Knight" in the title is a sales hook, more than anything else—an excuse for Miller to work up a grinning sugar-high, smash all of DC Comics' toys and kick over the sandbox. The best-remembered sequence from *DK2* is actually a sex scene between Superman and Wonder Woman, and Miller brings in every crazy Silver Age gimmick he can think of (if you don't happen to know what the Bottle City of Kandor is, a major plot point makes no sense).

If *Sin City* pushed the contrast level of black-and-white cartooning as far as it could go, *DK2* cranks the dial all the way in the opposite direction: its colors (by Miller's longtime partner Lynn Varley) are eye-gougingly bright, garish and blurry, and Miller's

linework is so thick and chunky it seems to have been drawn with a big knife—he never uses the *Sin City* standby of solid black where Varley can stick in a bombastic computer color effect instead. One advantage Miller finds in drawing characters with colorful, immediately recognizable costumes is that he doesn't have to be too precise about their bodies or features, so they get the same wild, gleeful distortions as everything else. It's a blow against the anatomical hyperrealism of mainstream comics, as vernacular and stylized as any art-cartoonist's work.

Still, Miller seems unclear on what kind of story he's telling, other than a really loud, not very serious one. There's cheesecake, presented in a way that poses unconvincingly as a critique of cheesecake; there's outright comedy, but his contempt for most of his walk-on characters gets irritating quickly. There's also some very flat characterization. In the first *Dark Knight* book, Miller's heroes had psychologies, and at least hints of interior life. In the sequel, they've got speech patterns, but that's it—they're inscrutable gods, clashing in the sky, the one-dimensional power fantasies superheroes are always accused of being.

Most of all, there's politics, posing as disgust with politics of all kinds. Instead of the blatant Ronald Reagan of *TDKR*, the U.S. president in *DK2* is nothing but an electronic construct, manipulated by the wicked Lex Luthor. The leftist hero Green Arrow and the rightist hero The Question are both objects of ridicule, along with witless television ideologues; there's also some satire about America's curtailment of civil liberties, although it feels pasted onto the plot. Miller tries to suggest that the story's politics are neither left nor right—a lot of ideologues, left and right, like to claim that they're presenting a "fair and balanced" viewpoint.

But if the story's glorification of violence and its dominion of the strong over the weak are so ludicrously out-of-proportion that they don't quite count as cryptofascism, Miller can't stop stacking the deck: his combatants are totally right-on or irredeemably evil in a way that allows for no moral quandaries at all, which is at least crypto-reactionary. More recently, he's gotten a little more overt about his politics. Back in 1984, *Batman: Holy Terror* was the first working title for a project that eventually evolved into *The Dark Knight Returns*; Miller recently declared that he'd be using it at last, for a story in which Batman takes on Al-Qaeda. (Oh dear.)

Unexpectedly, *DK2* has aged better than *TDKR*. The original *Dark Knight*'s earnest, controlled rancor feels a little tired now; the fun of the sequel is that Miller seems completely unfettered, like he's got no goal in mind but to make the biggest, gaudiest, most overheated comic ever. By its end, he's almost entirely sacrificed plot to spectacle—you can almost hear the "1812 Overture" in the background. If it's annoying on any level, for its ideology or its fannishness or its gaudiness, that's sort of the point: what it tries to do most is provoke a reaction. The blazing delight Miller obviously took in drawing it makes it easy to get swept along by his craft and boldness, and quash one's readerly objections until the book is over. At which point they all pop up again. ★

Douglas Wolk is the author of the Eisner- and Harvey-winning *Reading Comics: How Graphic Novels Work and What They Mean*. He writes about comics for *The New York Times*, the *Washington Post*, the *Believer* and elsewhere. http://www.douglaswolk.com/

Bob Andelman

"A Great Bamboozler": Howard Chaykin on Will Eisner

One of the interesting facets of writing Will Eisner's biography was determining the reliability of my subject's memory. Eisner was 85 when I met him in February 2002 and, with repeated exposure over the next almost three years, I came to believe his mind and recall were easily as sharp as mine—and I was half his age.

There were only a few stories that Eisner told me that gave me pause over that time, tales that didn't quite add up with independent confirmation. One of them was about an encounter he had with artist Howard Chaykin at a Barcelona comic book convention.

When I was dubious about his account, Eisner told me to call his old friend Joe Kubert. "Joe will confirm what I'm telling you," he insisted.

So I called Kubert, who got his first job working for Eisner at his studio in Manhattan's Tudor City in 1941. Kubert told me a lot of great stories, but he didn't exactly recall the

Bob Andelman's interview with Howard Chaykin first appeared on June 9, 2007, on Andelman's blog and news site, *A Spirited Life*.

Barcelona incident the same way that Eisner did. Here's the way I wrote it for draft of *Will Eisner: A Spirited Life*:

Eisner told a story about attending a comic book convention in Barcelona several years ago. He and several prominent artists, including Howard Chaykin and Joe Kubert, were talking about different comics. Chaykin mentioned *Blackhawk*, which he once illustrated.

"Will created *Blackhawk*," someone said.

"It was one of the few fascistic things I've done in my life," Will said. "It was one of the few fascistic things I've done in my life," Will said. Chaykin, as we'll see below, recalls Eisner going further, with Eisner saying he felt the same way about Chaykin's *American Flagg*.

"Fascist?" Chaykin said. "I'm one of the most liberal guys you'll ever meet!"

Eisner, as gentle and amiable as he was about most things, on occasion antagonized a fellow artist and this was one of those times. Chaykin felt Eisner was calling him a fascist and it made him quite angry.

"It looked like it was gonna get into a fistfight," Eisner said. "Joe Kubert finally separated us."

Sounds like a great anecdote. And across two years of being interviewed for this book, Will told many stories that were confirmed down to the final detail. But in this rare case, his memory of events was not shared by others who were there.

"Howie's the kinda guy that says a lot of things for effect more than anything else," Kubert said when asked about the incident. "It may have seemed to Will that it might have led to something. I'm sure it happened and that Will felt that way. But I couldn't imagine Howard ever getting into an actual fight with Will."

Eisner insisted the story happened the way he told it. He was pretty frustrated with me that I left it out of the book, in fact. But with Kubert deflating Eisner's version, there wasn't any point in going further and calling Chaykin.

Fast-forward to February 2006. I was a guest at Megacon in Orlando, promoting the book. On a break from my table, I dropped by to say "Hello" to artists Nick Cardy and Al Feldstein, both of whom I interviewed for *A Spirited Life*. To Feldstein's left was Chaykin.

When I bid adieu to Cardy and Feldstein, I dropped promotional postcards for my book at several booths. Seeing Chaykin was occupied with a bunch of autograph seekers, I dropped a postcard on his table and tried to move on quickly.

"Hey!" Chaykin called out to me. "Why the fuck do you think I'd care about a book by Will Eisner?"

Uh-oh.

Trapped—and with an audience, too—I introduced myself. Chaykin didn't have anything nice to say about Eisner, so I tried to excuse myself. Didn't work. Instead, I told Chaykin about the missing story from the book. That stopped him in his tracks. He couldn't believe Eisner would ever tell an unflattering story about himself.

More amazing for me, Chaykin confirmed the essence of the story and cussed Kubert for denying the seriousness of it. At that moment, the idea for extending the biography through a series of online interviews was born. There were so many people with Eisner stories to tell that I thought it would be fun to add to the legend.

Howard Chaykin agreed to be the first in the *Will Eisner: A Spirited Life Interview Series*. The following conversation took place by telephone on March 2, 2006.

Bob Andelman Do you recall the first time you encountered Will Eisner's work in any significant way?

Howard Chaykin Absolutely. That was the summer of 1966—the Harvey reprints. I had never seen the stuff before, and it absolutely boggled my mind. Wait—I'm wrong. The first time I was aware of it was in an article that ultimately became Jules Feiffer's book, *Great Comic Book Heroes*, published in the magazine section of the *New York Herald Tribune*. I'm pretty sure this predated the Harvey material. I could be wrong. Eisner did a strip about The Spirit working with John Lindsay for his re-election. Ebony objected to it because of his relationship with HarYouAct, a local civil rights group of the time.

Then I saw the Harvey material. I was impressed with that. It was very intriguing. I was really blown away by his drawing of women. I had no idea how much of an influence at the time he had on Wallace Wood, who I considered the archetype of drawing hot babes. Will's women were very sensual—a cross between Milton Caniff and Woody.

ANDELMAN How old would you have been in 1965?

CHAYKIN I was 15. I think those books came out in the summer of 1966, was that right?

ANDELMAN I think that is about right.

CHAYKIN I was 15 and a total geek. Hugely fat. Very unhappy. Archetypal comic book fan.

ANDELMAN Having been surrounded by them for the first time in years while promoting *A Spirited Life*, I am laughing.

CHAYKIN There's been an invasion and a successful conquest—with commercial slogans like "Nerds Fuck Things Up, Geeks Do It Right." I was totally asocial and living entirely in fantasy.

That was a great year for comics, with Joe Kubert's *Enemy Ace*, Bob Oksner's *Angel and the Ape*, and Nick Cardy, Denny O'Neil and Sergio Aragonés on *Bat Lash*.

ANDELMAN I was wondering if you were going to mention Nick Cardy. I was thinking that was a pretty big time for him.

CHAYKIN I love Nick's stuff. There's a bunch of guys, Nick among them, like Ross Andru, Frank Thorne, a few others. Nobody pays attention to them, nobody even acknowledges their existence. I just think their work is just brilliant.

ANDELMAN Let me bring you back to Will Eisner.

CHAYKIN By the way, did you like the guy?

ANDELMAN Yeah, I did, actually. He treated me extremely well.

CHAYKIN Because you came between him and the truth.

ANDELMAN I hope not.

CHAYKIN He obviously treated you well because you were going to be putting his life on paper, and he wanted to be revealed in the best light possible.

He was very competent at manipulating his own image.

ANDELMAN Well, I would agree with that to a point. I didn't have any restraints in terms of what I would say or what I would write or who I would talk to.

CHAYKIN I have to say, I am astonished he ever told you the story that brought us together in the first place.

ANDELMAN He treated me very well. There were only two rules that we worked with on this, and I was with him for about two and a half years doing this. The first rule was laid down by Denis Kitchen and Judy Hansen, his agents, and that was, "Do not ask him about family, do not ask him about children." And they wouldn't tell me why, they just said, "Don't." We were together about a year and a half, and at that point I think I had his trust. We were at his kitchen table and it was very late. He was never up past nine o'clock, but there we were, still talking, still talking…

CHAYKIN This was in Florida?

ANDELMAN Yeah. And I was asking him about some pictures on the refrigerator. There was a picture of him and Neil Gaiman and Art Spiegelman and Scott McCloud, and then he just started showing me the others, and then he said, "And this is my son." And I said, "I didn't know you had a son." And that was the night that he really came clean with me about stuff, that he had a son and a daughter and that his daughter had died of leukemia in 1969, she was 16, and that just destroyed him. They took all family pictures out of the house. Most people who knew him or met him after she died had no idea that he had children.

CHAYKIN I had no idea. I had met Will's wife a couple of times, and I am stunned.

ANDELMAN The thing was, I was told by Denis and Judy not to bring it up, so suddenly Will brings it up, and he says, "I know that you need to know about this, and I appreciate that you haven't asked, but I know you have to know," so he told me the whole story.

It turned out that *A Contract With God* was basically his response after several years, that was the first time he ever dealt with her death, that it wasn't about some religious Jew mourning the death of his daughter, it was about him mourning the death of his own daughter. And Denis has the originals and has been showing them this past year. In the book, the daughter's original name was Alice. So we talked about that.

CHAYKIN I am impressed by that, because he was so effective in controlling his own image and his own press. I think he was a great bamboozler. I think he manipulated the people who adored him, and used them to manipulate his own image. I really do.

ANDELMAN When did you start feeling that way about him?

CHAYKIN It probably traces back to the interviews, the "Shop Talk" stuff that he did back when Kitchen was publishing *The Spirit*. I found out that he was completely re-editing his side of the questions.

ANDELMAN Oh? I hadn't heard that before.

CHAYKIN I happened to be hanging with Gil Kane. Gil had ethical issues. I have no illusions. I loved Gil Kane despite his failings, okay? I take a lot of heat for this, but that's life. I learned a great deal about being a guy from Gil, including tying a necktie. He went absolutely bug-fuck when he read the "Shop Talk" thing he did with Will.

Gil was an extremely articulate man, a man who liked talking to a man who liked to talk. He was astonished and appalled when he found that Eisner had rewritten and re-edited his side of the interview, I guess to make himself sound more astute, I don't know. And that opened that can of worms for me, and I began to be aware, with *The Dreamer* and all that stuff, that he was reinventing the past. This guy created the modern system of the division of labor in the comic book business. He was a great businessman who passed himself off as an artist when it was necessary and as a businessman when that became necessary.

ANDELMAN The main issue that brought us to this point was Barcelona, but I kind of wondered before we got to that if you had any previous encounters with him worth noting.

CHAYKIN No. We had met in passing, at shows or conventions in San Diego. I always found it odd he moved to Florida. It seemed so "Jew-y." I am serious. Florida seemed an odd place for someone as cosmopolitan as Will.

ANDELMAN So kind of set the table for me in terms of Barcelona. Why were you there?

CHAYKIN I was a guest at the

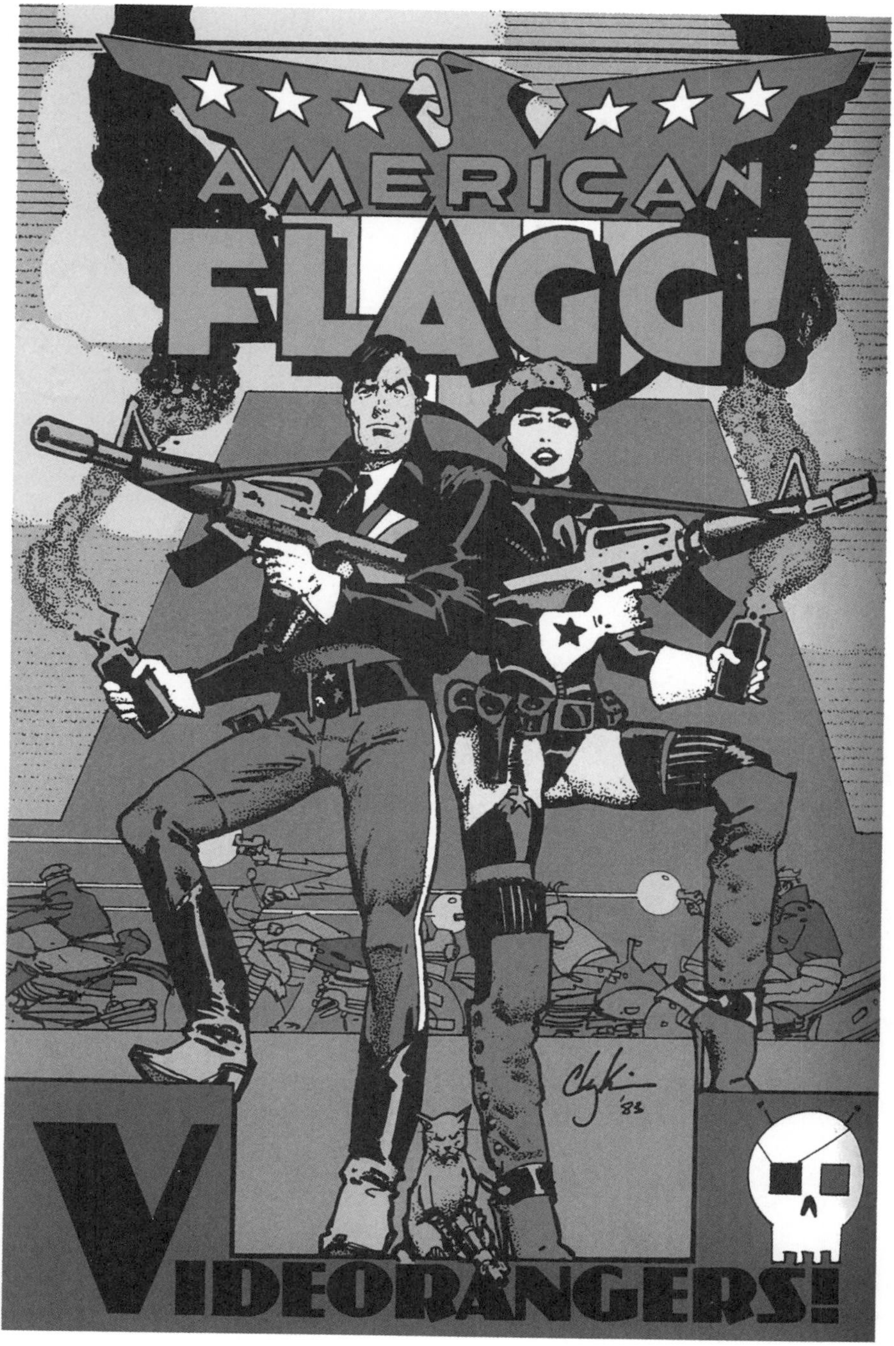
AMERICAN
FLAGG!
VIDEORANGERS!

convention. As per Joe Kubert's recollection and Will's recollection, we were talking about *Blackhawk*, but we got onto *American Flagg*, and Will accused me of producing fascist comics. I realized after the fact this was based solely on his interpretation of the cover imagery. I love fascist imagery, it's extremely powerful. I like what the Italians did, I like what the Germans did. I don't subscribe to their politics. I am a huge fan of Ludwig Hohlwein, for example.

ANDELMAN I'm sorry, who?

CHAYKIN Ludwig Hohlwein.

ANDELMAN I don't know his work.

CHAYKIN He was an advertising artist in Germany in the '20s and '30s who became a very important player doing posters for the SS. Amazing graphic designer. Very influential to this day.

ANDELMAN I will read up about him. I have probably seen the work, but I have just never heard the name.

CHAYKIN The influences on the covers for the *Flagg* books were poster art. I've never been happy with my cover work, but I think I finally achieved some measure of success with those covers.

I don't see my work showing any of the influence of Jack Kirby or Will Eisner. I have an enormous respect for Will's work. In the book I hope to write, I give Will credit for basically creating the vocabulary for the medium in which we are working. He codified the language. Up to that point, it was a series of experimental ideas. Then Harvey Kurtzman made it better.

Will would make pronouncements based on what little information he had.

He tended to imply he knew more about something than he did and frequently got away with it. He never read much contemporary comics stuff. He had no understanding of the context in which those covers existed, and yet he was willing to call me a fascist. And that's just something that I will not accept.

I am a child of liberal parents. I'm proud of my distinctly left liberal place on the planet. I have been called a left wing faggot on the Internet too often to accept otherwise. I am not a bleeding heart—I'm a Cold War liberal, a classic socialist Jew. I was raised in a predominantly secular home.

ANDELMAN I think that kind of brings us to what happened. I remember Will telling me, "I almost came to blows with Chaykin," or, "He almost slugged me," or something to that effect.

CHAYKIN I'm not going to hit anybody—but I was very annoyed. I offered Kubert $10 to kick his ass, and Kubert said that for $20 he would think about it. I was being facetious. I found him insulting and condescending. And I found his relationship with most people was profoundly condescending, yet they were willing to take it because he was so beloved a figure.

ANDELMAN Right. You were not planning to lay a hand on Will.

CHAYKIN Oh, come on. I don't do that sort of thing. I tend to shoot from the lip. I give credit to Jack Paar for having so profound an influence on my life.

One of the frustrations of working in

the comic book business is the constant misappropriation of the word "cynic" when skeptic is what they mean. I considered Will a cynic, if you will, willing to say and do anything to remain in the good graces of his audience. I don't think he was a bad guy, but he was condescending in a particularly German-Jewish way. I'm a Russian Jew, and I spent most of my boyhood being slum-lorded by German Jews, so I have my issues.

ANDELMAN Is there any part of you that wishes you could have had this conversation with him and worked that out?

CHAYKIN Not especially. I don't really care. The weird thing is, the two guys I feel are most responsible for the evolution of comics storytelling were Will Eisner and Harvey Kurtzman—and I never got along with either of them.

I have never outgrown my worship of Harvey's stuff. When I hire a new assistant I hand them the *Two-Fisted Tales, Frontline Combat* and *Terry & the Pirates*, to show them what they should be doing.

My personal feelings aside from Harvey, the work remains brilliant. I don't feel that way about Will's stuff. I will crack open Harvey's stuff and be amazed and intrigued by it, the *Mad* stuff, *Two-Fisted Tales* and *Frontline*. That rarely happens with Will's stuff. It's pretty, but I don't really care. The only time I think about Will Eisner is in a conversation like this.

ANDELMAN So you have read my description of what happened in Barcelona between you, Will Eisner and Joe Kubert. Is there anything you would fill in with the gaps of what was going on?

CHAYKIN He was not referring to *Blackhawk*, he was referring to the *Flagg* covers.

ANDELMAN All right.

CHAYKIN And Joe did not separate us. I literally—facetiously—offered Joe $10 to kick his ass, and Joe said, make it $20 and we will talk.

ANDELMAN And that was in front of Will.

CHAYKIN Yes. We were kidding. I was pissed off, but not pissed off enough to lay a hand on an old Jew. Frankly, Kubert could have kicked my ass. Twenty minutes ago, I was talking about Joe with my assistant. Joe could still take me apart and put me back together any way he wanted. I ran into Joe in the lobby of the hotel at a San Francisco convention, and he gave me a shot to the chops with his knuckles; he rattled my teeth. Joe is an incredibly, physically powerful guy. He is in amazing shape.

But no, there was no danger of any fisticuffs. On the other hand, I think what Will said was something he pulled out of his ass, because he knew nothing about me or the work. All he was basing it on was his cursory impression of the *Flagg* covers.

The assumption Will made was there was him and everyone else—that the everyone else is doing work that's by nature secondary to his vision. His dismissal of Jack Kirby is a classic example of this. I'm not a huge fan of Kirby's, but I acknowledge his place in the pantheon. Will never thought very highly of the work. I am sure you know this.

ANDELMAN It was never actually said to me.

CHAYKIN Will regarded Jack as a guy who just turned the pages out.

ANDELMAN If so, I think that had a lot to do with where they started together, and that is what Jack was doing at the beginning, and I don't think he ever saw him any differently, but…

CHAYKIN Like the work or not, Jack is the center of the universe in the evolution of modern work. The man was able to spew out work of astonishing, consistent quality over a period of fifty years. That's mind-boggling.

ANDELMAN After Barcelona, as you walked away from that situation, obviously your view of Will was changed. You went from just having a casual familiarity and knowledge of him in that sense to, "Boy, I really can't stand this guy."

CHAYKIN I was not happy with this character.

ANDELMAN Were there other things that happened between then and now that grew that, or was it just…

CHAYKIN Well, we were together again in Brazil in 1993 or 1994, and Kubert was there again. Joe is always a character in this story!

ANDELMAN What happened in Brazil?

CHAYKIN Eisner was baiting me. I don't remember the specific details. Eisner was traveling stag, his wife didn't

come down. There was Jules Feiffer and his wife, Kubert and Muriel, Jose Delbo and his wife Mabel, me and my wife. Will baited me. I think he did so because he felt he could. Jules calmed down the situation and I appreciated that, because there was no reason for me to lose my temper.

I had a prickly relationship with Will that lasted until he died. The last time I saw Will was at an Eisner Awards at the San Diego convention. I'm an early riser, a go to bed at 10:00 o'clock guy. It was 11:30, and I am having to be social and comfortable and conscious while I was exhausted. I wasn't all that thrilled to be there in the first place. I am a guy who never wins these things. I want the attention as much as the next guy, but by the same token, I don't care that much about the enthusiasm of others. If I did, I would probably have done different work, so I accept the fact that I am the architect of my own adversity. By the same token, at 11: 30 at night, I want to be in bed.

Will was there. We were cordial. He understood that we were not people who were close.

ANDELMAN Have you encountered anyone else over the years who has had similar exchanges with him?

CHAYKIN Gil Kane.

ANDELMAN What did Gil say about him?

CHAYKIN He felt very much as I did.

ANDELMAN Did Gil ever tell you any specific stories?

CHAYKIN Not really. We had a shared antipathy. Will was made a saintly figure before he died. This guy really was a talented artist, but a major portion of his career was played in the same ballpark as Jack Liebowitz and Victor Fox. He may not have been as big an asshole or mobster, but the guy was ethically compromised in his own way.

ANDELMAN After you are gone, do you think there is someone out there who will have any similar feelings toward you?

CHAYKIN In terms of my behavior?

ANDELMAN Well, yeah, or anything. You are a very strong personality. You say what is on your mind.

CHAYKIN I'm roundly despised by people who don't know me, but I believe I'll be held in fairly high regard by most people. I'm not really worried.

ANDELMAN Okay, I'll ask. Who is the guy who is more widely despised?

CHAYKIN I think John Byrne is more widely despised than I am.
  As for how I'll be remembered, I'm a cult figure. I never became a star, and I'm comfortable with that.
  I live a small life. The work speaks for itself. I'm ashamed of some of it because I take credit and blame equally. And I am bitter about some stuff and okay with others, but as I get older, I get less bitter, because I give less of a shit.

ANDELMAN As you look ahead, put on your forward-looking glasses…

CHAYKIN As I become the old Jew as opposed to the late middle-aged?

ANDELMAN There you go. How do you think the industry and the greater group who might have some knowledge of Eisner, how do you think he will be regarded in twenty, twenty-five, fifty years? Will people even remember him?

CHAYKIN Well, does anybody remember Lou Fine, does anybody remember Hal Foster? The industry is very much a reflection of contemporary culture. ★

Bob Andelman is the author of the biography, *Will Eisner: A Spirited Life*. He is also the host and producer of Mr. Media Radio: http://www.mrmedia.com.

In a career that dates back to the early 1970s, **Howard Chaykin** has worked as a comics artist, comics writer, illustrator, and screenwriter. He continues to work in the comics field, maintaining his reputation as a sweet-natured pain in the ass.

Alan Moore

"There is White and There is Black and There Is Nothing in Between"

My name is Alan Moore, I'm a comic writer and magician living in Northampton.

I probably first encountered Steve Ditko's work when I was seven or eight. I probably wouldn't even have known it was Steve Ditko at the time. There was a kind of elegance, a tormented elegance to the way that his characters stood, the way that they bent their hands. There was something even in the nine-panel page grids that he used to habitually use that brought a kind of claustrophobia, a kind of paranoia to the work. His characters always looked very highly strung. They always looked as if they were on the edge of some kind of revelation or break down. There was something a bit feverish about Steve Ditko, and I pursued my love of Ditko well into adulthood and it became a kind of low level addiction.

Jonathan Ross' interview with Alan Moore appears in the documentary
Searching for Steve Ditko, directed by Jonathan Ross, first broadcast September 16, 2007.
[©2007 Hotsauce TV Ltd.]

And there was something about the way that Ditko handled a superhero in *Spider-Man* which made a feature of the urban landscape. In *Superman* and *Batman* buildings were just to be flown past. But as with Jack Kirby, Steve Ditko brought this quality to his cityscapes that had real character. It was a slightly paranoid and slightly shadowy character, but that suited very much the kind of introspective, often melancholy mood of a lot of those early *Spider-Man* episodes.

Doctor Strange's entire universe, with all of these psychedelic, floating giant mouths, and cubes, and spheres—you suspect that probably Ditko was investing an awful lot of his own personal symbology in just the odd floating shapes in the background.

Very odd piece of work in that Steve Ditko, who was politically very conservative, was suddenly the idol of a whole generation of hippies who were reading some kind of drug parable into these colorful other dimensions that Doctor Strange was zipping through, all without ever leaving his Greenwich Village apartment. He would just be sitting there on the floor in a trance while imagining that he was battling the Dread Dormammu in some kind of zone of the nether dimensions.

Steve Ditko has got so much of his DNA in all the characters that he created. I mean I know that there were good issues of *Spider-Man* after he finished the book with issue 35, something like that. I know that John Romita did some very good work on *Spider-Man*, but I kind of lost interest with the first non Ditko issue because the character was so much a part of Ditko's world that it looked kind of dull when it was an ordinarily muscled man in a *Spider-Man* costume.

There was something about Ditko's characters where I began to wonder whether they had come to him in dreams. There was something so odd about them that they looked like the kind of almost nonsensical characters that you might see the name of, or the image of, in a dream, and jot it down when you woke up.

Anybody who had even committed the merest of crimes was wandering into this poisonous gray area. They were tainted and they could only expect the kind of terrible punishment that his Mr. A was likely to mete out to them.

One of the stories that I remember hearing, I think from Marv Wolfman, about Steve Ditko, was him going to visit Steve Ditko when I think Steve was living above a thrift store, somewhere in New York. They'd had a pleasant conversation and before Marv Wolfman left, Steve Ditko said, "I just wanna show you something." And he took a little white empty calling card, and took a magic marker, drew a line down the middle, and shaded one half of the card in black, and said, "There is white and there is black and there is nothing in between."

[Re: *Watchmen*] The most unpleasant right-wing character is Rorschach. He almost ends up as the hero of the book. He's certainly the character who seems to have the most ferocious integrity. Even if his politics are completely mad, he has this ferocious moral integrity that has made him one of the most popular characters in the book. And obviously, that ferocious moral drive and integrity, that was kind of my take upon Steve Ditko.

Somebody had been interviewing Ditko and had said, "Have you ever heard of this book, *Watchmen?*" And, he said, "Oh, wh-what's that?" And they said, "Well, it's got this character called

Rorschach." And he said, "Oh yes. Rorschach. He's like Mr. A. Except he's insane." *[Laughs]*

[Re: Ditko's *Hawk and Dove*] The Hawk side of the equation is perhaps a little bit non-intellectual, perhaps a bit headstrong, but he's a big rugged can-do action hero. The Dove half of the equation is a simpering, effete character, in a lackluster blue and white costume. And all he does, he doesn't get into fights, he stands around and agonizes about the need for violence. It was obvious where Ditko's sympathies lay in the equation.

Basically the only thing that The Creeper had going for him was his freakishness. He just used to sort of jump around in a yellow and green and red garish costume laughing, and this seemed *[Laughs]* to be his major super-power, that he could laugh at will.

I mean, Steve Ditko as far as I understood it, has lived in some very reduced circumstances throughout his life when Marvel, who have been raking in money hand over fist with characters that he created, or co-created—but which essentially in my heart were Steve Ditko creations.

Steve Ditko's drawing was completely expressive on its own and the way that he told it in these very small panels with the very small figure of Spider-Man crushed under this immense weight of machinery, it told you everything that you needed to know.

That sequence made it kind of obvious that it was mainly the visual dynamics that were powering the scene. Yes, Stan Lee was putting balloons in that said "I must try harder… no use, can't do it …" and things like that.

Steve Ditko was an original voice both in his drawing style and in his writing and his politics. I would say that today's audiences, if they're going to see things like the *Spider-Man* films, they should be painfully aware throughout every moment of the film that this is a character that was created by this extraordinary artist, Steve Ditko. ★

Alan Moore is a writer from Northampton, England, whose comics include the groundbreaking *Watchmen*, *V For Vendetta*, *From Hell*, *Lost Girls* and *The League of Extraordinary Gentlemen*, among many others. His latest work includes *The League of Extraordinary Gentlemen: Century* from Top Shelf and *Dodgem Logic*, a fanzine created by Moore and published by Knockabout.

Peter Bagge

Spider-Man Sucks

I don't like superhero comics, and never did. Well, like all little boys, I certainly liked the CONCEPT of a superhero, and did my fair share of towel-bedecked backyard "flying" when I was 5 or 6 years old—my main source of inspiration being the old live-action Batman and Superman TV shows, both of which I still find campy and garish and thoroughly entertaining. But the DC comics featuring the same characters during that time (c. mid '60s) seemed suffocatingly lifeless and dull to me. The art was so stiff and formal, and the stories were told in this very deliberate step-by-step manner, like an instruction manual on how to assemble a ham radio kit. In retrospect I find these same comics rather amusing, the way they so carefully and earnestly describe the most laughably absurd and implausible scenarios imaginable. I doubt the authors were going for irony, however, so even in retrospect I'm reluctant to praise them for the unintended effect their work would have on me 40 years later.

This situation was very frustrating to me, since I loved comic books in general, and still do. I love the feel and format of them, and I could be very forgiving when it came

---

to the content or lack thereof, as I'd mindlessly wade though mountains of Archie, Sad Sack and Dennis comics. Yet then as now, the comics shelves were dominated by superhero titles, and due to the sheer preponderance of them I gave many of them a try. Yet as I got older my resistance to them only increased. Those COSTUMES, for one thing. These characters were supposed to be Men of Action, yet they looked like effeminate clowns! I suppose I could make the requisite "gay" wisecrack here as well, but to be honest superheroes and their appeal aren't really a gay thing at all, which makes them even more pathetic. They'd at least make a lot more sense to me if they were!

The one line of titles that showed some promise for me back then were the new Marvel comics, particularly the titles drawn by Jack Kirby, such as *The Hulk* and *The Fantastic Four* (I also preferred characters like The Hulk and The Thing, since they DIDN'T look like effeminate clowns!). Kirby's art really stood out from the crowd in those days: it was so lurid and full of life; gruesome yet beautiful. It jumped off the page! I also liked all the wisecracks the characters made, in part because it seemed like a wink to the reader that yes, what we're asking you to believe here is patently absurd, but play along with us anyway...

What I DIDN'T like about Marvel titles, however, was that all their titles were serialized. Not only was this a shameless trick to hook you into buying the next issue (which was obvious to me even as an 8-year-old), but after plowing through a solid twenty-two page story I wanted some sort of resolution. I wanted "The End," NOT "to be cont."! This approach also made the stories FAR more involved and convoluted over time, asking the reader to become far more invested in the characters than I could possibly ever want to be. The sad thing is, this scam paid off, many of their readers DID make that investment, and all the other superhero publishers followed their example. Thus a huge separation was made between dedicated superhero comic fans and the rest of society, as them term "casual reader" became something of a misnomer. This was also the beginning of a distinct and recognizable class of humans who now make up the core of comic fandom, though terms like "nerd" or "comics geek" didn't exist at the time. Instead I used to think of them simply as "weird creepy guys who have no friends."

So now these "heroes" in psychedelic ballet costumes also all had complex, convoluted personal lives, to go along with their "professional" woes. Gone too was Stan Lee's snarky wise-cracks, as he replaced himself with younger writers who not only grew up on this stuff but who also totally BELIEVED in The Marvel Universe, and wanted the reader to totally believe as well. The suspension of disbelief required to become thoroughly engrossed in these comics had now reached a level that bordered on the psychotic, and the most psychotic of all Marvel's "flagship" title and character, Spider-Man.

I was turned off by Spider-Man right from the start. For one thing, his costume is particularly ugly (in my opinion, anyway). I also hated the artist who originally drew and co-created the series, Steve Ditko. This statement will read like sacrilege to most comic fans, who will prattle on forever about Ditko's "compositional skills," which he indeed did have. But that was ALL he had. The way he drew FACES, for one thing... I'm told Ditko is and always has been a bit of a shut-in, and I believe it, since I have

to wonder if he ever really studied another human's face long enough to get a real feel for it. What he drew instead were COMPOSITES of faces, as if he were a space alien who needed someone to verbally describe what a human looks like, or what a "smile" is. This stiffness and formality extended to the entire human figure, giving everything a cold lifelessness that I could not find less appealing.

What I now DO find appealing about the early Spider-Man comics is Stan Lee's writing. Lee is a bit of a whipping-boy among hardcore comic fans, since they feel he gets way too much of the credit for creating the Marvel Universe over Ditko and Kirby, which is true (though if you ever read anything that the latter two scripted by themselves you'd have to admit that neither of them had a clue how to tell an engaging—let alone coherent—story). Stan "the Man" also has this arrogant, Rolex watch-flashing, Miami-tanned mobster persona that's very easy to loathe. Yet when you read the early Spidey comics it's also obvious that one time Stan Lee was some scrawny, sci-fi loving Jewish kid named Stanley Leiber, and who most likely adopted a gruff, wiseguy exterior purely as a defense mechanism at first, until he eventually BECAME that gruff wiseguy. "Stan the Man" is Stan Lee's greatest fictional creation of all!

My point is, Peter Parker IS the young Stan Leiber, probably even more that Stan Lee was aware of at the time. It's like the miserable, insecure young Stanley just sort of leaked out of him, consciously or not (and I think not, even if he claims otherwise). Unfortunately, he also felt obliged to make his stand-in, Peter Parker, look and act like a total goy, and a very handsome one at that, which makes it a harder for me to buy into all that loneliness and alienation jazz. Well, I suppose I'd feel pretty alienated too if I was the only Iowa farm boy to ever grow up in the heart of Brooklyn, but then you all already know by now how much I stink at all this suspension-of-disbelief stuff.

What's really annoying about Peter Parker, however, is the relentless POUTING he indulges in. Except for when he's in costume, he rarely gloats or even expresses a single moment of joy over his superheroic exploits. Instead all he can do is dwell on the downside of his chosen profession. He's a real glass-half-empty kind of a guy, totally in need of a serious bitch-slapping. He was at his worst whenever he was around one of his beautiful girlfriends, at which point his pout-o-meter would go through the roof... All these endless "misunderstandings" that went way beyond his never-ending I-can't-tell-her-I'm-Spider-Man dilemma. I remember this one story where a college-aged Peter Parker stood up a girl, and when she confronted him about it he said nothing—he just stared at the ground the whole time with this wounded puppy dog expression until she stormed away. Only rather than being out all night fighting crime, it turns out he was up all night cramming for an big exam! "But why tell her that," pouted Ol' Pouty Petey. "She wouldn't understand." She wouldn't? What's not to understand?!? But God forbid he should miss a single opportunity to feel sorry for himself, even if that opportunity is totally self-created.

At this point you're probably wondering how a self-described Spidey-hater like me would know so much about the Spider-Man "canon." The reason is that I was hired by Marvel several years ago to do a one-shot Spider-Man comic, in my own style and with my own "take" on the character. I know, I couldn't believe it either, but this was back when Marvel was struggling financially and were willing to take a shot at anything (a situation that quickly resolved itself for them, ironically, by the enormous success of the first Spider-Man movie that came out shortly afterwards). My "take" was to use Spider-Man as an allegory for the whole Stan Lee vs. Steve Ditko back-story, which involved actually reading all the issues they did together. I also threw a whole lot of ME into the story, and what I was going through at the time, which was rather self-indulgent on my part, but who cares. My editor told me that the readers of the regular Spider-Man series hated its very existence, since it messed with the fragile suspension-of-disbelief thingie that their pathetic existence so relies on, so to this day I have no idea who DID buy it!

Reading superhero comics beyond adolescence seemed REALLY weird to me. Sure, I understood the appeal that these escapist fantasies can have for some fat ugly kid who can't throw a baseball. But then, me and my friends were hardly a bunch if "winners" ourselves—we were all covered in zits and sucked at sports, too! But none of us retreated into some total make-believe fantasy world starring a bunch of "heroes" who more closely resemble the type of guys that beat you up every day. We were in the process of finding and BECOMING ourselves, and not FLEEING from ourselves. It makes as much sense to me as a teenage girl playing with Barbie dolls—not merely collecting and dressing them, but acting out scenarios with them as well, the way little girls do. Superheroes are kids' stuff, f'r cryin' out loud!

Yet what was considered nerdy and pathetic when I was a teen is now totally acceptable and "cool" in our current infantilized society. For example, the other night I caught a bit of an awards show on MTV where the young actor who recently played Batman in the movies was sharing the stage with the young actor who'd played Superman in the latest film incarnation of that character. At one point the Batman actor commented on how the character he plays is much cooler than Superman, which elicited cheers and jeers from all the heavily tattooed rappers and rockers in the audience. The odd thing was, none of it was tongue-in-cheek or played up for laughs. Everyone was being dead serious regarding this comparison. This country has gone insane.

It's not just the nerd-ification of America that would explain the huge popularity of so many superhero movies lately, however. For one thing, the genre lends itself extremely well to all those computer-generated special effects—effects that also serve the dual purpose of obliterating dumb stories, bad dialog and idiotic premises. They also break a lot of the old comic books "rules" by, say, letting the hero get laid now and then, or by having the characters make jokes re: the absurdity of their entire existence, thus expressing a certain self-awareness that rarely occurred in the comics, if ever. This sort of rule-breaking drives many of the true believers crazy, and I'd be willing to give them a certain amount of sympathy because of it, if they weren't also the same people waiting on line for days to see these movies. Still, it's amazing how slavishly true these big budget Hollywood flicks are to the superhero source material, Spider-Man in particular, especially when you consider how much they'll mess with everything else. As a non-superhero cartoonist stuck in a superhero dominated industry, I'd love to see them completely mess with Spider-Man purely out of spite! Yes, I'm bitter, and so what. Spider-Man still sucks! ★

Peter Bagge is the creator of Buddy Bradley, whose adventures have been chronicled in the seminal indie comic *Hate*, published by Fantagraphics Books, Inc. The cartoonist also has had comics published by Marvel, DC and Dark Horse, and has a social commentary strip that runs in the libertarian magazine *Reason* (collected in 2009's *Everybody Is Stupid Except For Me: And Other Astute Observations*). His work has also appeared in *Hustler*, *Mad*, *The Weekly World News* and the *Oxford American*.

Donald Phelps

Letter Of The Law: Ditko's *Mr. A* Period

Steve Ditko's major, and (though its influence may be visible only intermittently) enduring contribution to the American comic book has been as pioneer and colonist of his own terrain: his definition and redefinition of reality. That is, not an alternate reality—as in what is commonly recognized and presented as "fantasy" in its comic-book and Hollywood manifestations—but Ditko's ongoing, always inchoate perception of the world. In its diverse, often calamitous progress (as it were); far beyond the bounds, requirements or talents of many comic-book artists.

Ditko's *Mr. A* has been furnished and utilized by its creator as an articulation of our world's current and immediate realities, and, in his ongoing dry yet resonant voice, a polemic against what he sees as the world's malignant deceits: its false peace offerings; its two-faced reassurances—to wit, about moral issues that many of us prefer to assume are dead, or at least *hors de combat*.

"Letter of the Law: Ditko's Mr. A Period" appeared in *The Comics Journal* #258 (February 2004). [©2004 Donald Phelps]

In one of those paradoxes whose validity he often seems ill-disposed to acknowledge, Ditko has effected his own local liberation of the comic book through the exigencies he has (in common with many a good frontier governor) invoked. His graphic style surges and pounds with contrasts between the ubiquitous black and white (to which Mr. A has lent symbolic trenchancy). Outstanding is the writhing, teeming partnership of razor-stroke lines (now serpent sinuous; now Art Deco angular) and churning compositions. The drawings are now commandingly stark (as in the repeated upright postures of Mr. A, acting as hero/emcee) and flow aswarm with borderline chaotic cascades of faces, intricately attitudinizing bodies—and words.

Words supreme; well beyond the hip chatter and arcade barker hyperbole of familiar superhero texts. Words at large, and words writ large. Blocks of text; torrential bold-faced proclamations of moralistic nouns: "Lies," "Deceit," "Dishonesty," "Corruption"; in stormy montage—interspersed with cascading black dots, like a volcanic ash overflow. Reproduced headlines—"Teens Terrorize Streets, Subways," "Crime in City Soars"—all contribute to the inundating scripture of Mr. A's and Ditko's nonstop meditation/proclamation; surmounted again and again by the glowing, defiantly all-white figure of Mr. A, and/or his calling card: a simple rectangle, halved by divisions black and white. No pernicious grays need apply.

Mr. A was as committed a moral absolutist as was, say, Harry Julian Fink's Dirty Harry Callahan; save that Mr. A very seldom if ever engaged in gunplay; and in private life, he was an ethically devout newspaperman of mythic lineage, named Rex Graine. Amid the baroque horde of costumed superheroes, Mr. A's simple uniform (his mask was a protective helmet of contoured steel) was as a Puritan rallying cry for sober reality. That phrase "steel helmet" recalls to me, as it may to others of my generation, Gene Evans as the misanthropic Sergeant Zack in Samuel Fuller's spitting-tough Korean War film. Unlike Sergeant Zack, however, Mr. A was no misanthrope: simply a devotee of ancient moral/rational canons—well supplied with adrenaline.

Although (in the two-part fiction-clad diatribe against the UN) Mr. A allows a fleeing hitman (impersonating him) to plunge to his death, the overtone of his moral realism is far removed from that of death-dealing bravos like Spillane's Mike Hammer, or Donald Hamilton's Matt Helm. Mr. A is Steve Ditko's legate, and perennial personal message bearer (one refrains from citing Jeremiah; considering Ditko's/A's express scorn for organized religion).

Ditko's rousingly dogmatic tone may seem virtually to demand the title "Crusader," although certainly not in the counter-realistic sense embodied by Batman and others of his like. Yet, I have never seen the word so much as used by Ditko. His reticence, I suspect, comes from the association of crusaders with gratuitous force; something Ditko has explicitly rejected again and again, while subscribing to retaliatory (justified) force, e.g., criminal oppression.

In truth, Mr. A is a frontiersman in an age-old tradition: maintaining, declaring and defending his reality, which is moral reality itself. That sounds like a spacious enough office; but, for Ditko the artist, space is a steadfast, if often combative, partner. His stance is unflinchingly and unapologetically parochial; insisting on the momentous relevance

of moral issues; insisting also on the potency, dignity and explosive potentiality of language; all as viewed through the localizing lens of the comic-book narrative, familiar at least in its outlines, with which Ditko has survived from the '60s onward.

Ditko's reflections on what he projects as the epidemic of sickly moral acquiescence in his world repeatedly leaps the boundaries of familiar political ideology, as well as those of popular genre. His didactic passion eventually created what amounted to a new genre. *The Question* is an amalgam of discussion (always through and with himself) and visual broadsides, the latter of which offer same latitude to the saturnine frisks and rollicks of Ditko's humor. Although not conspicuous in *Mr. A*, such humor is always imminent in Ditko's tumultuous compositions, the ever-present upheavals of conspiracy and betrayal. The frenetic tumblings and chargings recall free-for-all sequences from Preston Sturges' comedies of the '40s; recall in turn Sturges' darkest satire, *The Great Moment*. The film's theme (articulated in the career of Dr. William Morton, dentist and perfector of anesthesia) was the tragically farcical undoing of entrepreneurial genius by elastically scrupled collective interests. The bitter preface originally written by Sturges was replaced by a populist-placating homily. Steve Ditko might happily have signed his name, right underneath Sturges', to the first.

One is reminded that the sharpest edged iconoclasm and radical opinion often find a medium not in conventional satire, but in farce. The spirit of farce can often be sensed buzzing and circling through the backgrounds of Ditko's crime-smasher narratives. An average page, detailing labyrinthine intrigues and crazed spirallings of action, suggests a frenzied giant puppy, shaking the crystalline lines of the drawing. A succession of panels on a single page may present a patchwork quilt of veering perspectives: incursions of *décor*—desk corners, pillars in hotel lobbies—may turn a simple scene into an obstacle course. A view may be telescoped through successive doorways, as in the camera work of a Gregg Toland or Lee Garmes.

Like a cheerful poltergeist, a note of tipsy elation joins Ditko's polemic energy; and on infrequent but memorable occasions, blossoms as humor. The humor of "Midnight

Special," a 1967 *jeu d'esprit*, is appealing and eerie, with the surreal tone of Magritte. A tier of strip-like panels is beautifully etched in blacks, grays and silvery whites; a single white ray slashes the night, like the ray of righteousness on which Mr. A takes his stand. Here, however, the mood is grotesquerie muted into quaintness by the decorous beauty of Ditko's drawing.

In a similar, though broader comedic tier "The Break-Out" (1974) takes an oblique shy at costumery; that all but indispensable accouterment of many Ditko colleagues and rivals, and infrequently engaged by Ditko himself. The dreamy weirdness of the earlier cartoon is replaced by the floppy jauntiness familiar in the work of *Mad* masters Jack Davis and (Ditko's patron at *Witzend*) Wallace Wood. Ditko may also be found, in his 1973 one-shot *Masquerade*, taking costumed heroics on a notably lighthearted romp; featuring boy-and-girl masqueraders in a screwball Hollywood setting. The co-ed adventure of the pair is staged by Ditko as a "meet-cute" sitcom. Their expedition against studio conspirators takes place amid a surreal visual hubbub; including an endlessly chortling exec, and another who spits out acronymic phrases, defined in footnotes (NOIGEI—"NOw I GEt It").

A dimly resonant echo of the '30s seems to permeate Ditko's work occasionally; like Masquerade's hark back to the Hollywood of *Boy Meets Girl*, Ditko's reflections on present-day moral quiescence sometimes suggest the comic-book advertisements familiar to readers of Sunday supplements from the '20s through the '50s. The old term "thinking out loud" aptly apostrophizes the open-letter tone of his perorations. Despite their haranguing inflections, they are basically intimate; addressing individual readers with a tone not of the bully pulpit, but of the lecture platform in a small auditorium. Beneath their earnestness is the amateur's security: not smugness, but the unpretentious confidence of trust in a limited but sure terrain.

Disagree one may and should, with numerous tenets; for example, his opposition on his often-visualized scroll of mercy and justice. Likewise, he is explicitly anti-Intellectual, anti-Humanitarian and anti-Religious. All of the above values are lampooned in flaringly baroque caricatures, often attended by hordes of slavish worshipers. My favorite is the Neutralist: a little man in black-and-white striped policeman's attire, whose huge-toothed smirk and black glasses recall the ethnic caricatures of Japanese military officers during World War II. Familiar ideological fences, however, are resolutely trampled. Scratchy comfort is left for freelance capitalism in Ditko's caricature of the "Pragmatic Businessman."

Ditko's work as entertainer, fabulist and edifier is fueled by a raw vigor, a creative crudity that accords with his graphic acumen curiously but effectively. His broadside brashness and bodacious literalness recall such allegories as Swift's "A Tale of a Tub," or Hawthorne's "The Celestial Railway." His relation to language suggests that of a frontier father: solicitous, yet hard-handed; insisting that manners and clothes be sober, responsible, functional. Ditko insists on the potency of language; but also that such language be stringently monitored. Robin Snyder's *non pareil* commentary on Ditko cites the late Richard Weaver's aphorism: "Ideas Have Consequences." Ditko affirms and safeguards the concreteness of language, against what he depicts as a deluge of kitschy collectivist cant.

One of my favorite non-Mr. A episodes is "The Case of the Silent Voice." A disgruntled scientist avenges himself on crooks who have cheated him with a specially constructed ventriloquist's dummy (resembling an embalmed vaudeville comic) that when triggered, belches forth accusations against the betrayers. The polemics, however, are composed of solid letters, which batter their targets to death. As giddy as the concept sounds, Ditko's volcanic drawings lend a macabre piquancy. I recall panels from Mesmer's *Felix the Cat* in which Felix floats to safety on dialogue balloons, and does battle using exclamation marks as clubs. Another recollection furnished me, however, is a somewhat darker one; though easily as pertinent. A long-ago story by Robert Graves, "The Shout," dealt with an ancient lethal weapon of Australian tribes: a super-stentorian shout, which, though inaudible, could kill from immense distances.

That memory, I believe, underscores the constant bulky phantom of primitivism that is never far distant from Ditko's work. One bears in mind Ditko's imago of Illicit Force: a towering, mostly naked fellow of boulder-like muscles whose forehead is all but submerged between eyebrows and hair. In other words, a veritable model for The Hulk, whom Ditko co-authored with Stan Lee. Ditko utilizes the Primitive conspicuously as an avatar of reactionary savagery. A 1974 fable, "The Captive Spark," shows a progressive cave-dweller, discovering fire and the deployable benefits of nature, later exiled and denounced by his fellow troglodytes.

Such hardshell reaction, for Ditko, is inseparable from the Collective. Yet, *vide* The Hulk, Ditko also sees Primitivism as not only a possible but a necessary alternative identity for the hero who finds civilization actively threatened by barbarism. This perception puts Ditko close enough to the costumed-hero tradition to underscore his difference from it. He does not see the identity embodied in a costume as a "superior" or "more…real" identity in comparison with the rational being who adopts it. His instances of costumed champions—excepting perhaps the "Masquerade" fugue—are closer kin to the phantoms in *A Christmas Carol* than to Batman or Green Lantern. They are like armed images of conscience.

"The Screamer" (1974) routs a shrieking, vilifying throng of present-day Neanderthals (who are themselves manipulated by scheming politicos) as they lay siege to the citadels of ever-benign industrial science. The Screamer, an aerial acrobat wearing tights and a casque-like helmet, discountenances the Luddite hordes with a Tarzan-like yodel that streams like a banner across several panels.

The somber tones, muted by The Screamer's acrobatic élan, deepen with The Void, the adopted identity of Brad Dole, a personable young assistant DA. Even as his name connotes, The Void is an angel of death—which, however, he does not dispense but only forecasts. Suave in black tights and hood with a hollow-eyed mask, The Void seems an odd persona for the smiling and amiable Brad; who, moreover,

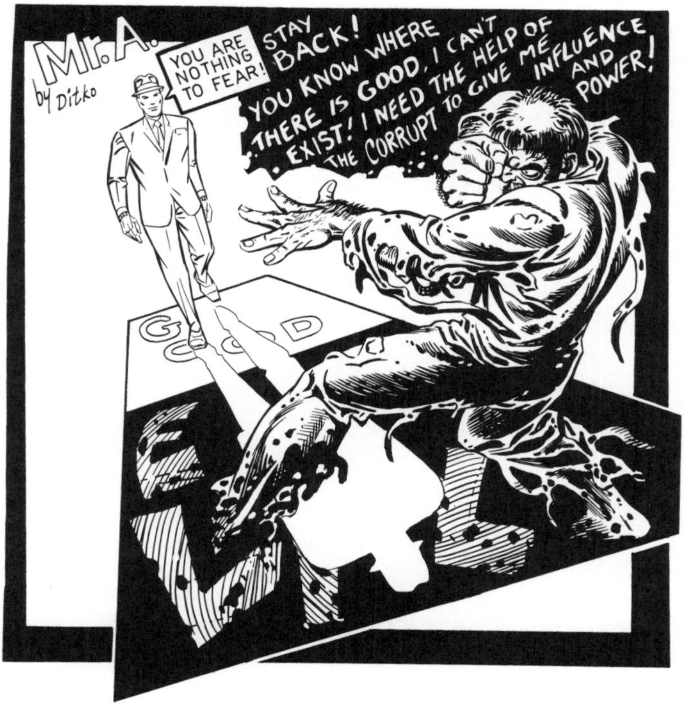
Mr. A.
by Ditko
YOU ARE NOTHING TO FEAR!
STAY BACK! YOU KNOW WHERE THERE IS GOOD, I CAN'T EXIST! I NEED THE HELP OF THE CORRUPT TO GIVE ME INFLUENCE AND POWER!
GOOD

as something of a rarity among Ditko's heroes, has a female friend: his fiancée, whose father—a criminally embroiled retired lawyer—is The Void's latest interviewee. When need be, The Void acts as two-fisted crimefighter but his preferred weapon is an icy vapor that immobilizes his targets. The warning he embodies is of a death more than physical. His unspoken motto is the old proverb: "The wages of sin …"

The most versatile and visually eloquent explicator of Ditko's canons is probably D. Skys. (Yes, he is a Hollywood actor.) Fretful at demands by his studio bosses that he portray nerds and losers, D. Skys withdraws from film work to assist his brother—a model for those proposed roles, who is being harassed by thuggish loan sharks. Overriding his brother's whining demurrals, Skys adopts a series of characters; each one the altertype of a distinct criminal. When the loan-shark enforcers turn physical, Skys, as a Viking warrior greets them as "Fellow Barbarians!" The mob boss "Spot" Kleaner is a germaphobe, as both name and image unequivocally inform us: A panel after Fritz Lang's gothic heart depicts "Spot," in black overcoat and black glasses seated in a white-lit cubicle surrounded by black night. Skys offers to him the character of a bearded, filthy derelict.

The apogee of Ditko's work and Mr. A's career, which it closes, is the 1976 "Death vs. Love Song." It is the ultimate encounter of Ditko's two chosen forms: allegory and comic-book narrative. Death would appear to be the terminal costume figure, following The Void; instead, this black-uniformed apparition—his skull face possibly no mask—dwells like a fugitive in a ruined church, somewhat recalling The Phantom of the Opera. He ventures into the adjoining graveyard to wistfully caress a certain tombstone. At night, he enters the city to strike down youth and beauty—two young lovers; a young mother with her infant—and stalk Love Song, a young nightclub chanteuse; no operatic Phantom he. The episode is totally pantomime. Abandoning verbiage, Ditko stages what amounts to a comic-book Armageddon. The atmosphere is of miasmic evil: Mr. A's calling card is seen turning all black. The episode's rhythms are those of film montage. It is a triumph of Ditko's powers in the field of vernacular fable that he has helped cultivate through the comic-book medium: the recharging of conventions, through the profession of his keenly perceived and often bitterly nurtured convictions about reality. From this, the smithy of his passionate imagination, he has forged an armature and exemplar of possibility for the often flaccid, clueless medium of superhero comic books. ★

Donald Phelps has been writing about the arts for 40 years, published his own guerilla cultural magazine in the '60s, and has appeared in various literary, political, and film magazines such as *Film Comment*, *The Nation*, *The Comics Journal*, *Pulpsmith*, Jim Stoller's *Moviegoer* and *The New Leader*. He has published three books of literary and cultural essays: *Reading the Funnies* (on comic strips), *Covering Ground*, and *The Word and Beyond*.

Ben Schwartz

"Like a Prairie Fire, Even Hotter: Harold Gray, Politics, and the Not-So-Funny Funnies"

In the 1982 movie *Annie*, billionaire munitions industrialist Oliver "Daddy" Warbucks arrives in Washington to meet the Roosevelts, whose calls he usually refuses to take. They want his help organizing the New Deal, which he thinks a preposterous scheme with no hope of success. But Warbucks goes for the sake of his ward, Annie—it's her first chance to see the White House. A musical being a musical, all it takes to melt his heart is Annie singing "Tomorrow," that anthem of stagestruck preteen girls everywhere, with Franklin and Eleanor.

FDR was certainly on the mind of Little Orphan Annie's creator, cartoonist Harold Gray, during the 1924–68 run of the strip. He despised FDR and let his comic's estimated thirty million daily readers know it. Liberals attacked Gray, not only for his views, but for expressing any serious opinion in the comics—a pivotal moment in

"Like a Prairie Fire, Even Hotter: Harold Gray, Politics, and the Not So Funny Funnies" first appeared in the Sept./Oct./Nov. 2008 issue of *Bookforum*.
[©Ben Schwartz & *Bookforum*]

moving "the funnies" onto more mature ground. In a nice bit of election-year timing, IDW debuts its multivolume *Complete Little Orphan Annie*, with *Will Tomorrow Ever Come?* ($40), which covers 1924 to 1927. (Volume 2, *The Darkest Hour Is Just Before the Dawn*, arrives in October.) This maiden volume gives us a chance to reappraise Gray, one of the most controversial cartoonists of his generation—and, via his career—American conservatism. For as modern conservatism struggles to define itself—if the Bush era's big-spending, government-empowering, internationally crusading GOP can be called conservative—Gray's strip about a little orphan girl in a cold, cruel world is the story of where that movement, and modern graphic literature, began.

Harold Lincoln Gray was born January 20, 1894, on his parents' farm in Kankakee, Illinois, and grew up idolizing his namesake, Lincoln, and Theodore Roosevelt. He worked on the farm until he entered Purdue, and dug ditches to pay the bills. Graduating in 1917, he taught bayoneting in World War I and returned to Illinois to seek work in his chosen field, cartooning. In 1920, he landed a job assisting the *Chicago Tribune's* star cartoonist, Sidney Smith. It put Gray on the front lines of a comics revolution. The funnies, at thirty years old, trafficked in comedy and fantasy, with talking animals, wisecracking goofs, and junior sociopaths like the Katzenjammer Kids. With Smith's family comedy, *The Gumps*, the *Tribune* pioneered book-length story lines (serialized daily), cliffhangers, and realistic characterization. Like postwar movies, which were expanding from shorts to features, the medium's novelty had worn off, and fans wanted something more.

Thus, in 1924, Gray offered *Little Orphan Annie* as a radical departure—a serious, often bleak drama. Annie suffers in Miss Asthma's orphanage, beaten and hired out as labor. When the social-climbing Mrs. Warbucks adopts her, it's to impress Society with her charitable nature. But seven weeks in, "Daddy" Warbucks appears and is smitten by Annie's pluck. As his name indicates, he's a war profiteer, dealing in arms, mercenaries ("my wrecking crew"), big-money political fixes, and wreaking vengeance on enemies with his own bare hands—a comic-strip complement to *There Will Be Blood's* ruthless tycoon, Daniel Plainview.

Gray's is an indifferent America. He has Annie shuttling from Miss Asthma's like a plow mule, fleeing (or ditched by) her nasty "guardians," causing the Warbucks' separation, and being held hostage by a murderous hobo who uses her for sympathy when panhandling. After she gets locked in a freight car to starve and freeze, bandits beat and shotgun her. Her optimism, often parodied as naïveté, is a lonely light in what comics critic Donald Phelps rightly calls "an epic whose tone is almost doom-laden beyond articulation." By 1926, Gray and Smith's popularity allowed for an innovative mass-market series of hardcover reprints. Today, we would call them graphic novels.

Jeet Heer, in Volume 1's extensive biographical piece, sees Gray as a progressive Republican, celebrating individualism, grit, and racial, ethnic, and religious diversity. He loathed con men, hypocrites, and snobs, especially those posing as moral reformers. "I hate professional do-gooders with other people's money," he once wrote. In 1932, the Depression brought to power one of the world's great professional do-gooders, FDR. Roosevelt's aggressive new liberalism transformed Gray into the new breed of

Republican: a pro-business, small-government tax cutter. Feeling that the New Deal destroyed rugged individualism with its programs designed to uplift, Gray spoke out. He never named FDR in *Annie*. But in 1934, when prosecutor Phil O. Bluster jailed Warbucks on phony tax charges, readers knew why. Inspired by fugitive Chicago millionaire Samuel Insull, then in Europe evading the IRS, Gray torched the New Dealers he saw as hounding businessmen for their success. Alone, Warbucks wonders aloud, "Is this the answer to ambition?"

One liberal, the *New Republic's* Richard Neuberger (later a Democratic senator from Oregon), shot back. Deriding Warbucks's soliloquy as "Hooverism in the funnies," he dismissed Gray as a pawn of the *Tribune*. Neuberger especially deplored Gray's politicking to millions of children, "the voters of the next generation." In fact, while the *Trib* urged Gray to write for adults (telling him, "Kids don't buy papers"), they valued *Annie* more as a merchandising cash cow than for his politics and feared losing readers.

Gray followed his pro-millionaire saga with a remarkably full-throated anti-union story line. In it, Annie befriends a homeless scientist, Eli Eon, inventor of Eonite, a cheap, easy-to-produce, indestructible material. Warbucks envisions it ending the Depression. Millions will work to mass-produce it, creating materials for housing that millions more will build. A corrupt union, led by John L. Lewis look-alike Claude Claptrap and liberal, long-haired journalist Horatio Hack, demands Warbucks give Eonite "to the pee-pul" or they'll strike. Their workers burn down Warbucks's factory (he hadn't gotten around to building it out of Eonite yet), killing Eon. The secret of Eonite, and to ending the Depression, dies with him.

Gray ran this as FDR signed the Wagner Act on July 5, 1935, giving unions the right to organize and represent workers. In August, Gray's union rioted. In September, the *New Republic* denounced *Annie* as "fascism in the funnies." In Huntington, West Virginia, Lewis's coal-mining power base, the *Herald-Dispatch* dropped *Annie* as "alarmingly vindictive propaganda." The *Tribune* quickly ordered Gray to "stop editorializing." Gray was no fascist. He hated big government, right or left. Ten months before Pearl Harbor, Gray undercut his employers at the isolationist *Tribune*. Warbucks, then overseas arming and organizing an antifascist resistance, escapes from a foreign concentration camp and returns home, eager to arm America for the upcoming war. Predictably, the right protested, also demanding Gray keep his politics out of the "funnies." Gray felt muzzled by such dictates, but he and the other *Trib* cartoonists who followed Sidney Smith's realist style had made a mark. In 1939, the *New Republic's* Heywood Broun wrote, condescendingly: "These strips, whether we like it or not, constitute the proletarian novels of America. They are scanned by millions. To those who cannot read the long words of literature the comic strip is extremely valuable. To those who cannot read any they are indispensable."

Responding to a 1943 fan letter from his congresswoman, Republican Clare Boothe Luce, not a proletarian by any standard, Gray predicted the success of socially engaged comics like *Li'l Abner, Pogo, Doonesbury, Maus, Palestine,* and *Persepolis,* writing: "There is a tremendous opening in such a venture for the one who breaks ground and first enters that forbidden field. I'd like to be that guy. A strip that is properly handled has tremendous power…A properly handled political strip would go like a prairie fire and be even hotter…Please give my regards to our RULER when you see him."

Gray's right-wing devotees included Luce, Ronald Reagan, Jesse Helms, Henry Ford, and the editors of *National Review*, but the scope of his work is too great to label him simply a political cartoonist. He sought to capture whole communities, not just issues. Millions admired him as a storyteller, including John Updike (who wrote Gray fan mail as a teen), Cynthia Ozick, Pete Hamill, Gloria Vanderbilt, and cartoonists Robert Crumb and Chester Brown, who have adopted elements of Gray's style as their own.

Will Tomorrow Ever Come? concludes with a classic Gray plotline, as Annie uncovers a gang of bank robbers—masterminded by a community activist and local banker, Mr. Mack. Eventually, Warbucks saves Annie, but Gray doesn't end on their embrace. Warbucks realizes the case against Mack won't hold up on a kid's testimony, no matter what Annie suffered. A gang of murdering thieves will go free. It's here that Warbucks gives Annie a cynical look at what runs the world. For once, she's not smiling. "Leapin' lizards! It doesn't seem right," she says. "'Daddy' told that senator to use his pull to get Mack and his gang punished—yuh'd think you wouldn't have to use pull to convict birds as guilty as those guys…In story books th' law always punishes th' crooks without anybody helpin'—I guess most story books must be the bunk—"

Gray died in 1968, but his tomorrow finally came. *Doonesbury* won a 1975 Pulitzer for political satire (a first for a strip), *Annie* the musical premiered, and Will Eisner collected four short stories as *A Contract With God* in 1978, reintroducing readers to the "graphic novel." Finally, Reagan's 1980 election meant conservatism had won voters over from their New Deal allegiance—sold on Reagan's smiling optimism, just the way Annie did it. ★

Ben Schwartz lives in Los Angeles, CA. He is not the stand-up comic/comedy writer Ben Schwartz, the ESPN sportswriter Ben Schwartz, nor *The Atlantic*'s literary editor Benjamin Schwarz. To clarify, he is the not-a-stand-up comic comedy writer from Suck.com that's worked with James Cameron and Ivan Brunetti, a baseball commentator for *Can't Stop the Bleeding*, and a contributing book critic/journalist/humorist for *The New York Times*, *Bookforum*, *Salon*, *The Washington Post*, and soon, *Vanity Fair*. Oh, yes, and *The Atlantic*. But he isn't those other guys. In fact, this Ben Schwartz is currently writing *The Lost Laugh*, a history of American humor set between the World Wars for Fantagraphics, and *Home By Christmas*, a biopic of Larry Gelbart and Bob Hope, until very recently, with the late Larry Gelbart. OK: clear?

Jeet Heer

Drawn From Life

A father and son take a walk through the woods in the fall. Their forms are distinct from a distance. The father, Walt Wallet, is puffy and rumpled while his adopted son Skeezix is slight, with a young boy's litheness. Alive with curiosity, Skeezix asks "Uncle Walt" why the fall leaves change color. The answers that Walt provides are less important than the tone and texture of the scene, a leisurely communion between parent and child that asks to be savored. Yet even in the pleasures of the moment, there is an undercurrent of sadness as well. The falling leaves remind us that change is a constant part of experience and one day the son will have a life apart from the father.[1]

---

1 This scene is reprinted in Bill Blackbeard and Martin Williams' *The Smithsonian Collection of Newspaper Comics* (New York: Harry N. Abrams, 1977), p. 109. It is worth noting that the current revival of interest in Frank King's work is directly traceable to the Smithsonian volume, which educated a generation of younger cartoonists (notably Chris Ware and Joe Matt). See for example Joe Matt, *Peepshow* #12 (April 2000) p. 8.

"Drawn from Life" is an expanded version of Heer's introduction to
Walt and Skeezix: 1921 & 1922.
[©2009 Jeet Heer]

This bittersweet moment appeared in Frank King's *Gasoline Alley* in a full-page Sunday strip late in 1930. King famously drew that day's art in a "woodcut" style, which perfectly suited the autumn mood of the strip, a delight in the surface pleasures of life mixed with a melancholy awareness of human transience. With its evocation of complex emotions, *Gasoline Alley* was one of the greatest comic strips of the 20th century. It belongs in the same select league as George Herriman's *Krazy Kat* (which explored the intricacy of love and hate) and Charles Schulz's *Peanuts* (that dead-pan study of childhood loneliness and rejection).

Yet, while *Gasoline Alley* enjoyed great popularity in its heyday during the 1920s to the 1960s, until now Frank King hasn't received the ample appreciation often bestowed on Herriman and Schulz by fans of good cartooning. The reason for this neglect is readily apparent: as a strip that dwelt on the daily travails of ordinary people, *Gasoline Alley* needs to be read in bulk to be appreciated.

The rhythm of *Gasoline Alley* is not the yuk-yuk gag a day humour of *Dilbert* nor the nail-biting melodrama of *Dick Tracy*. Rather, *Gasoline Alley* achieves its hold on the audience by being ruminative and cumulative: to catch the mood of the strip you have to imagine yourself as the new kid on the block, slowly getting to know the familiar neighborhood characters and easing yourself into their social circle.

Yet aside from a few scattered exceptions, King's version of the strip hasn't been available to those who missed it in its first newspaper appearance. By reprinting the peak years of King's work, this series aims to restore Frank King to the pride of place he deserves in comic strip history

Frank King was among the most autobiographical of cartoonists. Bits of his life and the lives of his family, friends and neighbors shows up refracted in the characters and storylines he created. To understand *Gasoline Alley*, we need to understand the background of the man behind it.

Born in 1883 in Cashton, a small town in the Kickapoo Hills of Wisconsin, Frank Oscar King really grew up in the nearby town of Tomah, where his family settled shortly after his birth. King's family were middling people: his father John J. King had worked as a carpenter before becoming the co-owner of the King Bros. General Store in Tomah. Aside from his parents and younger brother Leland, King's childhood was spent surrounded by an extensive family in and around Tomah, including uncles, aunts and cousins.

In his spare time, John J. King (whose stern patriarchal visage was tempered by a bushy walrus mustache) served as circuit preacher for the Congressional Church. In unsettled and sparsely populated areas, as Wisconsin then was, circuit riders would travel to places without fixed churches, preaching in living rooms of farmers and around work camps. It's difficult to find any traces of a religious upbringing in Frank King's work, but, like his preacher dad, the cartoonist was always happy to travel. Both King himself and his characters had the wandering spirit, especially eager to take excursions into the countryside and the open road.

The geography of King's childhood would show up in *Gasoline Alley* in casual references to Tomah and the Kickapoo Valley, places that seemed within short driving distance of where Walt Wallet and Skeezix lived. In the early 1930s, Walt Wallet would recall details of a fictional Wisconsin childhood with details surely drawn from King's actual memories. "When I was a boy I used to drive with my parents in a horse and buggy 35 miles over into Kickapoo Valley," Walt tells Skeezix on an autumn Sunday drive through the country. "The first night we'd stop with cousins in Kendall and finish up the second afternoon. Now we can do that much and cross two or three states in a day."[2] Walt here is exalting modern speed and progress, but there is a whiff of nostalgia for his "horse and buggy" childhood as well.

In an equally nostalgic 1955 essay which is reprinted in this volume, King recalls an idyllic small town boyhood of hi-jinks and antics, often in the company of his "kid pal" Walt Drew.[3] Drew, three years younger than King, had an older sister named Delia who was the same age as the future cartoonist. King would eventually marry Delia and use Walt Drew as the inspiration for Walt Wallet.

The King family were technophiles, in love with new gadgets like the camera and the automobile. Such machines had the glamour of novelty and they lent themselves to tinkering. They were fun for those who like to use their hands. Leland King would become an engineer while Robert King, Frank's son, would be a photographer. To this day you can see the descendants of Frank King fixing up antique cars in the outskirts of St. Louis, Missouri.

Because his family were early shutter-bugs, King's childhood and youth is amply recorded in many photos. Despite the fact that these photos were taken in the late Victorian era when most people froze up in front of the camera's gaze, the Kings always appear relaxed, not afraid to be caught in candid moments. The young King was frisky, prankish and artistically inclined. The walls of his bedroom, circa 1900, were covered with photographs, drawings and cartoons (including a risqué pin-up of a well-endowed woman and a knock-off of Frederick Opper's Happy Hooligan, the hero of a fresh new comic strip). In a series of mug-shots King, with his hair flowing wild like a mad orchestra conductor, makes funny-faces (according to the caption in the family album he's pretending to be drunk).

King started cartooning early. In 1898 the *Tomah Herald* published King's decorative line-drawings of a Hispanic lady and soldier. The following year he won a prize in a national art contest for high school students. While still shy of his 19th birthday, he was working full time as a staff artist for the Minneapolis *Times*, where he wrote and drew the weekly "Junior Times Nursery Rhymes." His early animals clearly bore in the influence of T.S. Sullivant, a prominent cartoonist he would soon meet.

While living in Minneapolis, King lost an important link with his Tomah past when his father died in Cashton in 1903. Henceforth, King would never return to Tomah except as a visitor.

---

2 This 1934 strip can be found in Chris Oliveros, ed., Drawn & Quarterly, volume three (Montreal: Drawn & Quarterly, 2000), p. 173.

3 Frank King, "My Home Town. Where Gasoline Alley and I Grew Up," Chicago Tribune *Magazine*, (May 22, 1955), p. 28-29.

In 1905 King studied at the Chicago Academy of Fine Arts. Photos from these school days show a raffish young man enjoying the bohemian pleasures of hanging around with artists in the big city. In one class photo almost all the sitters are clowning around with props, ranging from an easel to a dangling skeleton (King himself seems to be carefully pouring a drink). While attending school, King worked on weekends at the Chicago *American*.

King would later note that studying at the Academy gave him a sense of artistic self-worth, so he would feel ashamed when he briefly did hack commercial work like advertising illustrations for patent medicine. "My work at school began to show some promise (so the teachers told me) and I felt that my talents deserved a better outlet," King said.[4] King's artistic pride fueled his restless, analytical approach to cartooning.

Unlike many other cartoonists of his era, he wasn't content to stay with one style or approach. He was always looking at what other artists were doing and refreshing his work with new techniques. A photograph of King during this period shows him intently fixed before a canvas, paintbrush in hand. In the 1906 Chicago city directory, King listed himself as an artist.

King's usually light-hearted self gave way to seriousness when focused on an artistic problem. He always kept a sketchbook close at hand, even at home. A true artist, he regarded the world around him as raw material that needed to be captured in his work.

Especially in his apprenticeship years before creating *Gasoline Alley*, King was always keenly mimicking the style of other artists in order to expand his own range as an artist. From 1906 to 1909, he worked at the Chicago *Examiner* where he got to draw alongside an old hero, T.S. Sullivant. Aside from Sullivant, King's early work shows that he was paying attention to Winsor McCay, Claire Briggs, and Thomas Nast, among other cartoonists. King also kept attuned to developments in the art world outside cartooning circles. He was interested in everything from Japanese ceramics to Parisian painting. Knowing references to cubism and modernism would occasionally pop up in his comic strips.

As a cartoonist, King was very much a newspaperman. In the days before technology made it easy to reproduce photographs, illustrators like King did more than supply cartoons to provide comic relief from the news. Rather they functioned the way photo journalists do now, traveling with reporters and sketching breaking news like bank robberies, murder trials, and the visits of celebrities and foreign dignitaries.

In those years, King was in the thick of a fiercely competitive newspaper world, with nearly a dozen daily papers screaming for the attention of Chicago readers. In 1909 he was hired by The Chicago *Tribune*, which was building itself up to be the city's leading paper, in part by emphasizing features such as daily cartoons. King would stay with the *Tribune* until his retirement in the early 1960s. The Tribune gave King ample room to stretch his muscle. Aside from the usually court-room dramas, he also created a host of briefly lived comic strips, with titles like *Look Out For Motorcycle Mike* and *Augustus* (about a henpecked husband).

---

4 King interview in Martin Sheridan, *Comics and Their Creators : Life Stories of American* (Boston: Hale, Cushman & Flint, 1942).

At the *Tribune*, King worked alongside Clare Briggs, who became an especially formative artistic influence. Briggs specialized in a low-key slice-of-life comic strips. One Briggs-inspired strip drawn by King shows a driver frustrated at being cut in by another car, with the headline "Is this your pet peeve?" This headline speaks to the way observational humor builds a common ground with the reader's experiences. These were strips that would often focus, peevishly, on the everyday irritations and annoyances of life, which are meant to be seen as widely-shared frustrations which are too minor to require reform but too frequent to pass by unmentioned: traffic jams, small marital spats, dealing with difficult clerks or bureaucrats, not being listened to by your kids. These were the topics of everyday conversation. Like the old saw about the weather, everyone talks about pet peeves but no one does anything about them. But the very act of describing such an irritation, letting off steam through complaining, serves as a minor balm.

From Briggs, King learned that everyday life was an endless source of material. A cartoonist didn't need to always use extreme exaggerations to make a point: sharply observed moments of daily life could more easily resonate with readers. Briggs also had a style worth emulating: a confident pen-line, precise in conveying details but not afraid being homey and craggy. Inflected through King's own sensibility, this would become the *Gasoline Alley* style as well.

King's most memorable achievement during these apprentice years was the Sunday strip *Bobby Make-Believe*, which he started in 1915 and continued working on until 1919 (when it was taken over by other hands). A wistful fantasy about a day-dreaming boy, the strip was clearly influenced by Winsor McCay's *Little Nemo*. From McCay, King learned how to structure the Sunday page as a coherent unit and carry through the logic of a fanciful idea from beginning to end. If King didn't achieve the architectural grandeur of his distinguished predecessor, it has to be said that *Bobby Make-Believe* shows an understanding of childhood that McCay lacked. Unlike Little Nemo, King's Bobby seems like an actual boy with the genuine aspirations and fears of childhood. Many of the ideas shown in *Bobby Make-Believe*, along with a recurring focus on childhood daydreams, would re-appear in the Sunday *Gasoline Alley* strips.

In 1914, King started doing a regular black and white full page feature called *The Rectangle*, a coat-rack title that let him hang his various flights of whimsy. Often he would take a common word (for example, "hyphen") and spin it off for a page of puns and competing usages. In 1918, tucked away in a bottom corner of *The Rectangle*, King quietly introduced a new feature, *Gasoline Alley*.

Originally, *Gasoline Alley* detailed the weekly meeting of a group of automobile-owners who liked to hang around and chat about the endless hassles they have with their cars. In this incarnation, the strip offered the same pleasures radio listeners now get from the NPR show *Car Talk*, the frisson sensation of overhearing colorful characters wrangle over mechanical problems. Within a few weeks, the cast of the strip started gathering names and personalities: Walt, a portly bachelor with a tuft of forelock; Avery, who is always chomping on cigars and pinching pennies; Bill, recognizable by his jutting chin and dangling cigarette; and finally Doc, whose oval

glasses and spiky beard make him look like a large mosquito.

In its early days, *Gasoline Alley* was a masculine comic strip, focused on men and their cars. Aside from Walt the three other main characters were married (Avery to the pudgy Emily, Bill to attractive Amy, and Doc to Hazel, whose blank eyes matched her husband's glasses and anticipated Orphan Annie's famous face). Yet the women were marginal to the strip, usually seen in the background gossiping away while the men bantered about "flivvers" and home-brewed liquor (prohibition had started casting its long shadow in 1920). While talking cars, the men often wore grease-covered dungarees and overalls, definitely not dressed for mixed company.

Occasionally King would mix up the names of the wives (calling Emily Amy for example), indicating that they were interchangeable and un-important. One running joke had the male members of the cast being harassed by their wives, causing the happy bachelor Walt to throw up his hands in amused exasperation and exclaim, "I'll say I know when I'm well off." When Amy gave birth in 1920, it was done entirely off-

panel. Two years later, when a single woman moves into the Alley, the male denizens, especially Walt, were aghast at this encroachment of femininity into their space.

Amy's pregnancy was the first sign that *Gasoline Alley* was moving in a more domestic direction, but this trend greatly accelerated in February of 1921 when Walt became an instant family man after finding a baby boy left on his doorstep. Eventually named Skeezix, the little boy changed the tone and temper of the strip as rompers and baby carriages replaced carburetors and mufflers. Much of the humor of the early Skeezix is in seeing Walt try to apply his car-orientated mind to the task of raising of baby. In the process, the "old bachelor" (as his friends call him) is slowly domesticated, even going to lectures and baby-contests where he is surrounded by young mothers.

In unfolding the gradual change in Walt's personality, Frank King displays a deft hand, especially in the playing out the long courtship with Phyllis Blossom which starts in 1922. With a mixture of pride and bashfulness, Walt tries to hold on to his bachelor freedom as long as he can, slowly being enticed by Phyllis's charms. In having Walt waver and totter, love-sick one day and glowering the next, King demonstrates his unique combination of comic delicacy and psychological realism.

In transforming *Gasoline Alley* into a domestic drama, King may have been acting at the behest of his boss. According to newspaper folklore, Captain Joseph Medill Patterson, co-editor and co-publisher of the Chicago *Tribune*, encouraged King to introduce a baby into the strip in order to widen its appeal. (Other accounts credit Patterson's cousin and co-publisher Robert R. McCormick). Yet there are reasons to be skeptical of this standard account. The fact is, Patterson was a bit of a credit-hog and liked to take the applause for most of the innovations introduced by his cartoonists. The theme of family life and childhood had long intrigued King (witness *Bobby Make-Believe*) and the relationship between Walt and Skeezix had a personal resonance for the cartoonist.

To understand the origin of Skeezix, we have to take a closer look at King's own family life. In 1911, King married Delia Drew, his childhood sweet-heart. As we've seen, Delia's family had strong ties to Tomah. Her father ran the Bank of Tomah, where she worked before her marriage. Slightly higher than the Kings on the social hierarchy, Delia had attended a posh finishing school. She and her husband married relatively late for that era, when they were both 28 years old, perhaps because it was only then that Frank had settled into a secure career at the Chicago *Tribune*.

Prior to his marriage, King had moved around frequently in Chicago, living in an array of inexpensive apartments, rooming houses and as a boarder. But settling into married life, King started moving into more upscale residences. In their early married days, the Kings lived in apartments on the south side of Chicago, on Calumet, and later on Washington Ave. (a street later renamed Blackstone). These were upwardly mobile neighborhoods, despite the fact that laundry could be seen billowing outside.

The apartment on Calumet was a three-story brick building, close to a public transit elevated railroad that could take King to his downtown office. With a landscaped courtyard in the front, the Kings would have enjoyed an airy and bright view. The Blackstone building, done in the picturesque craftsman style of the times, was newly constructed when the Kings moved there either at the end of 1912 or the beginning of 1913. Again the Kings had easy train access, this time one a commuter rail, to the city's core. Both the Calumet and the Blackstone apartments had the additional advantage of being near a major public park. Spaciousness and close access to nature to the open air would characterize all the homes King would own from this point on.

The King household was comfy and middle class. In their living room, they had a piano were they played the *Ziegfield Follies* and other popular tunes. (It's not clear whether the piano was for Frank, Delia or both. Frank was certainly musically inclined, and played the violin.)

Delia was pregnant in 1912, but unfortunately the child was stillborn. Unnamed, their first child was buried in the family cemetery in Tomah. At that time King did a heart-rending little sketch of a baby, simply titled "our child." The still-birth seems to have marked both Frank and Delia. Afterwards, the theme of baby-loss would often appear in King's work. A fanciful strip that King did while still in the shadow of the still-birth shows a science fiction future where babies are produced cleanly and hygienically on an assembly line (one of the little tykes is a dead ringer for the yet uncreated Skeezix).

The loss of her first child seems to have aged Delia. In her high school she possessed a willowy beauty, keeping her thick-flowing hair tight on her head like a turban. If she ever let her hair go free, she could have posed as a Gibson girl in an early 20th century pin-up. By the time she married in 1911, she was a little plumper, but still very lively. A photo of the newlyweds shows Frank, wearing overalls, hanging over a fence-door like an overgrown Tom Sawyer, while his wife looks at him with a wondering contentment. Yet by 1920, when she's only 37, Delia is all together graver, looking matronly and stern, more like Frank King's mother than his wife. (In many of King's comic strips, a hapless husband with a roving eye for female beauty would be kept in check by a dowdy wife.)

The loss of their first child was tempered by good news on February 13th, 1916, when Delia gave birth to a boy, whom the couple named Robert Drew King. The young boy would grow up in the first house his parents owned, a newly built home in Glencoe, a semi-rustic suburb of Chicago that hugs the Lake Michigan shoreline. Within a quick train-ride to the city but secluded enough to enjoy its own thick forest and beachfront, Glencoe was prime Chicago real estate. While it was below Evanston and

Lake Forest on the city's social pecking order, it still had a distinguished ambience. Frank Lloyd Wright had designed several houses and a railroad station in Glencoe. King was conscious of Wright's presence, making an allusion to the celebrated architect in *Gasoline Alley* (Sept. 1, 1921). By Glencoe standards, the King house was fairly modest; unlike some of their neighbors the Kings didn't have a mansion. Still, the family had plenty of open land around the Glencoe property, where they seemed to enjoying gardening.

Owning a home in Glencoe was a sign of the Kings family's increasing prosperity, which was steadily ticking upwards, especially after the creation of *Gasoline Alley*. In 1914, the *Tribune* paid King $3,750 per year; in 1916, $5,000; in 1918, $6,250; in 1919, $10,000; in 1921, $15,000; in 1925, $22,500. Aside from the *Tribune* money, King also gathered in royalties from *Gasoline Alley* toys and books, which proliferated in the 1920s.

In their Glencoe home, the Kings enjoyed a cheerful domestic life, enriched by the fact they had relatives nearby. Especially beneficial for King's imagination was the presence of his brother-in-law and old Tomah friend Walter Drew. Plump, baggy-eyed, occasionally wearing a sailor's hat, and in the habit of hanging out at garages where cars were being fixed, Robert King's "Uncle Walt" was of course the model for Skeezix's "Uncle Walt." Around 1918, King would go from Glencoe to an alley near 63rd and St. Lawrence, where Walt Drew hung out with some buddies and tinkered with cars. Walt was an electrical engineer and one of his close friends was a locomotive engineer Bill Gannon, whom King claimed inspired the *Gasoline Alley* gang member Bill. Indeed, the term close friends doesn't begin to describe Walt Drew's relationship with Bill Gannon. From 1911 until his death in 1941, Walt Drew lived with Gannon and Gannon's wife Gertrude (Gertie), even as the couple moved through several residences. Walt would remain a bachelor all his life, so the Gannons seemed to have been his surrogate family.

It's easy enough to find parallels between King's life and the strip: Skeezix was introduced on Valentine's Day 1921, just a day after Robert King turned five. In 1921, the Kings (plus Walt Drew along with Bill and Gertie Gannon) went on a vacation that took them to Yellowstone National Park as well as Colorado and Wyoming. The *Gasoline Alley* gang make a similar jaunt that same year. King in fact drew the strip on the trip; in a photograph we can see him cartooning away outside a tent. While traveling, King would carefully mark each spot he visited just below his signature. (He also claimed the cost of his trip as a business expense on his tax return.) The Kings even drove a car with the same license plate as Walt Wallet: 354.

And, of course as Frank King and his family grew older day by day, so did the characters of the comic strips. King was the first cartoonist to forgo the convention of comic strip time (whereby "Little Nemo" will never be "Big Nemo"). He created a strip that in its incremental accretion of everyday events mirrored the experience of all his readers.

Yet the divergence between real-life and the comic strip is equally significant. *Gasoline Alley* is about a father who has a warm, loving relationship with his adopted son. The actual King family was more complicated. According to Drewana Schutte, Frank King's granddaughter, Delia was made skittish by the presence of children. In 1922, Frank and Delia sent their son Robert to boarding school. Aside from Delia's nervous condition (perhaps traceable to the death of her first child), the Kings may have been influenced by the fact that Delia had gone to finishing school.

When Robert grew up and had his own family, he would tell his daughter Drewanna that "I never knew my parents. I only saw them in the summer." Robert never talked about *Gasoline Alley*, and his daughter Drewanna only found out about the strip as a teenager.

If Frank and Delia King had a troubled relationship with their son, this experience shows up in oblique ways in *Gasoline Alley*. Throughout the early years of *Gasoline Alley*, Walt is fearful of losing Skeezix. The very fact that Skeezix was a foundling means that his status as Walt's son is always provisional and open to challenge (a problem explored in storylines throughout the 1920s).

In the Sunday pages reprinted in *Drawn & Quarterly* volume four we see the following little narratives: Walt leaves Skeezix outside a store in a crib and his maid Rachel takes the baby away, causing Walt to go into a tizzy about kidnapping (p. 99); Walt gets soot on his face, leading Rachel to think that a "big black cullid man is stealin' Skeezix!" (p. 102); Walt dreams that gypsies have kidnapped Skeezix (p. 107); Walt dreams that he's grown old like Rip Wan Winkle and Skeezix doesn't recognize him (p. 108); Walt can't find Skeezix because the boy has traded places with a Peublo Indian tyke (p. 123). [5]

The major plot narrative of *Gasoline Alley* in the 1920s was a long-running court case in which Walt had to defend his custody of Skeezix against the claims of a decadent opera singer, Helene Octave, who claimed to be the boy's mother. One complicating factor in the narrative is that Octave is close friends with Phyllis Blossom, who during this period goes from being Walt's girlfriend to his wife.

In the April 27th, 1926 daily strip, Walt hugs Skeezix and reflects on the forces that might drive them apart. "Well we men have got to stick together," Walt says. "We won't let anybody come between us and keep us apart, will we?" To which Skeezix replies: "Not anybody—Mam Octave or Auntie Bossom or anybody." (Referring to Phyllis Blossom as "Auntie Bossom" is a nice touch since she is often shown to be a bossy fussbudget who dominates over her husband and servants.)

In this little vignette we see the gender politics that underlie *Gasoline Alley*: father and son are allied against the threatening forces of womanhood. The misogyny of the strip is complex: Walt finds that he needs a wife to complete his happiness, yet he always yearns to return to the all-male island of happiness he has when he is alone with his son. Women, whether in the benign form of Phyllis Blossom or the malevolent shape of Helene Octave, threaten Walt's deepest happiness. To be a fretful father always afraid of losing his child is Walt's fate.

Tapping into his own memories of childhood as well as the experience of being a father, King created a strip about both the joys and anxieties of family life. The

---

5 Chris Oliveros *Drawn & Quarterly, Volume four* (Montreal: Drawn & Quarterly, 2001).

pleasures are easy enough to recognize: Walt adores Skeezix, even as the tot is tearing down the house. But *Gasoline Alley* is an emotionally nuanced strip, so we should attend to the darker shadows that King also sketches. Throughout the early years of *Gasoline Alley*, Walt is fearful of losing Skeezix. King and his wife themselves knew something about losing a child.

Whatever he might have drawn from his personal memories, the emotions that Frank King explored are universal. All parents worry about their children, who always grow up too quickly and get independent lives. From the child's side of things, there is always a gap, slight or large, between our experiences and those of our parents. Even those who have good relations with their parents find themselves occasionally flustered at the gulf between generations. *Gasoline Alley* is a comic strip by a father who is intensely aware that time moves on and childhood could easily be lost. Yet in his strip King clung to happy memories as tightly as possible, using his masterly pen-work to limn fleeting moments. The long walks between father and son that are so lovingly rendered in *Gasoline Alley* are moments we all wish we could have. ★

Jeet Heer is a Toronto-based journalist focusing on arts and culture. He is the co-editor, along with Kent Worcester, of *Arguing Comics: Literary Masters on a Popular Medium* (2004) and *A Comics Studies Reader* (2008). With Chris Ware and Chris Oliveros he is editing a multi-volume series reprinting Frank King's *Gasoline Alley* comic strip, under the umbrella title of *Walt and Skeezix*. He has contributed to many volumes reprinting old cartoonists such as George Herriman, Winsor McCay, Harold Gray, and Milton Caniff, among many others. The winner of a Fulbright Fellowship (2000-2001) and the Thomas Inge Award (2002), Heer is currently pursuing his doctorate at York University, writing his thesis on "the cultural politics of Little Orphan Annie."

Sarah Boxer

George Herriman: The Cat in the Hat

> We call him "Cat,"
> We call him "Crazy"
> yet is he neither.

—*George Herriman on* Krazy Kat

George Herriman's comic strip *Krazy Kat* is its own country. The borders are forbidding and you have to accustom yourself slowly to its landscape and its lingo. But once you're in, there's no looking back. You can't imagine a world without *Krazy Kat*, and it is almost impossible to tell outsiders what it is like. Fans of the strip often end up going native, speaking like Krazy—with lots of *K*s and a strange accent—as if that explained everything. It's a heppy, heppy lend.

There is no comic strip simpler on its face than *Krazy Kat*. In its thirty-one-year run (from 1913 to 1944) the plot never changed much. Ignatz Mouse, sadist supreme, aims to bean Krazy Kat, soulful innocent, with a brick, and usually succeeds. Krazy Kat takes the brick, even seeks it out, as a missile of love. And Krazy's secret admirer, the police dog Offissa Bull Pupp, throws the errant mouse in jail. All's well.

Yet despite the repetition—maybe even because of it—*Krazy Kat* is endlessly energetic, perplexing, and deep. There isn't a dull line in *Krazy & Ignatz*, the ongoing series of slim volumes collecting the complete full-page strips, published by Fantagraphics. (This, by the way, is the third attempt a publisher has made at the complete *Kat* comics.) In its recent appearance in the "Masters of American Comics" exhibition organized by the Hammer Museum and the Museum of Contemporary Art in Los Angeles, *Krazy Kat*, one of the oldest in the bunch, looked as fresh as Chris Ware's *Jimmy Corrigan* or Gary Panter's *Jimbo*.

How does *Krazy Kat* stay forever young? The easy answer is: animals. Animal characters don't get dated the way human ones do. The deeper answer is: flux. In *Krazy Kat*, Herriman made everything indeterminate. He set the strip among the rocky outcroppings of Monument Valley, opening up the funnies to vast, abstract spaces. (Yes, he beat John Ford there.) He made the trees, rocks, and moons shift shape from frame to frame for no apparent reason. His free-floating design of the page, with its mad array of wheels, zigzags, and frames within frames, kept changing.

And then there's that Krazy language. The Kat speaks a dialect that is distinctive yet elastic and impossible to pinpoint. Yiddish? "Ooy-y-y- Sotch a noive." Creole? "S'funna, but I dun't see no stomm—the sky is klee—blue an' bride wit' sunshine—not a cloud in it." Brooklyn-Italian? "Jess fency, Offissa Pupp, the tree of us, riding around tigedda—like boom kimpenions." At one point, Krazy asks Ignatz: "Why is lenguage?" and then answers the question: "lenguage is that we may mis-unda-stend each udda."

The ceaseless flux drove readers crazy back when Herriman was still alive. If it hadn't been for the ardent support of the newspaper publisher William Randolph Hearst, *Krazy Kat*'s earliest and most important fan, the strip would probably never have survived. As Bill Blackbeard, the editor of the Fantagraphics series, noted in 2002, Hearst often fought with his editors to keep the strip running:

> They claimed that they received endless letters complaining about this mystifying comic, which they had difficulty answering since they found it mystifying themselves.

The strip, of course, stayed. Hearst gave Herriman a raise—apparently against his will. And a happy band followed Krazy religiously, including Ernest Hemingway, F. Scott Fitzgerald, Gertrude Stein, Pablo Picasso, H.L. Mencken, Edmund Wilson, Walt Disney, T.S. Eliot, Frank Capra, Willem de Kooning, Philip Guston, and Charles Schulz. The critic Gilbert Seldes, an early fan, gave Krazy a boost in "The Seven Lively Arts," his 1924 essay arguing that the popular arts deserve as much critical attention as the classical ones. There Seldes called *Krazy Kat* "the most amusing and fantastic and satisfying work of art produced in America today," and called Herriman a "great ironist" who "understands pity" and belongs with Chaplin, Cervantes, and Dickens.

Shortly after Herriman died, in 1944, more critics came to call. (You can read many of them in *Arguing Comics*, a compilation of literary essays about the funnies.) In 1946, the poet E.E. Cummings saw *Krazy Kat* as a "meteoric burlesk melodrama of democracy…a struggle between society (Offissa Pupp) and the individual (Ignatz Mouse) over an ideal (our heroine)." In 1948, Irving Howe drizzled on the parade, faulting *Krazy Kat* for being a mass-culture product that allowed people to get a thrill from its "safe violations of traditional orders." But the parade continued. In 1959, Jack Kerouac found in Herriman's strips some of the roots of the Beat Generation: "It goes back to the inky ditties of old cartoons (Krazy Kat with the irrational brick)." In 1963, Umberto Eco wrote of "a certain lyrical stubbornness in the author, who repeated his tale ad infinitum, varying it always but sticking to its theme," and called Herriman a Scheherazade who creates "a genuine state of poetry, an uninterrupted elegy based on sorrowing innocence."

In 1971, though, the *Krazy* world changed, as Jeet Heer points out in "The Colors of Krazy Kat," the introductory essay to the 1935-1936 volume of *Krazy & Ignatz*. While researching an article on Herriman for the *Dictionary of American Biography*, Arthur Asa Berger, a sociologist and the author of a book on *Li'l Abner*, got a copy of Herriman's birth certificate from New Orleans. And this is what he reported in the *San Francisco Chronicle:* Although George Herriman, the son of George Herriman, Jr., from Paris, France, and Clara Morel Herriman, from Alsace-Lorraine, died Caucasian, in Los Angeles, in 1944, he was born "colored," in 1880.

For some readers, the news made an instant difference. Ishmael Reed, for instance, dedicated his 1972 novel *Mumbo Jumbo* to "George Herriman, Afro-American, who created *Krazy Kat*." Others remained unmoved. Bill Blackbeard recently pointed out that in New Orleans in the late nineteenth century, "colored" was code for "all dark-skinned furriners such as south Italians, Greeks, etc." In 1996, M. Thomas Inge, in an article titled "Was Krazy Kat Black?" argued that Krazy's creator was indisputably "of mixed race," a Creole with some African ancestry, but to designate him an African American "is to accept as valid the scientifically and morally inappropriate categories of a racist society." He added: "people should be allowed create their own identities."

And that's what Herriman did—with his hat and his cat.

The first rumblings about Herriman's heritage began when he was still alive. In the still indispensable 1986 book *Krazy Kat: The Comic Art of George Herriman*, Patrick McDonnell, Karen O'Connell, and Georgia Riley de Havenon reprint a newspaper column (circa 1920) where Tad Dorgan, Herriman's friend and fellow cartoonist, reveals his puzzlement about Herriman's race: "He looked like a cross between Omar the tent maker and Nervy Nat," Mr. Dorgan said, referring to Omar Khayyam and a cartoon tramp. "We didn't know what he was, so I named him the Greek." The tag stuck.

Then there was Herriman's hat, which he wore indoors and out. Although he once told a friend that he kept it on to hide a growth on his head, the few photographs that exist of a hatless Herriman reveal something else: "kinky hair, all slicked down," in the words of Robert Beerbohm, a man who collects hatless Herriman pictures.

Now, sixty-three years after his death at age sixty-three, Herriman's blackness is, in most quarters anyway, secure. He is, for instance, listed in Henry Louis Gates and Kwame Anthony Appiah's *Africana: The Encyclopedia of the African and African American Experience*. Yet, as Heer notes, all is not settled. In fact, "virtually everything about Herriman and *Krazy Kat* is still being debated." How much did Herriman know about his heritage? Should he or history decide his race? Does it matter? And how does it figure in *Krazy Kat*?

If Herriman knew he was black, he certainly did not flaunt it. There's no shock there, given the historical moment. In 1880, the year of his birth, Herriman would have been considered a "free person of color" (neither black nor white) in New Orleans, as *Krazy Kat: The Comic Art of George Herriman* notes. But by 1886, the year his family left New Orleans for Los Angeles, the lines between black and white had hardened. Segregation was becoming commonplace. Jim Crow laws were on the rise. And by the turn of the century, when Herriman was a fledgling cartoonist, the newspaper bullpens, Heer notes, "were open to immigrants but not to blacks," and at least one of Herriman's friends was openly racist.

How did he respond? Oddly. He made cartoons that seem a little racist themselves. In 1902, sixteen years after moving from the South and eight years before *Krazy Kat* first appeared, Herriman drew a cartoon called *Musical Mose*, in which a black man repeatedly tries and fails to "impussanate" a white man. In one installment, Mose masquerades as a Scotsman. When some white women discover he's black, they beat him up. Mose moans, "I wish mah color would fade," and returns home. His wife is not sympathetic: "Why didn't yo impussanate a cannibal?" she asks.

Musical Mose ended after only three episodes, and Herriman went on to create other comic strip heroes (mostly human ones) with other obsessions: *Professor Otto and His Auto, Acrobatic Archie, Major Ozone's Fresh Air Crusade, Rosy Posie – Mama's Girl, Baron*

Mooch, and *The Dingbat Family* (later renamed *The Family Upstairs*), a strip about a city family obsessed with the people living on the floor above them. In one *Dingbat* episode, Mr. Dingbat joins the Ku Klux Klan just so he can raid the apartment of the family upstairs. (It turns out that the Klan chief lives there.) Oh dear, or, as Krazy would say, Fuwi.

In 1910, Herriman finally found his inner cat. At the bottom sliver of one *Dingbat Family* strip, he drew in a cat and mouse, just "to fill up the waste space." Seldes described the advent of the animals:

> On their first appearance they played marbles while the family quarreled; and in the last picture the marble dropped through a hole in the bottom line.

The marble dropped indeed: Krazy and Ignatz were born. On July 26, 1910, Herriman had the mouse bean the cat for the first time. And after a month or so, Krazy Kat fell in love with her tormentor. She kissed Ignatz Mouse as he slept. "SMACK!"

Herriman, cartoonist in a hat, became Herriman, creator of *Krazy Kat*. It took a few more years, until October 28, 1913, for *Krazy Kat* to become a strip in its own right; it took another three for the strip to fill a Sunday page; and color came in 1935. But *Krazy Kat* had already taken over its maker's life. As Adam Gopnik once put it in these pages:

> Writing a biographical study of George Herriman is a bit like choosing to write a biographical study of Fra Angelico; once your hero takes his vows and enters the monastery, there's not a lot to say.

Herriman was absorbed in and into his work for the rest of his life.

His self-effacement means that his characters, especially his title character, are often asked to stand in for him. That seems to be how he wanted it, and they don't seem to mind. Over one photograph of himself, Herriman sketched in his characters. They look toward their creator and say: "Him? Oh, just a nobody." In other words, "Look at us, not him."

So, what do we know about Krazy?

Krazy looks kind of feminine, but there are signs that she's not. Ignatz sometimes calls Krazy "he," as in: "He comes… His doom is nigh" or "Dawgunnit!! It IS him!" Krazy claims to be confused: "I am confronted with a serious quandary," Krazy tells Ignatz once. "Y'see I don't know whether to take unto myself a wife or a husband." At another point, Ignatz's wife and kids can't figure out whether to call Krazy "Uncle" or "Aunt." They try out both. Krazy doesn't answer to "Uncle," but the name "Aunt Krazy" turns his head: "Kollin me, dollins?" Herriman himself never settled on Krazy's sex:

> I don't know. I fooled around with it once; began to think the Kat is a girl—even drew up some strips with her being pregnant. It wasn't the Kat any longer; too much concerned with her own problems—like a soap opera. Know what I mean?

Yes, we do. Sex is to Krazy as race is to Herriman—indecipherable, dangerous, interesting. And pinning it down ruins everything. As Herriman himself put it:

Krazy was something like a sprite, an elf. They have no sex. So that Kat can't be a he or a she. The Kat's a spirit—a pixie—free to butt into anything.

What about Krazy's race then? Well, she is definitely black, with a few—or not so few—crucial exceptions, as when Krazy gets doused in white paint or in white flour, or goes to a beauty shop to become a blonde, or switches character, name, and skin with Ignatz, who, in turn, becomes "a l'il eetiopium mice, bleck like a month from midnights."

Come to think of it, blackness and whiteness, ink and paper, invisibility and appearance, often are the explicit subjects of the strip. In "George Herriman's Black Sentence" (2000), an essay in the literary journal *Mosaic*, Eyal Amiran analyzed a *Krazy Kat* strip from 1919 that seems to prefigure the title *Invisible Man*. A dog (dogs are always the plebes) puts Krazy on display before an audience—that's us—to prove that a black cat standing in front of a black sheet is indeed invisible. Krazy first shows us that she's actually there by opening her eyes wide; then she shuts them and disappears. Next she makes herself appear by drinking a bottle of white milk. And finally she becomes invisible again by drinking a bottle of black ink. Here black is not only "the ink of the narrative," Amiran writes, but also Krazy's black blood, her skin color, and "a disguise for itself."

So, is this Kat just a black cat or ethnically black too? The question may sound like sheer nonsense, but not in Krazy country. You should know that all cats in *Krazy Kat*, whether they live on land or in sea or air, are related and all are black in color, including cousin Katbird, cousin Katfish (who runs a kind of undersea railroad ensuring the safe passage of anyone in trouble underwater), and (yes!) one Uncle Tom who is fond of singing minstrel songs: "Bugs is in the taties—weevils in the kottin—weasels in the hen koop—honey, times is rottin."

Krazy is black in all ways. In fact, Herriman once placed Krazy Kat in exactly the same scenario as Musical Mose, black impersonating white. Krazy goes to a beauty salon and when she emerges, all white, Ignatz falls in love with her, not realizing who she is. Krazy coyly drops her handkerchief with the initials KK on it (just one K short of the Klan) and Ignatz looks surprised. Krazy turns to him and explains: "My initchils—mins "Krazy Ket"—y'know that dunt you dollin?" Ignatz runs for a brick and Krazy wanders off, saying: "L'il tutsi wutsi thinks because I change my kimplection I should change my name."

Imagine coming across this in 1935 in the funnies. With the lightest of touches, Herriman delivers a thunderclap, declaring skin color irrelevant to identity and suggesting that those who don't agree might want to join the Klan. Or to look at it another way, it's exactly what Herriman might have said had he ever come out: You think I should change who I am just because of my skin color? Herriman reused this exact strip three years later, in 1938, and, oddly enough, in the retread Krazy turns not white but light blue. Did Herriman decide that Krazy's whiteness was too much of a race statement, especially in a color strip, where white really stands out? Or did he just figure that in a color strip where black is rendered as blue-black, white would logically be light blue?

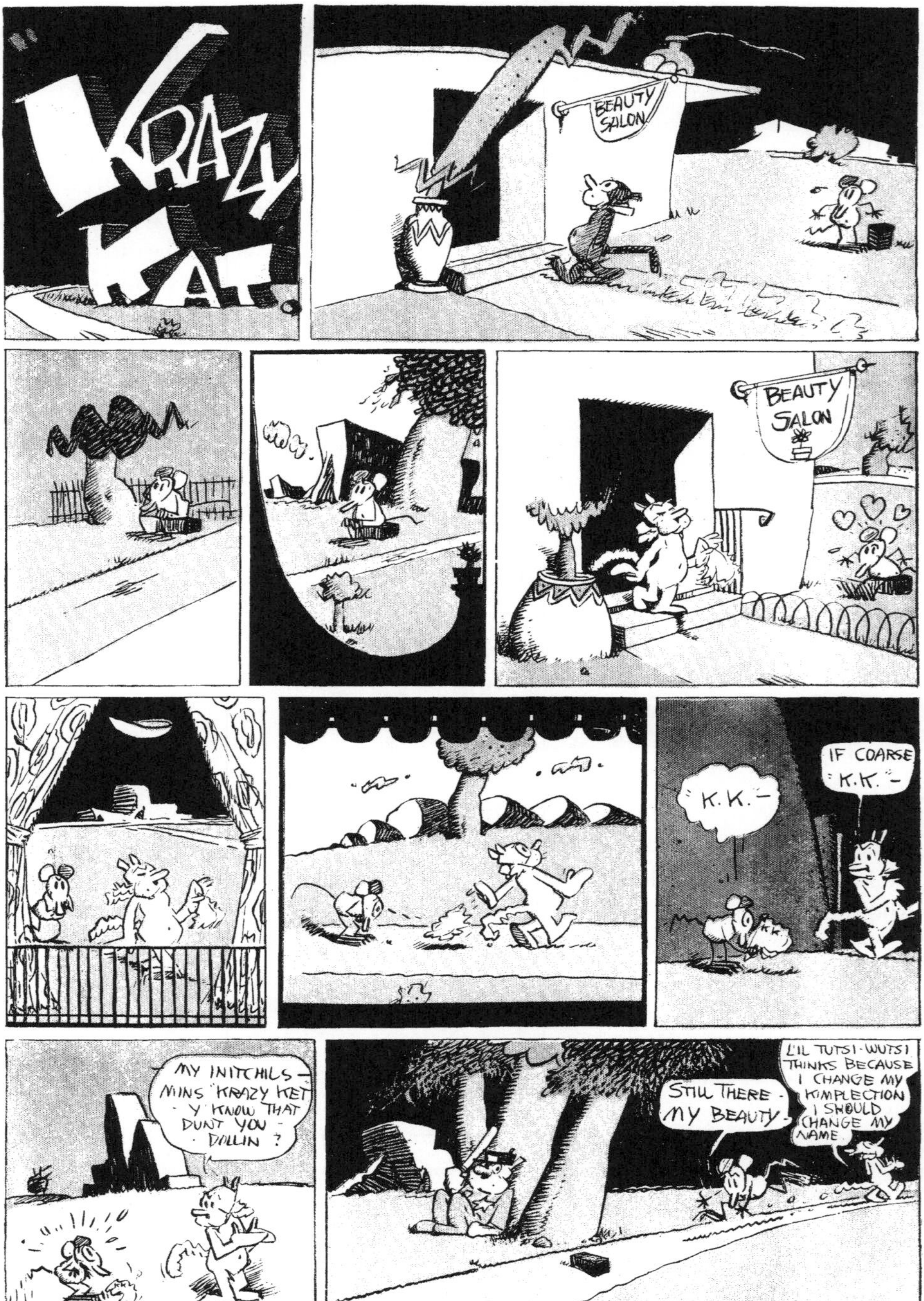
"KRAZY KAT"
BEAUTY SALON
BEAUTY SALON
K.K.–
IF COARSE K.K.–
MY INITCHILS–MINS "KRAZY KET" – Y KNOW THAT DUNT YOU – DOLLIN?
STILL THERE MY BEAUTY–
L'IL TUTSI-WUTSI THINKS BECAUSE I CHANGE MY KIMPLECTION I SHOULD CHANGE MY NAME.
10-6
HERRIMAN

What these questions show is that Herriman, under cover of Krazy, could play with color as freely as he pleased or, to put it his way, he was "free to butt into anything." In a strip from 1935 (the first year *Krazy Kat* ran in color), he put the shoe on the other foot, making Ignatz black and Krazy racist. Black Ignatz tries to bean the Kat with a brick and Krazy is uncharacteristically irritated. "I got a great care who I issociate wit – y-y-y sunboint koffa kake," Krazy says, and then kicks Ignatz into a lake: "This will titch soitin pippils to keep in their own social spears." Now, that's some cat—a black-colored (or black/colored?) masochist who suffers only white male sadists!

To complicate the racial issue further, Herriman laid out an ancestry story for Krazy and Ignatz that places Krazy neatly between black and white, between Africa and Europe, in Egypt: Way back in "the Egyptian day," a "noble roman rodent—Marcantonni Maus," Ignatz's ancestor (and, at least nominally, the ancestor of Art Spiegelman's *Maus*), fell in love with Kleopatra Kat, Krazy's forebear. Since Marcantonni Maus couldn't write, he hired his buddy Ptolemy Hoozis to chisel him a love note in brick. He tossed the brick to Kleopatra Kat, and when it accidentally bonked her on the head, he was hauled off to jail by a bunch of dogs (presumably ancestors of Offissa Pupp). That is why, Krazy explains, it is now Ignatz's "Romeonian custom to crease his lady's bean with a brick"—and why Krazy loves it.

Herriman, you see, was not shy about giving his characters ethnicities, or implying them anyway. Kolin Kelly, the dog who makes the bricks, is likely Irish. (Tossed bricks, I'm told, were once called Irish confetti.) Mock Duck, "oriental and launderer deluxe," is Chinese. And Ignatz, the li'l skeptic who doesn't believe in Santa Claus and whose sons are named Milton, Marshall, and Irving, is, I'd guess, Jewish. (Never mind that Ignatz is not a Jewish name and that he occasionally marches around in a kind of Klansman's garb; Krazy does that too.)

Herriman is even bolder when it comes to class. In one strip, some of Coconino's citizens, Walter Cephus Austridge, Terry Turtle, Gooseberry Sprig, Ignatz Mouse, and Kolin Kelly, are all smoking "at the Klub" and boasting about their royal roots. And who should come waltzing by but Krazy Kat, singing like an old-time minstrel about "the old haunted house and the cellar unda neet it, and the dear old wash-boila ee-e-een which I was 'born'"? The other animals are appalled: "Oh, that us aristocrats has gotta breathe the same air as a wash-boiler bred boor—s'awful."

In the end, we get the real score from Joe Stork, the "purveyor of progeny to prince and proletarian," who also happens to be the keeper of all genealogical truths. (By the way, Joe Stork is black. And one blogger has recently suggested that his name may be a sly reference to the 1917 pro-eugenics movie *The Black Stork*.) Joe Stork tells us that, in fact, all the animals, regardless of what they say, are lowborn. So, the only thing that distinguishes Krazy from the rest is that she hasn't any shame. She is above and below lying or caring. She sings out her story in her bastard dialect. She was born in a cellar. So what?

Is that Herriman singing from down there? Not exactly. Herriman did care—about color, class, race, and all matters of high and low. This is something that comes through in the very architecture of the strip. Remember that Krazy Kat and Ignatz Mouse didn't arrive full-blown on the page on October 28, 1913. They were literally born low. The first time they appeared, in the summer of 1910, they were playing under the floorboards of the Dingbats, who were, in turn, living under the family upstairs.

Herriman, both before and after he created Krazy, was obsessed with up and down. For him, almost every torment—whether it's loud neighbors, tossed bricks, beatings from racists, pangs of conscience, the Ku Klux Klan, or the delivery of babies by Joe Stork—comes from above. Ignatz is almost always higher on the page than Krazy. (Hey, that's how gravity works!) But down below is where the soul of the strip is. That's where Krazy was born, where she abides, and where she is the foe, unconscious of course, of everything that rises.

In one 1922 strip, Joe Stork stands on a high cliff and tells Krazy about ectoplasm. "When you flop into a trance your 'ectoplasm' passes out of your body—and soars out into the limitless ether, to roam willy-nilly, unleashed, unfettered, and unbound." Krazy is bowled over and a little disturbed: "Whooy—" she says. "Just imegin having your 'ectospasm' running around, William and Nilliam, among the unlimitless etha— golla, it's imbillivibil." So, when she thinks she sees Ignatz's ectoplasm floating upward (actually, it's only an Ignatz balloon), she dives to save it from the ether and in the process pops it.

Another full-page strip, dated July 21, 1918, zeroes in on the line that divides up from down. It begins: "Perhaps one of the finest portrayals of an 'horizon line' ever published—perhaps." Ignatz stands above the line and Krazy below it. Then, from under there, Krazy Kat tickles Ignatz's feet, first with one hand, then two: "L'il Tickil foots, how easily titillated he is. Tickle, kitchi, kitchi, ticki, ticki, ticki." The mouse shouts at his tormentor, "Daw gawnit!!! That was awful."

Here the order of nature is totally upset. The horizon line, for starters, doesn't act like a horizon line. The only thing the line does do is separate tormentor from tormented, and there too the usual order of the strip is violated. This time the torment comes from below, from Krazy. And Ignatz can fix the situation only by cutting the offending horizon line with an ax and using it to hog-tie Krazy. Krazy sighs, "I am love's keptive, bound by horizon lines."

In December of 1938, toward the end of Herriman's life and strip, a strange thing happened. The little sliver of basement space that had been the birthplace of Krazy and Ignatz opened up again. Herriman created a new underworld and filled it with enigmatic codas commenting on the strip above, much as he had done when Krazy and Ignatz were infants under the floorboards. Sometimes those slim bottom strips include a periscope that never quite manages to peer into the world above.

In one 1940 comic, in the panel under the strip, Krazy talks into a bent tube. "Helloi," he says, and "Helloi" comes back to him. He responds: Mus' be my 'eggo'." Given his accent and the pipe, Krazy probably means, "Must be my echo," or perhaps, "Must be my ego." In other words, "It must be me." (Or maybe was he talking about waffles? Eggos had just hit the market a few years before.)

Herriman's last Sunday page, which ran in the paper of June 25, 1944, exactly two months after his death, shows Offissa Pupp watching bubbles emerge from a pool.

He thinks Krazy is under there drowning and dives in to save her. But the underpanel shows Krazy safe, floating on her back in the underworld and holding up a sail with determination as ripples spread from her in the calm water. It's a fitting end. She is under her own power but going nowhere, idling in the "waste space" as Herriman called it, the breeding ground of endless subversion, waiting for the next breeze. ★

Sarah Boxer is a critic and reporter whose work has appeared in *The New York Times, The New York Review of Books, Slate, Artforum,* and *Smithsonian.* She is the editor of an anthology of blogs, *Ultimate Blogs: Masterworks from the Wild Web* (Vintage, 2008) and the author and illustrator of a cartoon novel based on Freud's case histories, *In the Floyd Archives: A Psycho-Bestiary* (Pantheon, 2001).

"All right, have it your way—you heard a seal bark."

John Updike

Thurber's Art

James Thurber once told a newspaper interviewer, "I'm not an artist. I'm a painstaking writer who doodles for relaxation." Yet the drawings rival his writings in their fame and lasting appeal. By the mid-1930s, his cartoons had become staples in *The New Yorker,* where Thurber had been publishing Talk of the Town pieces and signed humor since 1927. Until blindness overtook him, he illustrated his books—his comic masterpiece, *My Life and Hard Times* (1933), and his insouciant *Fables for Our Time* (1940), and his ardent, 430-word, pre-war "parable in pictures," *The Last Flower* (1939). The author as his own more or less naïve illustrator had twentieth-century precedents in Clarence Day, Max Beerbohm, and Hilaire Belloc. Nineteenth-century writer/artists like Goethe, Thackeray, Victor Hugo, and Oscar Wilde date from an age when drawing lessons were an intrinsic part of a gentleman's education. Thurber surely drew as a Columbus, Ohio, schoolboy; but an accident at the age of eight led to the loss of one eye and to

---

"Introduction to the Perennial edition of Is Sex Necessary?," "Thurber's Art," from *Due Considerations: Essays and Criticisms* by John Updike. [©2007 John Updike] Used by permission of Alfred A. Knopf, a division of Random House, Inc.

"That's my first wife up there, and this is the present *Mrs. Harris."*

limited, deteriorating vision in the other, and his development as a picture-maker was arrested at a lively, winsome primitivism. Some of his best-known cartoons, indeed, were the product of a carefree ineptitude: the one captioned "All right, have it your way—you heard a seal bark" originated, by his own testimony, when an attempt to draw a seal on a rock came out looking more like a seal on the headboard of a bed. A similar improvisation titled "That's my first wife up there, and this is the *present* Mrs. Harris" turned a woman crouching at the head of a badly drawn staircase into one crouched, or stuffed and mounted, on a bookcase. And in the cartoon captioned "You're not my patient, you're my meat, Mrs. Quist!" there seems no reason why the mustachioed medico leering down at the alarmed bed-ridden woman should be standing on a chair except that Thurber—who after White stopped inking-in for him drew directly in pen and ink on the paper—had neglected to make him tall enough for his feet to reach the floor. In his 1950 preface to his first cartoon collection, originally published in 1932, Thurber recounts how White, discovering him working at such refinements as crosshatching, exclaimed, "Good God, don't do that! If you ever became good you'd be mediocre." Yet one should not underestimate Thurber's conventional skills: in the drawing captioned "Well, what's come over *you* suddenly?" he took care to darken the other woman's shoe to show that the husband has been transfixed by a game of under-the-table footsie. Some of his captionless spots for *The New Yorker,* and his illustrations for his 1945 children's book *The White Deer,* carried out in Conté crayon when his failing sight no longer permitted pen and ink, show a care and balance considerably removed from the scratchy slapdash of his captioned cartoons.

Many of the captions provoke hilarity only because Thurber drew the picture: imagine *"Touché!"* by any other artist, or "What have you done with Dr. Millmoss?" Nor would his many treatments of what he called, in one droll yet ominous sequence, "The War Between Men and Women," be funny if the interchangeable men and women—"with the outer semblance," Dorothy Parker said, "of unbaked cookies"—were any more finely formed. The utterances so breezily illustrated the savor of his sexually vexed first marriage to the stately Ohio beauty Althea Adams, and of its boozy dishevelment: "When I realize that I once actually *loved* you I go cold all over"; "Everybody noticed it. You gawked at her all evening"; "This gentleman was kind enough to see me home, darling"; "With you I have known peace, Lida, and now you say you're going crazy"; "I'm helping Mr. Gorley with his novel, darling"; "Your wife seems terribly smart, Mr. Bruce"; "Your husband has talked about nothing but you, Mrs. Miller"; "You keep your wife's name out of this, Ashby!"; "That martyred look won't get you anywhere with me!"; "Have you forgotten our little suicide pact?"; "Have you seen my pistol, Honeybun?"; "If you can keep a secret, I'll tell you how my husband died"; "Which you am I talking to now?"

Thurber's childish drawings served up advanced adult fare; his men and women were libidinous to an extent that pressed *The New Yorker*'s youthful prudery to its limit. The Library of Congress is in possession of an exuberant pencil drawing, on lined paper, that didn't make it into mass circulation—the impending copulation of unbaked cookies. Thurber's head buzzed with not only sex but literature, especially the Victorian sort memorized in the Columbus, Ohio, of his youth. Nineteenth-century chestnuts like Longfellow's "Excelsior," Sir Walter Scott's "Lochinvar," Tennyson's "Locksley Hall," and Whittier's "Barbara Frietchie" became weirdly endearing, with unexpected pockets of pathos, when he illustrated them, as did such literary cartoon captions as "I come from haunts of coot and hern!" and "I said the hounds of Spring are on Winter's traces—but let it pass, let it pass!"

Thurber's drawing feels unstoppable, like the speech of a man who does not know a foreign language very well but compensates by speaking it very fast. His technically challenged style delivered a shock amid the opulently finished, subtly washed, anatomically correct *New Yorker* cartoons of mostly, in those days, art-school graduates; his more crudely amateurish successors in contemporary minimalism demonstrate by contrast how dynamic and expressive, how oddly tender, Thurber's art was—a personal art that captured in ingenuous scrawls a modern man's bitter experience and nervous excess. ★

As **John Updike** often noted, as a boy his earliest artistic ambition was to be a cartoonist. Born in Shillington, Pennsylvania in 1932, Updike grew up in the golden age of newspaper cartooning and admired such strips as Harold Gray's *Little Orphan Annie*, Al Capp's *Li'l Abner* and Milton Caniff's *Terry and the Pirates*. As a teenager he often wrote passionate fan letters to his favorite cartoonists. A sense of the visual informs Updike's prose, as can be seen in the many famous novels and short stories he wrote before his death in 2009. One can continue to cartoon, in a way, with words," he once wrote. "For whatever crispness and animation my writing has I give some credit to the cartoonist manqué."

Seth

John Stanley's Teen Trilogy

In the mid-to-late-1980s, I was attempting to educate myself on the history of cartooning and doing it in a very haphazard manner. I was looking at just about anything (even vaguely related) that passed under my nose—gag cartoons, children's books, girlie magazines, comic books, old engravings...you name it. Over a decade later, not much has changed. I'm still doing the same thing and I still have no logical study plan. I just follow wherever my interest leads me.

Back then, I was buying a lot of old humor comic books (seemingly for no good reason, since most of them were pretty terrible). I would leaf through a back-issue bin and if something grabbed my eye, I'd take a chance and pick it up. This is a poor method of finding quality work. I optimistically believed that there was more good work out there then there actually was. Somehow I had gotten the idea that humor comics of the '50s and '60s contained a lot of forgotten gems. This was clearly erroneous. Besides *Sugar and Spike*, ACG's *Herbie* and some good *Nancy* reprints, I found out that the

This is an updated version of "John Stanley's Teen Trilogy," which first appeared in *The Comics Journal* #238 (October 2001). [©2009 Seth]

majority of old humor comic books are dreck. Mixed in with this more generalized misinformation was the more specific error of believing that Dell comics had published a lot of good work. It's easy to see how I might have thought this: Dell published all the Barks work and all the Little Lulu comics. Surprisingly, though, they didn't publish much else of value. In fact, 90% of their line seems to have been licensed material hacked out by nameless second-string comic artists. Even the books licensed from the daily strips (*Peanuts*, *Beetle Bailey*, etc.) have very little to recommend in them. At best, the original artist may have drawn the cover. The insides were half-assed hackwork, cranked out and meant to be quickly forgotten. Which, thankfully, they have been.

However, in this random search through the dusty back-alleys of comics history, I did unearth a few titles that I had never heard of but that I immediately recognized as quality work. I began collecting *Melvin Monster*, *Thirteen (Going on Eighteen)*, and *Dunc and Loo*. I did not recognize that these comics were by John Stanley. I should have known immediately, since the covers on many of these issues were actually signed "Stanley," but I was ignorant enough at the time to simply have registered this as some other artist whose name was Stanley.

It's not like I wasn't familiar with John Stanley's work, either. I'd read every volume of *The Complete Little Lulu Library* (from Another Rainbow) that would have been out by that point. I'd devoured them. In fact, if I had compiled a list of favorite cartoonists at that time (and I did, several times) his name would have been near the top (and it was). I was highly enthusiastic about his work and if you had known me then, you'd have heard his name pop up in my conversation all the time. Still, it took me a few issues before I realized that these comics were by John Stanley. I remember clearly when it happened. I was reading *Dunc and Loo* #8; the final story in this book was a six-pager where the character Loo gets his head stuck in a little flying saucer. The pacing, the humor, the subtlety mixed with manic exaggeration—the giant "YOW!" on the fifth page—suddenly my eyes opened and I realized who had done these comic books. I didn't own a comic-book price guide at the time but I quickly acquired one and it confirmed what I had noticed. I must say, I consider it a real feather in my cap that I started to actively collect these comics before I realized who created them. It gives me some hope that my natural taste isn't entirely poor. Eventually, I discovered another book to add to the list: *Kookie*. I spent the next few years tracking down every issue of these series and, in time, I acquired them all.

Let me backtrack for a second, because you might be asking "who is John Stanley?" As I've already said, he's the artist behind Dell's long run of *Marge's Little Lulu* (and

Marge's Tubby). From 1945 to 1959, Stanley wrote and drew this much-loved and highly esteemed series. Other artists handled the finished interior art, but the rest was all Stanley. If that's unclear—he wrote it, broke it down, penciled it and completed the finished art for the covers. Irving Tripp inked the finished interior pages. Honestly, I cannot impart how wonderful those Lulu comics are. So much has been written about Carl Barks and the profound influence his duck stories had…but I sometimes I wonder if, for Barks, you had to be there (as a child, I mean). I've always had a problem seeing in Barks what everyone else sees. Maybe it's my intense dislike of those Disney characters, but I've never been able to read enough Barks to get to the point where I understand what everyone is talking about. My point in bringing this up is that I've never had this problem with John Stanley and I simply do not understand why his name is not mentioned as often as Barks's. But it isn't. I'm sure that, like Barks, Stanley created these Lulu comics with the least pretentious of motives yet somehow his natural genius turned them into real works of art. I don't know how anyone could read those Lulu stories without being bowled over by their immense charm and cleverness. Undoubtedly, though, someone right now is shaking their head in amazement at my inability to see the same thing in Barks.

Back to the point. After issue #135 of *Little Lulu,* the book passed into other hands. Stanley stuck around for a few more years, producing *Dunc and Loo, Kookie, Thirteen* and *Melvin Monster* (and a couple of other minor works) before leaving the field for good. Apparently, he didn't have very fond memories of his years in the salt-mines of Dell, since he seems to have rather strongly kept his distance from the world of comics fandom, consistently resisting interviews and avoiding conventions (smart fellow). I have some bits and pieces of biographical information around the house…but it's unimportant. It doesn't matter what high-school he attended or what year he wrote a *Choo Choo Charlie* comic book. What matters is the wonderful, funny, smart work he produced. I'm sure when he wrote these disposable comic books he could never have dreamed that, half a century later, grown adults would still be looking at them. It's an odd world.

The four comic-book series of interest that he did after *Little Lulu* are *Dunc and Loo, Kookie, Thirteen* and *Melvin Monster.* I won't be discussing *Melvin Monster* in this article—it doesn't really fit in with the other titles. Thematically, the first three fall into the demographic of "teen comics" whereas *Melvin Monster* is more or a product of that '60s monster craze that included such things as *Famous Monsters Magazine!, The Addams Family* and those great Aurora model kits. Stanley's four series were published by Dell and ultimately I have to assume that they were all failures since they were each unceremoniously canceled. *Melvin* had 10 issues, *Dunc and Loo* eight, *Kookie* a mere two. *Thirteen* came the closest to catching on—it had 29 issues and outlasted the other books by several years. However, the last four issues were reprints, which was a sure sign that the book was losing money. Then it was gone.

Not long after this, John Stanley apparently went to work in an industry that produced plastic rulers. I wonder if he noticed any difference?

Dunc and Loo

Of the three series I'm discussing, *Dunc and Loo* began the earliest, starting in Oct. 1961 (running a close second is *Thirteen*, starting one month later). At one point, all three series were going at the same time. *Dunc and Loo* ran for eight issues, starting out as *Around the Block with Dunc and Loo* but slimming down to just *Dunc and Loo* by the fourth issue. That mouthful of a title is a telling point, because the series really was about the block they lived on as much as Dunc and Loo. Like all of Stanley's work, *Dunc and Loo* is a thoroughly urban comic book. It takes place downtown, in an inner city area. Everyone in the book lives in the same low-income apartment building; if the setting were a little grittier you'd be tempted to call it a tenement. They live in a slum in the same way that Ralph Kramden lived in a slum. It's a nice slum.

Thirteen had a slightly more suburban setting to it—but not much. When the characters ventured off their nicely manicured street, they were immediately downtown. The same goes for *Little Lulu*. Lulu lives only blocks, at best, from downtown. There are always high-rises and buses (or streetcars) nearby in a John Stanley story. Stanley's characters clearly live in a city in the same way that the *Peanuts* characters clearly do not. Schulz's children are strictly suburban…and in some manner, that makes them more a part of our modern experience. Stanley's characters come from a world before Levittowns—they reflect an urban experience more rooted in the 1930s than the 1950s and, I suspect (knowing very little about Stanley's upbringing), reflect something of his experience of growing up in the earlier decades of the 20th century in America. None of this, of course, is overt—it's all just lingering around in the background.

Dunc and Loo are a couple of girl-crazy teen-agers. Dunc is the good-looking one and Loo is his Jughead-ish friend. The apartment building they live in, The Airy Arms, is the main locale for the stories and the secondary hangouts are Sid's Candy Store and the nearby street corner. There are a variety of nutty secondary characters. This mix provides the set-up for the entire series. Oh yes, there is one other element to the mix…the love interest. In the very first issue (on the first page, yet) we meet the romantic interest of the next eight issues; the blonde and beautiful Beth O'Bunnion. In the words of love-struck Dunc, "Beth O'Bunnion: Wouldn't you just know she'd have a beautiful name?"

The clearest and most recognizable feature of John Stanley's work is the remarkably clever use of the formula. Most comic-book writers work with a formula and that's why comic books are so deadly boring. Issue after issue of the same thing over and over again, John Stanley was different. He would devise a formula and then wring variations out of it that were endlessly interesting and inventive. Back during his years at *Little Lulu,* he returned over and over again to the same situations (or plot devices) for his stories. If you are familiar with those comics you will know just what I'm talking about. Lulu's imaginary tales that she told to Alvin are a classic example. Tubby's "Spider" stories, the "Little Men from Mars," Lulu babysitting Tubby, "Mumsday," I could go on and on. Stanley returned to these themes repeatedly for years, sometimes (like the Alvin stories) every issue. Basically, though, what we have here are a variety of scenarios that he could endlessly reinvent, always surprising you by finding a new wrinkle on this well-worn theme. Not unlike Schulz's annual Lucy/football gag (except a lot funnier).

In the comic books that followed *Lulu*, he continued the same pattern. He even structured the books themselves following a distinct formula. In each of these series, Stanley broke the books down into several short stories (usually five or six pages long) with each focusing on a specific character (or pair of characters). It's a rigid but surprisingly effective set-up. For example, in *Dunc and Loo*, Stanley might start off the issue with a five-pager titled "Dunc and Loo." Then following it would be a solo piece titled "Loo," then another solo story called "Dunc," then another "Dunc and Loo" and finally he'd finish off with a "Petey" story. Issue to issue, the set-up might vary; there might be two "Loo" stories and no "Dunc" or three "Dunc and Loo" stories, etc., etc.. The same pattern was going on over in *Thirteen*, with stories alternating between Judy, Val, Wilbur and Judy Jr. (or combinations thereof). This formula was followed a little less strictly in *Kookie* mainly because the series was cut short before a really good repertoire company of characters could fully develop. Even so, the stories varied between Kookie at home and Kookie at work and the characters Bongo and Bop.

What sounds at first like a rather monotonous method of organizing storytelling was, in fact, a marvelous vehicle for developing characters. In *Dunc and Loo*, this device allowed the two boys to go to their separate ways and interact with other characters. This helped to keep things fresh. We could watch Dunc pursue his romance with Beth or follow Loo's dealings with his various oddball friends, like Stoop or Birdboy. Imagine Jughead having a life outside of Archie. Admittedly, it wasn't much of a separate life—but was enough to keep things lively. It's no mystery where this approach came from. Stanley had been using it consistently for years in *Little Lulu*—and it is one of the real strengths of that series. Here's the pattern: you'd get a couple of Lulu stories, then a Tubby, then a Lulu and Alvin and sometimes an Alvin solo piece, too. Stanley knew how to have a large cast of characters that functioned well in a group *and* were interesting separately.

It seems obvious that by publishing these three comic series, Dell was hoping to cash in on some of the success of *Archie* and its various copy-cat comics that seem to have been very popular at the time. I'd like to know the actual facts about this: Who came up with the ideas for these comics? Was it Stanley or was it an editor? Either way, as cold-bloodedly as these comics may have been conceived, there is no mistaking the fact that Stanley either created the characters himself or immediately put his stamp on them. I have to admit right now that I like *Archie* comics quite a bit and I have hundreds of issues of *Archie* and its various spin-off titles. I can even tell you which years are the good years (1959 to '65, incidentally) but, I have to say, these characters are weak ciphers when compared with those John Stanley injected with vitality. Val, Judy, Dunc, Loo, etc.—these are not complex characters by any stretch of the imagination, yet they have an inner life lacking in the Archie gang. Can you, for one second, imagine Reggie alone in his room? What would he be thinking? It's not very exciting, is it? You would not say the same thing about Val (of *Thirteen*). You would have no trouble imagining any of Stanley's teens and their private world.

It might be because Stanley was interested in eccentricity. His characters are natural oddballs, peppered with personal quirks. Loo, for example, has an ivy-league suit that he's very attached to (even though people fall over laughing when they see him in it) and he gets his hair cut at a dog-groomers (he's cheap). At first glance, this may seen no more potent then Jughead's obsession with hamburgers—but it's different. It's hard to explain why. In eight short issues of *Dunc and Loo*, I have a deeper sense of these characters as people than in the hundreds of *Archies* I've read.

I think the answer is those words I used earlier: inner life. There is a sense that these characters have thoughts. Like Tubby from *Little Lulu*—you knew what he thought of himself. You knew he had a high opinion of himself even though no one else shared it. Loo is a lot like this. As he says in issue #5—"I dunno, Dunc…maybe I laid it on just a little too thick…when I said I was tall, dark and handsome—what'll she think when she sees I'm not dark?"

Loo's personality is the clearest in the book. In fact, Stanley's interest seems to gravitate toward Loo pretty quickly, leaving Dunc to act as the straight man, for the most part. Loo is the more eccentric of the two. He's an awkward, funny character—a geeky guy with a little pork-pie hat who does things his own way without realizing what an oddball he is. Stanley obviously liked this kind of character a lot since he tries to recreate him at least twice more over in *Thirteen*. Stanley understood that real eccentrics do not think they are odd—they think they are normal. Clearly, Stanley's sympathies ran toward behavior that was excessive. Think of Uncle Feeb from *Tubby*…or Tubby himself. In *Dunc and Loo*, the side characters are all filled with quirks. There's Mrs. Klobble, who rides the elevator constantly (with a chair, table and teapot) because all that going up and down "confuses her metabolism," There's Stoop, the super-strong lummox and there's Birdboy, an obsessed pigeon enthusiast who lives up an the roof. They are thinly written characters but I have no doubt that given another 10 issues, Stanley would have fleshed them out into strongly funny creations or reinvented them entirely.

Beth is easily the most bland of all the characters in the series and yet even she had her odd qualities. She is entirely unaware that her family is a group of Neanderthals ("Monsters," Dunc calls them). Her brother, Buddy O'Bunnion, is a terrible, low-brow thug who repeatedly harasses Dunc and Loo at every opportunity (shouting "I'LL ROON YA!") but Beth doesn't see it. She thinks he is a "riot" and brings him along for every date with Dunc. The O'Bunnion family themselves are just plain funny. That's one of Stanley's great talents. He was a funny writer. He had an absurd sense of humor and know how to set up a gag, building it to its ultimate conclusion (and usually its deflation, too).

He took his time with a gag and didn't mind using the space sequentially to put it over. Usually, he only allowed himself five pages to tell a story, yet he would gladly give over two pages to slowly set something up. In issue #3, Stanley uses two full pages for a silent sequence where Loo, exhausted from lack of sleep, walks into the public library, then slowly and methodically climbs a ladder and brings down books over and over until he finally climbs up the ladder and disappears. There is a silent panel, then a big panel showing shocked library patrons being disturbed by ear-shattering snoring.

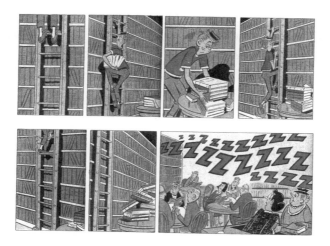

Only then does Stanley show what Loo has been up to by cutting to a shot of him sleeping on the top shelf.

Compare that to the majority of humor comics of the time. They wouldn't have given that gag more than two panels. This kind of thoughtful storytelling is a Stanley trademark and can be found throughout his work. Combine that with a real love of slapstick and you have an action-based humor that is unusual for the comic-book medium. Oh sure, if you look around in comics you'll find plenty of characters hitting each other over the head with baseball bats (or whatever) but Stanley has a sophisticated quality to what he's trying to put over. It's reminiscent of a good Laurel and Hardy bit: antic, anarchic…but smart. These gags were paced carefully and they usually paid off.

Pacing…you could make a good case for this being the key word in understanding Stanley's work. Like Kurtzman, the brilliance seems to come through in the storytelling. The characters and the jokes are funny, but it's how the story is told that makes it work. In issue #4 there is a very effective sequence where Loo is "fighting" Buddy O'Bunnion by running around the block so quickly he can come up behind him and hit him on the head. Here—it's clearer if you just look at it:

That's the thing—the storytelling is very clear. Logically set up and paced for laughs. It's the storytelling style of a born cartoonist—not fancy, but sequential. It's naturalistic, too. Exaggerated, no doubt, but one panel logically follows the other. The beauty of his understated approach is that you rarely notice it while you are reading the story. It flows by as effectively as to be almost invisible. If you have ever read any of the Weisinger *Superman* comics, you will recognize the opposite approach; panels jump wildly about, one minute you are in Smallville and the next on the moon. This doesn't happen in a Stanley comic and Stanley's way is simply a superior way to tell a story,

However, I don't want to sell his verbal humor short either. He was good with words and could turn a phrase nicely. Example: "Hedwick's no chick—she's a chunk." Another good line, this time from #6, where Loo is reading to Stoop from his favorite comic book *Maxie Mouse* (in which Maxie is being tricked into marriage): "Why would Maxie Mouse want to marry her Loo? She's built like a mouse!" That's funny stuff.

Stanley's humor had a nice absurd slant to it and, just like the formula he used to organize the stories in his books, he liked to set up absurd scenarios he could return to again and again. Unfortunately, the runs of these comics are too short for most of them to have been developed much. In *Little Lulu*, he had had the time to build his formulas and variations, but here we just see the early beginnings of what could have been richly humorous running gags. In *Dunc and Loo* #4, he introduced a baby named Snapper who had lots of potential. Snapper, of course, snapped at anything—eating hockey pucks and biting fingers. He was so deadly that his older sister, Birdy, had to wear gloves and carry him around by the back or his head (a funny and absurd image in itself). She spends the story trying to find a safe place to set him down. She tries hiding him in a pile of melons at the fruit stand but he bites the shoppers as they pick through the produce. The drawing of his perfectly round head, with its angry eyebrows, sitting among the round melons is a riot. Later she tries burying him up to his neck in a sandbox—another wonderful image. You can easily see the opportunities for Stanley to have come back to this situation again. Another such Stanley absurdity is the game of "soccim" in issue #7. The players are only shown as a whirling-dervish of arms, legs and faces as they maniacally work their way through the neighborhood. Birdy describes the game to a passerby; "Well, it's played on roller-skates with hockey sticks, baseball bats, table legs, two by fours, six by eights, nine by twelves—" "Do they play with a ball?" he asks. "Sometimes they do and sometimes they don't. Today they're playing with a ball—there it is—over there!" She says, pointing to an abandoned ball by the curb while the game carries on its merry way down the block like a tornado wrecking everything in its path. A lot of this humor has a high level of hysteria that builds with funny details. Observe:

Like I keep saying—it's funny stuff.

I mentioned Kurtzman earlier and in many ways, Stanley and Kurtzman have a lot in common. For one thing, they both had wonderful, bold, simple drawing styles. And in both cases they worked with collaborators to such an extent that their artwork tended to be overlooked. Much like Kurtzman, people tend to think of Stanley as a writer first, more than an artist (as if you could separate the two in a cartoonist). In *Little Lulu*, Stanley's beautiful page layouts were finished up by Irving Tripp and over in *Tubby*, Lloyd White handled that task. In both cases these collaborators seem to have been there mostly to slick up the rough edges of Stanley's style. Their individual styles are evident but the clarity of Stanley's look still shines through. The same is true in *Dunc and Loo* (and *Kookie*) where he is working with Bill Williams. Williams adds a surface gloss to Stanley's drawing but doesn't mess it up with a lot of extraneous brushwork.

There is a bit too much Mort Walker in Williams' style for my taste (what was once called the "Grand Rapids school of art"—all noses and feet) but he was very faithful to Stanley's line. Incidentally, where Williams really shines is in the two absolutely knockout covers he paints for *Kookie*.

I don't think that people have a clear idea of Stanley's artwork because of these long-time collaborations. In fact, in the price guide, the listing for *Thirteen* contains a question mark after the word "art" in reference to Stanley having drawn it. *Thirteen* is one of the purest sources of his uncollaborated artwork—and it goes unrecognized. It almost doesn't matter who he's working with though—the beauty of Stanley's art is how he paces a page and how he composes a panel. The rest is all gravy. There are some *Nancy* giants that Stanley did, from around the same time, where the art is finished in a very bland, perfunctory manner—but the strength of Stanley's breakdowns is so strong that those pages are still a thing of beauty.

Speaking of beauty, I think you'd be hard-pressed to find more lovely comic-book covers than the scores of those drawn (and inked) for his massive run of *Little Lulu*. Those covers define the essence of clever (and tender) sight gags. Every illustration I draw falls painfully short of such artistry when I think of those covers—and I always do.

Kookie

Of the three series, *Kookie* is undoubtedly the weakest. As I write this, I can't help but feel that I'm being unfair to John Stanley—he only got to produce two issues of *Kookie* and they were promising. Unfortunately, two issues was not a long enough run to fully develop his characters. It's a shame, too, because the setting of *Kookie* was so filled with possibilities for a cartoonist of his caliber. *Kookie* actually started later than *Thirteen* (Feb. 1962) but because of its short run I'm going to discuss it before the meatier 26 issues of *Thirteen*.

Kookie, the title character of the books, is a beautiful shapely blonde and technically, she probably doesn't fit the age group for a "teen" comic. She's out on her own (with a roommate, Clara) so I'm guessing she's probably in her early 20s. She is a nice normal girl, a little on the ditzy side, living in the heart of a Greenwich Village-type scene, working in a hip coffee house and surrounded by beatniks. The "scene" that Stanley has come up with is chaotic and fun but Kookie herself is the least interesting person in the mix. Whether he planned it that way or not, Kookie fills the role of an observer. Given time, I suspect another character would have risen to the lead spot and Kookie would have been delegated to the role of sidekick (not unlike Dunc). As it stands, Kookie remains a firmly dull character.

The good news, though, is that almost all the characters around her are interesting. This beatnik world that Stanley has chosen for his setting is loaded with comic types; I should, however, point out right away that his beatniks have little to do with the real thing—they are stereotyped beatniks of the first order, wearing berets, never bathing, quoting lame poetry and talking bop-talk. They are the same sort of beatniks you might find in the movies, television or gag-cartoons of the time. I have to assume that if by

1962 beatniks were considered a good subject for a teen comic book, then culturally they must have already been thoroughly passé.

The media image of the artist/beatnik of the '50s *is* a funny image. Looking at the beatniks and their attempts at non-conformity from the perspective of a square, kiddie-comic book artist, it's easy to see how they would view such an image as inherently humorous—even absurd. Stanley's characters are full of such nonsense. In issue #1, there is a very amusing five-pager where Bongo and Bop (two archetypal beatniks) go for a walk in the city park because they want a whiff of "that fresh air the squares are always yakking about." Once they're inside the park and start breathing it in, they begin to lose touch with their beatnik identities; they toss away their berets, straighten their postures, become kind and polite and decide to shave the moment they get home. Luckily for them, as they exit the park they get a good deep breath of the exhaust from a city bus and revert back to their hipster selves. It's a cute piece, mildly satirical in that it pokes fun at the perceived hollowness of the motives behind the beatniks' rejection of "straight" society—it's almost making the beatniks out to be victims of an urban lifestyle. But really, it's just a fun take on these types. In Stanley's world the beatniks are almost a separate species. They are simply natural oddballs—overgrown children who happen to love bad art and poetry for no logical reason. They do not represent any form of "true rebellion." They are harmless and sanitized.

Yet the situation is still humorously vital. So much of this vitality comes from that fascination with eccentricity I mentioned earlier. Every one of the characters in this book is a total eccentric (except Kookie) and the best one of all is Kookie's boss at the coffee house: Mamma Poppa. She's a typical Stanley type—a big, brash, overweight woman of enormous strength and a short fuse. She's an exaggerated figure just waiting to go over-the-top. Back in *Dunc and Loo*, Sid the candy shop owner filled the same role. Momma Poppa is rude, overbearing and most interestingly, oblivious to the oddness of her customers. In issue #2, she kicks out a loud Russian but says: "Your friend can stay if she wants to—she seems more refined…" Only then is she informed by Kookie that this guy's friend is an enormous bear. Mamma Poppa replies, "Kookie, I can't put everybody who comes in here under a microscope." Later in the same story, when the restaurant is unexpectedly sprayed with a big bomb of DDT, she breathes in a deep breath and runs to expel it under the kitchen sink—"I'm OK. I was just holding my breath. Didn't want to let all that high-grade DDT go to waste!" Still later in that same story she does a hilarious two-page dance for a visiting sheik. Here's a couple of panels:

Ten more issues of *Kookie* and I wouldn't be surprised if Mamma Poppa hadn't become the main character of this series.

An interesting point about the beatniks Bongo and Bop—well, actually, not about them so much as the position their stories hold in the book—that being, the back of the book. This is actually a unique facet of Stanley's formulaic set-up of these comics. Each series had a particular set of characters who hold the final spot in the comic. In each case, the characters were part of the neighborhood of the title character but they never actually interacted with that character. In other words, Bongo and Bop (for example) were beatniks and they obviously were part of Kookie's scene but they never appeared in any story with her or any of the other characters. Over in *Dunc and Loo*, the back-up was Petey, the local shoeshine boy. And while you might have seen Sid's candy store in his stories, the character Petey never showed up in the other segments. Again, over in *Thirteen*, there is exact same situation with a character called Judy Jr. (I'll talk more about her later) who never interacts with Val or Judy (*Thirteen*'s main characters) even though she is undoubtedly Judy's younger sister. It's an odd stylistic choice—but one I find fascinating. It adds a slightly greater level of depth to the world that these characters inhabit. To bring up Archie again—imagine if in the back of every *Archie* comic there was a story about some kid from Riverdale, a kid who never spoke to any of the Archie gang (and they were never even shown) but just happened to go to the same school. It's an interesting device.

A final comment about *Kookie*. Of the three series, this one carried the most potential for developing Stanley's satirical side. The beatnik setting lent itself more fully to a Kurtzman/Elder style of clever, meaningful and pointed nonsense. Certainly, these two issues do not deliver on that promise but there are hints of it here and there. At the very least, you often come across the same sort of hilarious throwaway gags that Elder packed his work with. Here are two examples from a funny story in *Kookie* #2, where Kookie is exploring a sidewalk art fair. On the first page she stops to look at a painting of a fat, thuggish woman in a rocking chair. The painting's title: "Wrestler's Mother." A couple of pages later, she passes a booth where a man is using a tattooing needle. The sign over his head reads: "Your social security number tattooed on a bratwurst—40¢."

Thirteen Going On Eighteen

Dear reader, it crosses my mind that you might be young enough to be unfamiliar with this old chestnut of a saying, "thirteen going on eighteen." I recall it from my childhood, but then, my parents were always old. It refers, of course, to the propensity of youth to act older than its age. If you look around today you might see that this phrase could be highly useful again in our modern world and is due for a revival. Although, perhaps now, "forty going on eighteen" would be even more useful. Sorry—off topic.

To prepare for the writing of this article I reread all 26 issues of *Thirteen* and it was a good experience. I had never previously read them all in one sitting and it gave me an excellent opportunity to see the series evolve. It begins weakly, builds to competence, then to inspired competence and finally the strip takes on a life of its own where it sparkles with the same sort of brilliance that *Little Lulu* did. While rereading the first quarter of the run, I caught myself thinking, "Is this series as good as I recall?" but by the midway point I was laughing out loud and remembering why I so thoroughly love this comic. I really do.

Val and Judy are as real to me as other beloved cartoon characters like the *Peanuts* gang, Walt and Skeezix or Maggie and Hopey. Stanley so ably breathed life into them that they seem to exist outside of the crumbling yellow pages of these old comic books. There's a moment when characters become deep enough that they are no longer just "lines on paper." A wonderful alchemy occurs where they seem to continue living even after you close the book. I'm sure you can think of some book or character that evokes this exact feeling in you. Even among the most talented cartoonists, only a few pull off this stunt. I'm certainly not talking about familiarity here. Cartooning has long relied on the concept of the continuing character and if you read 50 issues of *anything* you will achieve a feeling of familiarity; That's something else. I'm extremely familiar with the character of Dick Tracy, for example, but I don't for one second feel that Chester Gould brought him to life. When I close the book, Dick Tracy ceases to exist. It doesn't matter that *Dick Tracy* is a brilliant comic strip. It's just the opposite with *Little Orphan Annie*—Gray gave her life. Was Gray more talented than Gould? I don't think so. It's just a different experience. I'm not exactly sure why it happens when it does—but when it does, you know it.

Before I ramble on about this unexplainable nonsense, allow me to change subjects and give you the basic details about *Thirteen*. To begin with, this book is the most "teen" of all his teen comics. The main characters are Val and Judy, two 13-year-old girls who are entirely boy-crazy. They live in a nice middle-class area and attend the same high school. Billy (Val's main love interest) lives next door and they have known each other since they were toddlers. Judy has a "boyfriend" named Wilbur (a direct clone of Loo) and Val has an older sister, Evie. The contents of the book are comprised of the interactions between these main characters and a series of walk-on parts. It's set in the present (which would have been the early 1960s then) but the setting is so bland and innocent it could have been 1945. The boys are all dressed in nice suits with sharp haircuts and the girls are little ladies. Admittedly, the early '60s wasn't much different from 1945 in certain neighborhoods, so I won't hold Stanley to blame for that. The first hint that these stories aren't set in 1945 shows up late in the series with a few references to The Beatles.

Unlike every other comic book trying to cash in on the Archie craze, Stanley seems to have made it a point not to use their formula. First, there is no true rivalry between Val and Judy. In fact, unlike the equally attractive Betty and Veronica, Stanley has initially gone out of his way to make Judy unattractive (more about this later). His girls have a real friendship. They mock-betray one another and snip behind each others' backs—but there is a genuine love between them lacking in the bitchiness of Betty and Veronica. God knows what little girls learned from the horrible Betty/Veronica relationship—Stanley's teen comics are what they should have been reading. Second, there is no Archie gang to speak of; in fact, the book is surprisingly vacant of secondary characters. Billy, the boy next door, almost functions as a third main character. This leaves only Evie and Wilbur, who rarely mix with anyone else (except Judy and Val, respectively). There are no choc-lit shops, no jalopies and no Mr. Weatherbees. There's no school, actually. You rarely see any of the characters in school (except at a dance): Almost all the action takes place at Val or Judy's house. Typically, Stanley has set up a very small world where he can play with his variations and minutiae.

By tossing out that *Archie* world of teendom, Stanley has set himself the task of trying to write a funny book about a "real" 13-year-old girl. That is a difficult project and I wouldn't wish it on my worst enemy. It doesn't look too good for Stanley in the beginning either. Those first few issues are very weak. I must admit, I was a bit embarrassed reading that first issue—it's mortifying to watch a middle-aged man try to write cutesy dialogue for a teen-aged girl and fall flat on his face. Yet those issues fail for an additional reason: the art. I didn't know for the longest time who they got to finish the art and that was lucky for this unnamed cartoonist because I had nothing good to say about him. He was terrible. Several paragraphs back, I mentioned that it *almost* doesn't matter who Stanley collaborated with—it mattered here. This artist is so incompatible that he effectively kills every gag. I can see the usual pacing and composition under this guy's work but it's as if everything is poured in concrete. It's horribly stiff and dead.

Not too long ago I discovered that this nameless artist was Tony Tallarico. I feel bad knowing his name because I still can't find a single nice thing to say about his work here. In issue #2 there is a pretty good sequence where Val is trying to get rid of this pesty boy (Sticky Stu) by pretending they are star-crossed lovers. Stanley might have pulled this off if he'd drawn it himself but take a look at how painfully this reads because of Tallarico.

Compare this with any of the other art in this article and you can see how this poor collaboraton sucked all the vitality and humor out of these issues. Truthfully, though, even if Stanley had drawn those first couple of issues, I doubt he could have totally saved them. The book doesn't really come together until the fourth issue and by the sixth it's become pretty good. By the eighth issue it's priceless and it just continues to get better all through the run. This really makes me wonder what could have become of *Dunc and Loo* and poor *Kookie*. It took eight issues to get *Thirteen* rolling—*Dunc and Loo* only had eight.

Stanley takes over all the art chores with the third issue; I don't know why. If the comic-book industry were a logical place, it would merely have happened because someone recognized that Tallarico was really wrong for this comic-book series. However, in the confused hack-world of the time it could have been for any reason—they might have decided Tallarico was urgently needed over on *Lobo* or *Bewitched* or perhaps he found a better page-rate at some even worse comic company. Who knows? I'm just thankful that Stanley's art gets a chance to be showcased. I'm a genuine fan of his clear, loose, brushwork and his sparse use of background detail.

In the early issues, Judy is quite a different character than she will finally become. For one thing, she's about 200 pounds heavier. It's an interesting transformation. Initially, I suspect Stanley was trying to create a foil for Val to act against. Val, the typical cute little blonde, would be provided with a different "type" to work with: Val would be boy-crazy while Judy could be food-crazy (Judy still seemed young enough that she wasn't interested in boys yet.) Strangely, like a lot of Stanley characters, she had tremendous physical strength (shades of Little Lotta) which looked like it was going to be the source of a lot of her gags. She was tough, mean and a bit of a bully (see Judy Jr. later).

I have to wonder if the editors at Dell—wanting more of a *Betty and Veronica* comic—didn't send down an edict, "slim down that girl!" because by issue #4, she has dropped 100 pounds and in another two she is the same dress size as tiny Val. Nothing is said about it in the comic, however—she just gets lighter. Her earlier weight is never referred to again. The interesting thing in the transformation is that even after she is made blander in appearance, she's still pushy, rude and mean-spirited. Once the ball gets rolling on this series, Stanley manages to achieve what he failed to do with Kookie and Beth O'Bunnion—succeed at the unlikely goal of writing "real" girls. Both Val and Judy are vain, melodramatic, egotistical, selfish, histrionic, self-pitying, demanding and downright mean. Oh, yes, they can often be cute, funny, warm and nice, as well. Take it with a grain of salt, but these girls are not Betty and Veronica; they feel authentic. When I say the girls are "real," don't mistake that for any attempt at "realism" in their portrayal; the book tries hard to be funny and Stanley sets up absurd situations just the same as all his other work. A lot of the humor relies on Val and Judy's quirky behavior and wildly overdone attempts to get boys to pay attention to them, or in Judy's case with Wilbur (her stand-in boyfriend), to get him *not* to pay attention to her.

There are a couple of earlier failed attempts to set up a Loo-type character in *Thirteen* (Sticky Stu being one example) but when Stanley introduces Wilbur in issue #5, he has what he's looking for. Wilbur and Judy's Saturday night dates become one of those key Stanley features, appearing every issue. This again sounds like a rigid idea that could become boring and repetitive very quickly, but it doesn't happen that way. The chemistry between these two strongly eccentric characters is fun to watch. It's overwrought and manic…and most unexpectedly (because Wilbur is such a "big" character), Judy is the one who shines.

Just like Loo, Wilbur is a cheap, self-obsessed, overgrown boy, interested only in eating and watching TV. Judy literally can't stand him. She directs some sympathy toward him but most of the time, she treats him as nothing but a pest. While Judy has slimmed down her waistline, she still retains the unpopularity she had earlier. Wilbur is the best she can do and she resents it. In her own words, "Maybe he'll grow on me…and my loathing for him will turn into something finer…like mere dislike." Or in another story, where she says to Val, "Hey why don't you start by coming along with Wilbur and me?" "Three's a crowd, Judy…" replies Val, "OK," says Judy, "The first chance I get, I'll leave!" Wilbur *is* a dope and it's hard to feel sorry for him. Judy is rude right to his face and he's too dim (or thick-skinned) to pick up on it. In one story, he actually does take offense at her insults and grudgingly admits, "Maybe I'm not the handsomest guy in the world." To which Judy replies, "Maybe, he says!" Yet throughout the series, it's Judy you feel sorry for. You keep hoping some nice good-looking boy will ask her out.

Stanley throws Wilbur a crumb in one unusual episode. Judy has run into an old grade school chum, Lisa, and inevitably she has begun bragging (lying) about how fabulous her boyfriend Wilbur is; how good-looking, what a great personality, etc. etc. Near the end of this two-pager, Judy's eyes widen and she dashes off unexpectedly in mid-sentence. Just then we see Wilbur come running after her, gangly arms flailing, shouting, "Wait up Judy, it's me, Wilbur." Lisa stands by, in the last panel, and says, without a trace of sarcasm; "He *is* fabulous." It's unexpected…and funny. There's plenty of clever humor to recommend in this series—too much, in fact. I had a hard time narrowing things down here. Most of it comes from Val and Judy. It's always amusing to see one of them putting their foot in their mouth or dying from teen-age embarrassment. The dialogue is usually at a high level of hysteria. Example:

Val—"Oh, I know! This is only a nightmare! A hideous nightmare! Isn't it Judy? Tell me it's only a hideous nightmare!"

Judy—"I will not, Val! What would I be doing in a hideous nightmare?"

Admittedly, there *are* a lot of the typical sitcom style mix-ups and misunderstandings that form the basis of episodes. And in the hands of most comic-book writers this would be unbearable but Stanley has the right stuff to lead things to a funny and satisfying conclusion 90% of the time. A lot of the material in this series is very slight, too (it *is* a comic about 13-year old girls) but Stanley has such a light touch, he makes the work still readable and engaging to a grumpy middle aged man living in the early 21st century, like myself. That's quite a feat of craftsmanship.

I wish to return for a moment to the lovely negative qualities of Val and Judy's personalities. Judy's quick sarcastic wit and jaundiced attitude probably makes her the more appealing of the two, but they are both delightfully monstrous. Val is terrifically self-centered, often mooning over herself in the mirror and wondering why no one is telling her how strikingly beautiful she is. There is a charming episode where she is rolling about on her bed for two pages filled with self-pity over her "lost love" ("Oh-h-h, that this should happen to one so young—so vibrant—so BEAUTIFUL!") Within a page or two, her sister Evie comes to the rescue and comforts her with a heartfelt confidence about her own romantic problems. Evie's little speech ends up with the line "O-oh, my poor, poor, shredded heart." Val's natural kindness causes her to respond thusly:

For the most part, Stanley knows to stay away from any real "teen-age love." This is the early '60s, an era where 13-year-olds still waltz at school dances. Love interests are "crushes" and the only romantic kiss in the whole series (between Val and Billy) occurs while they have paper bags over their heads (don't ask.) There is a slightly "goopy" segment in the first half of the series: about an on-again/off-again romance between Val and a boy named Paul Vayne, but thankfully Stanley realizes (I'm guessing) that this stuff is treading too closely to soap-operatics and steers away from this material for good. He keeps the emotionalism defused with that great teen-age hysteria I keep mentioning.

For physical comedy, this series also stands at the top of the heap. Someone always appears to be engaged in a desperate sprint somewhere or they are just about to be engaged in one. Everything is at a high antic state and like anything visual, it's impossible to describe. Something gets lost in the translation. Instead, take a look:

That third character-revealing panel is genius. It's that marvelous pacing again. Stanley may have sweated over these details—but he sure made it seem effortless and off-the-cuff.

A lot of the physical humor acted to break up the monotony of the "teen romance" theme that predominated the book. He didn't overstate it, but it's clear that Stanley put forward a real effort to come up with ways to keep his material fresh. He varied his narrative approach throughout an issue, sometimes having a completely silent story following a talking-heads strip. One of the really good formula set-pieces he developed was a series of four- or five-pagers about Val's dreams that showed up every issue or two. These were dream "dates" (what else, she was boy-crazy) and the absurd world of dreamland allowed him to go off in all kinds of nutty directions. He also had an excellent set of at-the-beach stories that were a lot of fun. Stanley had a real arsenal of storytelling weapons, both subtle and sledgehammer, that he could deploy to keep things exciting. Reading this series is like a lesson in journeyman writing—there is a lot of craft on display here.

I can't end this article without a little bit on *Thirteen*'s inspired back-of-the-book character: Judy Jr., it's never explicitly stated just what her relationship to Judy is—she could either be Judy as a child or Judy's little sister—but I'm guessing it's the little sister. We never see them together…but then, we never see a lot of *people* in these comics. Where are Judy's parents, for example? Judy Jr. was designed back in the first issue and just like her big sister, she was made a fat girl (about 5 or 6 years old, I'd guess). When

Judy got slimmed down, they left Judy Jr. alone and she remained a little butterball.

Judy Jr. is a horrible child. She's not a cute little mischievous Dennis the Menace-type. Judy Jr. is someone else's bratty kid that you have to pretend to like. She is mean and selfish and (like Tubby) a complete egomaniac. This could be acceptable if she kept to herself, but that's not the formula Stanley had in mind. He's given her a nice little boy to be the target of all her aggression; Jimmy Fuzzi. Every episode, Judy Jr. tracks him down and taunts, harasses, intimidates and physically assaults him. He tries in vain to avoid her, but like a juggernaut she plows through whatever obstacles he places in her way. Stanley actually captures that look of fear in Jimmy's eyes as she approaches. He's like the proverbial deer caught in the headlights. Every so often Jimmy will get the upper hand and Judy Jr. will receive some minor comeuppance…but most of the time, he suffers in silence till the final panel. These Judy Jr. stories are among the most solidly formulaic that Stanley ever did and yet they prove my point about his great talent, I could read a whole book of them.

Believe me, I could keep rambling on about these comics. It would actually be rewarding to see this series discussed on an issue by issue basis but this isn't the place for it. Yet take my word—this work deserves notice. I feel a genuine connection with them. To tell the truth, I'm honestly surprised that in the more than 30 years since these comics saw print, no one has really bothered to write anything about them. Even *Tubby* and *Lulu* get short-shrift if you ask me. Without doubt, these abortive final efforts by John Stanley rank in the upper echelon of commercially produced comic books. They certainly tower above most of what was published in this field during the twentieth century and, in my honest opinion, *Thirteen* sits easily next to *Little Lulu* as John Stanley's finest work. Funny, smart, lovely work—not to be forgotten. ★

Seth is the cartoonist behind the long-running comic book series *Palookaville*: a new hardcover version of which will appear later this year. His Books include *Wimbledon Green*, *George Sprott*, *Clyde Fans* and *It's a Good Life if You Don't Weaken*. He is the designer for *The Complete Peanuts*, *The John Stanley Library*, *The Portable Dorothy Parker* and *The Collected Doug Wright*. His cardboard city of Dominion is currently touring Canada.

Jonathan Franzen

Schulz's Gifts

Was Charles Schulz's comic genius the product of his psychic wounds? Certainly the Schulz depicted in Rheta Grimsley Johnson's authorized biography, *Good Grief* (1989), was a mass of resentments and phobias that seemed attributable, in turn, to emotional traumas in his youth: his unpopularity at school, his skinniness and pimples, the rejection of his drawings by his high school year book, the death of his mother on the eve of his induction into the Army, the little red-haired girl's rejection of his marriage proposal, and so on. The man who became the best-loved artist on the planet was increasingly prone to attacks of depression and bitter loneliness. ("Just the mention of a hotel makes me turn cold," he told Grimsley.) Although he left his native Minnesota, he replicated its comforts in California, building himself an ice rink whose snack bar was called "The Warm Puppy." By the 1970s, he was reluctant even to get on an airplane unless someone from his family was with him. Here—the armchair

Jonathan Franzen's essay originally appeared as the foreword to *The Complete Peanuts 1957-1958*.
[©2005 Jonathan Franzen]

psychologist might think—was a classic instance of the pathology that produces great art: wounded by adolescent traumas, our hero took permanent refuge in the childhood world of *Peanuts*.

But what if Schulz had chosen to become a toy salesman, rather than an artist? Would he still have lived such a withdrawn and emotionally turbulent life? I suspect not. I suspect that Schulz the toy salesman would have gutted his way through a normal life the same way he'd gutted out his military service. He would have done whatever it took to support his family—begged a Valium prescription from his doctor, had a few drinks at the hotel bar.

Schulz wasn't an artist because he suffered. He suffered because he was an artist. To keep choosing art over the comforts of a normal life—to grind out a strip every day for fifty years; to pay the very steep psychic price for this—is the opposite of damaged. It's the sort of choice that only a tower of strength and sanity can make. The reason that Schulz's early sorrows look like "sources" of his later brilliance is that he had the talent and resilience to find humor in them. Almost every young person experiences sorrows. What's distinctive about Schulz's childhood is not his suffering but the fact that he loved comics from an early age, had a gift for drawing, and was the only child of good parents.

This is not to say that the depressive and failure-ridden Charlie Brown, the selfish and sadistic Lucy, the philosophizing oddball Linus, and the obsessive Schroeder (whose Beethoven-sized ambitions are realized on a one-octave toy piano) aren't all avatars of Schulz. But his true alter ego is clearly Snoopy: the protean trickster whose freedom is founded on his confidence that he's lovable at heart, the quick-change artist who, for the sheer joy of it, can become a helicopter or a hockey player or Head Beagle and then again, in a flash, before his virtuosity has a chance to alienate you or diminish you, be the eager little dog who just wants dinner.

On page 183 of *The Complete Peanuts 1957-1958* (March 2, 1958), you will find a strip in which Snoopy grabs Linus's blanket in his teeth, swings Linus round and round in the air, sends him flying skyward, and reflects: "I'm the first dog ever to launch a human being!" This strip probably refers to the Russian space dog Laika, who was launched in November 1957, but it could also serve as a description of the volume as a whole. In the 1960s, Peanuts would break free of gravity altogether—achieve a degree of popularity for which there was not remotely any precedent, abandon all pretense of depicting realistic children and animals, and attain the stylistic escape-velocity at which an artist is no longer shadowed by any precursor but himself. What launched the strip to such heights was, above all, the character of Snoopy. The years 1957 and 1958, which this volume covers, find Snoopy being transformed from a cartoon dog into the I-am-what-I-am of later years. These are the years when his snout reaches maximum extension, double or triple its original length. He still sheds fur, fetches balls, chases birds, and licks people for no reason; but now, for the first time, he does things that aren't conceivably doglike; he stands on Schroeder's piano and plays a violin; he suits up for baseball. Meanwhile, the children's personalities are settling into their now-familiar contours, and Schulz is developing the longer narrative sequences and archetypal gags (Linus's blanket, Charlie Brown's kite, Lucy's competition with Beethoven, Charlie Brown's "pencil pal," the baseball sequences) that characterize his breakthrough work.

One long-running gag, given treatment in multiple strips for the first time in 1958, is Charlie Brown's yearly failure to get any valentines. In *Peanuts, A Golden Celebration*, published shortly before his death, Schulz told a Valentine's story from his own childhood. When he was in first grade, his mother helped him get valentines for everybody in his class, so that nobody would be offended by not getting one; but he felt too shy to put them in the box at the front of the classroom, and so he took them all home again to his mother. At first glance, Schulz's story recalls a strip on page 97 (Aug. 12, 1957): Charlie Brown peers over a fence at a swimming pool full of happy kids, then he goes home and sits by himself in a bucket of water. But Schulz, unlike Charlie Brown, had a mother on duty—a mother to whom he chose to give his whole basket of valentines.

A child deeply scarred by a failure to get valentines would probably not grow up to draw lovable strips about the pain of never getting valentines. (A child like that— one thinks of R. Crumb—might instead draw a valentine box that morphs into a female body part that devours his valentines and then devours him, too.) Beneath the conventional narrative of Schulz's childhood failures is the story of a happy young man oversupplied with parental love. His little family's closeness gave him strength; its closedness probably helped estrange him from the world. Love feeding art feeding estrangement feeding forgiveness: the gifts Schulz was given became his gift to us. ★

Jonathan Franzen won the National Book Award for Fiction for his novel *The Corrections*. He is the author of *The Twenty-Seventh City, Strong Motion, How to Be Alone* and *The Discomfort Zone*. Franzen also writes for *The New Yorker*.

Daniel Clowes

"A Mozart of Zaniness"

Unfortunately for you, poor reader, I have nothing to offer in the way of biographical data or useful information. I have never met Mr. Elder, and know very little about the man himself beyond the sketchy details of various fanzine articles. My only claim to any kind of personal relationship is a life-long obsession with his work, which began with the discovery of a copy of *The Mad Reader* on my brother's floor in 1965, and has continued unabated to this day. I once had the pleasure of spending an afternoon with an old crony of Elder's, a fellow artist from the EC days, who, after about five minutes of small talk, launched unprovoked into a series of Will Elder stories. He presented these startling accounts, mostly of deranged (often borderline-illegal) practical jokes and crazy stunts (one example, if I recall correctly, had Elder walking around a restaurant with a firehose asking people what kind of salad dressing they wanted), with such polish and glee that it seemed like he had thought of nothing else in the intervening 40 years. I went home, amazed and baffled. How could such a man as Will Elder exist? This was a force of nature, a Mozart of zaniness, a vessel from which a seemingly

---

Daniel Clowes' introduction to *Will Elder: The Mad Playboy of Art*. [©2003 Daniel Clowes]

endless cascade of insane humor poured forth, not only onto Bristol board, but into the minutiae of his daily life! And somehow, by some unlikely combination of genetics and environment, he had also within his makeup the patience, conviction, dedication, and control to have produced some of the most perfectly-realized, technically-astounding work ever seen in comics! And magazines!

For me, the great beauty of Elder's artwork comes not from its style, but from its stylelessness. Unlike virtually all of his peers in the comic book/strip/humorous illustration field in the 1950s, his work is blissfully free of distracting tics, gimmicks, short-cuts, and flashy techniques. Despite the back-breaking labor inherent to his method, there is a disarming modesty to his work (something you wouldn't expect from the extroverted joker of his colleagues' anecdotes). Visually, Elder articulates his Milt Gross/Marx Brothers-Yiddish vaudevillianism not with slapdash expressionism, but with a Hogarthian eye for landscape and detail. In some ways, he is more a descendant of Bosch and Breughel than of Foster and Crane, but there is a very palpable sense of the history of comics flowing through his brush-line, implemented not with a fannish slaver, but with the engaged dispassion of a bemused biologist. It is this half-step of distance that makes him such a great (an understatement—he is the best ever) dismantler of his fellow cartoonists. He tackles the big names (Gould, Capp, King, Crane) with such effortless accuracy that the original invariably looks a little tepid next to its Elderized doppelgänger. His facile duplication of every stylistic flourish makes even the most unapproachable technical achievement seem mannered and not just a little suspect. Most impressive though is his handling of the solid but undistinguished B-list craftsmen (e.g. Ken Ernst), whose tiny failings would surely evaporate under the heat of a lesser imitator's scrutiny. His ability to capture the odd stiffness of *Rex Morgan* or the prosaic joylessness of *Charlie Chan* with a precision that is neither cruel nor forgiving is nothing less than astonishing. That he could duplicate the technique of Rockwell better than any of the master's esteemed peers on the faculty of the Famous Artists School is remarkable. That he was able to infuse this duplication with his own very personal sense of profound uncanniness and inspired absurdity (it still seems "edgy" and subversive—and, yes, funny—after 50 years) is practically unfathomable. And why does the humor still work so well? First and foremost, Will Elder is a funny guy—a rare commodity for which there is no substitute. The best of his work has a timeless quality, even when referring to long-expired source material, that seems to come from something very personal. While the main figures may convey the information necessary to follow the story (often beautifully so, thanks to the sure-handed rhythms of his frequent collaborator Harvey Kurtzman), the backgrounds are literally cluttered with information about the artist himself and the very specific urban culture from which he has risen. There is no sense whatsoever, as in the work of other detail-obsessives, that Elder is showing off or overcompensating, but rather we see the graphic results of a struggle within the artist to keep his own expansive consciousness engaged and amused. The detail does nothing to slow or disrupt the reading process and can be read as mere texture by those too tired or cross-eyed to engage with the full effect. It is there to be enjoyed, in whatever measure the reader chooses. As someone who has read "Starchie" 1100 times, I can say with certainty that there are still new gems to be found with every inspection. And, surprisingly, underneath it all there is a certain undeniable "tastefulness" to his mockery. The work is critical without snarling disdain or sycophantic gushing (as in every *Mad* parody of the past 20 years). If Elder makes fun of Modern Art, for example, we feel that he does so with a full understanding of his subject. There is a moral hierarchy in place, but it is one in which humor takes the top spot. The drawings are laden with brutal realism, but the work is infused with such a generous spirit that we never suspect the artist of having any particular agenda beyond the longing for a few fleeting moments of "reality" in which the interplay of chaos and control is orchestrated as beautifully as in one of his panels. And this is where he earns our love, we the readers of comic books and dirty magazines, for this indomitable generosity and good will, for providing an intimidatingly high level of inspirational material for every artist and humorist, and for allowing us to share intimately in his crystal-clear vision of a world gone mad. ★

Daniel Clowes was born in Chicago in 1961 and studied art at the Pratt Institute in Brooklyn, New York, though he considers himself to be largely self-taught. After producing seven issues of the cult comics magazine *Lloyd Llewellyn* in the second half of the 1980s, Clowes launched the generation-defining *Eightball* (1989–2004), an anthology of short-form and longer, serialized stories which were later collected into graphic novels, including *Like a Velvet Glove Cast in Iron*, *Ghost World*, and *David Boring*. A movie adaptation of *Ghost World*, released in 2000, garnered excellent reviews and a shared Best Adapted Screenplay Academy Award nomination for Clowes. Clowes' original graphic novel *Wilson* will be released in May 2010 by Drawn & Quarterly; in 2011 Pantheon Books will publish a significantly expanded (and uncensored) version of his 2007 New York Times Sunday Magazine serial *Mister Wonderful*.

Ken Parille

"What's This One About?"

A Re-Reader's Guide to Daniel Clowes's *David Boring*

In Daniel Clowes's *Ice Haven*, one of the story's many protagonists, the young Charles, rants about nature and sex. Unable to express his forbidden longing for an older stepsister, he yearns for the day when technology will allow him to satisfy his sexual desires without other people. Charles rails against nature because natural urges cause him so much pain: "Nature is not beautiful," he proclaims. "Only the artificial and the man-made can be truly beautiful" (15). Although Charles's rants are played in part as comedy, they express a philosophy at the heart of *David Boring*: an aesthetics that elevates artifice over nature. Instead of creating a fiction governed by verisimilitude, Clowes emphasizes the perversity and playfulness of fiction. *David Boring* follows its own logic and not nature's. The narrative never violates possibility as Clowes's *Like a Velvet Glove Cast in Iron* does (with three-eyed women and dogs without orifices),

---

This is s a revised version of "A Re-Reader's Guide to *David Boring*,"
which appeared in 2005's *Comic Art* #7. [©2009 Ken Parille]

but it repeatedly plays with believability: whenever a "lucky penny" changes hands, something unlucky happens; an Oceana police detective has the unlikely name of "Lt. Anemone"; and random objects share an unusual and symmetrical number. Yet the book's coincidences, puzzles, and clues are more than just intellectual games. They are part of a powerful emotional drama: David's quest to untangle the mysteries of his absent father's life by obsessively re-reading a comic his father created. *David Boring* is a detective story in which the solution to every mystery lies in artifice of the book and the conspiracy between author and re-reader.[1]

Always an astute reader, cartoonist Chris Ware has said of *David Boring* that "a lot of things are hidden in the narrative, in the overall structure of the book. The more you take apart Dan's book, the more complicated it gets. I think it's one of the greatest comics ever written" (Kim 1). As Clowes developed the materials that would become *David Boring*, he worried about "the level of readers," many of whom he believed lacked the kind of attention that someone like Ware brings to a text: "To me, that's the big problem... There aren't too many people who are actually willing to pay close attention to this stuff and read it carefully" (Howard 29). Comic readers, Clowes noted, have been raised on rapidly consumed and disposable narratives, and "as my stories get more and more complex, some people are complaining. They want them to be easy to digest, fun little comics" (Juno 106). While Clowes's first long narrative *Like a Velvet Glove Cast in Iron* was partially improvised, he described *David Boring* as "the most complex I've ever gotten in terms of writing something in advance" (Phipps 1). He "hope[d] people will sit down and read it carefully, because there's a lot more to it...than anything else I've ever done" (English 8). *David Boring* shows in its protagonist a version of the slow and careful reader who will be able to understand such complexity. As David reads *The Yellow Streak and Friends Annual* he models an approach to comics in which interpretation takes far more time than reading: "I allow myself to read only two panels a night, very closely" (45).[2] Clowes also imagines a reading process where re-reading happens, not just after a first reading, but throughout every reading. Unlike film, in which the viewer relinquishes control to the forward motion of the technology, comics allows the artist to "tell stories where you can introduce information that requires [the reader] to go back three pages and look at a panel" (Howard 31). And the clues, hidden narratives, and visual puns in *David Boring* remind us to read more carefully and to re-read repeatedly, assembling seemingly disparate information into complex patterns.[3]

---

1 Many of Clowes's stories dramatize the author-reader relationship. In "You," images of readers as money-grubbing parasites and scornful critics hover over the cartoonist as he works. See also "Just Another Day" and "King Ego." "I write for an imaginary audience based on versions of myself," Clowes has said. "I presume that everybody is going to get everything... But you never know what they are going to relate to" (Strouss 9).

2 It's important to note that, in David's case, the value of such close reading is in doubt; he never tells us if it helps him.

3 For Clowes, this way of reading echoes the process by which *David Boring* was created: "I get words in my head, just phrases—the name David Boring...popped into my head when I drew a character I saw on the subway once... [Y]ou get these images and notions and words in your head and they all sort of mix together and create linkages between each other" (Hunter 66). In *PLG*, Clowes talks about writing *David Boring*: "it's very similar to [reading] a detective story, where you have these clues you need to put together" (Lementhéour 32).

Clowes has said that "it's sort of essential to read [*David Boring*] three or four times," and nowhere is the need for re-reading more urgent than in discovering and interpreting the narrative's many puzzles (English 8). Just as Professor Karkes and Wanda Kraml play a game of arranging pictographs to form different words and David faithfully deciphers the daily "Cryptic Word Quiz," Clowes plays a number of games with his readers.[4] Many objects in the story appear to function as clues that could be assembled into a solution. Yet some of the clues and puzzles lead us, not to an answer, but to questions of fiction, the comic page, and interpretation. Just as David is about to be shot, for example, Clowes leaves a visual pun as a clue for us in the seventh panel on page 36. David holds a set of keys in front of a car: car + keys = Karkes. This pun is not a clue in the traditional sense because, although it names the assailant, it's not evidence related to the crime. Instead, it's an artificial clue, a kind of in-joke between author and re-reader. This visual pun is actually the second such car-key pun.[5] On page 34 David finds pieces of Karkes's homemade game of cartoon images: a drawing of a car, another of two keys, and a third of a wand with an "a." David takes these and other game pieces with him to Hulligan's Wharf, where he looks at them and wonders who shot him: "Why waste time thinking about it? This isn't a murder mystery" (43). Yet, the three pieces that appear in the panel with this narration—a car, a plus sign, and two keys—solve a mystery; and as an additional clue, Wanda tells us in the prior panel that "my professor says it's not love if you're not willing to kill for it" (43). David assembles the drawings in an attempt to determine what the possible combinations can tell him about Wanda, apparently not recognizing that, if arranged properly, they identify his assailant.[6]

By the time the first clue appears, Clowes has given us enough information to solve the mystery. We have been introduced to Wanda, who had apparently mentioned

---

4   Karkes, a professor who discusses limericks with his students, may be based on the scholar Gershon Legman, editor of *The Limerick* and author of *Rationale of the Dirty Joke*. Clowes refers to Legman's anti-hippie tract *The Fake Revolt* in *Like a Velvet Glove Cast in Iron* (64). The tract's subtitle, "The Naked Truth About The Hippie Revolt," is echoed in the subtitle of Clowes's *Modern Cartoonist*: "The Naked Truth."

5   The book has numerous visual puns. For example, as David studies his father's comic, he says, "I allow myself to read only two panels a night" (45). In the next panel, David is framed within two panels at night; the windows of the house on Hulligan's Wharf (itself a play on "Gilligan's Island") are analogues for comic panels.

6   Although there's a great deal of evidence to indicate that Karkes shot David, the comic stops short of telling us this directly. Another crime, the murder of Whitey, is never solved. Or is it? When David views Whitey's body in the morgue, he says the "dent in Whitey's forehead looked like a gigantic thumbprint" (9). In a dream recounted in Act Three, David says, "I watch as Whitey's head is crushed by a giant thumb from the sky. It belongs to god" (103). David also notes the police are "calling [Whitey's murder] an 'act of God,' I guess" (15). So, did Clowes, the god-creator of *David Boring*, kill Whitey?

Professor Karkes in the conversation on the airport shuttle. The game pieces, unlike the visual pun on page 36, could work as standard clues for both readers and characters by suggesting that Karkes and Wanda were romantically involved, creating a love triangle, with jealousy as Karkes's motivation for shooting David. Yet it's unlikely that many (if any) readers could make all of these connections on a first reading; because comics is a silent medium, we read "Karkes" but are unsure how it's pronounced, making it improbable that we would understand such information as clues.

While these clues could eventually be recognized and decoded by any diligent re-reader, Clowes creates interpretive puzzles in *David Boring* that are far more obscure and difficult to untangle. One such puzzle involves repetitions of the number 333. We first see it on *The Yellow Streak* cover, next as the number of Wanda's apartment building, and last on the three movie lobby cards for "Crime and Judy" that appear between Acts 2 and 3. The purpose of these 333s is difficult to determine; their repetition and placement give them significance, but what exactly do they signify? Does it make sense to call them clues? And if so, what problem can be solved by decoding them? Are they related to any of the plot's mysteries: Who killed Whitey? Who shot David? Where's Wanda? *The Yellow Streak* was drawn in 1968, Wanda's address appears to be random, and the nature of the lobby cards is unclear. Are the cards design material that Clowes added as transitions between acts, or are they for the movie that David is writing, and if so, has he created them? Has he noted the 333 connection between his father's comic and Wanda's address and symbolically linked his own narrative with these objects? (If so, he never tells us.) Within the world of the story, the only reasonable explanation appears to be coincidence: these numerical repetitions are random and therefore can't be clues to anything.[7]

This explanation, however, seems unsatisfactory, for Clowes has deliberately connected these objects. Maybe the 333s are more like prompts than clues, asking us to consider the relationship between the three things associated with the number: *The Yellow Streak*, Wanda, and "Crime and Judy." David obsesses over each. He constantly re-reads his father's comic, stalks Wanda and fetishizes women with a similar body-type, and repeatedly interprets his life as if he were starring in a movie he had written. *David Boring* suggests that David's interest in his father's comic, his fetish, and his desire to tell his story share an origin in the troubled family dynamics of his early upbringing. But it doesn't tell us much more. Maybe the 333s are just a joke, sending us on a fruitless search for a solution that never comes. Talking about *David Boring*, Clowes laughingly said "I don't like to manipulate the audience unless it's in a very sadistic way, where they are not rewarded in the end" (Lementhéour 32).

---

7   Randomness and order are important concepts for Clowes: "a lot of the artists that I am interested in… are trying to give some cohesion to…the seeming randomness of the world, trying to put all of the pieces together" (Howard 32).

333 has an aesthetic meaning that's crucial to the art of *David Boring*. It's a numerical representation of the nine-panel grid (three rows of three panels), a standard comic book page layout. Numerous pages in the book use this exact grid, no page has more than three rows, only seven of the more than 340 rows exceed three panels, and only one page (interestingly, page 33) has more than nine panels. So, almost every page has three rows, and at least one row, though usually more, contains three panels. In this sense, then, the nine panel grid is the 3x3 "template" behind nearly every page.[8] (One particularly interesting nine panel grid is page 16, where the center panel has a 333, as if commenting on the page itself). While many mainstream and alternative comic artists reject what they see as the constraints of the grid and rectangular panels, Clowes embraces the kind of traditional page layouts and panels used in the superhero, crime, humor, and horror comics he read while growing up. Although Clowes's short stories have a wide assortment of layouts (including many strict 333 grids), *David Boring*, like his long narratives (*Like A Velvet Glove Cast in Iron, Pussey!*, and *Ghost World*), relies heavily on versions of the 333 template. A sign of the book's visual narrative practice, 333 signals Clowes's connection to and appreciation of his pulp predecessors and influences.

The notion of 3 is also a fundamental organizing principle behind the comic's origin and its structure. Clowes "initial idea was for a character who had three wives in three different cities. It was based on my childhood, where I had to spend my time in three separate houses" (Hunter 67).[9] The three acts—as Clowes calls the sections of *David Boring*—were originally serialized in three issues of *Eightball*, and like Clowes David plans to write a film that follows the "3-act structure" (73).[10] David connects his interest in the traditional three-part form to the aesthetics of his ideal woman with a pun on narrative and physical notions of "structure": she, like a work of art, must have "the timeless allure of a classical structure" (8). This pun implies that the energy driving David's interest in narrative is sexual, and another numerical pun connects his preference for a kind of woman's body with the structure of *David Boring*. When Dot sees a woman who matches this type, she says to David, "Holy 36-32-48, Yellow Streak," three numbers that correspond to the page counts for the book's three acts.[11] The structural significance of 3 also refers back to the 3x3 nine-panel grid and is reinforced

---

8   For the seven rows with over three panels, see pages 5, 12, 14, 33 (two rows), 34, and 91. The opening pages of each act vary from the 3x3 template: see 1-3, 37-38, and 69-72.

9   Clowes says that *David Boring* "came together from this mass of notes I had in these three different notebooks" (Lementhéour 28).

10   There are numerous parallels between the films of Dot and David and *David Boring*. A movie frame shown in the last panel of page 4 reappears (from the opposite direction) in the last row of page 111. Another film image—Dot holding two guns (96)—reappears on the third lobby card and prefigures Dot's shooting of the two Oceana police officers on page 112. David's description of a film they wanted to make could describe *David Boring*: "Our big idea was to make a pornographic epic...a complex narrative, where the sex was a natural part of the action. I was going to be the main star" (16). Similar parallels occur between *David Boring* and *The Yellow Streak*. The last panel of page 35 shows a full page of *The Yellow Streak*, the layout of which mirrors the *David Boring* page upon which it appears: the *Yellow Streak* panels that appear as full panels occupy the same grid location on both pages. On page 35, The Yellow Streak warns Testor he is in danger. Though David doesn't realize it, he is also in danger. On the next page he is shot.

11   Thanks to Adrian Tomine, who told me of this connection.

by other references to the number, such as a sign for a business named "Trident" (11), mentions of "World War Three," and a bullet striking a character's forehead three times. In all of these ways, the world of *David Boring* echoes the symbolic and ordered artifice of fairy tales, which often show a similar obsession with structures, objects, and actions occurring in 3s.

With these strange and improbable 3s and 333s, *David Boring* stretches believability by creating numerous instances of repetition that, if we approached the comic as a realistic text, might strain our ability to accept it as natural or believable. Whereas *Like a Velvet Glove Cast in Iron* lunged headfirst into impossibility, *David Boring* takes place in a world that seems like ours. Yet Clowes's narrative is indebted to the imaginary worlds of fairy tales, pulp fictions, and B-movies, with the book's strange coincidences, doublings, wordplay, and self-reflexive narrative. The many puzzles involving names and numbers emphasize this pulp artifice, yet they do more than just reveal the playful "hand" of the author in the way that much metafiction does—they speak to larger thematic concerns.[12] For example, the names of the only two beers seen in the book— "Elba Light" and "Blight Ale"—are anagrams of each other and of *Eightball*. The wordplay here gets at the simultaneously humorous (light) and apocalyptic (blight) tone of the book and its narration. A similar pairing occurs with two publications: *Utopia* and *Distopia*. An image in David's fetish book comes from *Utopia*; the magazine and a torn-out page are seen in panel 1 and 2 of page 14, and the removed page appears in David's fetish book in panel 1 on page 23. Karkes's academic article, which includes an analysis of the fetish book, appears in the journal *Distopia* (78/4). These titles parallel the opposition set up by the beer names (light and utopia, blight and distopia), pairs that seems to be connected to the romantic duo of David and Wanda—David's apocalyptic skinniness seeks and find its antidote in Wanda's utopian fullness. All of these pairs reveal the novel's obsessive interconnectedness, for in the fictional world of *David Boring* everything seemingly refers to everything else.

David Boring also features a system of references between itself and comics history. Thematically, David's butt obsession and some of *David Boring*'s pages (especially 26) have their pornographic roots in the 1940s and '50s, when, according to '50s anti-comic book crusader Fredric Wertham, "run-of-the-mill comics [gave] special emphasis in whole series of illustrations to girls' buttocks. This is a kind of fetishism (sic)" (178). Wertham (whose work Clowes has adapted into comics) also records the comments of a boy whose sexual fantasies come from the comics he reads: "I think of girls twisting their heels on my chest and face" (182).[13] The cover of *Eightball* 20, part of which appears in *David Boring* between pages 36 and 37, echoes this fantasy: Dot chokes

---

12   Just as Clowes figuratively appears in the comic through various puns and puzzles, the hands of creators literally appear. David imagines Whitey being killed by god's thumb, which descends from a hole in the clouds (103). This image parallels a scene in *The Yellow Streak Annual*'s backup story, "Allergy." In the only panel from this story we see, an artist's hand emerges from the clouds and starts to erase the title character: "I'm sorry I ever created you, you obnoxious pest!!" (98). When David reads this panel, does he imagine that this is how his father eventually felt about him?

13   A similar image appears on the title page of Clowes's *Orgy Bound*. See Clowes's adaptations of *The Show of Violence* and *Seduction of the Innocent*.

Manfred while Iris twists her heel into his face and chest. Numerous characters' names and fictional types recall important comic artists and cartoon characters. David shares a last name with Wayne Boring, a famous Superman artist of the post-war decades, whom David explicitly alludes to when introducing himself in Act One. (Is it intentional or coincidental that David Boring works as a security guard and Wayne Boring worked as a bank security guard?) The cover of a comic likely drawn by David's father echoes a common scenario from Will Elder and Harvey Kurtzman's *Goodman Beaver* (75).[14] When David describes his mother's destruction of the "innocent color-dots" of his father's comic book, he draws our attention to a traditional method of coloring comics, and *The Yellow Streak* panels are colored in imitation of this method, which uses small "Benday" dots to create a field of color. And just as David's name refers to a well-known comic artist, the name of his best friend Dot recalls, not only a coloring method, but a famous Harvey Comic's character, "Little Dot," a girl obsessed with dots, ironically the very things that color her. In his manifesto *Modern Cartoonist* Clowes identifies "the hag" as a superhero and horror story archetype. Two characters in *David Boring* fill this slot. Wanda is called "a hag" by Dot, who sees her through the lens of cartoon and fairy tale types as the villain in David's story, and the villain in *The Yellow Streak* is called "the hag" by the comic's hero (95). By featuring a character who operates as "the hag," the world of David's narrative imitates the cartoon world of his father, as if David unintentionally replays scenes from his father's comic. And even after the narrative has ended, Clowes continues to link the text to its tradition. The book's movie-style closing credits refer to numerous cartoon characters and artists: Batman's alter-ego "Bruce T. Wayne," cartoonist "Jack Davis," a man with the first name "Popeye," and even "Kim Lee," the name of a minor character in Clowes's then yet-to-be-published *Ice Haven*.[15]

Another of *David Boring*'s minor characters, the private detective Purcell Howe, appears in two ways in the comic, and as with the multiple 333s, the nature of this reappearance—as coincidence or intentional act—is unclear. We first see Howe as a picture on the back cover of *The Yellow Streak*, a 1968 advertisement for his work in missing persons cases (63). Howe then actually appears, when David and Karkes hire the "semi-

---

14   On the comic's cover, a boy on a beach says to a girl, "Excuse me, miss. You dropped something!" (75). This scene recalls a gag from *Goodman Beaver*: he follows Annie Fannie (who is wearing only a towel) and says, "Oh miss - You forgot your clothes!" (Elder 90).

15   Clowes ties his stories together into a loosely connected world by reusing unusual names: Hal Hoffen-kamp is a game show host in *Like a Velvet Glove* (78) and a talent scout in "Little Enid" (0), stories written over a decade apart; "Hulligan's Wharf" is a television show in *Like a Velvet Glove* (70) and the island retreat in *David Boring*; and a character named "Prof. Boring" appears in *Lloyd Llewellyn*. Clowes has said that "people are always thinking things are anagrams that aren't," and names like "Wanda Kraml" seem almost deliberately chosen to suggest such an origin (Silvie 60). Perhaps this name implies a playful manipulation of the readers who would try to decode it, thinking it might reveal something about the character.

retired private investigator" to help them locate Wanda (83). Did David remember the ad from the comic (which by this point has been ripped into pieces, with many of the fragments lost) and seek him out because he represented a way for him to connect his narrative with his father's? Given how much time David has spent re-reading the comic, it's hard to imagine that he wouldn't have noticed Howe's

ad. But David and *David Boring* are silent on an interesting question. Symptomatic of Clowes's approach, he withholds information that readers might want to know, that would help them to understand if the hiring of Howe was only a coincidence.[16]

Perhaps the book's most complex series of "reappearances" involves numerous female characters, most of whom are objects of David's sexual interest. David alerts us to some of these parallels when he refers to a "resemblance between Wanda Kraml and my favorite scrapbook girl," claiming that "the genealogy of this infatuation can be traced back to…their prototype (my perfect cousin, Pamela)" (15). But he represses another important similarity, the one between Wanda and his mother. Indeed, his mother's face is drawn in the panel on the prior page directly next to this comment, and Wanda's face first appears four pages earlier, placed in a similar position (right side of an even-numbered page, directly facing the reader) and drawn at the same size. The kind of reader who, as Clowes hopes, will "go back three pages and look at a panel" might notice this resemblance and the careful positioning of the faces.

The extensive series of resemblances between female characters is as follows: David's mother looks like David's cousin Pamela (with whom he had his first erotic encounter), both of whom look like Wanda, who in turn looks like her older sister, Judy, who looks like the image in his fetish book that David identifies as his favorite. David says that Judy is "perfect" and "the original of Wanda," but the actual original—the first in the series—may actually be his mother, a fact perhaps too disturbing for David to contemplate, or at least to acknowledge to us. It seems that David would rather proclaim his originality than understand the origin of his obsession. He even describes himself as an "original": "I'm David, your eponymous narrator. David Jupiter Boring, the first" (2). David is eager to tell us that, like a comic book title's "first issue," he does not imitate or repeat anything. He claims independence from his father, while remaining in bondage to his fetish.

16   A symbol for the ambiguity of Clowes's narrative method could be the image of the back of Whitey's head on page 5. If we could see Whitey's expression in panel 7, it might help us determine if he is telling the truth about the lucky penny's origin. Clowes's stories sometimes frustrate our desire to make such determinations by withholding information, a technique that leaves greater interpretive room for the reader.

ON JANUARY 26TH, AFTER A PERIOD OF INCREASING REMORSE, DOT FINALLY BREAKS DOWN. "WHAT HAVE I DONE?" SHE SAYS, "I'M A MONSTER!"

The origin of David's butt fetish can be traced in parallels that go beyond the facial and figural resemblances of these women. In the book's most absurd, and therefore most meaningful parallel, David's mother's hair is connected to his obsession, for the buns in her hair resemble a woman's butt, a parallel Clowes says "was…intentional" (Silvie 65). The hairstyle also evokes an atomic explosion, especially as drawn by David's father, whose *Yellow Streak* panel on page 115 prefigures Wanda's hair in the first panel on page 83. These two images are further joined by sound effects; in the first, the "boom" of the explosion, and in the second, the "boom" of David's beating heart as he watches a videotape of Wanda, a sound that first appears when David first sees Wanda. Moreover, David refers to Wanda's hair style as an "apocalyptic hair-do," suggesting that he is aware of the parallels, and possibly even of a connection between his sex drive and death drive (100).

In these parallels, Clowes outlines the genealogy of David's butt fetish as a fixation tied to the sexualized hair-do of his mother, though the reason for this fixation—the trauma or conditions in which the association of hair and butt originated—is never articulated. In *Modern Cartoonist*, Clowes mentions Freud's explanation of a fetish, showing that it's not only connected to the missing phallus of the fetishist's mother, but more importantly for our purposes, to the trinity of author-comic-reader:[17]

> Comics have an inherent energy to them, entirely divorced from content; a near electric charge that we would be hard-pressed to define. This built-in aesthetic, what we might call the 'fetish-value' of the comic, manifests itself both in terms of the creator, who often will obsess over every balloon pointer and panel line in his unwinnable struggle to create the perfect object, and the reader…who covets the artist's creation. (7)

These ideas about the comic's "fetish-value" play out in *David Boring*'s creation and design. David's fetish book is a standard marbled "composition book," and Clowes's

---

17   See *The Yellow Streak* panels on page 35 for a visual metaphor of the maternal phallus.

design for the book's hardcover imitates this style.[18] And we are reading Clowes's fetish book. As he also says in *Modern Cartoonist*, "the best comics are usually done by a single creator, often an obsessive-compulsive type who spends hours fixing things and making tiny background details 'just right'" (7).[19]

To understand these "tiny background details" and the comic as a whole requires a fetishistic reader, who, like the artist, should confront the story as if every minute detail is important and related to other details. Since the comic book is a fetish object, *David Boring* is therefore a fetish object about fetishes that should be read by a reader who is governed by fetishistic principles of interpretation, principles that involve uncovering hidden meanings, identifying complex parallels, and creating links between similar and dissimilar objects and actions.

When Chris Ware noted that "a lot of things are hidden in the narrative," perhaps he was thinking of what I will call—after David's phrase "The Wanda Affair"—"The Beard Affair." A love triangle with an unhappy ending, this narrative barely registers as a subplot. It's almost never visible in the book's foreground, taking place largely in the corners, shadows, or backgrounds of numerous panels in Act One and Three. Only one of the three characters in this subplot speaks, and then only briefly. The narrative is built from the kind of "background details" over which Clowes says the artist should obsess, and the credits at the back of the book give these characters names that speak to where they operate in the panel: "Mr. Beard" as the "Background Man" and "Mrs. Beard" as the "Background Woman." The credits also identify the third party of the triangle as "Mr. Beard's Friend," played by "Gladys X." "The Beard Affair" is a sketch for a fuller, though unwritten story that readers must flesh out for themselves.

Because this plot is so submerged and hasn't been commented on by readers, it's worthwhile to recount it. As David greets Whitey at the airport, we first see the Beards at the arrival gate (page 5/panels 1-2). We know it's them from a sign held up by a chauffeur, and we can correlate the sign to information in the credits, which lists the cast in order of appearance, alerting us to this affair and helping us to unravel it. Later, we see Mr. Beard and X in Dave's diner and at a bar (16/8, 17/1, 19/1). Then, the Beard

---

18   As a child Clowes was obsessed with *Mad* magazine, and the cover of the first edition of *David Boring*, like numerous *Mad* covers, imitates a composition book. See *Mad: Cover to Cover*, 19.

19   David believes that, because *The Yellow Streak*'s stories were written and drawn by a single person (his father), the comic can reveal facts about its creator in a way that a collaborative comic (the approach used in most commercial comics) cannot. Clowes prefers the single-creator method because it allows for the undiluted expression of the artist's ideas. The cover of *The Yellow Streak* features a device called a "2-D Ray." Perhaps this represents the process by which psychological reality is translated into a comic: the cartoonist's pencil becomes the ray.

I HADN'T SEEN WHITEY IN A YEAR BUT HE CALLED OCCASIONALLY. THE LAST TIME WE SPOKE, IN A FAILED ATTEMPT TO COAX AN INVITATION, HE MENTIONED "A GREAT HOUSEWARMING GIFT" HE HAD FOR ME···

WHAT'S WITH THE HAT?

narrative directly overlaps with David's, as Mr. Beard and David talk in the diner, interestingly enough, about "narrative disruption" (35/6, 36/1-3). We next find Mr. Beard and X in Act Three, again at Dave's (81/6-7). Later, as they walk in a park (86/1), Mrs. Beard sees them (86/2). They walk past, seeming not to notice her (86/3-4). Having realized that her husband is having an affair, Mrs. Beard visits a divorce attorney (93/2-3). Mr. Beard tells his problems to a bartender (94/7), and finally, Mrs. Beard flirts with a man in a bar (99/1, 99/3-4).[20]

Why would Clowes create such a deeply hidden narrative that functions independently of the main plot? It seems natural to ask in what way "The Beard Affair" resembles other aspects of *David Boring*—as David has already suggested, "astute readers" will note "resemblances." This plot doesn't directly affect David, though it does echo numerous affairs in the book: David's father's possible extramarital affairs (hinted at by the love triangle in *The Yellow Streak* with The Yellow Streak, Florence, and the Hag, and by the comment of an acquaintance of David's father on page 75). Is Clowes saying that Beard is an older Boring, or that all relationships end badly? Is decoding "The Beard Affair" a reward for readers who stay through the credits? Or maybe there is no payoff: the plot doesn't mean anything. Perhaps a rationale for the subplot comes back to the notion of creating a text that places demands on readers, for "The Beard Affair" is certainly hard to figure out. It demands that we read the credits carefully, re-read every panel to see if any of the three characters appear, and then fill in the blanks of their story. Perhaps this plot is really about the need for a type of close re-reading that examines each panel with care and contemplates the possible meanings of its contents.

"The Beard Affair" is almost solely confined to the visual margins of *David Boring*, but the plot of Whitey's "lucky penny" operates at its center. Like the coincidences I've discussed, this plot challenges believability by employing the kind of improbable series of events typically found in crime and detective fiction, pulp genres that often flaunt their sub-literary artifice. In *David Boring*, the transfer of the "lucky" penny from character to character happens with a calculated regularity throughout the three acts. In a manner reminiscent of fairy-tales, each exchange of the penny—and of the bullets or bodily fluids that inevitably follow—seem to generate the plot, magically creating and linking its numerous acts of sex and death.[21] The regularity of the exchange and the resulting "punishment" suggests the hand of an author who pulls the strings of his characters

---

20   Mrs. Beard also appears in the lower left-hand corner of the first lobby card.

21   For other "cursed coins," see Clowes's version of an Irish folk tale, "A Fairy Frog." For a fairy tale narrative driven by a coin's exchange, see Hans Christian Anderson's "The Silver Shilling." In this story, as in *David Boring*, characters disagree about the nature of the coin (lucky or unlucky), which is also made into a "lucky" necklace (258).

for the readers' and his own enjoyment. When asked if he believed in god, Clowes said, "I tend not to, but then I think there is probably some master puppeteer up there laughing at us. There have been too many miserable coincidences in my life when I thought, "There has got to be somebody making this happen just to amuse himself at my humiliation" (Lementhéour 34).

To signify its importance, Clowes places the first exchange of the penny in the first narrow panel of the comic and in the first row to have more than three panels. When Whitey gives David the penny as a gift, David doubts his

claim that it's a "lucky penny," thinking instead that, when David asked Whitey about a gift he had promised, Whitey improvised a story about the only object in his pocket: "I've had that with me ever since my father died…I know it probably doesn't mean much to you, but I…Anyway, I hope it brings you luck" (5). Whitey links the penny to his father's death, just as the narrative links it to a host of deaths and crimes. Even before we see the lucky penny, we are set up for its role by two crucial moments on *David Boring*'s first two pages. In the story's opening panel, David begins the narration by invoking his own luck: "by some miracle of circumstance" (1). This phrase is echoed by the first line of dialogue, in which Dot asks David if he was successful in his quest for sex: "Any luck?" (2). In the first five pages, Clowes carefully ties the lucky penny and the notion of luck to the book's plot, narration, and dialogue.

When Whitey leaves a bar with a woman, he tells David, "Wish me luck, li'l buddy… It's my first time without the lucky penny!" (6). That night, a luckless Whitey is killed. The next exchange happens from David to Wanda shortly after they have sex for the first and only time. "It's my lucky penny," he says as he gives it to her, thinking it made their sex possible: "I made it into a necklace. Believe me, it works!" (30). Yet almost immediately after receiving it, Wanda ends her relationship with David and disappears, and a few pages later, a drunk and devastated David is shot in the forehead. While recovering at Hulligan's Wharf, David has sex with Mrs. Capon (David's mother's cousin), who puts the lucky penny necklace on shortly before the act. Soon after, she is dead. When the police recover her body, they keep the necklace for evidence, and Mrs. Capon's daughter Iris receives it from a detective romantically interested in her. Iris then gives it to Dot (they are having an affair), who gives it to David, who gives it to Judy, whose angry husband takes it from her and gives it back to David when assaulting him. When we see it next, David asks Dot to throw it in the lake. She refuses, saying "are you kidding? This is for real…Do you know how lucky you are?" (113), a question that brings us full circle to her opening question, "Any luck?" (2). This symmetry, like that of the number 333, shows Clowes's authorial hand, reminding us that fictional narratives can achieve an ordered and artificial perfection that real narrative often don't. David refers to this kind of balanced construction when he notes the "narrative symmetry" of actress Emily Ransom's appearance at the opening of Act One and the closing of Act Three: "Such narrative symmetry cannot bode well. This must really be the end" (108). And it is, for the book ends eight pages later. Questions of luck begin *David Boring*, animate a carefully constructed plot thread, and bring the book to a close.

An even more precise example of symmetry occurs in David's narration on the book's opening and closing pages. In the fourth panel of the first page David speaks of living in the present and ignoring concerns about the past or future: "I believe in 'experiencing the moment' in its present tense, without dwelling on bygone associations or a tragic aftermath" (1). In a parallel location—the fourth panel of the last page—he makes a strikingly similar claim about present, past, and future: "We've been trying to live peacefully, without regret or foreboding, mindful of a return to living in the present rather than for an imagined future" (116). Perhaps such symmetry, like the almost unbelievable chain of exchanges of the penny, suggests that David may be a manipulative and unreliable narrator, telling us his story in a way that is too self-conscious, too perfect to be believable.[22] Maybe David, not Clowes, planted the 333s…

Though much of my reading has focused on the book's construction, the comic is more than just an exercise in artifice. The achievement of this and many other Clowes works (such as *Like a Velvet Glove Cast in Iron* and *Ice Haven*) lies in the balance Clowes strikes between artifice and emotion. While some readers have accused *David Boring* of exclusively dramatizing malaise at the expense of a broader set of emotions, this criticism overlooks David's varied emotional states, such as boredom, joy, anger, devastation, and fear. His narration and dialogue express these feelings in tones that have their own affective register, including austere seriousness, pretentiousness, genuine vulnerability, and what Clowes calls "adolescent self-satisfaction" ("Conversation" 2). The plot, too, is driven by intense conflicts, in particular by love triangles that lead to violent confrontations: Karkes shoots David over Wanda, Paul Lowenstein assaults David over Judy, and Dot and Iris attack Manfred. Such triangles even animate the narrative in *The Yellow Streak*, which centers on a conflict between the Yellow Streak, Florence, and the Hag. Much of *David Boring*'s pathos comes from the family triangle of David's ongoing struggle with his mother and his father. The comic develops this triangle in numerous ways, the most interesting of which is through David's thoughts about fatherhood.[23]

Shortly after having sex with Wanda, David excitedly mentions that "no precautions of any kind were taken" and then fantasizes about marrying her and having a child (27, 31). In a box in her abandoned apartment, he sees a birth control pill container, ending, for the time being at least, his chance at paternity. Yet their sex does produce a child, albeit a fictional one. David says that "the eerie boy" who haunts his dreams is their

---

22   David's middle name is Jupiter, the supreme god in the Roman pantheon. Perhaps we should see David, and not Clowes, as the supreme creator of the artifice in *David Boring*. The first three letters of his middle name appear as part of a sign visible in the first panel of page 27. Has David left this partial signature, in the way that an artist would sign a drawing, to acknowledge authorship?

23   The book's two-page title spread dramatizes a love triangle with David, Wanda, and god; this triangle is echoed on the cover of *The Yellow Streak*, which pictures Testor, The Yellow Streak, and the hag.

"neglected ghost-offspring" (78). The eerie boy is also the psychic offspring of David's ongoing struggle with his father. David dreams that he is alone in a theater watching a movie in which he and the tearful eerie boy fight. This dream reveals the depth of his anger and sadness toward his father by replaying the oedipal struggle, but with David in the paternal role. The importance of the eerie boy and this struggle is emphasized by the construction of the page on which his birth appears. At 13 panels, page 33 is the only page of the comic that exceeds nine panels.[24] This visual tour-de-force unites many themes that run through *David Boring*—the exchange of the penny, David's fetish and his encounter with Pamela, his germ phobia, his masculinity, his relationship with his mother, his stalking of Wanda, the numbers 3, 13, 33, and 333—and ties them directly to one of the comic's most moving tropes: anxieties about fatherhood.[25]

Clowes has talked about the origin of the main character in paternal terms: "I wanted to create a character who would be my son…and I created David Boring" (Polvino 49). "The challenge," he said, was "to give life to a decent 19-year-old" (Rolston 1). Clowes figures himself as David's literary father by blending facts about his own life into David's father's biography. David tells us his father "started in 1961 (?) and did a bunch of stuff for a small Connecticut publisher: a detective thing, some humor stuff, a teenager strip" (45). These facts are drawn from Clowes's biography: he "started" in 1961 (he was born April 14 of that year); his first title, *Lloyd Llewellyn*, is "a detective thing"; the early *Eightball*s are largely "humor stuff"; and *Ghost World* is "a teenager strip." Clowes draws our attention to a reference to his birthday in *David Boring* on the "about the author" text on the second hardcover printing's dust jacket. After mentioning his birth date, Clowes writes, "see p.17," a page where David discusses events "on April 11th" and the "obscure religious holiday" that occurs "three days later." On April 14, do the characters celebrate the birth of their creator?[26] Once again, Clowes asks us to make connections between *David Boring* and the world, in this case between the book and notions of authorship, paternity, and autobiography.[27] A literary modernist principle famously expressed by Gustave Flaubert claims that "the author in his book should be like God in his universe: everywhere present and nowhere visible." Yet in *David Boring*, the artist is everywhere visible: in a character's biography, seemingly random dates, puns and puzzles, and perhaps, even in the subway. Clowes has said that a young man he saw on the subway inspired David Boring. When David and Wanda talk in the subway on page 43, is that Clowes standing next to them and then walking away, his

---

24   Like the unlucky penny, the symbolically charged number 13 appears throughout *David Boring*: David sits in row 13 on a plane, the 13 visible on the overhead luggage rack (14). Wanda and David have sex for the first and only time on their 13th date, and David's prescription bottle has the number 13-1300 (58). Another 3 number, 30, also has significance; David walks toward track 30 on page 104, and four pages later, sits in seat 30, the number randomly selected by a spinning wheel.

25   David's father's comic has clearly affected David's dream-life. David "used to have nightmares about being attacked by giant microbes," and an image from *The Yellow Streak* shows Testor under assault by giant germs (24, 14).

26   In the story "Eightball," Clowes is called "sir god Eightball" and interacts with his characters (24).

27   In another connection between Clowes's life and *David Boring*, "the first panel," Clowes noted, is "the date I started working on the story" (English 8). When expressed as numbers, David's birth date and time form a pattern: 5/6/78 at 9:10.

back toward us? The credits list "D. G. Clowes" as one of the "featured extras," leading us to wonder if this scene replays David's birth in Clowes's imagination.

A part of the comic's emotional content comes in a form more difficult to discuss than the issue of fatherhood—which we all recognize as emotionally charged—because it depends on each reader's reaction to the comic's images. Though I can't necessarily convince you that the panels that affect me (such as the bullet heading directly toward the reader at the end of Act One, or the eerie boy on page 54) should likewise move you, I can say that *David Boring* is deeply interested in the power of static images to evoke strong responses. In *Modern Cartoonist*, Clowes discusses this power:

> Study and contemplate the nature of pictorial stillness. What does the still picture have to offer a narrative that the moving one doesn't? Find and study an intriguing movie still from a film you've never seen, then watch the movie to see how and why it falls apart and loses its compelling mystique. (12)

Because this mystique is crucial to *David Boring*, like the important notion of luck, it's introduced early. On page 3 Dot asks David to identify his favorite woman in the fetish book. When David points to her, an incredulous Dot replies, "Really? But it's only a drawing...Are you being serious?" As his fixation on panels from *The Yellow Streak* proves, David takes drawings very seriously. The artifice of a drawn and perhaps imaginary girl can be more compelling and closer to perfection because the artist doesn't collaborate with reality and therefore isn't limited when creating an image. The power of these drawn images, Clowes says, finds its origin in our first encounters with art:

I KNOW A BIT ABOUT HIS CAREER BUT NOT MUCH: HE STARTED IN 1961 (?) AND DID A BUNCH OF STUFF FOR A SMALL CONNECTICUT PUBLISHER: A DETECTIVE THING, SOME HUMOR STUFF, A TEENAGER STRIP... JUST DRAWING, THOUGH ...

> The average child in his or her formative years has his earliest 'artistic experiences' with cartoon drawings... By the nature of the medium alone [cartoonists] can connect a reader to feelings engendered by his earliest and purest artistic experiences. (*Modern Cartoonist* 10)

Clowes sees in his childhood reading experiences a goal for him to emulate as an artist: "As a child, I was so haunted by certain images in the comics I had, that I would go into fits of depression/crying etc. for days based on a single panel... My dream is to... be able to inflict the same sort of thing on my readers" (Green 1).[28] And it appears he was successful. In a letter printed in *Eightball* 20 (Act Two of *David Boring*), a reader refers to page 26—one of the book's three pages without dialogue or narration—as one of the "most horrific/poignant pages in the history of comics."

Throughout *David Boring*, David figures himself as the book's author, directly addressing his readers and identifying himself as our "eponymous narrator" (2). We are reading a comic, but as far as we know, David isn't a cartoonist. In fact, he dismisses the medium: "I'm better than my father. Movies are better than comics" (75).[29] Should we think of David as an author in the same way that we consider first-person narrators of prose

---

28   For Clowes, an image can be so powerful that he builds a plot around it:

> [W]hen I was working on [*David Boring*], I just had this idea of [David] having this hole in his head...I didn't have any idea of where that came from...but I was very obsessed with getting that into the comic somewhere, and so I had to...write backwards and get that bullet-hole in his head...[P]eople said 'Why didn't it just kill him?,' but somehow it didn't concern me...I just thought that was a great cartoon image. (Lementhéour 32)

(Compare the image of a wounded David in the center panel of page 48 with the center panel of page 98.) The image of god in *David Boring* is based on an animated cartoon Clowes saw as a child; when he saw the image decades later, he said "it was so strong to me [that] it was like seeing an actual photograph of god" (Lementhéour 33).

29   *David Boring* dramatizes not only David's conflict with his father, but as Clowes has said, a "struggle between comics and film," and "the supreme creator that you can be in comics that you can't really be...in film" (Stephens 5).

END OF ACT ONE...

stories to be? When we read *The Catcher in the Rye*, for example, the fiction is that Holden Caulfield, not J. D. Salinger, is the author. This fiction is easy to assent to in prose, but is much more difficult in a comic, unless the narrator draws. David compounds this problem by relating his story in the present tense. How is this possible? Does he draw it as he narrates it and not tell us? Is this story fundamentally unreliable, like an Edgar Allen Poe story that ends with the first-person narrator claiming to be drowned in a maelstrom? Such questions, however, may be misguided, for they seem to demand that fiction be closely tied to reality.[30] Should we, then, just ignore these questions about narration and authorship because they are unanswerable, or because they show a failure to accept the artificial nature of fiction? Perhaps these interpretive cruxes are simply functions of the elaborate artifice of *David Boring*, of which *Ice Haven*'s Charles would certainly approve. When David re-reads *The Yellow Streak and Friends Annual* he asks

---

30 In addition to highlighting the artifice of comics, *David Boring* shows how strange or unbelievable real life can be. It may seem absurd, for example, that an Oceana detective is named "Anemone," but these kinds of things happen.

unanswerable questions that erase the boundary between artifice and reality: "What other adventures have [the characters] had? What do they do between panels? Where are they now?" (74). The empty spaces between panels represent a time not narrated; we know—or believe—that something "happened" in those interstices, but such events are forever inaccessible to us. When we read *David Boring*, we are subjected to a kind of interpretive vertigo. Is David a reliable narrator? Was there a terrorist attack? Are the 333s prompts, clues, or a joke?

David Boring is a highly organized fictional world in which this kind of ambiguity is everywhere and solutions are nowhere. Clowes has said "I like the idea of clues and mysteries, but I hate the solution in a detective story. I find it always very dull" (Lementhéour 32). And precisely because there are no conventional solutions in the book, there are always reasons to re-read it. The artifice of puzzles, anagrams, unexplained coincidences, and hidden narratives helps to create a deep connection between reader and comic because we are continually provoked to ask questions about these features and to re-read knowing that more are to be found. The comic's complexity is its generosity. In this reading of *David Boring*, I have tried to answer questions about the artifice of the book that ultimately may be unanswerable. But given the comic's obsession with interpretation, this kind of questioning seems appropriate, for it engages the book on its own terms. Wanda Kraml asks, "What's this one about?" (51). David and *David Boring* answer by repeating a phrase used by Holden Caulfield: "It's kind of hard to explain…" ★

Ken Parille teaches at East Carolina University. His essays have appeared in *Comic Art*, *The Boston Review*, and *The Believer*, and he has authored three books, *Boys at Home: Discipline, Masculinity, and 'The Boy-Problem' in Nineteenth-Century American Literature*, *50 Essential Guitar Lessons*, and *Daniel Clowes: Conversations* (with Isaac Cates). Parille's Daniel Clowes bibliography is available at DanielClowesBibliography.com.

Andersen, Hans. "The Silver Shilling." *Hans Andersen's Fairy Tales*. Trans. L. W. Kingsland. Oxford: Oxford University Press, 1985. 255-259.

Clowes, Daniel. *David Boring*. New York: Pantheon, 2000.
—. *David Boring*. 2nd ed. New York: Pantheon, 2002.
—. "David Boring, Act 2." (*Eightball* 20.) Seattle: Fantagraphics, 1999.
—. "Eightball." *Eightball* 9. Seattle: Fantagraphics, 1992. 23-24.
—. "A Fairy Frog." *Eightball* 11. Seattle: Fantagraphics, 1993. 13-15.
—. *Ice Haven*. (*Eightball* 22.) Seattle: Fantagraphics, 2001.
—. "Just Another Day." *Eightball* 5. Seattle: Fantagraphics, 1991. 17-20.
—. "King Ego." *Eightball* 12. Seattle: Fantagraphics, 1993. 12.
—. *Like a Velvet Glove Cast in Iron.* Seattle: Fantagraphics, 1993.
—. "Little Enid." *Twentieth Century Eightball*. Seattle: Fantagraphics, 2002. 0-1.
—. *Modern Cartoonist*. Seattle: Fantagraphics, 1997.
—. *Orgy Bound*. Seattle: Fantagraphics, 1996.
—. "Playful Obsession." *Eightball* 5. Seattle: Fantagraphics, 1991. 21-23.
—. "Seduction of the Innocent." *Lout Rampage*! Seattle: Fantagraphics, 1991. 54–59.
—. "The Show of Violence." *Lout Rampage*! Seattle: Fantagraphics, 1991. 49-53.
—. "You." *Twentieth Century Eightball*. Seattle: Fantagraphics, 2002. 101.

"A Conversation with Dan Clowes." *Bold Type* Sept. 2002: 1.

Elder, Will. *Will Elder: The Mad Playboy of Art*. Ed. Gary Groth and Greg Sadowski. Seattle: Fantagraphics, 2003.

English, Austin. "Parody and Perplexity with Daniel Clowes." *Indy Magazine* Sept. 1999: 9.

Green, Bartholomew. "Dialogue: Clowes." *Dolomite* 24 (1998): 1-3.

Howard, Dave. "An Interview with Dan Clowes." *Don't Touch Me* 6 (1997): 25-35.

Hunter, Andy. "Dan Clowes & Chris Ware." *Mean Magazine* (Nov./Dec. 2000): 66-68.

Kim, Jin David. "Clowes & Ware." *Varsity Review* 16 Oct. 2000: 3.

Jacobs, Frank. *Mad: Cover to Cover*. New York: Watson-Guptill, 2000.

Juno, Andrea. *Dangerous Drawings: Interviews with Comix and Graphix Artists*. St. Paul: Juno Books, 1997.

Lementhéour, Rudy. "Dan Clowes." *PLG* 37 (2003): 27-37.

Phipps, Keith. "Worldly Things: The Art of Dan Clowes." *The Onion: A. V. Club* 19 Feb. 1998: 11.

Polvino, Lynn. "Dan Clowes: Dean of Underground Comics." *Shout Magazine* Dec. 2000: 47-49.

Rolston, Elana. "Creators Dan Clowes and Chris Ware Merge the Bizarre and the Mundane in their New Works." *New Times Los Angeles* 14 Sept. 2000: 1.

Silvie, Matt. "The *Velvet Gloves* Are Off: A *Boring* Interview with *Ghost World*'s Dan Clowes." *The Comics Journal* 233 (2001): 52-77.

Stephens, Chuck. "Uncle Superman: David, Jimmy, and the Shmoedipus Complex." *San Francisco Bay Guardian Literary Supplement* Oct. 2000: 5.

Strouss, Lisa. "Chris Ware and Dan Clowes: Indie Comics Gods Hit the Road." *Robot Power* 20.5 (2000): 6-11.

Donald Phelps

A Child's Garden of Detritus:
The Cartoon Chronicles of Lynda Barry

Besides the numerous convulsive alliances (siblings, cousins, amorous couples, school chums) that are scrutinized by Lynda Barry's five category-defying cartoon narrative presentations and all-out spectacles, her work engages a perpetual, often fiercely competitive partnership: image and text. In the present generation of American cartoons, the contentious marriage has been adjusted and at best revitalized by the emergence of the cartoon strip as correspondence. "Biography" is now an acknowledged category. However, in Stan Mack's vignettes from the steam rooms of the advertising industry, or the serpentine excursions of Jim Woodring, one sees autobio broadened into psychodrama or public meditation. Such are the progeny of those 1950s innovators, Jules Feiffer (whose stand-up cartoon sequences widen their sights within the first year beyond satire on pre-Woody Allen psychopiffle) and Charles Schulz, whose *Peanuts* delivered an elegant variation on kidspeak, and forecast the TV phenomenon of "talking

---

"A Child's Garden of Detritus: the Cartoon Chronicles of Lynda Barry" first appeared in
The Comics Journal 2003 Winter Special

heads." Throughout the ensuing decades, the texts of certain major (if not uniformly famous) cartoon strips introduced reflection on the nature of the language employed, on its substance—a signal difference from loquacious comic strips of the '20s and '30s, like Sidney Smith's *The Gumps*, or Harold Gray's *Little Orphan Annie*, in which the dialogues and monologues sometimes distend their balloons to resemble a mid-Victorian air regatta. Their concern, however, was almost entirely with the dramatic goings-on of the story. Until recently, there remained largely untouched any attention by comic strips to the possible soundings of text as literature. One hears little, in today's litcrit marketplaces, of either "tone" or "texture" at any literary level; both have often seem consigned to that possibly terminal detention camp Elitism.

"Tone" might be defined as the vocal resonance, the extra-specific significance of language; "texture," the sensuous autonomy of language: the value, the peculiar coloration, that distinguishes artistic precision from mere specificity. Both may be observed emerging, albeit irregularly, in cartoon work from America's last five decades. Both may be found a fortiori, in the 1980s–'90s work of Lynda Barry.

The Swinging Shepherdess

In roving burlesque manuals like the 1983 *Big Ideas* and *Leaving Mr. Wrong*, Lynda Barry is seen shlepperdessing an ungainly (and ungainful) cast of players on an expedition of surveillance and scavenging. Her terrain is the present generation's over-abundant spillage of bargain-basement bromides, popular myths straggling in from the expiring new age; an unstinting ever-present treasure trove of junk wisdom, scattered from the retail outlets of magazine ads and quizzes, TV ads and talking-head wisdom bees. All such are set forth by Barry, not with the nostril-pinched scorn of some uptown counterparts, but with a ripe sense of drollery and its chief component: a prankish curiosity (that sneaker-footed cousin of wonder). Also on hand is an equally vagrant, yet ever-hovering empathy; sugarfree, but warm and dry.

She dispenses sad little vignettes of women trying to impress closure on some blatantly wrong mister; trying to control weight in the face of a visit from a friend bearing a freshly baked pie; sparring with the temptation to gobble Ayds as though they were capsules of salvation. Their struggles mainly give rise to nightmares of a glutton's Hell, in which the Devil sentences them to monitor and devour endless doughnuts.

The drawing suggests the maladroit earnestness, the frantic gawkishness of young children's drawing; true, between the early '80s work, and the latter accounts of Marlys the girl impresario, the sweaty cachet of childhood is never entirely absent. But the lines in *Big Ideas* are wire-taut and unyielding. Most of her personae (usually seen in profile) suggest a bilious marriage of imitation Picasso and Art Deco, each at its respective worst; without the wriggling litheness that will mark Marlys, her family and chums. Those earlier bodies seem to have been posture-trained in jammed telephone booths. The bolster-like torsos of man and woman are canted toward each other; their beaky noses suggest a resemblance to infant birds seeking food.

More than anything else, these figures suggest human diagrams, ventriloquist's dummies for Barry's ever present managerial text. The text is the true star and the unifying force of the mock-didactic *Leaving Mr. Wrong*, and the mock-inspirational *Big Ideas*. Sometimes neatly printed, often written in laboriously dainty schoolgirl calligraphy, the text inundates and at times overruns the panels (when there are any). Like some familiar mold, it infiltrates the no-frills housing space, often squeezed into what seems like any available corner.

The texts are borne along at times by first-person narratives: a young miss on New Year's Day anticipates a *Wunderjahr* with fervid hope. Her sole visitor (in signature Barry fashion) is a burglar, who breaks in merely to deliver his own lament about his thwarted life ambition to be a filling station attendant. The burglar's *De Profundis* occupies most of the panel space, leaving room only for fractional glimpses of his bowed head, and the attentive profile of his auditor. Elsewhere, Barry, a self-confessed Capricorn native, lays down endless symmetrical columns of Dos and Don'ts for meeting, keeping, or shedding a man; dietary recommendations (two pages feature displays of "Basic Food Groups," including Chocolates, Fast Foods, Cool Gratifications, and Beverages); all illustrated with carefully labeled samples. Their range may be noted in the Beverage segment: a shot glass labeled "Filthy Roadhouse," a bottle tersely marked "Brewski" and a garden hose.

The texts don't override, but emphasize the domination of whiteness, which contributes to the overtone of cockeyed classicism. Even the occasional bedtime scenes are sharply demarcated; the sleepers' ovoid heads in clean relief against a rectangle of no-nonsense black sky. This linear tautness will change with the chronicles of Marlys. It changes even here, in a vignette entitled "Chuckie and Harry": a younger and (slightly but significantly) older brother enacting the litanies of pre-sleep squabbling. ("I wouldn't talk, Chump." "So who says I'm talkin' to you, Scrub.") Barry's juggling of dialogue balloons competes with Segar's *Thimble Theatre*. Moreover, her drawing of Chuckie and Harry invokes a warm, sbaggy, deeply shaded bedtime; the bodies, beneath blankets, are fully dimensioned. The same densely sketched intimacy follows in a segment called "Phobia-Phobia," dealing with schoolday terrors.

Such "exceptions" to Barry's style offer (as usual in such cases) a sense of its true capacity. Her overtone is an affable pedantry, its deadpan patience proof against the incongruities or absurdities of its content. It recalls somewhat those vagarious, faltering, yet dauntless lectures delivered in the printed essays and numerous short movies of Robert Benchley.

He, like Barry, took side excursions into his childhood. Barry's preoccupation with domestic props like dishware and makeup appliance recalls Benchley's usually calamitous sorties among typewriters and electric shavers; they share a decent reverence (nonsectarian) for food. Barry, who recounts the health problems of her pet turtle Gamora, might have willingly illustrated Benchley's "The Sex Life of the Polyp." (The very early sound films show Benchley with a white doll-like face, beady eyes and dainty moustache; which, with his puppet-like obsequious gestures, seem to propose him for Barry's company.) Of course, a chasm of history separates them. Benchley, the suburban homeowner, yields to the bedrock reality of Barry's rootless teetering fringe dwellers. Benchley's chuckle has died with him. The vaulting realities of loneliness, addiction, and disconsolate daydreams all outreach Uncle Bob's usually self-generated quandaries involving home repairs or dieting. Yet, the current of sturdy cheer in Barry's graphic journals suggests a private heirloom of gallantry from a man who kept sometimes uneasy house for his most private troubles.

Barry's bright eye is never averted from her sparrows. Those preposterously incapable-looking figures are drawn with a deliberate dry gravity, a muted, hovering pessimism that hangs around like an unsightly retainer.

And still another layer activates, lightens and sweetens her work: the recurrently perceptible shimmer of wonder; reminding us that her thrust is in truth neither the sheer chipper cynicism of Stan Mack, nor the file-rough satire of George Grosz (cited in a quoted testimonial to her work). Barry's theme as maintained and extended through her style is the foraging search of the starvling human imagination, accompanied by its little brother Hope, through the dreck-strewn fields of current popular culture.

In this regard, her text and pictures not only supplement each other, but join in a style that, like the best artistic styles, can encompass experience in its variety. Her comedy sometimes recalls to me the arid, grainy, achy look of B. Kliban's work in the '60s and '70s. Kliban's definitive forte was his mock iconography in single panels like that of the Virgin Mary seen by an automobile. Barry shares Kliban's cockeyed regard for popular objects of reverence (slightly fewer these days) and awe (only too plentiful and misdirected). A lonely lady hears chiding messages from her cigarette lighter (labeled "Capricorn"). Barry's take on a supermarket tabloid feature ("Now It Can Be Told: The Dead Are Trying To Reach Us!") lists uncanny phenomena: "Missing Caps on Your Toothpaste Tubes," "A Sock Is Missing After Doing the Laundry." In these pages, Barry is not a fantasist; but she acutely understands fantasy hunger, and the way pedestrian fripperies like the above may furnish flower boxes for meager but comforting blooms. (Benchley would have chortled at that last one.)

Babes Up In Arms

Marlys Mullen, the polycreative heroine and embodied Zeitgeist of three Barry collections, enriches and amplifies the bleak comic map set forth in earlier Barry works. Marlys' showcase volume, *The Greatest of Marlys*, is flanked by two others: *Come Over, Come Over* recounts the views, strivings and crystalizing reflections of Marlys' 14-year-old sister Maybonne. *The Freddie Stories* chronicle the demon-beset days and nights of the Mullen sisters' 14-year-old brother. Be it noted: Freddie's demons, unlike the canons of stereotypical teenage fiction, are not solely evoked by his sisters. They are numerous, persistent and alarming.

The two adjoining books enlarge and vitalize the wunderkind excursions of Marlys; furnishing supplementary perspectives ("perspectives" summarizes a major theme of all three books: the saga of the Mullens). Indeed, the trilogy offers a nurturing earth for the comedy of Marlys, which, with its scars and ridges, provides the terrain for a deeper and more resonant comedy. Yet, Marlys is the undoubted center of the triptych. Her presence blossoms like a sunflower from the cover of her own volume. Her figure, in red and yellow diagonal-striped dress, performs a dance of welcome: rubbery, ever mobile limbs swinging; her braids bouncing in the air like friendly snakes; she is surrounded by inserts, blazing like a Busby Berkeley meteor storm, of her siblings, and of (Arna and Albert Arneson) her cousins and next-door neighbors. It should be noted that many of Marlys' stories are told by Cousin Arna: Marlys herself is barely at the threshold of introspection. But hers is the cavorting muse of creativity. Her resilience (plus the extraordinary bulk of information conveyed through the girls' narratives) reminds me of that fine Irish novelist Roddy Doyle's beleaguered young hero Paddy Clark (*Paddy Clark Ha Ha Ha*). However, Marlys' mimicry and zestful adaptation of advice columns and schlock-movie synopses echo with a more tickling resonance, not only Barry's earlier work. They also shimmer with the remembered image of Penrod Schofield, Booth Tarkington's jimson weed. Like the memorable and too little remembered Penrod, Marlys gets her juvenile high from the popular prints. Penrod honored the fiddle music of pulp detective magazines by writing stories of his own. Counter to yet another dictum of pop teenage fustian, he and Marlys are burgeoning artists, rather than mere fantasists; more than juvenile Walter Mittys and Alice Adamses.

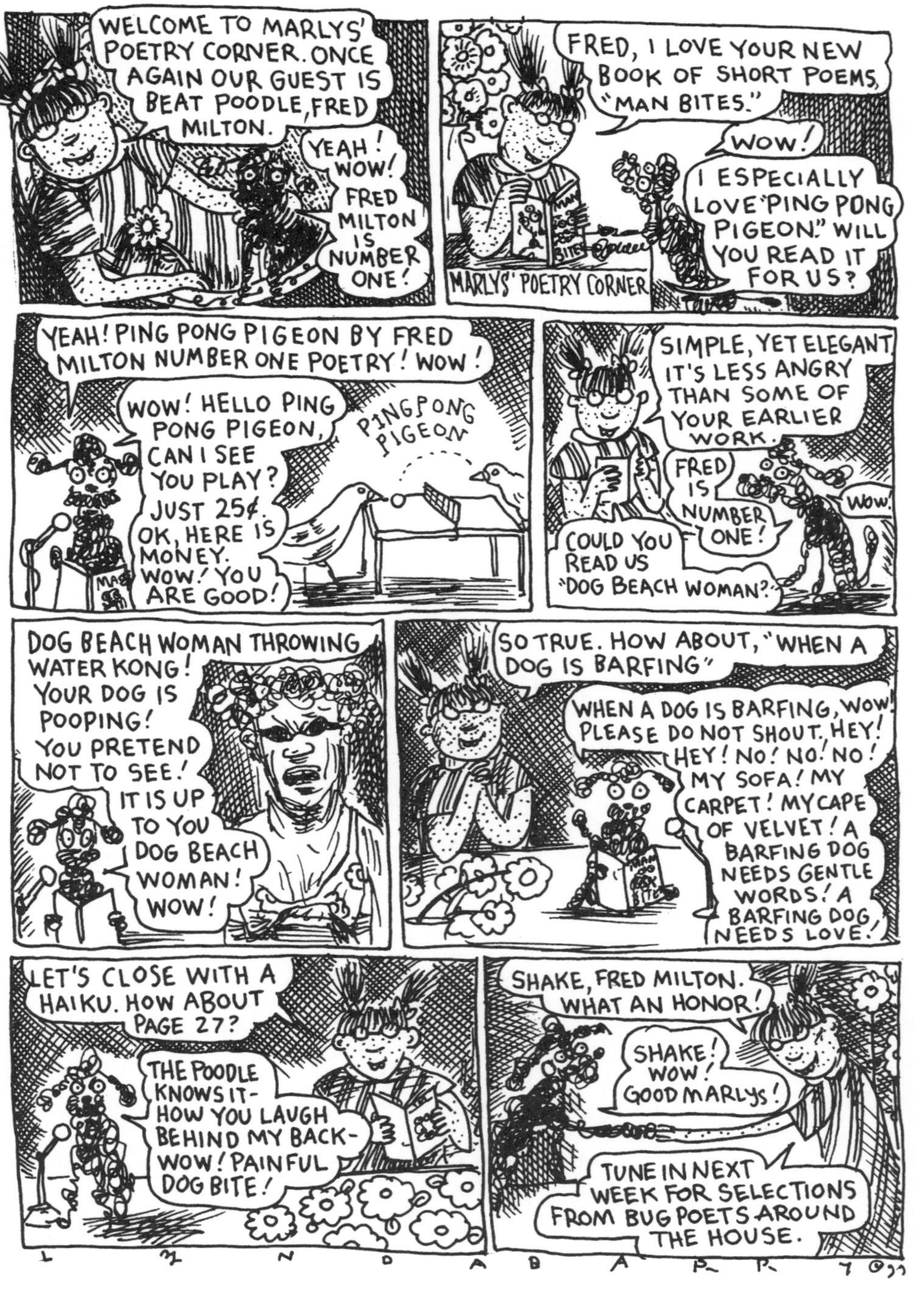
WELCOME TO MARLYS' POETRY CORNER. ONCE AGAIN OUR GUEST IS BEAT POODLE, FRED MILTON.
YEAH! WOW! FRED MILTON IS NUMBER ONE!
MARLYS' POETRY CORNER
FRED, I LOVE YOUR NEW BOOK OF SHORT POEMS, "MAN BITES."
WOW!
I ESPECIALLY LOVE "PING PONG PIGEON." WILL YOU READ IT FOR US?
YEAH! PING PONG PIGEON BY FRED MILTON NUMBER ONE POETRY! WOW!
WOW! HELLO PING PONG PIGEON, CAN I SEE YOU PLAY? JUST 25¢. OK, HERE IS MONEY. WOW! YOU ARE GOOD!
PING PONG PIGEON
SIMPLE, YET ELEGANT. IT'S LESS ANGRY THAN SOME OF YOUR EARLIER WORK.
FRED IS NUMBER ONE!
WOW!
COULD YOU READ US "DOG BEACH WOMAN?"
DOG BEACH WOMAN THROWING WATER KONG! YOUR DOG IS POOPING! YOU PRETEND NOT TO SEE!
IT IS UP TO YOU DOG BEACH WOMAN! WOW!
SO TRUE. HOW ABOUT, "WHEN A DOG IS BARFING"
WHEN A DOG IS BARFING, WOW! PLEASE DO NOT SHOUT. HEY! HEY! NO! NO! NO! MY SOFA! MY CARPET! MY CAPE OF VELVET! A BARFING DOG NEEDS GENTLE WORDS! A BARFING DOG NEEDS LOVE!
LET'S CLOSE WITH A HAIKU. HOW ABOUT PAGE 27?
THE POODLE KNOWS IT- HOW YOU LAUGH BEHIND MY BACK- WOW! PAINFUL DOG BITE!
SHAKE, FRED MILTON. WHAT AN HONOR!
SHAKE! WOW! GOOD MARLYS!
TUNE IN NEXT WEEK FOR SELECTIONS FROM BUG POETS AROUND THE HOUSE.
L Y N D A B A R R Y ©99

Perhaps the most heartening and challenging evolution in Barry's work here displayed is the multiplied scope and vigor of her style. The tightsphinctered lines and miniature fipperies of earlier books have given place to a writhing, rampant line, accompanied by raw shading and recurrent darkness. The effect is of an unceremonious, often mauling vigor. Barry resorts to distortion and foreshortening as freely as in her earlier urban comedies; here, however, the effect is of a squirming, rippling current of potential change. As the episodes progress Barry incorporates some of her more whimsical penchants in the children's seeking out, and befriending of eccentrics, fringe-dwellers, human oddities whether by nature's cruelty or election. (I recall one of Marlys' display pages as recreating the contents of a *Believe It Or Not* book by Bob Ripley. I can remember the original book.) The hallucinatory and near-autistic Freddie finds a corridor of peace in friendship with an autistic girl, from the "special class" to which he has been assigned. Even Arnold Arneson, the feral-faced and weasel-spirited brother of Anna, finds love with a harelipped girl (he reenacts their kiss and his ambivalent spasms with a hand-puppet rabbit). Marlys herself records interviews with the original Cyclops, and a hairy, faceless prehistoric man. She also documents the New Year's resolutions of socially unacceptable insects, including ants, termites and the ubiquitous cockroaches. These later episodes suggest Barry not backtracking, but newly encountering her own fantasy tropes. A frequent interviewee of Marlys in the later episodes is Fred Milton, a beat poet poodle: as assemblage of corkscrew ringlets, who utters sporadic exclamations of approval or disfavor in what seems to be the speech of a recent East Indian immigrant.

I have barely mentioned Barry's mastery and manifest love of language, consistently on view in the children's frantic makeshifts, their bubbling hyperboles, the vaulting rebirth of cliches. All serve to propel the embracing beauty of Barry's accuracy in a pedestrian epic of evolving spirit. I consign my epigraph to Maybonne: "It's mainly about how life can magically turn cruddy then beautiful-and then back to cruddy again, then it just keeps on evolutionizing you."

I seem to remember when that might have been a pretty good description of the novel. ★

Donald Phelps

Diary of a Teenage Rake:
An Appreciation of
Phoebe Gloeckner's Masterpiece

One important progenitor of the so-called graphic novel in its most vital, most valid form is probably *The Rake's Progress*, by the 18th-century artist William Hogarth. The work is a dark, sumptuous procession of teeming compositions and writer, ungainly, befouled figures: human, animal, architectural, in a seemingly limitless variety of postures; frustrated, stupefied, stunted even in their manifest lust and rage. The malign virtuosity of Hogarth's black traceries and bitter mischief of his "incidental" details offer a virtual textbook of grotesquerie, the snarled entanglements registered in nature, of the potentially awesome and the absurd.

Hogarth's great work effectively exemplifies the skitter-footed phrase "graphic novel"; even though most of Hogarth's words are explanatory captions. The structured, sequential narrative presents an authentic, amply consummated marriage of words and

---

images. The images, thanks to the vigilantly maintained form, acquire a purposeful, dynamic rhythm well equal to that of any printed sentences.

The Rake's Progress overstrides and supersedes genres. Unlike some present day claimants to the "graphic novel" designation, this is no commercialized fantasy; nor yet, a packaged, formulaic "realism" such as the term "genre" suggests. Though most of the drawing's content is substantially realistic, it deftly admits caricature (as the mighty critic Hazliff points out) in its torrent of mordant elucidations. It is no union of forms or media; rather, another autonomous form, another medium, propelled by the yoked team of observation and imagination.

The promise and exactions of the graphic novel have birthed an eloquent sisterhood within recent years: the work of Lynda Barry, dealing with 14-year-old Marlys, her sister Maybonne, and their brother Freddie has been discussed earlier in these pages. Phoebe Gloeckner's *Diary of a Teenage Girl* displays sharp stylistic differences from Barry's work; yet, too, a kindred range of perception regarding the data and colorings of a teenaged sphere; an accommodation both robust and delicate for teenage language, with a shrewd recognition of its diverse cultural influences; and a warm comprehension of the combined recklessness, cluelessness, and gallantry attending a young girl/woman's encounter with horrendous moral squalor: not only the promiscuities and dissipations of the street; but those masked or camouflaged within and by the home.

A major difference of emphasis between Barry's work and Gloeckner's is that of form: form as determined by each youthful protagonist/embryonic artist endeavoring to apprehend the scope, immediate and potential, of the social and by extension universal landscape in which she moves. "Apprehend": i.e., define and thereby possess by the same process; reifying through the exercise of definition, her own powers of creation and recreation.

Form is the evolving affirmation of identity through art. Lynda Barry's prevalent art, ministered by Marlys, Maybonne and Freddie, is that of the performer: profuse, ranging, reveling in grotesqueries that often betray a dark subtext: a bleakly dyslectic family scene, with a frantic, striving, alcoholic mother and an all-but-phantasmal father, himself an on-again off-again drunk. The comic strip is the God-given vehicle for that family and its Midwestern environs; where the father of Maybonne's school chum is glimpsed lewdly caressing his daughter.

The journals of Phoebe Gloeckner's heroine Minnie (Minerva) Goetze offers a misshapen domestic scene similar to Barry's. Minnie and her younger sister Gretel occupy a San Francisco apartment with their mother, who is separated from their father, an artist, as Minnie tells us (the father is represented by a pen-and-ink drawing, quaintly baroque, of a jalopy procession. According to Gloeckner's explanatory note, the drawing's real author was her own father, David). The girls veer and zigzag through their still-coalescent lives; not amid the trash-profuse grunginess of Barry's Illinois; but amid the glossy, casually bizarre and voraciously self-serving wilderness of 1970s-'80s San Francisco.

The cityscape, not available to Barry's youngsters, evokes from Minnie a different order of imaginative response: watchful, guarded, quietly but decidedly judgmental; within her home, furtive—concealing from her mother not only the urban adventures, but her burgeoning romance with the mother's lover. Yet Minnie's progress through the enclaves of San Francisco's bars and partying places is not, like that of Hogarth's rake, a progress of dissolution; rather, it is a voyage of assemblage, triply-motivated. Even as she lags and dawdles her way through school after school, to declining grades and attendance records, Minnie is earnestly concerned with charting the new nation of her identity, in the piecemeal, picaresque way eternally familiar to young adolescence. Gloeckner has in truth presented us with a *bildungsroman*: an epic of youthful identity as shaped through the challenges, abrasions, and precious, though infrequent, gifts of experience. A form of ancient familiarity; though commonly identified with male protagonists.

Interwoven with the quest for identity, in immemorial paradox, is the grasping at bogus, trial identities: disguises. Early in the book, Minnie mentions her attendance at churches of varying denominations, which she visits ("Today I went to the Russian church, with the big, gilded onion tops..."). She discovers the "Cosmic Conference": "You dial the phone number, and you are connected to the Void." The updated version of that older American tradition, the party line, furnishes Minnie with the comfort and excitement of an invisible community, along with the titillating trial balloon of a fictitious identity.

Interplaited with her quest for identity may be seen, here, two other, yoked concerns: the numb, hesitant articulation of faith; and the no less halting emergence (though with a clearly uttered certainty at the helm) of her chosen vocation: cartooning. Her faith, hinted of course in her church visits, is nurtured by no less likely a source than the lover she is sharing, fitfully, with her mother: Monroe Rutherford, an entrepreneur in athletic nutrients, provides her with an inspirational self-help tape by the West Coast self-improvement seer Earl Nightingale. But gleams of a much more advanced faith's coalescence appear in random, desperate prayers; in a glimpse of Jesus, sardonic-toned but touched with anguish, in her third serious cartooning effort. A full-page drawing of "Left Side of My Room" shows, affixed to the bedstead, lines from an old hymn; "I wonder as I wander." At the novel's end, she has rallied a sufficiently durable spiritual casing to enunciate silently, apropos Monroe, a cocky and pompous, yet serviceable mantra that her now-separated stepfather, the slickly pedantic Pascal, has vouchsafed her. Progress of a sort, indeed.

Much of Minnie's chronicle is reported in her own prose; lucid, often vernacular. The earthy hyperbole of Barry's youngsters is replaced by a mulling intensity. The burden of the narrative, however, is shared by the graphic portions of this graphic novel. These are by no means subordinate. To the prose account, the visual supplement consists largely but by no means entirely of comic book pages, grid-like tiers of panels, that take up Minnie's narrative in passages not covered by her first-person perspective erotic small talk and byplay with the many-faceted Monroe; devious, teasing phone conversation about her sometime lover's identity with her friend, the placid-eyed Kimmie (leading Minnie into the bathroom, where Kimmie is seated); encounters, in company with another, more diversely-seasoned friend: the ambiguous Tabatha, with a black pimp, and with the worldlywise drag queen Richie.

These mini-events, and certain larger ones, are not likely to be described by Minnie; certainly not in the detail which Gloeckner offers. Often, Gloeckner's alignments of angles, often claustrophobically close perspectives and successive small actions (Minnie squirming about for comfort in a car seat) or architectural intricacy (room-to-room rambles in Monroe's digs), seem to reflect an enlisting of movie techniques. Yet the corporate effect of the comic book supplements is of a tender identification, reaching beyond abstract concerns of technique, of Phoebe with her little sister-creation. She creates an auctorial presence recalling those of the Victorian novel's heyday. Such invocation of the past is, I think, well-buttressed by other examples from the book.

Phoebe Gloeckner is a fully accredited master of both art and science (i.e., biology); and her regard for the exigency of structure is thus fortified. So too, however, is the gentle ceremony which underscores the book's opening: a dedication, over strewn flowers, to her daughters; an epigraph, some verse extolling the child's vision, by one Libby Hutchinson (identified in the Notes as a poet and suffragette) and dated 1880. There is a cautionary note ("Don't read this, unless…") to the reader; a note recalling the book's inception (March, 1976); a title page of a doll-sized Minnie, shown against a sloping Frisco hill-street; and a similarly miniscule pair, Minnie and Kimmie: the former, plaintive, the latter beaming; both wearing grandma dresses with a poignant fragrance of nostalgia that recalls (from my own memories of a German grandmother) ancient genre woodcuts and prints.

With such formal officiation, Gloeckner not only clasps the hand of her sister-persona; she forecasts as in the vision disclosed by a benign angel of prophecy, the consummation of Minnie's own artistic career. Nor is there any very rigorous distancing of the two, in the art work with which the pages are interspersed: traditional captioned illustrations (a view like that of an American Primitive painting: Minnie and Mother in the kitchen); a drawing of a fish; a diagram in floral pattern of the Cosmo Conference. Likewise, Minnie's own work, probably drawn from Phoebe's recollective file: three fledgling comic-book pages, of respectively, A Walk Through the City; Identity Crisis Comix, featuring a nude trio of Melanie Higbeans (a sideswipe at three-faced Eve?) and

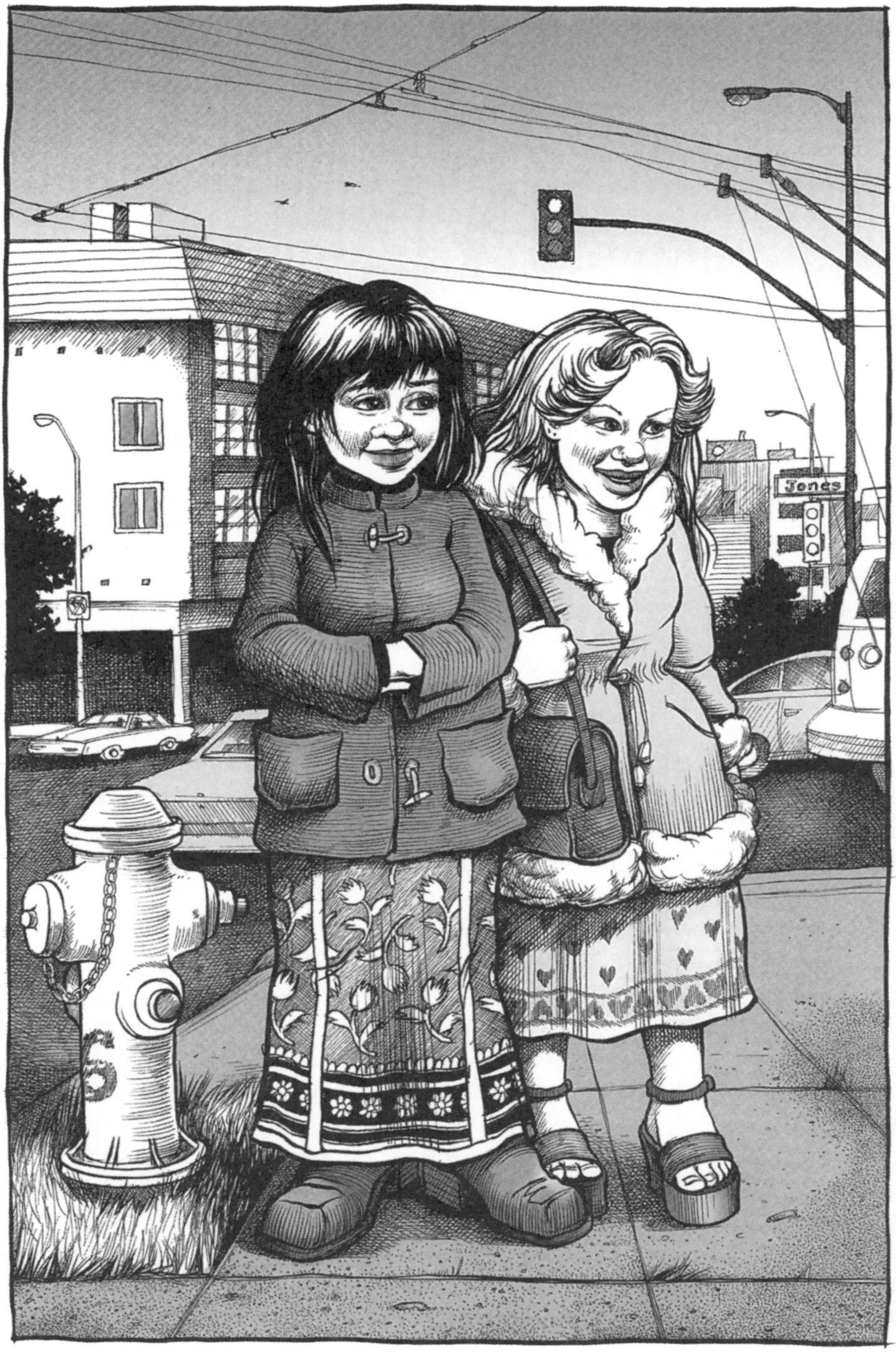
Jones

a serpentinely surreal depiction of a damned One Night Stand, with Jesus intervening against the grungy middle-aged couple.

We view Minnie's faltering but surely advancing command of composition, the distribution of blacks, and deployment of anatomies. We see no less surely (not only in her invocation of names) the benign sympathies of Robert Crumb and his fellow artist/consort, Aline Kominsky, both of whom contribute self-depictions to Minnie/Phoebe's art. Surely, too, the blocky, yet dexterously deployed literalness of Gloeckner claim kinship with those sober Crumb portraits of elderly jazz musicians, black and white? And her allusions to a doll's house past, his own acid-edged recall of America's overploughed grass roots.

Yet, such nostalgia as may be is countered by Gloeckner's vibrant and piquant cartography of 1970s-'80s San Francisco, a conglomerate of enclaves: each province, each street corner visited and appraised by Minnie, a cubicle of casual intimacy, nip of dissipation, spiritual adventure. Minnie/Phoebe interiorize each 'Frisco locale: each low-paneled view by Gloeckner is dominated by human figures (while settings are amply noted). Even Minnie's own comic-paged walk through the city highlights a street corner bar, a sinister late night canopied doorway, a huge-thighed woman descending from a bus, in film noir tones of gritty darkness. The domestic mingles with the exotic, the provincial with the rococo. Young Minnie's avid yet matter-of-fact account draws intimate ambience from the gaudy and dingy alike. Thus, Polk Street, known from Frank Norris's *McTeague* and Dashiell Hammett's Sam Spade, is seen here in the Palms Hotel, Crumb's longtime home; Market Street is the zone of hooker recruitment, with stalking, black-hatted pimps; on Walnut Street live the art-loving Golds, who display an Andy Warhol silk screen; while on Sutter Street is the Mt. Zion Hospital; probable permanent home for Minnie's late romantic attachment, the pitiably psychotic Fred. Against the souped-up, pulpy generalizations of 'Frisco, Phoebe/Minnie present us with a Minniecosmos.

And a diorama, coolly affectionate at times, lucidly just always, of 1970s-'80s popular culture. Norman Lear's renowned soap opera parody *Mary Hartman, Mary Hartman*; the non-mainstream comic art of Crumb, Kominsky and Justin Green (creator of *Binky Brown Meets the Holy Virgin Mary*; and represented here by a painting displayed at the Golden Boy Pizza in North Beach); Louise Lasser, Woody Allen discovery and star of the aforementioned *Hartman* series, to whom Minnie is often compared, to her resentment. Page 145 presents us with an olio of modestly priced candies (Good 'n' Plenty, Abba Zabba, etc.) preferred by Minnie; the olio recalls Manny Farber's table-top paintings of the 1970s and '80s.

Gloeckner's Minnie saga emerges as a chronicle of adolescence blessedly free of bogus sentiment or special pleading. I had originally thought of titling this piece: "Minnie Mouse at the Tower of Babel"; but, thanks to Gloeckner's example, I know where to draw the line. ★

Dan Nadel

What Went Wrong with the Masters Show

I really wanted to like "Masters of American Comics." The exhibition, which traveled from 2005 until early 2007, purported to be an in-depth look at fifteen American "masters" of the comics form. A roomful of Kirby pages to look at. Herrimans to immerse yourself in. And, from a non-fannish perspective, the promise of a focused, museum-quality examination of crucial American cartoonists. The art itself was certainly astounding, but what about the ideas? Great art alone does not always make for a great exhibition—context, arrangement, and critical texts are just a few of the other necessary components. And it's in these other areas that "Masters of American Comics" proved itself lacking. As an exhibition and as a book, it failed on two fronts: first, in imaginative scope, and, secondly, through a lack of critical seriousness that permeates and ultimately sinks the entire show.

"What Went Wrong With the Masters Show" first appeared in
Comics Comics #3 (Summer 2007).
[©2007 Dan Nadel]

Let's begin with my first complaint: Imagination. Why must there be a canon, and why fifteen? The curators have argued that by presenting a narrow canon, they've created baseline level of critical agreement that engenders further, focused studies on each artist. The point being that to move forward, critics and historians need to agree on who is most important, and then begin longer studies of each artist in order to elicit a deeper understanding of the medium. But is that really a great premise for an exhibition in 2007? After all, a canon by necessity enforces a set of values that may or may not be useful to further analysis of the medium. And are all of the included fifteen really so indisputable? I would argue that the canon they've created is actually restrictive and retrograde rather than an advance. What the curators have done is pushed a view of comics as a male-centric, genre-based, stodgy medium unworthy of serious examination. As usual, it pushes the idea of comics as a medium in line with modernist claims of technical execution and thematic richness. But in squishing comics into what the curators imagined was a museum-acceptable shape, this approach ignores the chaotic diversity and basic anarchy of comics.

The fact is, in this day and age, a new, comics-centric approach to the medium is needed, one born of intense examination and an organic evolution of ideas rather than the superimposition of another medium's and another era's values. The culture of comics is too fluid to pin down even the guidelines that would be needed to establish a common critical language. Terms like "technical mastery" and "formal innovation" are thrown around in the written materials, but I'm unsure exactly what they mean. An artist like Milton Caniff draws his formal techniques from film and his drawing style from pulp illustration. There's nothing wrong with that—it's how comics worked— but a little explanation of how that related to normative definitions of mastery and innovation is in order. For me, Ogden Whitney and Rory Hayes are, panel for panel, as much masters as Milton Caniff and Lyonel Feininger in their ability to create believable drawn worlds and arresting narrative images, but most would dispute that. All the more reason for clear understandings of terminologies and concepts.

Furthermore, why fifteen and not twenty? Or ten? Or five? The plurality of artists and styles (and cross-breeding) make it rather tricky, for me at least, to say that any one "canon" makes sense. Herriman, McCay, Kirby, Crumb, Panter: OK—these seem like reasonable foundation cartoonists. Not indisputable, but representative masters of the different aspects of the medium. But the rest? Oh, I don't know, it seems somewhat arbitrary at that point. I mean, Feininger, really? His career is interesting, if short, but there are handful of other artists from that period doing equally interesting comics. Feininger just happens to have the fine art credentials that make him appealing for this kind of show/plea: as if to say, "See, serious artists made comics too!" But in terms of innovation and influence, he is not terribly important. Neither are his comics more than marginally interesting in terms of their content—a mishmash of German kids' book tales and light fantasy. Beautiful yes, but significant? And Spiegelman? It's too early for him. As of now, he has produced a single important work in *Maus*, and has been a hugely important editor in comics. But a cartoonist on the level of Kirby, Panter, Herriman, and McCay? That simply hasn't happened yet. It may later, but up to this point, he has an extremely limited emotional and conceptual range and an inexpressive drawing style. And why include Caniff, and not Roy Crane? It goes on and on. I could punch holes in the choices all day, but fundamentally the curation feels lazy: why not at least nod towards pluralism and the case for open readings of history that go beyond "great men"? Instead, this organizing principle marks "Masters of American Comics" as dated and out of touch with contemporary curatorial and critical concerns. And if the idea of the exhibition was to facilitate further study of comics, the vision presented is pretty discouraging: fifteen dudes, most of whom write about male power fantasies and/or feeling sad.

Worse yet, there was no context. The "great man" march through comics history is not buffered at all by any sign of any other cartoonists (not to mention any other gender), or, indeed, the business and culture of the medium. Surely someone could have thought beyond the great man stomp and allowed in just a little bit of air. It's as though the "greatness" of the work was meant to be self-evident. There were, at least in the New York and New Jersey stop of the show, few captions, and absolutely no indication given of what exactly we were looking at it. How is the average art-engaged viewer supposed to know what an original comic page is, and how it related to the final printed product? It is never explained at all. On a very basic level, those viewers who weren't already familiar with comics history simply didn't know how to evaluate the work in front of them. When a viewer sees a painting on a wall, he knows more or less how it functions: paint on canvas to delineate form and texture and volume. Viewers approach with the assumption (more or less correct) that the artist controlled the work from beginning to end, creating a complete artwork ready for viewing as is and in a particular kind of art-space. Comics pages, created solely for reproduction, drawn under editorial and technical restrictions, are an entirely different animal. They beg numerous questions, including: How is a comics page not just a drawing? Why is everything drawn in outline? How did the anticipation of color affect the compositions? What kind of materials were used? How is a printed Sunday page different than, say, a lithograph or silkscreen? Where does the color come from? Who dictated the color choices, and who implemented them? Who inked all those Kirby, Eisner, and Kurtzman pages? Did Caniff have assistants? Why does Harvey Kurtzman appear to use so many different rendering styles? (Answer: Because the curators didn't bother to credit collaborators.) How is the creation of a comics page different from the creation of a painting or an etching or everything else in the museum? Hmmm?

And on a content level, why should we, the average museumgoer, take *The Fantastic Four* seriously when it seems so silly? What did Kirby do so well (and well enough to offset the pretty rough-going prose in 85 percent of his comics)? How do we measure Crumb's progress from toked-out psychedelic comics to historical tales of blues musicians? How do we reckon with the one-dimensional portrayals of women in nearly all the work? Or the simple absence of women from even the context of the show? What can one say about Kurtzman as a writer for comics, and why is he different than, say, Crumb? Where is E.C. Segar's drawing style rooted? Are they similar to Frank King's roots? (Answers: Bud Fisher, and yes—context context context.) How do we get from Kurtzman to Crumb to Panter in just twenty years? Or from Gould to Caniff to Schulz? Again, no satisfactory explanation is given in the exhibition and catalog.

Where is some mention of Roy Crane, without whom there's no Kirby or Caniff or Schulz? How 'bout Harold Gray? Where's Frederick Opper and the aforementioned Bud Fisher? And maybe, just maybe, if an artist as young as Chris Ware is included, women like Lynda Barry or Julie Doucet could be, too. In other words, where are the dozens of artists whose work contributed to and allowed the main subjects to exist? None of this would have required a larger exhibition. It all could have been accomplished with short prose placards and the occasional extra visual by a non-canonical artist. In an exhibition on, say, painting in the 1960s, all of these equivalent questions would be examined. I can't imagine it would be otherwise. So why not here? Comics history and aesthetics is an incredibly rich and under-explored subject, but you'd never know it from "Masters of American Comics."

This curatorial "silence" about the simplest issues relating to comics completely defeats the ostensible goal of building a discussion. On what grounds are we meant to construct the dialogue? There's no information—no components to work with. And without a discussion, the curators' claim to seriousness falls short, and makes viewers wonder if, perhaps, there's simply nothing to say. Perhaps the medium isn't worthy of an exhibition after all.

Unless, of course, one is meant to buy the accompanying catalog to taste those tender morsels. If so, well, then, we've just stumbled into my second complaint: lack of critical seriousness. This handsome volume (love those word-balloon chapter headings. Who thought of that? Ingenious! I guess we should be lucky the exhibition wasn't called Splat Boom Pow, though the net effect of its content is no different) holds some gorgeous reproductions of original art, as well as a tremendous amount of verbiage of uneven quality. If the execution of the exhibition only hinders its purpose, the book itself defeats the exhibition's premise.

Accompanying John Carlin's exhaustive essay narrating the historical arc of the show (long on formal analysis, though oddly short on the actual aesthetic and comics-specific context of the work—and riddled with factual errors) is a sheaf of mostly execrable essays by "celebrity" writers. It's easy to imagine the meeting that must have taken place to allow these essays to happen: "Well, the book needs a hook! I know, let's get famous people to write!" The problem with famous people is that, while charming, they don't necessarily know anything about the medium at hand. I am not famous,

THE POET HAS ABUSED HIMSELFE, LIKE AN ASS ƷT WERE SIMPLE INJURY TO HIS FREE HAND.

but if someone asked me to write an essay about, say, the work of Jonathan Safran Foer, I'd beg off, since, though I appreciate it as a reader, I don't really know enough about contemporary fiction to say anything valuable about it. So, what's his excuse for his essay on Art Spiegelman? It's a paean to his friendship with Art, and um, their long talks together, gentle massages, etc. It's a tough slog. And there's Dave Eggers' embarrassing defense of Chris Ware. Dave, Chris Ware is a genius artist—he doesn't need to be defended. He does, however, need insightful, non-smug prose about his work. Françoise Mouly's cringe-inducing essay on Crumb ("he's a good babysitter") fails to address even the most basic aspects of his work; Pete Hamill's upteenth regurgitation of his out-of-date appreciation of Milton Caniff; Jules Feiffer's rote appreciation of E.C. Segar (which should have been great given his past comics-history writing and his screenplay for Robert Altman's *Popeye*, but instead felt like something he'd written years ago and dusted off); Glenn David Gold's fan-boy appreciation of Kirby…and on and on, each one bad in wholly different ways. Only Robert Storr and J. Hoberman, on Gould and Kurtzman, respectively, acquit themselves admirably. And gee, I wonder why? Maybe because they're serious critics in touch with the art of cultural criticism and the medium in which they're dabbling. The use of "celebrity writers" defeats any claim the exhibition has to importance. If the curators don't take the subject seriously enough to ask solid, qualified scholars to contribute essays (and I should note, that these scholars would not be the only correct choice—just one of the many better options), why should we? And if the curators were unable to gather more than a handful of decent writing for the book, one has to wonder if the medium really is worthy of further curatorial efforts. Would the curators of that painting-in-the-1960s exhibition I hypothesized earlier find it necessary to commission non-art writers to "endorse" the work? The answer is obvious. Beyond the concerns of legitimacy, etc., the artists deserve better.

So, if the curators really want comics to be examined as a serious medium, the first step is not to establish a bullshit canon, but rather to be serious—avoid silly stunt casting, attempt to provide rudimentary information, and for heavens sake, try not to commission an exhibited artist's wife to write about another exhibited artist. Y'know, act like real, grown-up curators! Good luck.

In the wake of "Masters of American Comics," I've heard it argued that its failure proves that comics don't belong on walls, and I know plenty of cartoonists who reject and/or resent the idea of original comic art being shown in galleries and museums. I disagree. I think that the best hope of the serious study of comics lies with active participation by major institutions. So what if we need to adjust our eyes a bit, and look at comic pages as artifacts, like Grecian urns, statuary, and other objects that simply weren't made for the spaces they now exist in? It is true that comic pages will always pale next to paintings, drawings, and prints—these are objects made to live in and activate a particular space. Comic pages (with the notable exception of Gary Panter's) are not made with those concerns in mind. If paintings function to be looked at, then comics function to be, well, printed, and then read. These are two very different activities. But it doesn't mean comics can't exist in an institutional setting—just that new, more innovative ways to display them must be found. Treating them as drawings or any "normative" paper media just doesn't work so well. The effect of displaying them (accompanied by some text) to the public, outside of stores and homes, is invaluable—it allows the discussion to begin. If MoMA, the Whitney, and other museums began establishing collections, began devoting resources to the medium, a critical consensus could emerge—one that is not reliant on publicity hooks and canons, but rather the direct experience of a profound and multi-layered medium. ★

Dan Nadel is the author of *Art Out of Time: Unknown Visionary Cartoonists 1900-1969*, the co-editor of *Comics Comics*, and the owner of the packaging and publishing company PictureBox.

Reviews

Persuaded that this means a suicide on
her account, the Marquise faints.   *Her dog also.*

Chris Ware

Töpffer in English

In the winter of 1831, Johann Wolfgang von Goethe, creator and appreciator of all things Kunst, was feeling blue. His loyal attendants, sympathetic to the great man's depression, had heard of a taciturn Genevan educator who, in his spare time, wrote and drew farcical picture-stories to amuse himself and his students. So Frédéric Soret, tutor to the Duke of Weimar's children and translator of one of Goethe's scientific works, obtained one of these illustrated manuscripts and, placing it into Goethe's hands, stepped aside. Thankfully, the gamble paid off: Soret discovered that Goethe found the book "very amusing" and that it gave him "extraordinary pleasure," though he chose to take his pleasure in small doses, so as not to suffer "an indigestion of ideas." Soret also noted that Goethe thought the Genevan sparkled "with talent and wit," and "if he… did not have such an insignificant text before him, he would invent things which would surpass all our expectations."

Chris Ware's review first appeared in the Apr./May 2008 issue of *Bookforum*.
[©2008 Chris Ware & *Bookforum*]

The Genevan in question was Rodolphe Töpffer—the inventor of the comic strip. Born in 1799 to landscape painter (and occasional caricaturist) Adam-Wolfgang Töpffer, the young Töpffer did not follow in his father's fine-art footsteps, finding employment instead as a schoolteacher who conducted unusual open-air hikes to the Alps before eventually settling into a post as professor of literature at the University of Geneva in 1830. Despite reported vision problems, his abilities as a draftsman were considerable, and his travelogues from these trips are illustrated with lush, scribbled pen drawings. But it was his rough-hewn fictional picture-stories—the loosely doodled satiric improvisations about society, government, and education he began in 1827—that garnered him lasting fame. However fearful Töpffer was of societal reprisal for indulging in such tomfoolery as caricature (and however worried he was about how it would weigh on the career of a freshly minted university professor), he nonetheless grew cautiously bolder after Goethe's encouragement, passing out his hand-drawn books to select aristocrats, until it was generally known (wink wink) that the Genevan "RT" was the author of those amusing picture books everyone—especially Goethe—was talking about. One of the original manuscripts even includes a written exhortation to "please avoid crumpling, dirtying, or pulling the pages about, being careful to turn only by the edge," revealing just how "underground" these books really were. A cross-century connect-the-dots to the comix movement of the 1960s is almost too easy: Much of Robert Crumb's earliest work was done in sketchbooks and in letters, and a book-length full-color love note to his first wife existed for years only in sketchbook form, until the artist's subsequent fame compelled her to publish it (as *The Yum Yum Book* in 1975).

Twenty years ago, as an undergraduate painting student at the University of Texas, I'd occasionally seek artistic inspiration in the sterile discomfort of the campus fine-arts library by flipping through the pages of an oversize book published in 1973 and insanely titled *The History of the Comic Strip, Vol. 1: The Early Comic Strip: Narrative Strips and Picture Stories in the European Broadsheet from c. 1450 to 1825*. Although I was dutifully attending all my art classes, I was also trying, independently, to draw comic strips like those of Crumb, Art Spiegelman, and Ben Katchor: a sort of literary, self-revelatory picture-story aimed at adults. I had no idea what I was doing. Young, confused, and seeking my own voice, I needed not only all the helpful examples I could scrounge up but also a little-known source of readily stealable graphic ideas. Fortunately, this strange tome provided just that. Shortly after graduation, I discovered that the author, David Kunzle, had also painstakingly assembled a second, even more impressively huge and obscure volume that examined the nineteenth-century comic strip. (Its preface somewhat bitterly noted that "the 'scientific literature' of my discipline [art history] has tended to pass by Volume One"; a third volume, unsurprisingly, never appeared.) As years passed, I looked for other books to steal from, and Kunzle's interests turned away from comics. Who could blame him? In 1990, writing a serious study of comic strips would have been tantamount to writing an analysis of MTV's DJs.

I should have just waited another seventeen years. Now, when publishers acquire "graphic novelists" with a fervor usually accorded only real novelists and scholarly articles about comics appear nearly as frequently as tenured positions in colleges and universities, Kunzle has returned to the discipline he helped found—with not one but two new marvelous books that focus on the life and work of Töpffer, who not only was the first to codify the comic strip into its own visual language but served as the raison d'être for Kunzle's 1973 study. (Volume 1 *of The History of the Comic Strip* features an epigram by Töpffer on its frontispiece.) These new books constitute the first complete set of Töpffer's works translated into English, an unjustly late showing considering that the English-speaking world has long claimed that the flash-point invention of the comic strip was in 1896 by Richard Outcault's introduction of speech balloons emitted from a phonograph horn in his strip *The Yellow Kid*. The material is divided neatly into *Father of the Comic Strip*, a critical monograph on Töpffer's work, and *The Complete Comic Strips*, a 650-page hardbound collection of his published and unpublished picture-stories, translated by Kunzle from the original French. Thankfully, the volumes are devised such that it isn't necessary to have the monograph on hand to appreciate the comics: Kunzle divvies up information so there is little crossover, and all rudimentary biographical necessities are included to aid the casual reader (or art student hiding out in the library).

When Goethe tried to describe what he found so revolutionary in Töpffer's work, he primarily observed that the sequential pictures suggest movement, which "freezes and unfreezes in the spirit of imitation." In this awkward but prescient observation, Goethe nails the strange mechanism Töpffer had stumbled on and finds metaphoric resonance with one of his own earlier utterances: "Architecture is frozen music." Kunzle deftly summarizes this mechanism as speed—the speed of drawing, thinking, writing, printing—which even infects the movements of the characters themselves: "Speed, leaving all inessentials aside: that was his aesthetic philosophy in a nutshell, all nuts and no shell, all essence, no mere surface description. So the doodle, first fling of his unconscious, was drawn out into faces, figures and scenarios, careering haphazardly, a little blindly one might say, turning obstacles into launching pads, and logic upside down. Graphic and narrative trajectories remained open." From a Voltairean ensemble farce to a simple story of love-struck woe to a pragmatic tale of a husband and wife deciding how best to educate their children, Töpffer obviously enjoyed playing with the new toy he had invented. Reading back and forth between images, he was the first to discover how to make pictures move.

Töpffer was also among the first to move picture books. By borrowing a lithography method from the process theretofore relegated to advertising circulars and grocers' bills, he eventually upgraded from the salon and the circulated manuscripts to the commercial distribution of the public bookshop. Without having to resort to writing backwards on a lithographic stone, or, even worse, to the calculated tracing of wood engraving, he was able to self-publish cheaply and to self-distribute selectively. He also reaped a much more substantial profit without a middleman—thus becoming the first comic-book mogul, for better or for worse. Stan Lee, who has claimed that he wrote comics "to make a couple of bucks," would certainly approve.

Töpffer was also a serious critic, essayist, and apologist for his new medium, and among the most revelatory sections of Kunzle's monograph are the chapters on the

Mr. Pencil, who is an artist, draws from beauteous nature.

Mr. Pencil, who is an artist, views his achievement with a complaisance, and notes that he is content with it.

Mr. Pencil, who is an artist, notes that he is content with it upside down as well.

And even looking over his shoulder.

artist's "Essay on Physiognomy" and "Essay on Autography," the latter laying out Töpffer's method of cheap reproduction and how that technique allowed for more fluid drawing and consequent transference of ideas, as well as pointing toward a new way to approach fiction (that is, visually). Kunzle goes into welcome detail about Töpffer's process, quoting the artist's explanation of how one of his protagonists, and subsequently an entire story, emerged from idle doodling: "What gave us the idea of doing the whole story of Mr. Crépin was having found in a single stroke of the pen and quite by accident…the whole epic issuing much less from a preconceived idea than from a [facial] type and by chance." This passage is especially significant in that it clearly shows the difference between cartooning and simple illustration. As any moderately serious cartoonist knows, one can think until the cows come home, but the second one puts pen to paper, all bets are off—drawing, and looking, open a whole new world of possibility. As a capper, Kunzle explains that Töpffer preferred to call his works *histoires en estampes*, which Kunzle translates as "engraved novels" or—gasp!—"graphic novels." Was there nothing this Genevan didn't invent?

What strikes the reader immediately on flipping through Töpffer's work is his unusual sensitivity to human gesture, especially those gestures meant to influence or to deceive, something the writer Leo Tolstoy made regular use of forty years later and what continues to make his novels *Anna Karenina* and *War and Peace* feel so real and immediate. (The Russian novelist cited Töpffer's most popular prose work, "My Uncle's Library," as an early inspiration.) One of the fundamental tools of comics is the wordless re-creation of the rhythms of human gesture, most easily accomplished by maintaining a fixed scale of character from one panel to the next, so that the only changes the eye registers are in the variations of posture between the repeating figures (a style more commonly seen before comics began imitating the camerawork of movies). Töpffer uses this device frequently, especially on the opening page of "Mr. Pencil"—one of the eight principal stories contained in *The Complete Comics*—in which the main character, an artist, admires his own work, trotting around and coyly glancing at it from various viewpoints. Even without the explanatory text, the figure seems to come alive on the page, the rhythm of his actions revealing his self-satisfied disposition. By contrast, a different tone is struck on the first page of "Dr. Festus," where only the captions indicate that four years have passed between the first two panels. Such wild shifts in time and place, and even crosscutting, are everywhere in Töpffer; the sensation must have been particularly exciting and strange for his first readers, and the importance of these visual innovations should not be lost on historians of cinema, a medium that his work unquestionably prefigures.

The flavor of caricature that Töpffer regularly employs for his protagonists—jutting chin and squarish, bulbous, protruding nose (what I think of as the "Punch and Judy" or "Lady Elaine Fairchilde" school)—feels somewhat outmoded today. Like the archaic elongated s in eighteenth-century documents that reads as an f to modern eyes, Töpffer's anachronistic style potentially trips up the possibility for empathy with his characters. The story that employs a less exaggerated visual approach, "The History of Albert," thus ends up being among the most affecting. Unlike many of his other works that immediately explode into pandemonium, "Albert" is refreshingly no-nonsense. Seemingly a satire of the Swiss educational system from a child's viewpoint (Töpffer had ridiculed it in an earlier book from the parent's point of view), it soon becomes, quite surprisingly, a satire of identity. Even more amazingly, Albert literally grows up before our eyes—and self-righteously so: "His genius starved of air and space by institutions. Criticism, filthy vampire of the dawn of genius." Töpffer cannily presents Albert's heartbroken longings and frustrations with a specificity that could, through a few well-placed guitars, iPods, and a mod hairdo or two, apply to the youth of today. As the young man matures, he tries his hand at being a poet, a law student, a political activist, a medical student, a wine merchant, a grocer, an educator, a cocoa manufacturer, a tutor, a candlemaker, a business agent, a lamplighter, and a newspaper publisher before finally "finding himself" at story's end. Goethe's hope that Töpffer might "invent things which would surpass all our expectations" seems a potential best fulfilled by this tale.

A total of eight stories, dating from the 1820s to the 1840s, are translated, annotated, and reproduced, as well as a number of never-before-seen notes, fragments from unfinished works, and deleted scenes, making *The Complete Comic Strips* the true Töpffer boxed set. While all of his works were originally offered in landscape format (that is, horizontally), here they are presented sideways, in a vertically bound book. This means that all two pounds of Töpffer have to be read with the pages flipped up and held with one hand, like a school tablet. Fair enough, but that also means Kunzle's extraordinarily informative, lively, and necessary footnotes are buried (vertically) at the end of the volume, with no numbers or citations for cross-referencing. (Oddly, Kunzle himself thanks the publishers in his preface for printing the book "in a format oblong like the original albums.") Such a kvetch does not diminish the importance of these two remarkable books, however, which should be considered an indispensable part of any art or literature library. Kunzle has finally brought to modern readers stories that until now were, in a sense, unreadable. And Kunzle the scholar is anything but unreadable—those wary of academic writing should be instantly reassured by his genial, lively, and frank commentary. Töpffer, who disliked pretension, would have been quite pleased, I think. The Töpffer Kunzle conjures—believing in the democracy of his art, publicly self-deprecating, prone to magnifying minor slights in solitude—sometimes reminds me of the Charles Schulz in David Michaelis's recent biography. In fact, the Genevan artist is so familiar at times that it seemed I was reading a book about my own generation. It's clear that not only did Töpffer invent the modern comic strip, he also invented the modern cartoonist. ★

Chris Ware is the author of *Jimmy Corrigan: The Smartest Kid on Earth*, which received the Guardian First Book Award in 2001 and was included in the 2002 Whitney Biennial. A contributor to *The New Yorker* and *New York Times*, his work was also the focus of an exhibit at the Museum of Contemporary Art Chicago in 2006. He is currently serializing two graphic novels in his periodical *The ACME Novelty Library*, the 20th issue of which will appear in 2010.

Rick Moody

Epileptic: Disorder in the House

These days, it's easy to see the enormous influence that cartooning and comics have had on popular cinema. It's as if the Hollywood studios have no other source and no other style for their family friendly entertainments. Yet less well observed is the relationship between literature and comics. While there are worthy precursors, to be sure, the ascent of comics into the realm of the literary began in earnest in 1992 with the publication of *Maus*, by Art Spiegelman. And it's with the advent of Chris Ware's *Jimmy Corrigan*, or, *The Smartest Kid on Earth* (2000) that comics and comic artists became unavoidable in literary circles. Ware's masterpiece even burlesques this infiltration on its endpapers, in a mock newspaper article entitled "New Pictorial Language Makes Marks: Good for Showing Stuff, Leaving out Big Words."

Certain publishing houses are experimenting with this new form of expression, test-marketing carefully demographed entertainments, and then strategically aiming them at a less-educated and/or intellectually blunted segment of the consumer pool. The results, thus far, are encouraging. "Dumb people are eating it up," says our researcher. "They love it. Especially people who buy a lot of stuff. This could be big."

People *are* devouring the graphic novel, and across the whole range of human IQs. It's not at all uncommon now for readers of literature to admire Chris Ware or Julie Doucet or Joe Sacco or Joe Matt with a partisan vigor formerly reserved for renegades like Kurt Vonnegut or Richard Brautigan. It seems to me there are a number of reasons for this popularity. For example: comics are, at the moment, better at the sociology of the intimate gesture than literary fiction is. Literary fiction, obsessed on the one hand with defending itself against the popularity of cinema, is too preoccupied with story. On the other hand, in competing with poetry, it is occasionally dazzled by abstraction and cerebral firepower. Between the two once lay the novel of manners, in which we found Henry James perfectly depicting the way an American ingénue wore a dress, crossed her legs, and entertained a suitor. You infrequently read this kind of social observation anymore. But Chris Ware is great at drawing it. So is Chester Brown, for example, in his poignant graphic novel *I Never Liked You.*

Of course, it is inevitable that Europe and Asia should also capitalize on the ascent of the graphic novel, in the process supplying their own notions of the form. And so we have, for example, *Epileptic*, by David B. (the pseudonym of one Pierre-François Beauchard, from Montreuil, France), published in this country by Pantheon, who also brought us Spiegelman and Ware. Just as the European novel has a different set of concerns from its American relations, so does David B.'s story have preoccupations that we might not ordinarily find in a graphic novel. Well, for one, it's not a novel at all, but a memoir.

Historians of the graphic form will observe that, yes, Spiegelman, Sacco, Marjane Satrapi, and others (one stunning example is the recent prose/graphic hybrid *Diary of a Teenage Girl* by Phoebe Gloeckner) have all experimented with the autobiographical in their work, but in the case of *Epileptic* the autobiographical impulse has, in my view, more to do with what's happening in French writing these days, namely *l'auto-fiction.* If, against the advice of the *National Review*, et al., you should travel to the Paris of 2005, you would find there that the *roman à clef* of French literature has lately given way to a cottage industry in intimate accounts of the lives of French nationals. David B.'s story, which in the broad outline is about the desperate attempts of his family to deal with his older brother's chronic epilepsy, is consonant with this confessional impulse, but it also takes liberties with the subgenre. The young Pierre-François, for example, is obsessed with military history, and therefore interleaved with the particulars of his brother's lamentable story are the young artist's myriad designs of the invasions of the Mongols, his grandfather's experiences in WWI, tales of the Algerian war, the French Resistance, etc.

Moreover, because David B.'s brother began to experience the symptoms of his seizure disorder in the late Sixties, the family made use of the many alternative therapies available in the Europe of that time. So there are sad and hilarious passages in *Epileptic* about childhood in the macrobiotic communes of France. (Page 106: "Soon the entire commune is running entirely on guilt. The society we left behind has recreated itself. We have a macrobiotic cook, macrobiotic judges, macrobiotic cops.") David's parents also consult the Rosicrucians (page 202: "It's awesome, my brother, my sister and I are part of a secret society. Each one of us is given a grade."). They even experiment briefly with alchemy. All in pursuit of relief for their afflicted son.

In short, *Epileptic* constitutes something new: a graphic intellectual history. A design-oriented history of ideas. There are entire dreams illustrated here, in a disturbing and rococo illustrative style, with interpretations included, as if David B. is channeling Jung's *Memories, Dreams, Reflections* or Freud's seminal writings on the oneiric; there are allusions to May '68 and the role of the French intellectual in contemporary Gallic life, and there are ghosts in profusion, ghosts of Europe past. In particular, I should include here the ghost of the author's grandfather, a man of somewhat dubious ideas, who is rendered such that he resembles one of those beaked denizens of hell you find Hieronymous Bosch (page 145, e.g.: "You must explain to him that he has left this life behind and he must go into the Beyond in order reach his next reincarnation").

Because it is unafraid to dwell in detail on cultural and intellectual lineage, *Epileptic* feels as much influenced by Gide, Foucault, Malraux, and Barthes as it is influenced by Spiegelman. It is less graphic novel, that is, than *bildungsroman* on the coming of age of the artist as reader of continental philosophy, wherein brother Jean-Christophe's epilepsy, and its attendant familial disorder, is the fulcrum that forces Pierre-François to become author David B., spawning in the process his magnificent pictures, drawings at once full of the iconographies of both atavism and surrealism.

Here in the United States, it is perhaps fair to say that the memoir is a triumph-over-adversity genre. (The English title of this book, *Epileptic*, is an indication of this, since it's much less interesting than the French title, *l'Ascension du Haut Mal*.) We find many examples in America of the memoir of overcoming alcoholism, the memoir of incest survival, the memoir of discovering the joys of sodomy, and while some of these books are genuine and poignant, the result is that the memoir, hemmed in by the requirement of a predictable epiphany and triumph, becomes a pale shadow of the creative medium it might be. But just as the graphic novel has borrowed from and improved on the acute observational skills of the great literary writers past, so does *Epileptic* borrow from the great cultural and intellectual archeologies of French non-fiction writing of the last hundred years, all the while remaining both accessible and moving.

The graphic novel may originally have been aimed at "a less-educated and/or intellectually blunted segment of the consumer pool," as Chris Ware observed, but *Epileptic* proves that this relatively new form can be as graceful as its august literary forbearers. Just as recent novels by Jonathan Lethem and Michael Chabon have indicated how formative comics can be for writers who rely only on words, now comic artists are expressing their facility with the strategies and ambitions of the word-smitten crowd. This cross pollination is to be celebrated. ★

Rick Moody is the author of five novels, three collections of stories, and a memoir, *The Black Veil*. He plays music in The Wingdale Community Singers.

Robert C. Harvey

Fun Home: Literary Cartooning in a Graphic Novel

It's no good extolling Alison Bechdel's *Fun Home* as a literary achievement without taking into account the role of pictures in this graphic memoir. The maturity of comics as literature is evident, first, in the book's narrative technique. Bechdel the cartoonist's autobiographical recollections of her childhood and youth as Alison, the daughter/narrator, do not form a chronology: instead, they cluster thematically in chapters that examine her father's role in the family and his daughter's discovery of her homosexuality. In successive chapters, Bechdel returns, again and again, to pivotal events, each time exploring various memories that resonate from aspects of each of them. Her protagonist is her father, a high school teacher of English and, part-time, the small town's only undertaker, who spends his spare hours meticulously restoring the family's 1867 Gothic-revival home, working in the garden, or reading great works of literature. Alison's mother, also an English teacher, working on her master's degree and acting in community theater, is, compared to her father, a blank; her two siblings,

Earlier versions of "*Fun Home*: Literary Cartooning in a Graphic Novel" first appeared on the web magazine *Rants & Raves* in December 2006 and in *The Comics Journal* #281 (February 2007). [©2007 Robert C. Harvey]

likewise. We learn about the father's obsessive perfectionism in restoring the house in the book's opening pages, and Alison also tells us, off-handedly, that he killed himself and that he had sex with teenage boys.

When she returns to his alleged suicide, we learn that his death may have been accidental: he jumped, backwards, into the path of an oncoming truck and was killed. About his homosexual adventures, however, there is little doubt. He was a closeted gay all his life, but his wife knew, and she tells Alison soon after Alison discovers her own sexual orientation as a lesbian, which she does when she goes away to college. There, like any dedicated book lover—she is, after all, her father's daughter—she learns about lesbianism by reading about it first rather than by experiencing it with someone. When she tells her parents, they react like the two somewhat liberal intellectuals they are: the mother, without overtly condemning her daughter's waywardness, hopes she is mistaken; her father, his own orientation still a secret from the daughter, announces his belief that everyone should experiment. "It's healthy," he says. Almost immediately thereafter, her mother tells Alison of her father's predilection. Upon subsequent revisitings of these events, we learn that her mother started divorce proceedings soon after learning of her daughter's homosexuality, and then, just two weeks later, her father is killed by the truck.

As Alison circles again and again the key events in her life, she comes closer and closer to the preoccupation that compels her as a person and motivates her art—her desire for a closer relationship to her father, who, as she establishes very early, was distant emotionally, seldom, if ever, displaying affection for his wife or children. When she learns of his homosexuality soon after acknowledging her own, she hopes the coincidence will establish a rapprochement otherwise missing in their relationship. Instead, he dies. Alison assumes a cause-and-effect relationship from a sequential one: in her imagination, her revelation seems to have caused his death.

In the first scene of the book, Alison propounds a mythic kinship with her father, evoking Daedalus and his son, the doomed Icarus, who flew too close to the sun, which melts the artificial wings his father had devised for him and sends him plummeting from the sky. Her father, Alison says, embroidering the allusion, was a master artificer, "a Daedalus of decor" in his restoring passion. But, she goes on, ominously at this early stage in the book, "in our particular re-enactment of this mythic relationship, it was not me but my father who was to plummet from the sky." The book is laced with other literary allusions—to Henry James, F. Scott Fitzgerald, Shakespeare, Proust. Given her father's involvement with literature, the maneuver lends the narrative an appropriate ambiance. Long before the end of the book, we know her father's favorite novel is *Ulysses*, James Joyce's portrait of a complete man. "Ulysses," Joyce told the artist and critic Frank Budgen, "is son to Laertes, but he is father to Telemachus, husband to Penelope, lover of Calypso, companion in arms of the Greek warriors around Troy, and King of Ithaca." In his famed novel, Joyce intended to show "the complete man," man in all his roles, "from all sides." And in Joyce's enterprise, Daedalus again appears, this time as a young man, Stephen Dedalus—a son—whose odyssey results in his finding a spiritual father in the novel's Ulysses, Leopold Bloom, the cuckolded husband of the affirmative Molly, earth mother of us all. *Fun Home* moves from the mythic to the spiritual, but the flywheel of its dynamic is Alison's search for something real, a tangible relationship with her father.

The strongest thematic current in the book is the deceptive spell of appearances. The name of the book is the first clue: "fun home" is the Bechdel children's mocking shorthand for their father's "funeral home" occupation. The label that cartoonist Bechdel puts on the cover for us to see, the "fun home," is not the reality she shows us inside, which is scarcely fun. Moreover, the painstakingly restored house the family lives in "is not a real home at all but the simulacrum of one, a museum"; and the family, "a sham." In the father's passion for restoration, Alison sees telltale evidence that her father was "morally suspect" and had "a dark secret," saying: "He used his skillful artifice not to make things but to make things appear to be what they were not." This caption runs over a page-wide panel showing her father taking a photograph of his family, an idyllic tableau followed immediately by another, captioned: "He appeared to be an ideal husband and father, for example, but would an ideal husband and father have sex with teenage boys?" The mother's passion for the theater, for play-acting, is another manifestation of the artifice of appearance. And in real life, she plays a dutiful and loving wife even though she knows her husband prefers sex with other males. The father's death is another deceiving appearance: he seems to have been killed accidentally, but his daughter thinks it was suicide. Finally, the father's homosexuality is the central deception in the book: he appears to be what he is not, "an ideal husband and father." By this route, homosexuality itself acquires a cloak of deception: homosexuality is the reality contradicted by appearances. Gay people are not the sexual personalities their apparent genders announce to the world.

Alison's search for rapprochement with her father thus becomes a metaphor for her search for peace of mind about her own sexual preferences. She needs from him some sort of sign of approval or acceptance. The closest she comes is a conversation the two of them have in the car on the way to a movie one night a few weeks before he was killed. "When I was little," her father says, rather emotionlessly, "I really wanted to be a girl. I'd dress up in girls' clothes." And Alison says: "I wanted to be a boy! I dressed in boys' clothes." Pause. Then the telltale appeal for recognition: "Remember?" This barren but revealing exchange is not, alas, "the sobbing, joyous reunion of Odysseus and Telemachus," Alison notes wryly in captions accompanying the visualization of the episode. "It was more like fatherless Stephen and soulless Bloom having their equivocal late-night cocoa at 7 Eccles Street. But which of us was the father?" she continues. "I had felt distinctly parental listening to his shamefaced recitation."

And here, the function of Bechdel's pictures is crucial. The conversation is depicted in two facing pages, twelve panels of uniform composition on each page: we look into the car from the window on the passenger side, Alison in the foreground, and her father beyond her at the wheel of the car. The night outside is evoked with a black background hovering around the images of the father and his daughter. The monotony of the layout emphasizes the emotionlessness of their exchange. Alison's thoughts appear in white letters against the black. Her father's facial expression and his posture never change, suggesting the absence of emotion in his remarks. Alison, in contrast, gestures and looks around, her eyes, opening wide or squinting, accenting her comments and registering her reactions to what her father says.

In the best works of the cartoonist's art, pictures blend with the words to create a meaning neither achieves alone without the other. In that idyllic family tableau that Bechdel shows her father photographing, the picture shows us one thing—the ideal; the words announce the fraud. The picture without the words sustains the illusion; the words without the picture say nothing about the Bechdel family being the "sham." Together, the picture and the words create the reality of the family as Alison understands it. Bechdel's blend of the visual and the verbal here achieves yet another dimension in thematic depth: she shows us a photograph being taken, and a photograph is another "appearance."

Bechdel's attention to visual details gives endless nuance to her tale, usually a humorous embellishment. In the picture of her family at church, notice that her father is eyeing the choir boys as they pass—just as the accompanying caption reveals his sexual interest in them. Alison, standing next to her father, also looks at the boys, but not with the same interest. She seems bored, an emotion suggested by the depiction of her brother next to her: he is clearly nearly overcome with ennui, his eyes closed as if asleep, and his posture is the mirror image of Alison's. The visual details in the backgrounds of Bechdel's pictures usually reward our attention with the quiet hilarities of the human comedy.

The information conveyed by the visuals is not always subtle. In the book's most outrageous blend of word and picture, Alison records an early lesbian love-making with captions that evoke Odysseus in tandem with pictures that give the verbiage a musky double entendre that is altogether missing in either words or pictures independent of each other. "In true heroic fashion," she writes, "I moved toward the thing I feared"; the picture shows her face hovering over her lover's naked crotch. The verbal paean continues: "Yet while Odysseus schemed desperately to escape Polyphemus's cave, I found that I was quite content to stay here forever"; and the picture shows Alison up to her nose in the honeypot of her lover.

For the book, Bechdel has simplified her usual drawing style, eliminating the cross-hatching and slant-line shading that we find in her comic strip, *Dykes to Watch Out For*. Her line is simple, unadorned, flexing slightly but not obtrusively, a little bolder in outlines than in details. Her draftsmanship—anatomy, composition—is confident, accomplished rather than adequate; the pictures, nearly a tour de force of plain-line technique. In place of linear texturing, she has deployed a delicate gray-green wash, tinting the entire enterprise with a low-key hue.

In *Fun Home*, Bechdel often deploys her visual-verbal resources to create a tension that underscores the theme that things are not always what they seem or what we might want them to be. In a long sequence early in the book, the captions drone on, comparing the Bechdel home life to that of Jimmy Stewart's family in *It's A Wonderful Life* and to the mythic life of Daedalus. The pictures accompanying the captions show us what Alison means when she says Stewart's yelling at his family in the movie is "out of the ordinary." The pictures present an episode of Alison's home life, complete in itself: her father's fit of temper causes her to break some crystal she's handling and, fearing her father's reaction, she flees the house. The captions, meanwhile, carry on about Daedalus' famed labyrinth, concluding with a speculation about whether Daedalus was "stricken with grief when Icarus fell into the sea? Or just disappointed by the design failure?" The prose of the captions offers one story; the pictures, another. Together, they juxtapose a fiction and a reality, myth and fact, a happy abstraction and a grimmer actuality.

Alison frequently shadows her prose with her pictures, telling two tales simultaneously, juxtaposing two realities—two appearances?—which suggests that one may be more real than the other. Or, perhaps, sometimes both equally real. In a sequence at the end of Chapter 3, the captions fantasize about Alison's father and F. Scott Fitzgerald, imagining a mystic connection between the two. The pictures, however, show us an entirely mundane incident, Alison asking her father for money to buy some new *Mad* books. The episode concludes with a telling picture: we peer into the house from outside, seeing Alison and her father in the same room through two separate windows. The mini-essay of the captions, meanwhile, has reached its heartbreaking conclusion: that she persisted in believing that she somehow caused her father to commit suicide because it created a bond between them, a connection she longed for all her life. As we read these words, we see the father and his daughter, bonded, ironically, by the composition of a picture that completely separates each from the other.

In creating the book, Alison's method doubtless fostered the frequent occurrence of such double-vision passages of prose and picture. "The first thing I do," she told Margot Harrison at sevendaysvt.com, "is I write on the computer in a drawing program, which enables me to make these little text boxes and move them around, make my panel outlines" without any images. Then she adds pictures, sketching into the panels on the preliminary layout of the page. A cartoonist's sensibility kicks in naturally, then, resulting in pictures that have an ironic or satiric relationship to the verbiage. But however accidental the emergence of the double-vision sequences, they are integral to the meaning of the book as a whole, establishing a pattern of appearance and contradictory or alternate realities.

The culminating event to which the narrative wends is a Joycean meeting between father and daughter, a spiritual sharing, which, at last, is achieved more in Alison's memory than in fact.

In the book's last sequence, Bechdel returns to Joyce's *Ulysses* to marvel at her father's staying in the closet all his life. Referring to Molly Bloom's passionate and sexual affirmation of life, Alison writes about her father: "How could he admire Joyce's lengthy, libidinal 'yes' so fervently and end up saying 'no' to his own life?" The last three pages of *Fun Home* take place in a swimming pool, where Alison's father is apparently teaching her to swim. Or encouraging her to dive off the diving board. Alison admits her claim that her father is gay "in the same way I am gay, as opposed to bisexual or some other category, is just a way of keeping him to myself, a sort of inverted Oedipal complex." In the last analysis, however, "spiritual paternity," like that between Stephen Dedalus and Leopold Bloom, is more important than "consubstantial" paternity. She depicts her younger self poised on the diving board, her father in the water beneath her, and concludes: "In the tricky reverse narration that impels our entwined stories, he was there to catch me when I leapt." The picture shows her jumping off the diving board and her father with his arms up to catch her.

But did he catch her when she leapt, jumping from straight life into gay life? Very little in the book supports that conclusion. In fact, the book is about her longing for him to be there and being perpetually disappointed that he never was. Or was he? Throughout the book, Alison returns again and again to aspects of her father's life and their relationship. Gradually, through repeated approaches, she strips him of his pretenses, of his artifices. But she clearly loves him, and it's his approval she wants. That tenuous conversation in the car comes close but it's not enough. By the time Bechdel in creating the book gets to the last pages, she has been back and forth over aspects of her father's life, and her own, several times, entwining their stories in tricky reverse narration. In the book—in her imagination—he is a constant presence. He is "there" in her imagination if not, actually, in her life. But his imagined presence persuades her that he has been "there" all along: that he caught her when she leapt, even though, as we well know, he didn't.

Having lived, with Alison, through the elaborate charades of the book, the juxtapositions of alternate realities, of appearances and contradictory realities, we are ready, as is she, to accept the reality she constructs for us, and for herself. The last sequence in the book reveals, in its allusions to Joyce, the book's narrative strategy: Alison, failing to achieve a genuine connection to her father despite their shared homosexuality, consoles herself with a spiritual relationship. The book's last caption is the conclusion in this line of thought. But it is false. Like the book itself, the assertion on the last page is a devout wish but not a fact, an appearance but not a reality.

The reality is in Alison's basement studio. Rachel Deahl of *Publishers Weekly* visited the cartoonist in her lair. "I stand in her workspace and look at the rows of books lining her shelves. They remind me of the panels in her book, the pictures of her reading and her father reading, of them sitting in that massive house surrounded by print and pages, skirting discussions of their own lives by talking instead about Leopold Bloom and Stephen Dedalus, Odysseus and Penelope. Then I notice it. It's a black-and-white photograph of a young man. He's handsome, clean shaven and smiling. He looks familiar, and I think I recognize him from the drawings. I begin to ask, 'Is that...' 'That's my father,' Alison says. It's the only framed picture in her work area and one of the few in the house. But that seems as it should. After all, who could have watched Alison through this process other than her dad?" Her father is still a presence in her life, still "there," but only in a photograph, an appearance.

While homosexuality forms the core of otherness at the thematic center of the book, *Fun Home* could well be a tale of adolescent alienation. In the Bechdel household, each

OUR HOME WAS LIKE AN ARTISTS' COLONY. WE ATE TOGETHER, BUT OTHERWISE WERE ABSORBED IN OUR SEPARATE PURSUITS.

AND IN THIS ISOLATION, OUR CREATIVITY TOOK ON AN ASPECT OF COMPULSION.

family member is isolated from the others, each absorbed in his or her separate pursuit, a circumstance the cartoonist dramatizes with a telling cut-away illustration of the old house that shows each of the family engaged in a different endeavor, a diagram that is repeated on the cover of the book underneath the dust jacket. Alison's situation could well embody the typical adolescent's sense of profound aloneness coupled to an equally typical desire for adult approval and acceptance. *Fun Home* is more than a portrait of an emotionally barren family life: it is also a record of Alison's persistence in trying to find actual evidence of having shared life with a father she admires and loves, evidence that, in the last analysis, exists more vividly in memory than in fact.

Judging from the book, Bechdel never seems to have felt hesitant about her homosexuality: she apparently accepted her sexual orientation as a simple fact of life almost from her first awareness of it. She was about twenty when her father was killed, and she launched her alternative newspaper comic strip within a couple of years. Its title, *Dykes to Watch Out For,* is not just unabashed: it's defiant. Neither unabashedness nor defiance are marks of hesitancy or awkwardness; both are flat assertions. At first, when the strip started in 1982, it took the form of weekly (or bi-weekly) commentary on various aspects of the human condition—the joys of couplehood, "the rule" (never go to a movie unless it has two women in it who talk to each other about something other than a man), the party, great romances ("that never were"), the first sleepover, politi-cola ("the birth of an activist"), summer grooming tips ("at the music festivals, braid your armpit hair"), and so on. In "Depression," Bechdel speculates on the condition and its causes. Depression may be brought on by hormones or "because you don't have a girlfriend…or it's the inevitable result of living in a depraved society during the nuclear age" (the caption under a picture of Reagan on tv, saying, "I believe in Armageddon"), but "it's well known that even women with rich lovers and no political awareness are often depressed!" She illustrates various possible remedies—increasing sugar intake, sex, reclusive behavior—"but nothing works except waiting for it to pass…one day, just as inexplicably, you will wake up in a good mood."

Eventually, individual characters emerged from the nameless milieu Bechdel began with, evolving into the current manifestation with a cast of dozens of diversities, including various racial minorities and a lesbian (or bi-sexual) who has a child by her male housemate. The presence of personalities pretty soon produced plots and stories, which are now continuing from week-to-every-other-week, exploring the ever-changing combinations of lovers, politics and social issues, and such personal trauma as breast cancer. Bechdel's drawing style at the beginning deployed a fragile line of unvarying thinness and solid blacks deftly spotted throughout. The line acquired greater confidence over the years, becoming bolder when outlining figures, and Bechdel began using gray tones as well as a variety of texturing devices. *Dykes* is now one of the handsomest comic strips around, in or out of the alternative newspaper universe, and its storylines reflect current political events as well as social consciousness and personal crises. At least 11 reprint volumes have been produced; see amazon.com for a list. Doing the strip undoubtedly gave Bechdel the creative confidence to undertake the longer work of *Fun Home*, but the two enterprises are not at all alike in theme or substance except that each is assured cartooning about aspects of the human condition that matter. Serious literature for mature readers for whom sex is only a part of adulthood. ★

A freelance magazine cartoonist who has also published in comic strip, editorial cartoon, and comic book genres, **Robert C. Harvey**, Ph.D. (in English literature), is a comics chronicler who explores the artistry as well as the history of the medium. Among his books are *The Art of the Funnies* (1994), an aesthetic history of newspaper comic strips, and its sequel, *The Art of the Comic Book* (1996), showing how the latter developed from the former; *Accidental Ambassador Gordo: The Comic Strip Art of Gus Arriola* (2000), and *Meanwhile: A Biography of Milton Caniff, Creator of Terry and the Pirates and Steve Canyon* (2007). Harvey publishes regularly in *The Comics Journal* and in his biweekly online magazine *Rants & Raves* at www.RCHarvey.com, where he reviews current comics and reports news and lore about cartooning.

John Hodgman

Epics

(Kirby's Fourth World Omnibus; Kirby: King of Comics; Age of Bronze; Y: The Last Man)

In 1970, Superman went down a rabbit hole: a secret tunnel on the outskirts of Metropolis leading to a bizarre underground world inhabited by hippies, drop-outs and mutant creatures.

"Welcome to the wild area, brother," announces the first person he encounters, a bearded young man meditating atop a giant mushroom that spits poison gas. "You are now free to do your own thing!"

This was issue No. 133 of *Superman's Pal, Jimmy Olsen*—the first to be written and drawn by the comics legend Jack Kirby. And so, without knowing it, Superman (and the reader) had wandered into what would come to be known as Kirby's "Fourth World"—a weird saga of warring gods that for a brief moment hijacked the normally staid line of DC Comics and plunged it into bracing, beautiful oddness, and which is now fully and lovingly collected in the four-volume *Jack Kirby's Fourth World Omnibus* (DC Comics, $49.99 each).

Besides the psychedelic jump-start he gave to Jimmy Olsen, Kirby started three new titles—*The Forever People*, *The New Gods* and *Mister Miracle*. All chart the conflict between two families of the New Gods: those on the peace-loving planet of New Genesis, and those living in the warlike world of Apokolips. Apokolips is ruled by the evil Darkseid, who seeks the "anti-life equation" that will erase all free will in the universe but his own. Pitted against him is his son, the monstrous yet noble Orion, raised on New Genesis to love peace but ultimately doomed by his addiction to war.

It was a cosmic "epic for our times," with one foot in ancient myth and the other in the wildest science fiction. And unusually for a comic book story, it was designed to be told slowly, over many years, and to come to an end.

But it was also a personal epic. Kirby, as you ought to know, was the King. He got the nickname while working at Marvel Comics, where, with Joe Simon, he created Captain America. Later, with Stan Lee, he helped fashion a completely new, psychologically rich aesthetic in comics, reviving a flagging industry and unveiling a pantheon of pop-culture deities—the Hulk, the Fantastic Four, the Silver Surfer—that still walk the earth today.

But Kirby's share of the riches they generated was modest. Like nearly all comics artists of the day, he worked for hire. Born in 1917, Kirby (né Jacob Kurtzberg) was a pugnacious child of the Depression-era Lower East Side and thus far more likely to favor a sure paycheck over a smartly negotiated contract. (Often, there were no contracts at all.) By the end of the '60s, fights with Marvel over money and growing resentment over Stan Lee's celebrity led Kirby to an unthinkable defection to the competition.

DC, by contrast, offered him vast creative latitude and an almost overdetermined amount of credit. "KIRBY'S HERE!" shouted bold sunbursts on the cover of early Kirby issues. The Fourth World was to be his liberation—the place where he would at last get to do his own thing.

The results were startling. Kirby fans already knew that his art was muscular and kinetic, and in this collection, he's at the height of his powers. His characters are always in motion, leaping and punching at impossible angles, straining at the panels that try to contain them. Kirby's writing was the same way. His stories were linear—even primitive. But there is something powerful and melancholy and personal that weeps in Orion's epic, city-smashing rages.

At other times, though, the pages cannot seem to keep up with Kirby's astonishing imagination. Concepts, characters, subplots and themes are wildly thrown into the mix like drunken punches and then abandoned, never to be seen again: A whole city "hewn from the giant trees of a great forest"! Space giants lashed to asteroids! Werewolves and vampires living on a miniature planet in a scientist's basement (a planet with horns on it)!

In the biography *Kirby: King of Comics* (Abrams, $40), the King's longtime confidant and assistant Mark Evanier writes of Kirby that "when a new idea came to him, he jotted it down on a scrap of paper and, usually, lost it. Once, he got careless with a cigar, started a small fire in his workplace and lost over 50 concepts"—or, as his wife, Roz, put it, "'a whole day's work for Kirby.'"

Some of Kirby's concepts were beguiling. Mister Miracle, a warrior of Apokolips who flees to Earth to become a "super escape artist," keeps a "Mother Box" up his sleeve—a small, living computer that can enable its user to do almost anything, so long as it is sufficiently loved. In Kirby's world, all machines are totems: weapons and strange vehicles fuse technology and magic, and the Mother Box in particular uncannily anticipates the gadget fetishism that infects our lives today. (The Bluetooth headset may as well be a Kirby creation.)

But sometimes, his inventions were merely bizarre, driven by some opaque, unknown part of his brain. At one point, one of the Forever People, Kirby's band of dimension-hopping flower children, gives a small boy named Donnie one of his "cosmic cartridges"—a device at once resembling a bullet and a large, mysterious pill.

"I—it feels warm—like it was alive!" Donnie says as his features blur into the cosmos. "I—I'm everywhere at once—I—I see—everything—and everything moves—and makes a kind of beautiful noise!"

It's hard to know what a teenager would make of this. But Kirby was writing just as much for himself. He was 53 when he undertook the Fourth World, and a veteran of World War II. But as Evanier points out, and as is evident throughout this book, Kirby was deeply inspired by the young generation that was renouncing war around him. His understanding of the youth movement was perhaps idiosyncratic (in Kirby's world, the "Hairies" built their perfect society in a giant missile carrier they called "The Mountain of Judgment"). But they too were forging a new world; and the pleasure he clearly took in their efforts seems to have balanced the bouts of Orion-like rage. In one moment, Highfather of New Genesis turns to one of the young boys in his care. "Esak," he asks, "what is it that makes the very young—so very wise?"

"Tee hee!!" Esak replies. "It's our defense, Highfather—against the very old!!"

This is probably the only passage in the English language containing the words "tee hee" that has actually moved me.

This optimism pervades the first two volumes of the *Fourth World Omnibus*, and it helps the reader forgive its occasional excesses. It also lends poignancy to the failings of the second two volumes. For these are the books that document the premature death of the New Gods. By the 11th issue, as sales flagged, DC withdrew its Kirby mandate and the story ended, long before it was finished. Kirby was forced to wrap up as much of his saga as he could, in one rushed issue of *Mr. Miracle*, and then the wild area was closed.

There are no gods in the three volumes of *Age of Bronze* (Image; prices vary), Eric Shanower's triumphant illustrated fusion of the many legends of the Trojan War.

"I've gone so far as to shove the gods offstage," he explains in an afterword to the first in his proposed seven-volume series. "Not an original move on my part in retelling this story; it's been in and out of fashion for centuries—but a decision which I think is relevant to this 21st-century world where so many are quick to look beyond themselves for answers or to assign blame."

Instead, Shanower draws on intensive archaeological research and his own uncanny psychological insight to depict an ancient world that is wholly, tragically human.

Paris is not merely an abrasive, kidnapping cad; his tragedy begins when he realizes as a young cowherd that he is actually a prince of Troy who had been left for dead. It's his desire to prove his worth as a royal that causes his horrible overreach: the capture of Helen—half seduction, half abduction—that leads to the disastrous war with the Achaeans. Meanwhile, you could make an argument that Agamemnon launches the thousand ships to retrieve Helen either for reasons of antique honor or out of a calculating desire to plunder Troy's riches. But somehow Shanower locates both desires in his version of the Achaean high king, and he is transformed, suddenly, from competing literary interpretations into an actual person.

But it was always Achilles' choice that made the story seem as remote as the moon. A choice between a long life that goes unsung and an early death that is remembered forever? Unless you are 19, this is a no-brainer. But Achilles, of course, chases glory. And in one of many expertly drawn battle sequences, we see Achilles' skill and recklessness as he chases a young woman, the sister of a slain foe, almost playfully to the edge of a chasm. And then, in that queasy, silent stop-time that only comics can achieve, he watches her stumble, fall and die. It's a stupid, pointless death—one of many in the book—and in her fragility we suddenly appreciate the desire to somehow ennoble life's nasty, brutish shortness, even, irrationally, through war.

The initial sailing of the thousand ships led to the Achaeans' invading the wrong island. Weeks were spent making peace with the understandably peeved King Telephus of Mysia and burying the many dead, before a huge thunderstorm sent the Achaeans home for good. It would be years before the invasion could be launched again, and throughout the story, Shanower deftly shows us the horrible toll the war took on the Achaeans' families, fortunes, resources and nerves. (Perhaps the only thing that might rival the tedium of ancient war is the act of drawing a comic about it. Shanower began researching the first volume in 1991—it was published in 1998—and the latest, Volume 3A, was released just this year.) And then, of course, the worst toll of all: Agamemnon is told that before the fleet may sail again, he must kill his own daughter. How could Helen ever have been worth it?

The story of Iphigenia's slaughter makes up the slow, wrenching heart of *Book 2, "Age of Bronze: Sacrifice."* Patiently, with enormous skill and a palette of starkest black and white, Shanower reveals Agamemnon's torment. He is torn between a genuine fear of godly wrath on the one hand, and a mundane fear of his own army's rebellion should he disobey the godly command—one he knows may be wholly fictitious. This is the vise in which Agamemnon is caught, but it is Iphigenia who is crushed.

Not surprisingly, one of Shanower's most lively characters is Odysseus, the sharp-witted strategist and trickster who is Agamemnon's right hand. Before this dark section, it is easy to get caught up in the cinematic friendship they share, and indeed the long sequence in which Agamemnon recruits Odysseus and the other members of his crack team can't help mimicking the giddy fun of a heist film (this is, one might argue, the first heist film of them all).

So it is particularly affecting when Shanower recasts the legend of Iphigenia's magical rescue—how her body was switched at the last moment for a doe's, and her spirit was drawn to the gods—and transforms it into a story told by Odysseus to comfort Iphigenia's grieving mother. But this time, the trickster fails: in one single, stark panel, Shanower captures in Clytemnestra's face a shattered shore that the rosy fingers of myth cannot ever touch.

"How can I expect anyone else to recognize me after 20 years," Odysseus says at the end, referring to his own dark prophecy, "when after only four years I feel as though I wouldn't even recognize myself?"

Is this bit of self-analysis too modern for a hero of antiquity? Perhaps. But for all his historical research, Shanower's world never feels more convincing than when it reminds us that these humans—who died millenniums ago, if they ever lived at all— still feel painfully close.

In 2002, Brian K. Vaughan and Pia Guerra began their own epic journey, which recently wrapped with the final issue, No. 60, of *Y: The Last Man*. (These comics have been collected, thus far, into nine paperback volumes, with the 10th coming in July. They're published by Vertigo and priced from $12.99 to $14.99.)

It is the story of Yorick Brown, a recent college graduate who, like Mr. Miracle, is an escape artist. We first meet him as he hangs upside down, straitjacketed in his Brooklyn apartment. He is talking on the phone with his girlfriend, Beth, who is in Australia. "Do you ever think about destiny?" he asks as he slips his bonds and avoids asking her to marry him. "Why does fate choose one man over another?"

Something of a dummy, Yorick is completely unaware of the casual chauvinism of his question until, a few moments later, destiny makes its choice against all men. A plague runs through the world, killing every male mammal, mysteriously and all at once—except for Yorick (and his capuchin monkey, Ampersand). Somehow, he's escaped. As members of the world's better half seek to rebuild society, Yorick sets out to find Beth. Along the way, he's taken under the wing of a secret agent named 355 and relentlessly pursued by those who want to make use of the last man on earth—or destroy him for good.

It's this kind of gimcrack episodic storytelling that makes *Y* addictive and got Vaughan hired onto *Lost* last season. But there's more going on here. Like the best sci-fi writers, Guerra and Vaughan weave their story out of canny and provocative speculation over what an "unmanned" planet would mean. Yorick and 355's odyssey reveals a world in which the police and fire departments are annihilated, and supermodels take jobs as garbage collectors cleaning up the dead. But at the same time, the Israeli Army is the best-trained force in the world, and Australia—one of the few countries to allow women on submarines—rules the waves.

In addition, one might point out, such a plague would mean the almost total collapse of the comic book industry. That's one more reason to be grateful for Pia Guerra, whose

clear lines and expressive faces ground the work and make the death of billions of people what it should be: horrifying and sad.

At one point, in Washington, Agent 355 reminds Yorick that the death of every man on earth is not just a premise for an adventure. "They turned one of the monuments into an ad hoc memorial for all of the men," she says.

"Which monument?" Yorick asks.

"Guess."

(I don't think you need the picture to figure it out.)

Y, of course, stands for the Y chromosome, for the man, Yorick, and for the question that propels him. The book is full of these kinds of twisty double meanings and thematic echoes that reward careful reading. When Yorick catches the deadly Agent 355 knitting in Book 1, No. 5, for example, the presumption is that it's just an opportunity for some character-building repartee. ("What are you working on…rifle cozy?" he asks.) How could he expect the breathtaking payoff the scarf will provide by No. 56, five years and 1,400 pages away, as he and Agent 355 stand under another, far more feminine monument, the Arc de Triomphe? (And if that scarf isn't an allusion to Penelope's shroud in that other odyssey—the Odyssey—I'll eat my rifle cozy.)

No, Yorick surely didn't see it coming, anymore than I did. For by the time you know him well, you realize that Yorick, alas, really is a dope. This in part makes up for the fact that this story about billions of women remaking the world ultimately follows the journey of a single boy. Worse: a fanboy. For while Yorick may be immune to the man-killing disease, he's woefully infected by another contemporary plague—unceasing pop-culture references.

"Bad news, Frodo," he tells 355, explaining that the unusual engagement ring he bought for his girlfriend is not secretly the reason for his immunity, as he had thought. "Any delusions I once had about me being the protagonist of some predestined epic quest have gone the way of boy bands."

The story is told in real time, over five years, and as they pass, the initial reasons for the journey fade, like Helen, in memory. Yorick's search for Beth gets backburnered again and again. The need for an explanation of the plague becomes less pressing. Instead, the plot stops and asks its characters for directions. And where does it lead? To a graceful world in which women are getting along just fine, thank you. (Hint: In a world where the Roman Catholic Church is pretty much kaput, cloning becomes much less controversial.) Yorick realizes that his great escape amounts mostly to pure, dumb, Elvis-y luck. He realizes he is not particularly strong, nor particularly important, and in so doing he becomes what we used to call a man—and what I will now call: an adult.

Kirby imagined a different future for comics, one in which creators would own their own work. One in which they could tell ambitious personal stories with beginnings, middles and ends. And one in which the individual issues would be collected into books, which would be sold in bookstores, and kept forever. Indeed, that is exactly the success that both *Age of Bronze* and *Y: The Last Man* have enjoyed.

But before you conclude that Kirby, who died in 1994, was nothing but a doomed prophet, there is more to his epic. As recounted by Evanier in his biography and annotations to the *Fourth World Omnibus*, by the end of his life, Kirby was rightly lionized by the fan community. He would eventually win back a great deal of his original art from Marvel, and so he profited from it as a kind of retirement fund. And while the New Gods died, they nonetheless achieved a sort of Achilles-like immortality. Because Kirby did not own the rights to his creations, his characters were rediscovered and reinterpreted by new generations of DC artists. (Indeed, Jim Starlin is currently killing them off once more in his miniseries *Death of the New Gods*.)

Finally, in the early '80s, Kirby was given the chance to finish the story he had begun so long before. The graphic novel *The Hunger Dogs* provides the bittersweet coda to the *Fourth World Omnibus*. Given Kirby's age at the time, it's a remarkably accomplished, if uneven, work. But it is also surprisingly somber. Kirby's faith in youth's and technology's ability to change the world has evaporated somewhat. Esak, the smiling, tee-heeing child, has grown into a deformed monster, creator of a doomsday device of such unrelenting magnitude that it even makes Darkseid nostalgic. "Old age is snapping at our heels—reaching for the hunter and the hunted," he confesses to an old foe. "Perhaps I shall miss you when you've finally perished."

While many believe this final chapter is something of a rushed failure, it contains elements that are bravely, authentically tragic. And as Evanier points out, the very fact that it is being reprinted now, alongside successful works like *Age of Bronze* and *Y: The Last Man*, makes it a strangely happy ending. ★

John Hodgman is an expert. He lives in Brooklyn.
www.areasofmyexpertise.com

Amazon Readers

Was This Review Helpful To You?: Joe Matt's *Spent*

★ ★ ☆ ☆ ☆

Disappointing

October 23, 2007
by Barnaby Thieme (*San Francisco, CA*)

Having been a big fan of Joe Matt for many years, this collection came as a big disappointment to me. After reading it I've been forced to reluctantly conclude that in his last work he's taking the reader for a ride. Unlike his other exuberant, imaginative efforts, this is a claustrophobic, abrasive work that consists entirely of tight facial closeups and repetitive dialog that is all-too-familiar from his previous efforts. Matt's character has already been long-established, and he takes it in no new directions in this volume. On the contrary, his close introspection on his inability to form intimacy and his addiction to pornography have no counterpoint in drama, dialog, or action. The result is solipsistic and boring.

"Was this review helpful to you?" collected from the
Amazon Customer Reviews section of Joe's Matt's *Spent*.

This is a shame because as a long-time reader I have really enjoyed his previous work. The most emotion *Spent* got out of me was when Matt reflects on his previous efforts and confesses that he abandoned his planned ending to the *Fair Weather* arc of *Peepshow*. It would have involved a trip to the fair, but he gave it up because he was "too lazy to draw the crowd scenes." Looking back on that storyline (the name, they were building the fairgrounds throughout) I have to accept this, and it's simply depressing.

In this book Matt communicates to his readers in no uncertain terms that he has given up on his craft. He has become for this reader like the old friend whose destructive tendencies finally overcome your loyalty, and I feel something of that kind of disappointment reading this depressing work. After this read, Matt would have to completely reinvent himself to get my attention again.

★ ★ ★ ☆ ☆

It has problems (and so has Matt), but it kinda works...

November 24, 2007

By A reviewer (Europe) This book kind of works well with Matt's two previous book, as a dire warning about how it's easy to paint yourself into a corner unless you remember to grow as a human being. However, read on its own it's pretty depressing. Unless Matt can find a way to widen his scope, the world probably won't be desperately looking forward to any further books, but it DOES work as a suitable conclusion (or dead end?) to this series.

★ ★ ★ ★ ☆

Exceptional cartooning, but to what end?

September 2, 2007
By J Petrille (*New York City, NY*)

Joe Matt's work is truly dark. That word conjures images of *the Crow* or...what's that really stupid one? *Johnny the HOmicidal Maniac*. But in fact it would be pretty cool to be *the Crow*: you look cool and you're either getting vengeance or laid. Spent is about the true dark moments of the soul, which are usually alone and in dingy settings. Knowing the history of how he got here makes this all the more effective: he couldn't appreciate Trish (who is now, incidentally, married and a successful animator) while he had her, always lusting after someone not interested in him. Now Trish is gone and nothing's sprung up to take her place except the porn they so often fight about. That scene where he's about to make the Crumb shirt his new ... errr... rag... that's so powerful. Reading though, I asked myself: isn't he afraid of Trish reading this?

Anyway, Matt is such a great cartoonist. His characters are fluid and alive he somehow makes thirty pages of a three guys in a diner or a guy wandering around his tiny bedroom interesting and compelling. And frankly, without Matt's talented,

(deceptively?) simple cartooning, it would be difficult to make it through this very sad story.

It's a good thing he ended the story where he did, since approximately the next day he gets a call to turn his cartoon show into an HBO tv show and moves out to LA where young girls fawn over his 45 year-old carcass (don't believe me? Check out his MySpace page). What an unbelievable Deus Ex Machina: what hack dreamed up that illogical end to this pathetic character's story? Luckily Matt ends it where it 'll end for most losers: in their porn-cluttered boardinghouse bedroom.

My one negative thought on this was that I'd read the excerpt he did of *Spent* in the *McSweeney's* compendium a few years ago. It's like 6 pages: Matt edits his tape, finds the t-shirt, flashes back about Trish, tries to cheer himself up by planning on buying a slice of pizza, only to get seduced by the porn into not leaving his bedroom. Don't those six or so pages tell his story much better than this large graphic novel? WHat we get from the rest, though buoyed by his excellent cartooning, only takes away from that concision: do you care that Seth bullies Joe? I sure don't. Still, it's a pleasure to read in the hands of this virtuoso—you just don't want to *shake* those hands.

Really wish I liked this more.

August 7, 2007
By R. Bullock (*Philadelphia, PA*)

The good thing about "Spent" is that the graphic art is wonderful. The lines are nice and crisp, and Joe Matt clearly is a talented artist.

The bad thing is that—whether intentional or not—the protagonist Joe that he presents to us in "Spent" is such a dreary, pathetic drag. He is addicted to dubbing his favorite moments from porno films onto blank tapes (he's got hundreds upon hundreds of hours of tape as a result), addicted to saving money and watching it accrue interest yearly (he therefore becomes a somewhat reclusive miser, deathly afraid of spending any money despite the fact that he's got tons in the bank). He will spend money on long-sought-after collector's items that his friends want, if only to sell it back to them for several times what he paid. He spends too much time brooding over his torturous childhood (and it apparently wasn't that bad—simply your same-old-routine of young boy is nerdy and watches "contraband" porn and wishes girls liked him and boys didn't tease him so much).

I can spot the protagonist's self-deprecation in "Spent," and for the most part, I can appreciate that it has its place there. Certainly people like him thrive on such behavior. That's fine. I can understand that. But the lead here is such a unlikable guy, I found myself hoping it would pleasepleaseplease get better, or end more quickly than it did.

I am also willing to concede that, as a woman who was relatively popular in school, I simply may not be able to relate. For that reason (and because of the nice artwork), "Spent" gets three stars from me.

★ ★ ★ ★ ★
GREAT
November 26, 2007
by Bobby N. (*Melbourne, Australia*)

This book put a smile on my face. The voyeur in me couldn't put it down until I turned the last of its 120 pages. It's a breeze to read, and funny to boot.

I think its one of the best things I've read this year. It's just very entertaining & enjoyable. If summed up, the book shows little more than Joe talking to himself in his 1-bedroom dwelling, watching porn, and a few (real-world) conversations with his 2 cartooning friends Seth & Chester Brown.

But the WAY it's done is something else!

If you like R.Crumb's self-loathing comics, then I daresay you'll get a kick out of this book. I sure did. Joe's first collection of "Peepshow" (Called "The Poor Bastard") collects his life with his ex-girlfriend, and as such shows a more gregarious lifestyle (Well... as gregarious as Joe can get). This collection (Spent), shows his life "after'"the relationship is over. He's alone, and aside from brief chats with a friend or two, is largely introspective and contemplative.

Joe's art & writing are refreshingly clean & simple. Though blunt & honest, Joe doesn't just point at the world and say "You are to blame!" - (far from it) - In fact he's constantly pointing the finger at himself. He recognizes that he's the reason for his lot in life, but knows himself enough to accept it. You get the feeling that Joe is his own 'shrink', and getting it out on paper helps him makes sense of it all. (Though publishing it for the world to see took some balls!)

'Spent' really is like reading someone's diary. A beautifully drawn and funny diary. For the price, you really are getting a lot in a hard-bound and well made comicbook. I can't recommend it enough.

★ ★ ☆ ☆ ☆

Lack of Strong Narrative Is What Disappoints...Joe Matt Remains the Same!

December 5, 2007
by otternymph (*Sunnyside, Queens, NY*)

In a weird way, what disappointed me about Joe Matt was not his baldly honest and funny objectification of women and "Orientals" (me being both) but the black hole *Spent* was.

As other reviewers have smartly put it, this book was a let-down because there was no revelation, action or change in Joe Matt. But let's face it; we don't read Joe Matt hoping for him to emerge as some uber-man, we read him to relate, to feel good about our own pathetic moments, and even point our fingers. *Peepshow* and *Poor Bastard* were essentially the same story as *Spent*, but seemed as if "more happened" because they generally spanned over a greater period of time. Even if the character of Joe Matt didn't change from the beginning to the end of the book, we (or I!) did. There was a sense of satisfaction after reading each previous book because there was a narrative arc completed.

And that's the problem with *Spent*. A bunch of things happen: Joe tapes porn, Joe haggles a book with Seth, Joe gets upset about someone moving his toothbrush, but there's no cohesion. Finishing *Spent*, I'd neither learned or unlearned anything about Joe. This book could have simply not existed.

Which is too bad, because as laughably despicable a character Joe Matt is, there was such fun in reading him. Joe Matt the author is clearly a smart storyteller and brilliant artist, but surely he could have said more in this book. However, I definitely do not care to meet him in person! His MySpace page, as someone else pointed out, lacks the charming filter his artwork provides. To see him in life makes it all too real—his fetishes are no joke. As much as I chuckled over his episode with his Asian roommate, it's not as funny to see his half-dressed Asian female fans prancing about. They willfully play right into his desires, which is just wrong on too many levels.

I highly recommend *Peepshow, Poor Bastard* and *Fair Weather* instead, in that order. Happy reading!

★ ☆ ☆ ☆ ☆

Joe Matt: Please Stop Making Comics

September 20, 2007
By Velma JInky "Velma" (*California*)

Joe Matt has one great work under his belt, that being his first book, *Peepshow*. Each page was an experiment with how to most efficiently or interestingly use one page to tell a story. None of his following efforts have measured up. What's amazing is that it takes him two years to produce a new comic and the last few issues have just involved him pitying himself, walking around his apartment or jerking off. This is the product of a man who's best work is long behind him. *Spent* is a completely accurate description of Joe Matt. ★

C. Spinoza's *Pacho Clokey*

Nate Gruenwald

Nate Gruenwald prefers to remain anonymous.
C Spinoza's *Pacho Clokey* [©2000 Pachoclo Inc.]

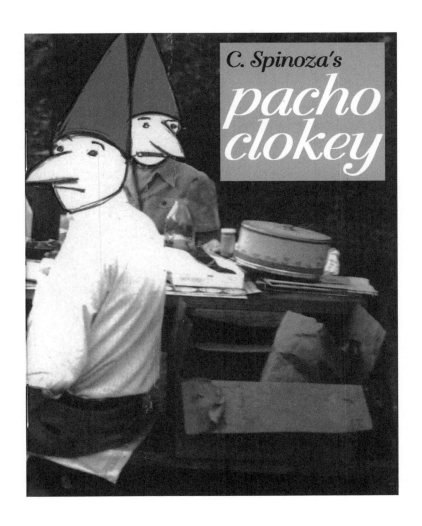

C. Spinoza's

pacho clokey

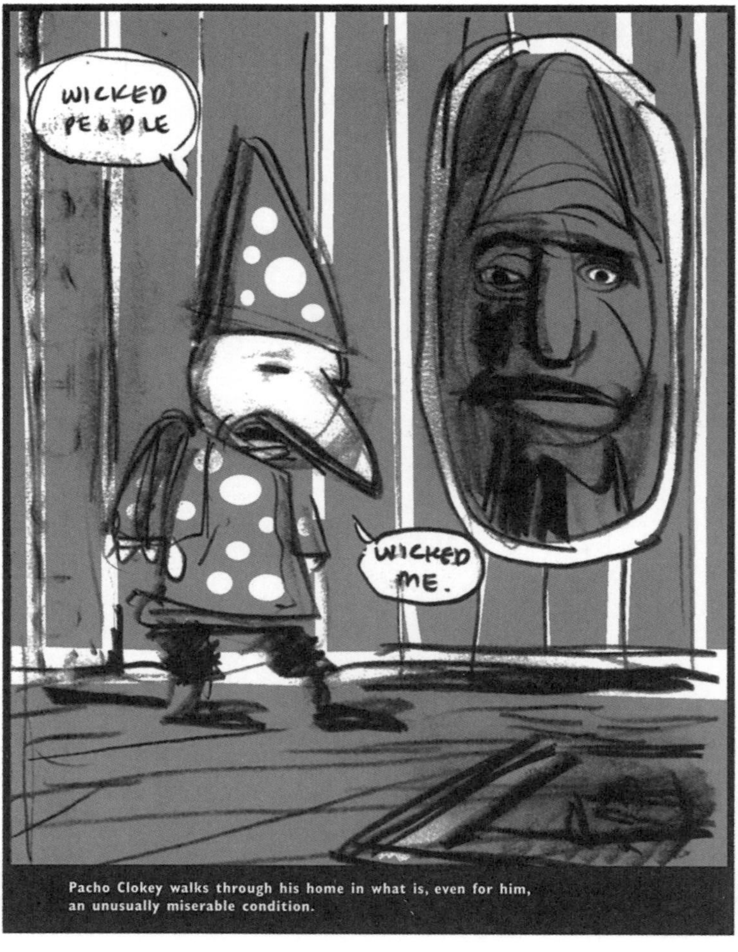
WICKED PEOPLE
WICKED ME.

Pacho Clokey walks through his home in what is, even for him, an unusually miserable condition.

His disturbed state has apparently caused him to wander up to a hilltop to clarify things. (the text here is cryptic and must be considered a temporary slug for something more comprehensive)

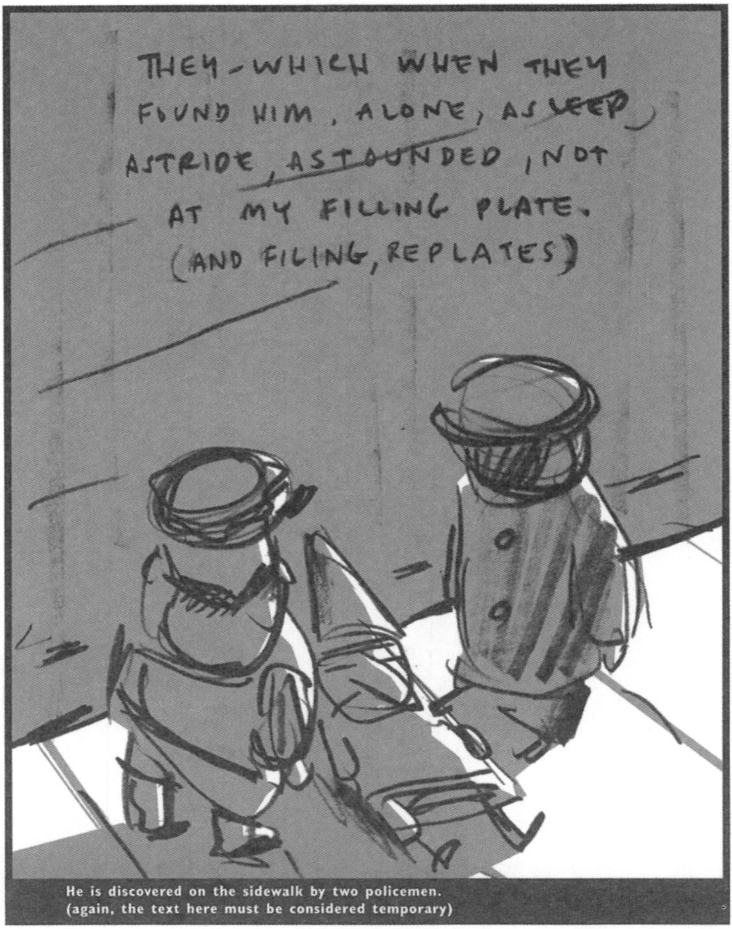
THEY-WHICH WHEN THEY
FOUND HIM, ALONE, AS LEEP,
ASTRIDE, ASTOUNDED, NOT
AT MY FILLING PLATE.
(AND FILING, REPLATES)

He is discovered on the sidewalk by two policemen.
(again, the text here must be considered temporary)

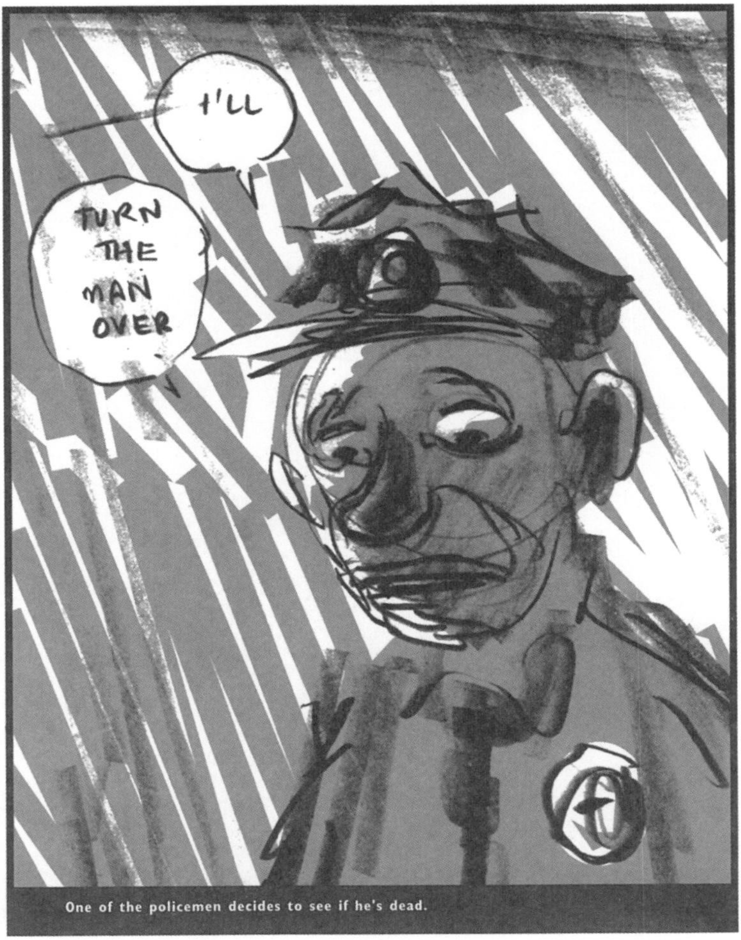
I'LL
TURN THE MAN OVER
One of the policemen decides to see if he's dead.

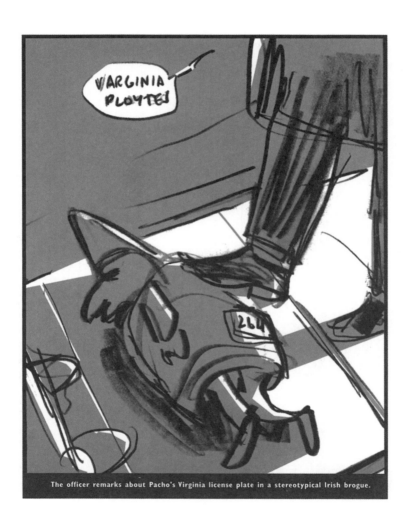

The officer remarks about Pacho's Virginia license plate in a stereotypical Irish brogue.

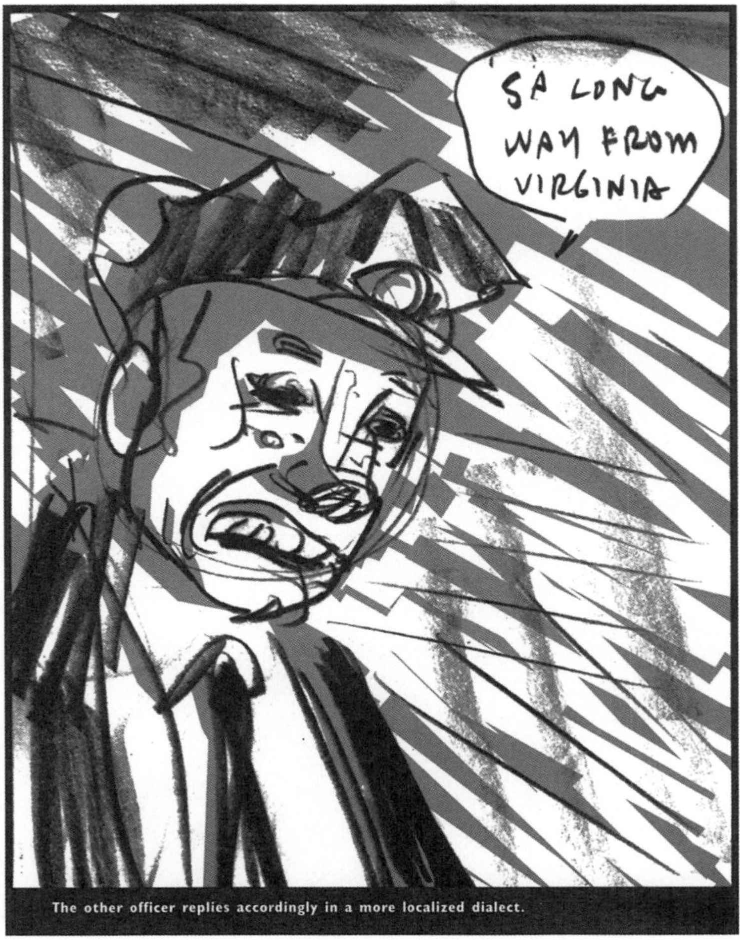
SA LONG WAY FROM VIRGINIA

The other officer replies accordingly in a more localized dialect.

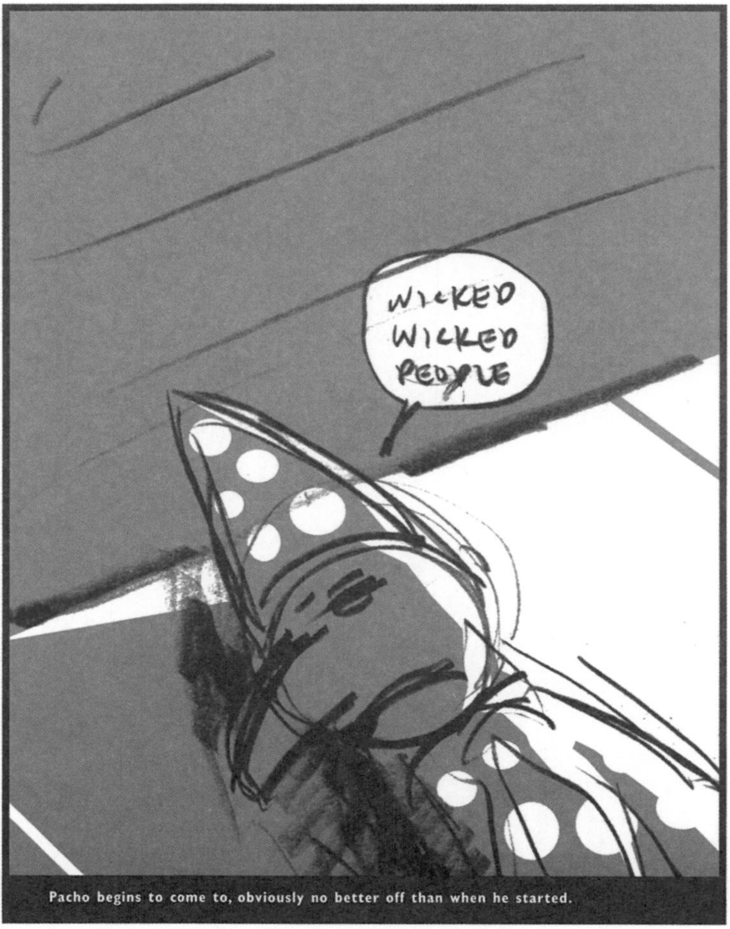
WICKED
WICKED
PEOPLE
Pacho begins to come to, obviously no better off than when he started.

This is yet another example of the acclaimed "circular storytelling" for which Mr. Spinoza was so well known.

The picture in the corner seems to suggest that Pacho's best days are behind him. Could this be a rumination on the author's own life?

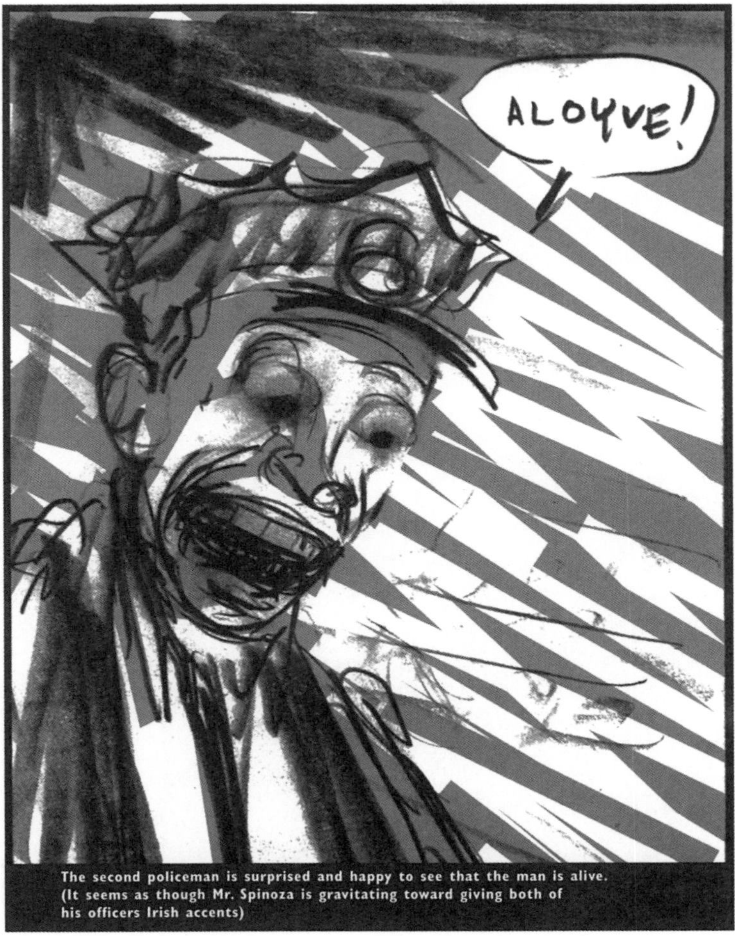
ALOYVE!

The second policeman is surprised and happy to see that the man is alive. (It seems as though Mr. Spinoza is gravitating toward giving both of his officers Irish accents)

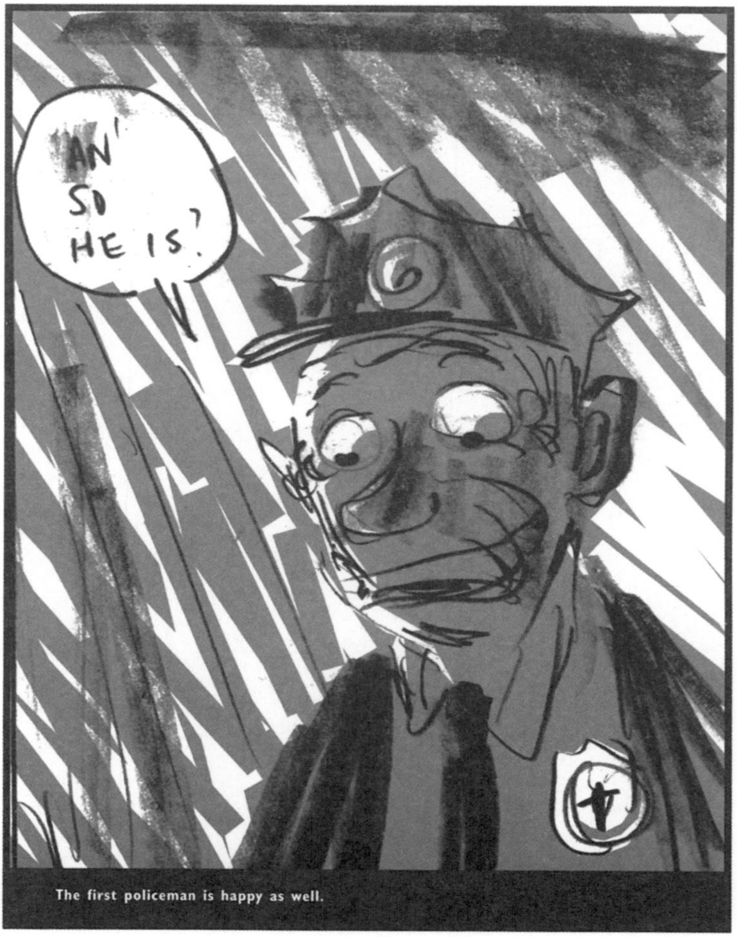
AN' SO HE IS'
The first policeman is happy as well.

He tries to be of some assistance.

Pacho becomes aware of the inevitable.
This kind of melancholic deduction is barely hinted at in the author's published work.

After seeing the identical outcome of every episode for 39 years, we know what will happen as well, but for Pacho himself to know, this is a revelation!

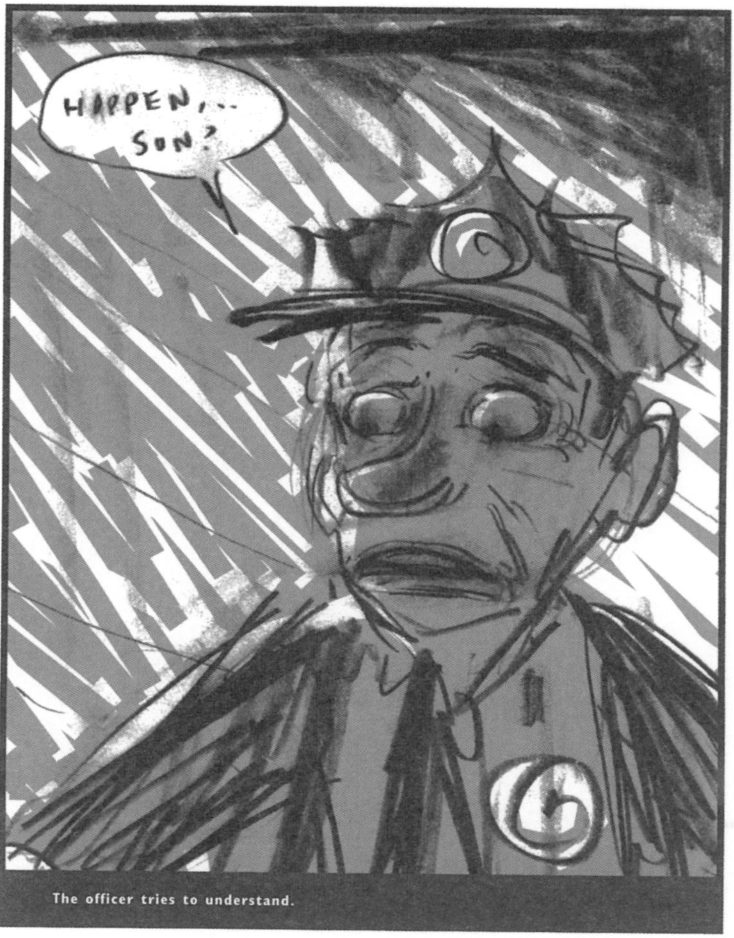
HAPPEN, ...
SON?
The officer tries to understand.

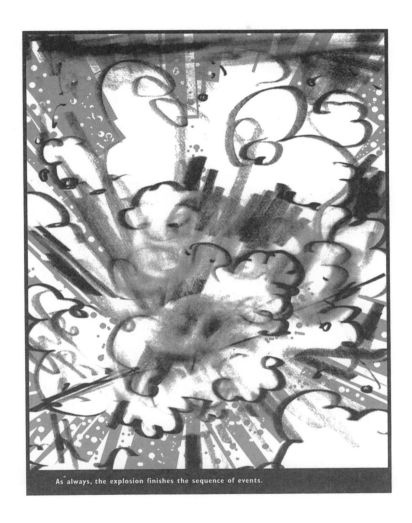

As always, the explosion finishes the sequence of events.

Interviews

David Hajdu

Persian Miniatures

The eons-old culture of the place we now call Iran first inspired comic-book artists as early as 1949, when the late Disney studio veteran Carl Barks wrote and illustrated a twenty-four-page adventure fantasy titled "In Ancient Persia" for Dell Comics. Lightly peppered with Middle Eastern arcana, the story makes reference to the historical cities of Kish and Susa, and it depicts the fictional Ali Cad scurrying to find the capital of Persia-Persepolis, which he recalls as a "roaring boomtown." Three time-honored cartoon gimmicks inform the narrative: a mad scientist, uncanny resemblances, and talking fowl. Ali Cad just so happens to be a double for the book's protagonist, Donald Duck, who is mistaken for the wholly caddish Ali and trapped (along with the former's nephews, Huey, Dewey, and Louie) in a nominal Persia that functions mainly as a source of whimsically grotesque exotica.

Comic books were not the place to look for more enlightened views of Iran, past or present, until recent years. In the late 1990s, Marjane Satrapi, an expatriate Iranian

---

"Persian Miniatures" first appeared in the Oct./Nov. 2004 issue of *Bookforum*.
[©2004 David Hajdu & *Bookforum*]

woman living in Paris, began writing and drawing what would become a series of quirky, veracious memoirs in comic-book form. Collectively titled *Persepolis*, they may well represent the first notable use of the word in comics outside the context of Donald Duck. While the books are named for a city of the first millennium BC, they are utterly contemporary and intimate accounts of Satrapi's life in and out of Iran. The first, published in America in April 2003, details her childhood in Tehran in the years prior to, during, and after the Islamic Revolution of 1979. The second, issued here in August, 2004, follows the author to school in Vienna, where she suffers a traumatic indoctrination into Western society and young adulthood, and then back home to Tehran, where she struggles to find her place in both a stultifying, bifurcated society and a doomed marriage of convenience.

Employing a pop medium associated with America to portray a complex, ancient culture of the Middle East, Satrapi has made her country—at least her loving view of it as a land of noble traditions and human passions misrepresented by fundamentalist extremism—appealing to Western eyes. She has upended the worst American stereotypes of Iranians as humorless jihadists on the axis of evil, putting a new face on her homeland: namely, Satrapi's doodle-like caricature of herself. With thick curlicues of black hair and a capital L of a nose (a couple of ovals with adroitly placed dots inside), the cartoon girl in the first *Persepolis* could have been an Iranian exchange student in Charlie Brown's class. *Persepolis* has now appeared in a dozen or so European countries in addition to the United States, and the two volumes have found a welcoming readership, particularly among those around college age who take their generation's wealth of ambitious comics and graphic novels as seriously as their parents took classic-rock albums. (None of Satrapi's work is available in her native Iran, where comics have been banned by religious authorities who view them as decadent.)

Much as *Persepolis* defies widespread preconceptions of its subject matter, it also challenges long-held prejudices against its medium. The books are not juvenile, but sophisticated, even in the first volume's referential use of its child narrator's often naïve point of view; they are not hyperactive and do not glory in violence, but progress at the mercurial pace of memory and depict the horrors of life under the Shah and the Islamic Revolution as a way of protesting them; they are not male-oriented, but absorbed with matters of womanhood (particularly the sexual inequity of Islamic fundamentalism); and they are not overblown or self-consciously arty, but simple, elegiac, artfully unaffected. At the same time, they are proudly comics and good at the things comics do best: The drawings have punch and clarity (the Guardians of the Revolution, who nab the young Satrapi for wearing a denim jacket and Nikes, look like ghouls; the shrouded school girls are interchangeable), and the story takes fanciful flights (at the start of the revolution, when Satrapi suddenly feels groundless, we see her

float into outer space; God visits Satrapi from time to time to have a glass of milk or talk about the weather).

Satrapi was promptly acclaimed in Europe, where arts institutions carry on a vaguely Marxist tradition of advancing parity between the high and the low. She won Spain's Fernando Buesa Blanco Prize for a literary work furthering peace, as well as most of the important honors for comics art in Europe, and pages from her books have been exhibited at museums and galleries in Paris, Berlin, and Lucerne. She has lectured on her work at the Royal Academy of Fine Arts in Naples and spoken at the elite Tschann Libraire in Paris. In the United States, it has been much the same; the first *Persepolis* book was praised in the book-review pages and made several best-seller and best-of-the-year lists. Soon after its publication, Satrapi began receiving commissions from the same sort of venues, including one for a *Times* Op-Ed-page comic about the 2003 Nobel Peace Prize, which had been awarded to the rights activist Shirin Ebadi, a fellow Iranian woman for whom Satrapi had served as translator on the day the prize was announced.

The *Persepolis* books entwine the stories of Satrapi's first twenty-five years and her country's contemporaneous history. The first words above the first book's first drawing— one of the author at age ten, a year after the Islamic Revolution—are "This is me..." But the art depicts what fundamentalism had brought upon her: Posing dutifully for a class photo, she is sitting with her arms folded, wearing the mandatory black veil and a plain, long-sleeved, button-down dress; in the second panel we see four of her classmates, all positioned and attired identically. This is my country, Satrapi tells us in pictures with as much value as words. Near the end of the first book, as Satrapi prepares to leave Iran for the journey to Europe and womanhood that makes up *Persepolis 2*, her father implores her, "Don't forget who you are and where you come from." Her books are proof that she listened.

The young Marjane Satrapi was a bright and troublesome girl, having been educated during the last years of the Shah's reign in relatively liberal, bilingual (French-Persian), secular schools. As she depicts herself in the first *Persepolis*, she was something of an

Iranian Pippi Longstocking, a free spirit who challenged authority in all forms that affected youthful life, be they parental, academic, religious, societal, or governmental. Initially sympathetic to the "cultural revolution" against the Shah, she defied her parents' orders to stay safely clear of public protests and joined a demonstration with her maid, only to be caught and roundly punished by her mother. After the fundamentalists imposed rigid new standards for dress and conduct (public and private), the adolescent Satrapi dared to ignore them, and (a) went out in public alone, (b) to buy bootleg cassettes of Kim Wilde and Camel, (c) wearing Nikes and a jean jacket adorned with a Michael Jackson button. (Nabbed for the last transgression, Satrapi was taken off the street and interrogated, although she escaped punishment by claiming that she wore the shoes for school sports and that Michael Jackson was really Malcolm X.) Defiant beyond recklessness, she was expelled from one school for striking the principal in a fight over a forbidden bracelet, then dared to question her subsequent overseers on matters of political dogma. Her parents, seeking to protect her from punishment worse than expulsion, sent her to school in Austria. She was fourteen.

Thus begins *Persepolis 2*, wherein Iran starts becoming a spectral presence in Satrapi's life. Seduced by Western pop culture and its romantic idealization of loners, outlaws, and the like, Satrapi goes through a series of phases much less common in Iranian culture than they are in the average American high school or college. She discovers sex and suffers betrayal; she makes gay friends; she takes up smoking and drinking; she does drugs and even deals a bit for a time; she becomes a punk...Exhausted by it all, Satrapi returns to Iran four years later, studies art, and, desperate for male companionship, submits to a marriage that she regrets before the end of her wedding night.

"The books are about me, and they are about my country, but we both change in the books, and I'm still changing—look, now I'm married again, and I'm happy, and I was so miserable before," Satrapi explains, relaxing in the front room of the airy, third-floor apartment in Paris's Marais district where she and her second husband, Mattias Ripa, a Swedish émigré, have lived for four years. Relaxing is a relative notion to Satrapi; she had worked all day on a Sunday, as she does nearly every day and most evenings, because she revels in it.

"It's not that I think working is the best thing in the world—I'm really passionate about what I do," she says. "If I cannot do it, I would die by my own hand. I'm very lucky that my husband understands." (Satrapi, in turn, has no interest in what he does for a living—nor the least knowledge of it. "Nobody wants to believe me, but I don't know," she says with a wink of a smile. "I prefer not to know. My first husband and I knew everything about each other, and we did everything together, and it was awful. This way, I can imagine, 'I wonder what he's doing,' and I think that's better.")

She teeters on the edge of the seat cushion of a brown leather armchair, seemingly prepared to lunge across the coffee table if need be. She smokes as she talks—and smokes as she snacks on sweet pistachios that her mother shipped from Iran—occasionally using one cigarette to light the next. "The point of the books is not just to say, 'Oh, look at me—I was cute, and I had black hair, and my parents, they were nice.' The point of the books is to show what a person is really like who comes from my country, because nobody outside of my country knows that there are normal people in Iran. I shit and fart, and I laugh and I make love.

"I don't really care what people think of me," Satrapi, now thirty-four, says. "But I care what they think of my people. I love my people, even though the ones in power right now are idiots."

Her parents, Taji and Ebi Satrapi, prosperous social idealists who deplored the oppression of the Islamic revolution but came to accommodate it, take pride in having instilled in their only child a devotion to independence that they have compromised in their own lives by remaining in Iran. "The most important thing for us was definitely independence," her mother says, responding to questions relayed and translated by her daughter. "We always wanted her to grow up as an independent woman with all that this may mean. In a country like Iran, with its patriarchal culture, a woman with an economical independence may also often be a happier person than a woman who is financially dependent on her husband.

"I remember her always saying, 'If I don't try to do it, how would I know if I can do it or not?' The word fear is something she doesn't know the meaning of."

Like her work, Satrapi's apartment is a mosaic of Middle Eastern and Western, high and low—a willful testament to cultural and aesthetic heterogeneity. Hanging from one wall are a small handwoven rug, a diorama of figures from Persian mythology, and a painting of one of her great-aunts—a Jean Harlow look-alike, posing in the nude; on another wall are a couple of vintage American advertisements with the slogans "The Man for Me is a Pipe-Smoking Man" and "I'm your best friend. I'm your Lucky Strike." On a third wall is a poster of one of Roy Lichtenstein's comics-inspired paintings, and on another is an array of palm-size stones onto which photographs of Satrapi's parents have been glued, gifts to the daughter in Paris from her mother's maid. An appetite for kitsch appears to run in the extended family.

Despite having read no superhero comics in her youth—and few other comics besides a Soviet-published title, *Dialectical Materialism*—Satrapi has been inclined to hero worship, as well as grand ambition, from an early age. Her book portrays each of her parents much as she sees herself today, as a flawed champion of a virtuous minority position. Her parents once fought to preserve their values of Marxist secularism; Satrapi, through her books, seeks to challenge the Western caricature of Iranians as malevolent zealots. "I always thought, I will grow up and I will fight for the freedom of the people—I will be like Che Guevara!" Satrapi says. "The fight that I'm making now is to show the people in other places of the world that a person in Iran can be very much more like them than they think."

The very fact that an Iranian female has written a graphic novel shatters perceptions, Satrapi has found. "A lot of people can't believe that a woman from my country could do such a thing—they think we're all idiots or maniacs and don't know about anything except how to hide behind a veil," she says.

The deftness with which she has lifted that veil to reveal herself, as well as Iranian life as she has seen and felt it, distinguishes Satrapi from the many artists of her generation who have done intimate memoirs in cartoon form. According to the comics historian

Trina Robbins, author of *The Great Women Cartoonists* and other books, "What most women, like most guys in the independent comics field, do is very boring, because an awful lot of the indie cartoonists, unfortunately, really have very boring lives, and they make these really boring real-time comics that say, 'Oh, I hang out at the coffee shop, and then I go to my job at the used record store…' Whereas the story that Marjane has to tell is so incredible and so powerful, and she tells it magnificently. It's a privilege to hear her story, and not another one about 'I hate myself because my thighs are fat and my boyfriend left me.'"

After her failed first marriage, Marjane Satrapi left Iran for the last time (so far) to study illustration at the Strasburg School of Decorative Arts. Following graduation, at age twenty-four, she moved to Paris with aspirations of writing and drawing children's books. Having grown up without much exposure to comics, she had not given them much thought one way or another. "I started reading comics late, really," she recalls.

In that, she has much in common with those around college age who have made *Persepolis* and other graphic novels a popular phenomenon, embracing a form many of them likely see as something new and their own. They are, on the whole, the first young adults since the invention of the comic book to have grown up without much connection to traditional comics; in essence, today's graphic-novel audience is the postcomics generation. Because of a radical change during the '70s in the way comic books were distributed and sold and, commensurately, how they were created and read—comics largely disappeared from magazine racks and re-emerged in hobby shops, where they mutated into specialty items for obsessives engaged in collecting and trading them (ideally, wrapped and unread). Publishers facilitated this shift into "direct sales," which liberated them from magazine distributors' irksome policy of returning unsold titles for credit. Although many kids have continued to buy comics (and sometimes read them), absorption with comic books has not been a common rite of American childhood for decades. Video games, being more kinetic as well as more suspect in the eyes of adults, have taken comics' place. Accordingly, when readers in their twenties today pick up graphic novels, they are inclined to do so without the prejudice of entrenched childhood associations.

When Satrapi first tried to create books for children, she failed magnificently; she wrote and illustrated fourteen titles for young readers and received 187 letters from publishers rejecting them all, she says. Satrapi remained blithely unimpeded. "She always had this self-belief," says her Swedish husband. "She was famous when I met her. Nobody knew it, of course." (Since the success of *Persepolis*, Satrapi has published four children's books in France, most of them revisions of her once unaccepted ones.)

Meanwhile, at her shared studio, five French artists, all about her age, were thriving in comics. Thanks to a friend of one of her friends, Satrapi had landed in L'Atelier des Vosges, an exquisitely decrepit space on the perimeter of the Place des Vosges that French comics enthusiasts regarded as the Parisian Bloomsbury of the art form. "It was an accident that I was lucky enough to be in the same studio with the best comics artists in France," Satrapi explains, sitting at her drawing board in the atelier late on a weekday morning. "The miracle of the thing was not that these people decided that they were going to make a movement—it happened that all of us were in the same studio, all of us around thirty years old, and I end up there. We were all talking all the time," Satrapi says, miming chatter and rolling her eyes. "I was telling my friends there about my life in Iran and the Islamic Revolution. They didn't know anything about my culture, and I didn't know anything about comics before I met them. One of them, and then two of them, then three of them, said to me, 'Come on, come on, come on—you should do a comic out of that.'"

L'Atelier des Vosges was and is a somewhat fluid assemblage of French comics artists who share working quarters, provide mutual stimulation and support, and publish themselves in a cooperative called L'Association, through which the *Persepolis* books originally appeared. Its membership has included some of the most esteemed names in European comics circles, including David B., Christophe Blain, Émile Bravo, and Joann Sfar. "We came, most of us, from fine art, from modern art, and we were trying to do comics," explains Sfar, whose children's book, *The Little Vampire Goes to School*, was a best seller in the United States. "We were learning our job together—there was no master and pupil. We are still learning, and we try to play together. Sometimes, we have two people draw the same story at the same time, to see the difference. We play and experiment and, most of all, please ourselves. But Marjane thought comic books were vulgar and something for kids. She was not interested until she realized, 'Okay, it's not a genre, it's a medium.'"

As Satrapi recalls, "Suddenly I started doing it, and they helped me a lot. I didn't know the language of comics. I had the drawings follow from right to left, like in my mother language. They all gave me advice. Émile Bravo told me, 'When you are drawing, be like a lizard—be perfectly still, but aware of everything around you. Don't waste your energy with a lot of movement while you're working. Be like a lizard.' There were things that I didn't know how to draw. Christophe said to me, 'A hand is like this…'"

Satrapi roughs out a one-page opinion comic about the Iraq war, commissioned by the Italian newspaper *Il Manifesto*. She has just begun and is testing designs for a panel depicting a grid of invading aircraft. Dispensing with drawing-class convention, she uses a marker rather than pencil; the ink, being less forgiving, "forces me to concentrate," she says. "Otherwise I would sit here all day and draw shit." At the same time, she employs a counterbalancing ritual to prevent her work from becoming overly self-conscious: She draws on the most inexpensive paper she can find. "If I use very good paper, I feel like I have to make a masterpiece," she says, "and the best way to make shit is to feel like you have to make a masterpiece. I feel now like the world is waiting for a masterpiece every time I put a brush in my hand, and that is a bad thing. Cartoonists shouldn't have to be too good.

"I never thought that I was good and that I had talent—I still don't," Satrapi says as she draws. "My understanding of anatomy has always been zero, because in the anatomy class I took in Iran, the woman was fully clothed. I didn't even know how an arm bends. I'm not really a very good drawer—I'm a good budgeter. I do the best with what I have."

Satrapi finishes her page, looks it over, shrugs her shoulders, and reaches for a cigarette. "The technical quality is not the thing that matters," she says, darting her eyes at the page on the table. "Cinema is reality, but reality is obvious. Nothing is more truthful than a drawing, because it's an interpretation.

"I like black and white better than anything, because there's no bluff in black and white. To me, color is extra information, and when you add color, whether or not the drawing is naïve, it makes something real about it. I write a lot about the Middle East, so I write about violence. Violence today has become something so normal, so banal— that is to say, everybody thinks it's normal. But it's not normal. To draw it and put in color—the color of the flesh and the red of the blood, and so forth reduces it by making it realistic. Black and white makes it abstract and more meaningful." Satrapi picks up the page she has finished and looks again at the maze of jet fighters she has drawn. She turns it upside down and gently pounds her fist on the back of the paper.

It is hardly a bad reflection on comic books that it took decades for the medium to be accepted as suitable for adults; to the contrary, it seems a testament to comics' resilience and adaptability. About a quarter of a century ago, the pioneering American artist and writer Will Eisner published one of the first book-length comics drawn from personal experience: *A Contract With God and Other Tenement Stories*, a collection of four loosely related stories about tenement life in the Bronx of the Depression years, inspired by Eisner's childhood. While American precedents for adult oriented, long-form comics date back to the era of *God's Man*, the wordless "novel in woodcuts" that artist Lynd Ward rendered in 1929 (antecedents for which can be traced all the way to hieroglyphics, if you want to get technical about it), *A Contract With God* prompted a generation of artists and writers to experiment with long-form comics, because the idea was good enough for the revered Will Eisner. "He was the most credible and loudest evangelist in the early years," recalls Paul Levitz, the president of DC Comics, who was a twenty-two-year-old comics writer and editor when *A Contract With God* was published. "Will was the guy who was an established figure, who stood up and said, 'This is the way of the future—these things are going to be for adults, and they are going to tell stories of intellectual worth.'"

Eisner's approach to making comics for grown-ups was vigorously transformative. "I believed that the medium had a capacity to go beyond the joke-book usage," Eisner has said. Unremitting in their determination to prove the point, his books have been serious above all—virtually purged of humor, in fact.

Satrapi and many of her peers, like the underground artists before them, see seriousness of purpose and lightness of execution as mutually compatible—indeed, the tension between the two, pulled to extremes, is the essence of their aesthetic. Robert Crumb's early influences included Little Lulu comics and talking-animal cartoons, and the ghosts of nursery school in his artwork make his darkly comic tales of drug trips and sadomasochism all the more disturbing. Art Spiegelman, much the same, extricates the Holocaust from the realm of abstract evil, thereby magnifying its horror, by rendering the Nazis and Jews as accessible cartoon cats and mice. Satrapi takes on adult subjects (Islamic fundamentalism) in sophisticated ways (interlacing her narrative with Iranian history, demonizing no one), while also exploiting the expectation of a good time integral to what used to be called "the funnies." (Her cartoon self trades jibes with God, whom she depicts as a look-alike for Karl Marx, but with curlier hair.)

When Satrapi looks up from her drawing table, she sees a found-object collage of novelty items: a poster of Bruce Lee, an assortment of children's stickers from a flea market, an "A for Anarchy" logo made out of a varnished sausage, a Russian circus poster depicting performers engaged in inexplicable feats. "What is he doing?" she asks, pointing to a contorted painted figure in something like a Gypsy space costume. "Or these people over here—you don't know really what is happening, either. If they do what they're doing, they are going to die, they are going to be like hamburgers. It's not possible. The artist took people for idiots. I think this is very, very funny." A short while later, Satrapi picks up a cell phone from her drawing table and starts carrying on a terse business conversation, during which a spray of water shoots onto my shirt from the phone, which I realize is a gag water toy. Satrapi roars.

Several days a week, Satrapi likes to sit in a sidewalk café around the corner from her studio and watch for amusing passersby. "This is the best place in Paris, because you can sit here and watch all the fancy people as they walk across the street," she says, squirming to get comfortable on the tiny iron seat. "You can tell this is becoming a fancy area, because the food shops are closing, and they are being replaced by clothing shops, because the rich people, they don't need to eat. The rich people, they eat air, and they shit bubbles. The rich people, all they need are make-up and clothes and shoes.

"I have to move, because it's become too fancy," Satrapi says. "Sometimes, I need to go out and buy something other than shoes."

Where would she go? No further than a "not so good" neighborhood in Paris, she says. Despite her fascination with American pop culture, as an artist, Satrapi feels bound to live in France. (Crumb has been living in Sauve, a medieval village in the south of France, for years, and his American friend and fellow comics artist Peter Poplaski is a neighbor there.)

"In France, comics are taken seriously, yes—but, at the same time, they are not such a big deal," Satrapi says. "Here, as a comics artist, you have respect, but at the same time, you are allowed to do some foolish stuff—they will excuse you.

"I know that I'm a very serious person, but I don't want to be thought of as a serious person. The fact of not being taken for serious, for me, gives me freedom. That's the only thing that I care about—being free, acting free, thinking free," she says as she snuffs out her cigarette. "That is the hardest thing and the most important thing." ★

Darrell Epp

"It Keeps Ending Up Looking Like It Was Drawn By Me": An Interview with Chester Brown

"Chet's skills as a cartoonist, his drawing ability, they're unparalleled, you know?"
—*Joe Matt*

Chester Brown started creating comic strips over 25 years ago, and since then has built up a body of work featuring a wide variety of subject matter—horror, comedy, non-fiction, even adaptations of the Gospels—as well as beautiful artwork. His first major project, collected as the book *Ed The Happy Clown* in 1992, told the story of a luckless clown who awakens to find that the head of a miniature version of Ronald Reagan from a parallel dimension has affixed itself to the head of Ed's penis. Ed goes on to encounter deadly pygmies, pygmy-hunters, vampires, vampire-hunters, zombies, werewolves, and mad scientists before solving his penis problem—sort of. Brown's next two books told autobiographical stories set in Chester's awkward adolescence. *The*

Darrell Epp's interview with Chester Brown first appeared April 22, 2002 on the website *The Two-Handed Man*. ©2002 Darrell Epp]

Playboy was published in 1992, and *I Never Liked You* was published in 1994. These two books are two of the finest graphic novels you could hope to find, due in part to the sparseness of the drawings and page compositions. One distinctive thing about Brown's drawings in these books is the lightness of his linework, which smartly complements the material. One gets the impression, viewing Brown's memories of some of his most awkward and confusing moments, of someone pressing lightly on a raw nerve or a loose tooth, and this idea is reinforced by a line that's spare and delicate, controlled with a surgical precision and deliberation. The fact that many professional cartoonists often seem unable to resist the temptation to over-render their drawings makes the effect Brown achieves in these books even more impressive. *The Little Man*, a collection of short strips spanning two decades, was published in 1998. Besides the entertainment value of the strips themselves, many of which are hilarious, what makes the book such a treat is watching Brown's skills as an artist improve from the earliest strips to the most-recent ones.

I interviewed Brown at his home on January 29, 2002, when he had completed the first six chapters of his biography of *Louis Riel*. For the benefit of any non-Canadians reading this, or Canadians who skipped history class to play *Space Invaders*, Louis Riel was a Metis (half-French, half-Native Canadian) leader who was instrumental in the negotiations that led to Manitoba becoming a province of Canada in 1870 (he even gave the province its name: Manitoba is the Cree word for 'The god that speaks'). Yet this man who was a Father of Canadian Confederation was executed for treason against Canada in 1885. In response to the great suffering the Metis Nation and the Plains Indians had endured under English Canadian rule, Riel led an armed uprising against English Canada. Complicated by Riel's messianic religious visions, hopelessly outgunned and outmanned, the Metis Rebellion was quickly put down, but the issues he fought for, the conflicts his name symbolizes, still haunt Canada today.

Two-Handed Man When did you first start thinking about doing a book about Louis Riel? And, what was it about him that appealed to you?

Chester Brown Well, any time I read a book, a history book or whatever, I'm kind of half-thinking about how it would read as a comic, so I was thinking the same thing when I was reading Maggie Siggins' book about Riel (*Riel: A Life Of Revolution*). Her biography was the first book I read about Riel, and the idea just kind of stuck in my mind after I finished it.

And what appealed to me about him? His story had a whole lot of interesting elements, the whole question of native rights, the question of whether he was crazy or not, all that stuff, and the whole religious part…there was a convergence of several different interests of mine.

THM I think it's the Siggins book that mentions the fact that in his early teens Riel spent some time at the Grey Nuns' Residence in Chateauguay Quebec, and of course you were living in Chateauguay when you were that age as well.

BROWN Yeah, yeah. I must've seen that when I first read Siggins' book but I forgot about it until I re-read it for the purpose of doing the comic book. It's my only personal connection to Riel.

THM It made me wonder if you had heard about him growing up at all, and since you've lived in both English Canada and French Canada, if you could talk about any difference in the way Riel is perceived in the two cultures.

BROWN Well, even though I grew up in Quebec, I don't feel like I lived in French Canada. There was an Anglophone community and a francophone community, and at that time—this would be the '60s and the '70s—the anglophone community around Montreal was very strong. I didn't speak French, and when I encountered French people, they spoke English. And I certainly never talked to them about Riel. I wasn't interested in him at the time. So I can't really say I have a take on the francophone perception of Riel.

THM So you were part of the anglophone migration out of Quebec that took place in the late '70s when Rene Levesque's separatist Parti Quebecois came to power?

BROWN Yeah, I guess the PQ got in around 1976, if my memory's right. My father stuck around to the point where both his sons had graduated from high school, and then he moved out. That was around the time I'd be moving out the house anyway, so that's what I did, I moved to Toronto.

THM I'm interested in the motivation behind the project. Was it mainly a chance to talk about Riel and the issues surrounding him, or were you more attracted to the personal challenge of doing a kind of project you hadn't done before, adapting a series of actual events into comics? Since you aren't using any sources that are new—

BROWN I know what you mean. Not too long before doing Riel, I had done this strip called "My Mom Was A Schizophrenic" and that had mostly involved taking all this material that I had read in various books and whatnot and condensing it into a short space—I think that strip is six pages long. And I had really enjoyed that. That was the most fun I'd had doing a comic book for quite a while, so I kind of wanted to do something like that again, where I had to do a bunch of research, and condense it all into a short amount of space, and doing a historical comic book made sense because the problem with the schizophrenia strip was that it didn't really have a story-line. And, you know, story-lines are good in comics, especially if they're longer strips. And history provides you with a story, the story of a person's life, or the story of whatever historical line you're following. So it made sense to do something historical, and I was thinking in those terms, probably even when I picked up the Siggins biography, that I might want to do a historical comic book.

THM Besides the Siggins book, how much research did you have to do? And, in how much detail did you have the project laid out before you sat down and started drawing?

BROWN I read a whole bunch of books about Riel. I'm not sure how many books it all adds up to, and I've continued reading since I started the project, because new books keep coming out all the time about Riel. Plus, I come across old ones in second-hand bookstores. So, before I started, I had read maybe 12 or 18 books, something around that number, and more since then.

THM In the notes for the first chapter, you said you had written a script for the entire project, of around 200 pages or something. How is that different from the way you normally work? Do you have a story written out before you start drawing, or do you write as you're drawing?

BROWN This is the first time I had really written out a full script, where I knew what was going to be said in every word balloon. On past projects, it varied a bit. *Ed The Happy Clown* was a lot of improvisation, just making it up as I went along, but even there sometimes I would get ahead of myself and write scenes that were coming up, or whatever. And the autobiographical stories, there I would have a plan of what I wanted to do, and what kind of scenes I wanted to include.

THM Is this project frustrating at all for the "writer" part of your personality, since you have to stick to telling events of a story that's already written? Does that ever feel limiting at all, or does it just feel like you're exercising different muscles?

BROWN It's pretty much what I'd been doing with the autobiographical stuff, too. There I was limited to what happened the same way I am with Riel. It doesn't feel like a great burden to have your story, to some degree, set. I am enjoying figuring out what I think is the most dramatic way of telling this set of historical facts. I'm not even thinking about, "Boy, it'd be fun if I could have

the ground swallow up Riel right now…"

THM It seems like the big albatross Riel had to carry around for most of his political life was his execution of Thomas Scott [depicted in Chapter Three of Brown's book. Scott was an Irishman captured after fighting against the Metis]—

BROWN Yeah.

THM —and he never seemed to show any remorse for it, just thought of it as something he had to do, yet it would always haunt him, always prevent English Canada from taking his concerns seriously. Do you think if he had spared Thomas Scott's life, there would have been less resistance in English Canada to viewing him as a "good guy"?

BROWN I don't know about that, because what he was seen as doing in 1885 is inciting an Indian rebellion, and that was definitely frowned upon. Whether or not he would have been executed or not, I think he still would have been seen as a villain. But then again, if he hadn't had Thomas Scott killed, who knows how things would have played out after that. Then, maybe, he would have been accepted as a Member of Parliament, he wouldn't have gone to Montana, he wouldn't have been in Saskatchewan in 1885, it's hard to say. It kind of changes everything, or it might have changed everything.

THM *The Globe & Mail* recently had a big 10-part series of reports on the current state of "The Native Problem" in Canada, examining the poverty and despair on the reserves, and their feelings of being overwhelmed when they try to make it in white society. The whole series was interesting and thoughtful, and then they wrapped it all up by recommending their solution to the whole mess: assimilation. And it was such a drag, such a typical response: "These people are a hassle, it'd be easier if they just ceased to exist…"

BROWN Tom Bethell's book *The Noblest Triumph: Property And Prosperity Through The Ages* convinced me that the West's wealth comes from property rights for individuals. If you look at poor countries, their property rights are either weak or non-existent—look at rich countries and they have strong property rights. If you accept this premise (and if you don't, you should really read Bethell's book) then it should be obvious why Indians in North America are so poor: weak property rights. People on reserves aren't allowed to buy, sell, or own the land they live on. This comes from their traditional respect for the natural world—no one should be able to own the land. This was one of the fundamental differences (perhaps *the* fundamental difference) between the natives of North America and the incoming Europeans. So, if they were to accept property rights they'd be giving up at least one thing that makes them culturally distinct. And it would go beyond that—reserves would cease to be reserves. If non-Indians could buy reserve land from Indians, then reserves would, over time, cease to be centres of cultural identity for Indians. This would mean assimilation.

THM But what if they don't *want* to be assimilated? What if, to them, their assimilation is their destruction?

BROWN I'm not for forcing anyone to do anything. But they should understand the consequences of the way they organize their communities. They aren't going to be able to keep their culture *and* enjoy the kind of economic growth that we see in the rest of the US and Canada. They can't have both—it's one or the other.

THM I'm curious about the way you change the layouts of your pages, from the individual issues the single chapters first appeared in, to the complete books, and what's behind these changes. Like, the issues of *Yummy Fur* that featured the material that would later comprise the *Playboy* book, those pages were a lot fuller, with a lot more panels per page, so the events weren't as isolated as they are in the book. You re-arranged all of the panels for the book, and the spaces you left between the different visual moments helped to draw our attention to the important stuff, and help with pacing, getting your point across, and being a more entertaining read. Why the difference in the layouts, between the stories in the completed book formats and in the serialized formats?

BROWN The thinking is, in the comic books, I should pack as much onto a page as possible, because, you know, it's kind of the cheaper format, and you want to give readers as much as you can for their dollar. With the book, because

THM Do some stories seem to demand certain types of layouts? It seems like your layouts are always complementing the content in some way. How much do you think about that when you're working?

BROWN With each of those projects I wasn't thinking about how the layout would really affect the story I was working on—it wasn't the content that was affecting the layout, it was, how I wanted to draw at that point in time. With *Riel*, I'm drawing in those squares, because, at this point in time, I'm really under the influence of Harold Gray, and I'm wanting to draw as much like him as possible. And you know, Harold Gray was the artist who drew *Little Orphan Annie*, and *Little Orphan Annie* was always in those little squares, so that's just how I want to draw right now.

THM Is Harold Gray influencing the way you draw figures, as well?

BROWN To some degree, yeah. Well, I'm trying to draw like him, but it keeps ending up looking like it was drawn by me. *[Laughs]*

THM What do you feel is your best work?

BROWN *I Never Liked You*. I think that's my best book. I think it works the best as a story, and I like the drawing. It works on both levels, for me at least. At this point, I think *Louis Riel* might surplant *I Never Liked You* as what I consider to be my best work, or it might be in second place, but I am certainly happy with how it's turning out.

THM I think I had heard that you were going to do a new version of *I Never Liked You*, with different layouts again…

BROWN They're pretty much the same layouts, but you know how in *I Never Liked You* and *The Playboy*, the background behind the panels is black?

THM Yeah.

BROWN I'm changing it to white. But to do that, I have to re-layout the whole book, so it took awhile.

THM In the footnotes at the back of *The Little Man*, you say one reason you wanted to switch from autobiographical stories set in the recent past to stories set in your childhood was to avoid any possible trouble with friends or loved ones who may object to the way they're portrayed in your stories, but beyond that, what is it about the time of adolescence that makes it such a rich area to focus on?

BROWN It's the intense emotions of the period, as you're figuring out sex and love and everything. Later on, you develop a bit of a better handle on that whole world, but in those early days you make so many mistakes, and you don't even know, you're still confused by it all, so it's bound to produce rich material for stories.

THM Where did *Ed [the Happy Clown]* come from? What's the origin of the story? How did that start off, and did it just balloon once you let yourself go with it?

BROWN Well, the first episode in the *Ed The Happy Clown* book, at the beginning there's a section called *Introductory Pieces*, and the first one, *Ed*

The Happy Clown, was just a strip that I started, I made it up panel by panel. [Opens up the *Ed* book] The first panel I drew was this one here: "Ed is happy." I had no idea where it was going, I just drew this clown, going to the hospital to entertain sick children, and then I just drew this second panel, where the hospital has burnt down, and it just kind of continued from there…I added the first panel later, with the mayor discussing the rat problem, I guess. This first strip was made up panel by panel, over about a week I guess, and that's really the way most of the book went, kind of making up stuff as it went along. At a certain point I kind of knew where it was going, or had ideas, but then again, the ideas kept shifting around, so to a large degree it was a work of improvisation.

THM That recurring feature where each chapter starts with the events of the end of the previous chapter, but being retold from a different point of view—when did you have that idea?

BROWN It's not so much that I got that idea at some point, it came up naturally because of the improvisational nature of the story I was telling. If I had known from the beginning where I was going, I probably would have intertwined various elements in different ways, but because I didn't know where I was going *[Laughs]*, it meant sometimes having to go back and go over the same ground from a different point of view, the point of view of the new character I had created, or whatever.

THM All of those classic horror movie tropes—the vampires, the werewolves, the zombies—had been used in comics before, but the way they were used in this book was quite different from the way they were used in *Tomb Of Dracula*, or something. Were you interested in subverting genre conventions and expectations? *[Brown thinks it over]* It's just, the way you used these things was different from the way they'd been used in the past.

BROWN Yeah, I guess. I just have a love for that stuff, the horror genre, so I guess I just wanted to do stuff with vampires and monsters and stuff.

THM Did they represent anything? Were they metaphors for anything?

BROWN *[Laughs]* No, no. I just like vampires.

THM I asked that because I read an interview with Alan Moore where he said the super-heroes in *Watchmen* were metaphorical stand-ins for the cultural signposts of the '80s, larger than life characters who represented philosophical ideas like the atom bomb (Dr. Manhattan) or anarchy (V), and that his stories were a place for these ideas to—

BROWN *[Laughs loudly for a long time]* Come *on*! I mean, he was doing stories about super-heroes because super-hero comics *paid money*! He was working for DC Comics—of *course* he was writing about super-heroes! I mean, I'm sure there was a metaphorical level going on, but that's not what was going on with me. I just wanted to draw some vampires.

THM So you think what Alan was saying there was just a scam to give the work an extra layer of—or a sheen of class it doesn't quite deserve?

BROWN Oh well, Alan Moore does have a sheen of class. He's a smart guy, and I'm sure there was a metaphoric level, I'm not denying that, but let's face it: the main reason he was doing a super-hero comic was because he was working for a super-hero comic book company. *[Laughs]*

THM Speaking of Alan Moore, was his *From Hell* book any influence on *Louis Riel*, in the sense of doing a major comic book re-telling of an historical incident?

BROWN It couldn't help but be some kind of influence. I love *From Hell*, and it came before I was doing *Louis Riel*, although it certainly wasn't the only historical comic book out there. It's a great book, but I'm not trying to do the same thing as *From Hell*. *From Hell* comes right out and says it's a melodrama, and I'm not trying to do a melodrama at all. My book is a lot more emotionally flat. But sure, on some level it's an influence.

THM With trying to be emotionally flat, is there any sort of conflict between properly re-telling an actual event, and making an entertaining comic book? If the emotional value is flat, what's there to hook the reader in the place of that?

BROWN You hope that the events themselves are interesting. I think that's what you have to hope for, that on a broad level it's an interesting story.

THM What were the main influences on you back when you first started getting serious about becoming a cartoonist?

BROWN Even at that point, Harold Gray was some influence on me. I started reading Gray's stuff probably as soon as I moved to Toronto. Other influences? I'd begun reading Crumb shortly before that, and other underground stuff, so that was an influence to some degree. Of course the Marvel and DC comics, they had been my main interests in my teenage years.

THM Religious imagery appears often in your work. Do you believe in God?

BROWN Have you ever read Emanuel Swedenborg? Emanuel Swedenborg was an 18th Century Christian mystic who influenced a whole bunch of people. He influenced William Blake, and Helen Keller was into him, and Johnny Appleseed, of all people.

THM There was a real Johnny Appleseed? I thought he was like Paul Bunyan or something.

BROWN Oh yeah, he was John Chapman. He went around the country, not just planting apple trees, but also giving out books by Emanuel Swedenborg, trying to spread the good news of Emanuel Swedenborg. Anyways. Swedenborg wrote a bunch of books on Christian theology. His most famous one is called *Heaven & Hell*. He claimed that for the last 27 years of his life, he lived not just in this world but also in the afterlife, that he could travel back and forth, so he was quite familiar with what Heaven and Hell were like. I've been religious for years and years, but without being sure exactly what I believed, or keeping my beliefs vague, you know. I don't know what's true and you can't know what's true. It seems like there's probably a God but I don't know what he would be like. Anyways, reading *Heaven & Hell*, it seemed to make a lot of sense. I've been reading a lot of his books lately. Right now I'm reading this one, which in this translation is called *Love & Marriage*, but it gives the full title below that: *The Sensible Joy In Married Love And The Foolish Pleasures Of Illicit Love*. I'm not really sure if I'm going to end up being a Swedenborgian or not, but it's interesting, and I'm taking it seriously.

THM Do you think your adult interest in religion is just a result of you having been raised in a religious environment? After rejecting traditional Christianity, are you now trying to get to the same place but by a different route, or something?

BROWN That could be. I am wondering, am I just looking for a way back into Christianity? Because to a certain extent I felt like I couldn't believe in Christianity. The doctrines didn't really make sense to me. And Swedenborg is a form or an interpretation of Christianity that makes more sense to me than regular Christianity. So…is that the only thing that appeals to me about it? And, I don't know. *[Laughs]* I try to work this out in my head…

THM You started doing comic book adaptations of the Gospels in 1987. Why did you begin with Mark, as opposed to Matthew, which comes first, or Luke or John for that matter?

BROWN Because, according to the popular theory, it was the first one to be written. There's a bit of debate about that; some say it was really Matthew, but the popular consensus is that Mark was the first one, so that's why I did that one

first. And I was planning on doing all four. Of course, I'm halfway or so, more than halfway into Matthew now, and I don't think I'm going to be getting to Luke or John. But you never know. My interest in Swedenborg might get me wanting to do Luke or John now.

THM How much is that work a personal religious exercise for you?

BROWN When I was doing Mark and Matthew, certainly at the beginning, it was a matter of trying to figure out what I believed about this stuff. I had been reading books about it, and reading the Bible, and it just made sense to take it over into my comic books and do an adaptation of the Gospels. It looked like a good way to figure things out.

THM So has the experience of repeatedly drawing the face of Jesus brought you any closer to him?

BROWN It wasn't a matter of trying to get closer to him. It was a matter of trying to figure out whether I even believed the Christian claims—whether or not Jesus was divine, all that.

THM Do you feel like you're getting anywhere with that?

BROWN Not really. I'm as confused as ever.

THM You're going to finish that project, when the Riel book is done?

BROWN I'm going to finish the *Gospel of Matthew*, yes.

THM As you said at the start, the Riel project is a nice convergence of several interests of yours, and maybe we should talk about Riel's own weird mental behaviour in light of your schizophrenia strip. One element that doesn't come through so clearly in your book is that, from the get-go he was super-religious to a degree that a 21st century person can't really imagine.

BROWN Right.

THM Praying constantly, writing poems to God as soon as he knew how to write. I think it's the Flanagan book (*Louis 'David' Riel: Prophet Of The New World* by Thomas Flanagan) that really deals with that—

BROWN Yeah, the Flanagan book is really the one that talks about his religious beliefs most thoroughly.

THM He had a world-view that sounds strange to "modern" folks, but in other cultures in the past, it was the prevalent one. To him, everything in the physical world could serve as a symbol of something spiritual or a message from above, and in that light, his own breakdown just seems like the normal way someone with his world-view might deal with a big nervous strain, and just calling it "crazy'''sounds like…a form of bigotry. And it seems like that response has a lot in common with the way our culture deals with schizophrenia—the situation doesn't involve a medical illness as much as it does a lack of understanding/tolerance on the part of the beholder.

BROWN Yeah. Most people today have a hard time getting into the religious mindset. It doesn't make sense to them, it just seems crazy.

THM When Riel hears the voice in Chapter Six, it kind of comes out of nowhere and there's no real precedent for it earlier in your book.

BROWN Right.

THM Did he have any weird mental episodes before that?

BROWN Besides what I describe in my footnotes, I don't think so. And you're probably right, that it does seem to come out of nowhere, because I don't mention how religious he was. It might make more sense if the reader knew that he had gone to university with the specific intention of becoming a priest, and I don't even mention that. Well, I do mention it, but it might have been better if I'd shown it.

THM I'm not sure whether you were thinking about this at the outset, but the Riel project does work as a pretty good "object lesson" about how what we accept as truth is sometimes just motivated by expediency and convenience, like labeling something as schizophrenia so we can treat it in a consistent way, and make things easier for us "normal" folk…

BROWN Also, I think one of the motivating factors for coming up with it is, they felt like they had to have an answer. The scientists at the end of the 19th century had people coming to them with this weird behavior, and they didn't know what was going on but there seemed to be a similarity. They needed an answer, so they made up one. I'm sure that they didn't think of it as "making up one." They thought they were identifying a set of behaviours, but yeah, they just wanted to have an answer.

THM How much can the problem of skyrocketing rates of mental illness be viewed as a result of a certain set of conditions in the culture as a whole? Maybe a breakdown isn't so much an indictment of a certain weak individual's failure to hold it all together. Maybe the culture itself is the proper culprit.

BROWN Yeah, I think that there's definitely a problem in the culture that results in the way that people have these breakdowns. That's the thing: in medicine, you're used to saying there's a problem within the person, and saying there's a problem within the culture, that's not a medical answer. Medicine has to look in one direction, so there's only one type of answer that they can find. It's hard for doctors to think in other terms, not even necessarily at environmental problems in the way that we understand them, but admitting that it's not a physical problem so much as a problem with how we act, how we do things.

THM So the psychiatric drugs are just treating a symptom, and not the real problem?

BROWN Yeah, I think so.

THM *[Checks disorganized notes]* I think I'm out of questions. Is there anything else you'd like to talk about, or say?

BROWN *[Laughs]* Yeah, please put a note in the introduction to this or something, and tell people that I don't live on a dirt floor.

THM What?

BROWN In the new issue of *Peepshow*, Joe says that I live on a dirt floor, and people should know that that's not true.

THM Why did Joe say you live on a dirt floor?

BROWN Why did Joe say that I lived in a place with a dirt floor? Just because he thought it sounded funny, so—*[Chester laughs]*. On the other hand, I think there are a lot of people out there who do think that the person in *Peepshow* is me, portrayed accurately. They don't take into account the fact that *Joe Matt is a lying bastard!*

THM Well, that's good to know. And hey, I'm here, I'm an eye-witness, and I can state for the record that: "Not only is Chester Brown one of the finest cartoonists working today, he does *not* live on a dirt floor." Thanks for having me over, Chester. ★

Darrell Epp is behind the website Twohandedman.com and has put together a book of poems, plays and stories: *Consolation Prizes*.

Gary Groth

"I Feel My Zaniness Is Based On Truth":
An Interview With Will Elder

Will Elder was born in the Bronx in 1921. As a child, he was known as a comic, a prankster, a class clown. He loved physical humor and imitated exemplars of the genre such as the Marx Brothers and Buster Keaton well into adulthood. (I once viewed a sketch he and Kurtzman did, circa the late 1950s, in which they both exhibited remarkable physical comedic skills—more Jonathan Winters or Red Skelton than Keaton or Chaplin, demonstrating a subtle, antic elegance that would have been perfect for TV at the time.) But he was also a skillful artist and, after graduating from the famous High School of Music and Art, he segued into commercial art and comics.

He learned the ropes by inking his pal Johnny Severin on Western material for Prize Comics in the late '40s, continued inking Severin's war stories (written by Kurtzman) at EC and, as we all know now, came full circle, finding his métier illustrating stories

Gary Groth's interviews with Yoshihiro Tatsumi, Will Elder, and Kim Deitch appeared, respectively, in *The Comics Journal* #281 (January 2006), *TCJ* #254 (July 2003) and *TCJ* #292 (October 2008). [©2003, 2006, 2008 Gary Groth]

for *Mad* and *Panic* from 1952 to 1956—four years of some of the most inspired work in the history of comics.

When Kurtzman left *Mad*, Elder left with him and followed him into three noble failures: *Trump, Humbug,* and *Help!*. *Trump* was the realization of Kurtzman's dream to produce a slick, upscale humor magazine—and Elder's contributions show a quantum leap forward into breathtakingly detailed painting and intricate black-and-white line-work that even surpasses the advertising parodies he had done for *Mad* (themselves a huge leap in technique from his earlier comics). After *Trump* folded after its second issue—publisher Hugh Hefner pulled the plug for reasons shrouded in some ambiguity—one of the contributors, Arnold Roth, cheered everyone up and suggested that they try again. So, they did. Roth, Kurtzman, Elder, Al Jaffee, and production man Harry Chester all ponied up some money and started *Humbug*, which they owned equally (along with Jack Davis, who ponied up art but no money). The idea behind the magazine was that each artist would own his own work as well as a stake in the magazine, and that each artist would benefit if the magazine took off. This lasted 11 glorious issues and failed for numerous reasons, most of which boil down to the fact that they were great artists and lousy businessmen. The artists lost their shirts. (Some of them even lost their art.) Elder continued to refine his technique, which he applied to television and movie parodies and the occasional illustration.

After *Humbug*, there was a lull, during which Elder drew illustrations for a variety of magazines, such as *Pageant*. Although many of these are stunning, most of them weren't of a humorous nature, and you can tell that his technique was in it but his heart wasn't. In the early '60s, Kurtzman started yet another humor magazine, *Help!*, that Jim Warren published. Kurtzman and Elder once again collaborated, this time on a series of strips starring the Candide-like hero Goodman Beaver, which represented some of Elder's best work to date. In 1962, Kurtzman and Elder began a 26-year collaboration for *Playboy*: *Little Annie Fanny*, which was entirely painted in watercolor and tempera—the first and surely the most virtuosic of its kind.

Will Elder is most widely known as Harvey Kurtzman's lifelong collaborator. True enough. But he was, in his own way, an autonomous artist—not unlike Jack Kirby during his most creatively fecund collaborations with Stan Lee. Elder's parodic work for EC holds up almost irrespective of the writing, which would fluctuate wildly. Kurtzman, who wrote the *Mad* stories, was far more sensitive to the graphic rhythms of visual storytelling than Al Feldstein or Jack Mendelsohn, who wrote the *Panic* stories, but it's a testament to the immanent hilarity of Elder's drawings that there's so little qualitative difference between the stories he worked on in the two comics tiles. Elder obviously reveled in the outrageous: he added immeasurably to the stories proper with jokes, gags, signs, all imbedded in the background, as well as just plain drawing funny. While researching Elder, I paged through the Russ Cochran reprints, flagging Elder's stories, and I discovered that the quickest way to spot Elder's work was by what I would call an absence of style. Wally Wood's, Jack Davis' and John Severin's work could be spotted a mile away—Wood's lush, sensual brushwork, Davis' angular figures and flailing limbs, Severin's rangy figure drawing—but Elder's work was characterized by an imitative approach in which what few stylistic mannerisms there are (exaggerated lips on the female characters, for example) were subsumed into the unique approach each strip required and hidden beneath a meticulous, almost anonymous graphic approach.

Elder continued to refine his inking technique throughout his collaborative work in *Trump*, *Humbug*, and the Goodman Beaver strips in *Help!*, even as the intrinsic humor of the drawing continued unabated. I have to admit that slogging through 26 years of *Little Annie Fanny* became a chore—the satirical quality is intermittent at best—but my interest was maintained mostly due to the lushness of the painting and what Kurtzman called Elder's "eye-pops," the details, nuances and gags hidden in the backgrounds of the panels. Remarkable too is how Elder is able to maintain the essentially exaggerated cartoony quality of the drawing with his meticulous, painterly technique.

Journal interview introductions always refer to the interview subject's modesty, generosity, decency, charm, and hospitality. This one won't be any different—except that in this case it happens to be true (my first and last attempt at Elderesque humor). This interview was conducted over the course of two months in late 2002. The first interview was conducted in Elder's home in New Jersey, the four subsequent sessions over the phone. We have tried to retain as much of Elder's spontaneous and absurdist sense of humor as we could on the printed page.

Gary Groth The first issue of *Mad* was published in October of 1952. Can you tell me what you know about how *Mad* came about?

Will Elder Well, it was during the Kefauver Committee, the hearings on juvenile delinquency. Of course Bill Gaines appeared and he spoke about "The Night before Christmas," which I, by the way, drew, penciled and inked. He said, "I'm going to get up there and tell them what I think." And he did. He said, "'The Night before Christmas' is poking fun at Santa Claus. Santa Claus is not a religious figure. It's a phony figure. It was made up by Thomas Nast, another cartoonist. He also invented the Democratic donkey and the Republican elephant." So the committee wasn't surprised but they figured out that

Gaines knew what he was talking about.

Gaines was going bankrupt really rapidly. But someone said, "Why don't we start a humor magazine or something that pokes fun at these characters that we've been advertising all of the time. Make a comic book that makes fun of the comic book." That was a very unique idea at the time. Now, it seems like it was a simple idea, but it wasn't. And it was a desperate idea, because we needed to find something that would keep us afloat. And because of that, we came up with a humor magazine that was going to be very irreverent and perhaps sell a few copies and it overwhelmed everybody. It did well. It didn't do as well as it did a few years later, but it certainly kept us afloat. And that's how *Mad* was born.

GROTH You mentioned "The Night Before Christmas."

ELDER That's correct. They thought that would be corrupting the youth.

GROTH That was also banned in Massachusetts.

ELDER Everything is banned in Massachusetts.

GROTH That I didn't know.

ELDER It has a notorious outlook on life.

GROTH What was your relationship with Harvey at this point, in 1952?

ELDER Well, Harvey would take me into his little room where he always took artists and discuss a story or whatever.

GROTH At the EC offices?

ELDER Yeah. Right down on Canal Street, somewhere around there. And he would say, "We just came up with the idea of a magazine called *Mad*. I think it's up your alley. If I were you, I would go put yourself into it and become an actor or become an actress, become an opera singer. Do whatever you want for yourself, but make it funny. It's got to be funny. And you can do it." He encouraged me like a football coach. Get out there and fight! That's the way I got myself wrapped up with *Mad*.

GROTH There were basically four revolving artists in *Mad*: you, Wood, Davis and Severin.

ELDER Johnny didn't hang around too long; he left for other pastures.

GROTH The first strip you did for *Mad* was called..."Ganefs"? [*Mad* #1]

ELDER Gah-niffs. It's an old German term, which means thieves. [Those strips] were more or less influenced by the early comedians of physical humor. Buster Keaton. Harold Lloyd. Charlie Chaplin. You can see that in the little guy who uses violence in his humor. Always flapping the big dumbbell... What the hell's his name? I can't remember his name. Oh, it's been so long. My God, it's over 50 years.

GROTH In the story? The character's name is Bumble.

ELDER Hello? *[Phone glitch.]*

GROTH Can you hear me?

ELDER Sorry I woke you.

GROTH The character, are you referring to Bumble?

ELDER Bumble. Right. That's it.

GROTH I want to get into some details with the stories you did for *Mad*. "Ganefs," for example. My understanding is that Harvey wrote the stories.

ELDER Right, for the most part, I had a lot of freedom with Harvey at *Mad*. He would write the stories and give me a lot of latitude and say, "make it funny, Will." So I would say that "Ganefs" in particular and "Mole" [*Mad* #2] were much more from the two of us, I think I came up with "Mole" and Harvey may have come up with "Ganefs." It's hard to know who did what after all these years, but I do know that Harvey gave me a lot of freedom to do whatever I wanted on the *Mad* stuff.

GROTH And he provided layouts?

ELDER Yeah. He would roughly set it

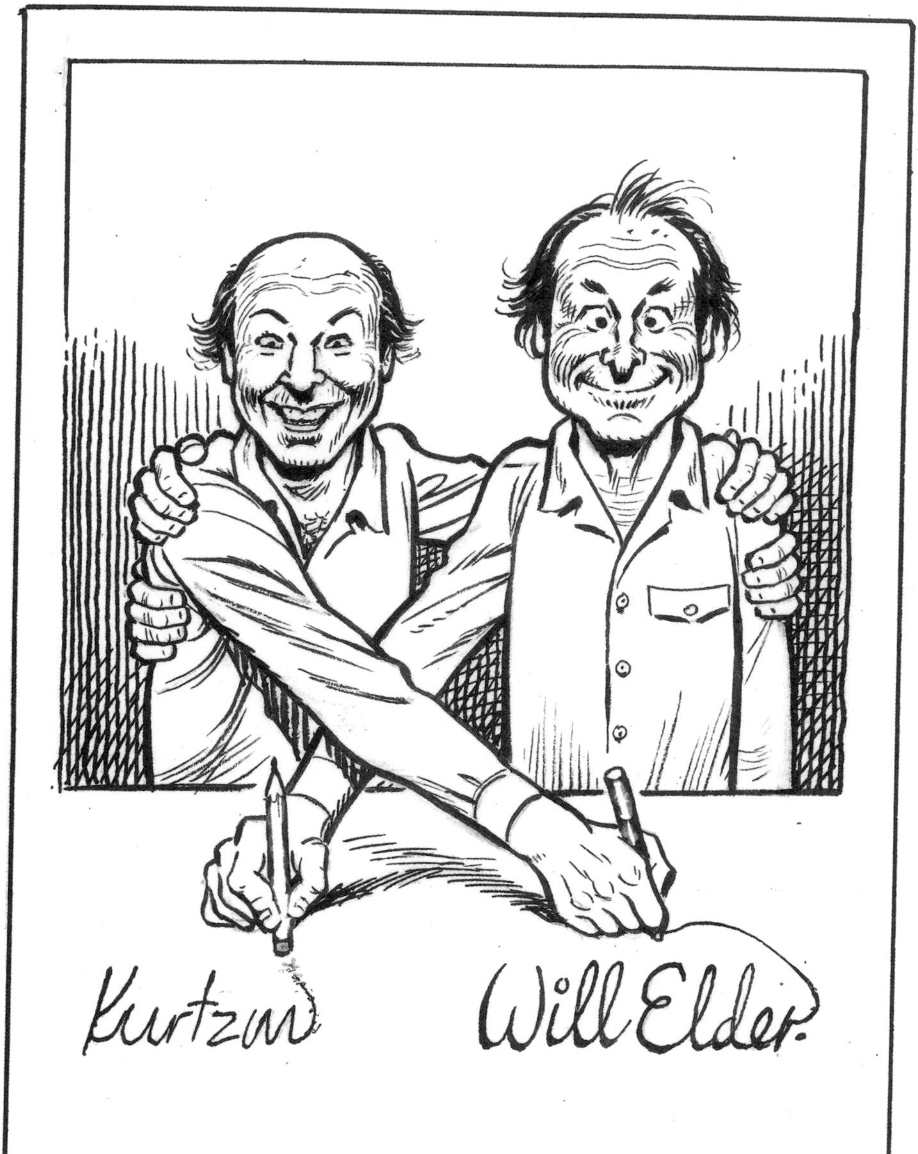
Kurtzman
Will Elder

down on paper in these little panels and written dialogue and sound effects. I would work with that as a base. Basically I would use that and start throwing my things in. And he never said a word, because he figured whatever I did would only enhance the humor of what he did. And it was a good combination. It worked well. Before you know it, I was throwing in the kitchen sink and the dumbwaiter. Every blessed thing that came into my mind, which ended up in a hilarious clutter, as he put it.

GROTH Was the lettering on the boards by the time that you started?

ELDER It wasn't finished lettering. No. It was just the story that was being told or that was being recorded on the paper.

GROTH When would the lettering be put on the artwork? At what stage in the process?

ELDER After I got through with the inking. They would either paste it on, and have balloons that were pasted on…

GROTH Oh, really?

ELDER Yes. Because I would try to leave room. I had to have the example of the lettering first, to see how many lines of lettering there would be so that when I made room for it eventually, it wouldn't cover up part of the pictures or part of the illustrations. I would leave a note where the balloon would go for each panel with the proper lines and size of the letters. So it wouldn't… beforehand it would be sitting in the right place in each panel, where the dialogue took place. Do I make myself unclear?

GROTH Very precisely. I assume that many, if not all, of the details in the work are yours?

ELDER I would say a good many of them. Yeah.

GROTH When Harvey wrote the scripts for the stories, did he also accompany that with a description of what was going on in each panel?

ELDER Yeah. He would reenact each scene. It was kind of peculiar and it was rather humorous. He would reenact each scene, he would tell you what every scene should have, what the situation was. His voice would change in order to express his ideas. It was fun. I would throw in a few ideas and he either rejected them or accepted them. Then I would take those ideas that I got from Harvey's re-enactment and go to town, adding as many things as I could think of to Harvey's basic layout.

GROTH Let me ask you a specific question which you might not be able to answer because you might not remember. I wouldn't blame you a bit, but let me go ahead and give it a shot.

ELDER I don't remember the shot.

GROTH In the story "Dragged Net!" which ran in *Mad* #3, I noticed things that you've drawn in the panel that wouldn't necessarily have been indicated in the script.

ELDER Right. Good thinking.

GROTH I'm wondering to what extent you took the script and visualized it differently than Harvey or another artist would, and to what extent Harvey gave you directions.

ELDER Every artist that worked for

Mad had a style. Harvey knew that. He prescribed certain stories to certain artists, to one of the four of us who was best-suited to that particular story. But Harvey would reenact the story in addition to the layout so the artist had the layout and Harvey's explanation to go by. I would listen very closely to Harvey's explanations, his reenactments and I would use that to embellish the story with my own ideas. Somehow he introduced Bernie Krigstein to *Mad*. Bernie was certainly not, to my mind, a humorous cartoonist. His work is very serious and very well done, but I found that he wasn't suitable enough for Harvey, for *Mad*. He did *From Here to Eternity* ["From Eternity Back to Here!" *Mad* #12]. There were a lot of things that he could have done better, because I've seen his work. His work, some of it is beautiful. The thing is, Harvey knew exactly what could be done by what artist and how he worked. And somehow it worked. It was a very good plan. It was a good way of organizing each one of us into doing what we best do.

GROTH You did "Starchy" in *Mad* #12.

ELDER Oh yeah. There were a lot of letters on "Starchy."

GROTH Which was actually remarkable. It seemed to me to be the most risqué strip that *Mad* published up to that time. You had Starchy smoking.

ELDER All the things that are wrong with people in society registered on those pages.

GROTH You had the principal chasing Betty and Veronica around.

ELDER Well, it happens. Some teachers prey on their students.

GROTH Right. But it was pretty unheard of to put that in a comic in 1954.

ELDER Yeah. But I feel my zaniness is based on truth. If it weren't that way it would be pretentious. It wouldn't be believed at all; all really great comedy is based on truth.

GROTH How are you able to capture the likenesses and the artistic styles of these strips? I'm thinking of "Starchy" and the Li'l Abner—

ELDER I worked like a b-a-s-t-a-r-d. I worked very hard, because not only was I challenged to do something interesting, very interesting, but also to show Harvey that he's got a guy whose doing hard work for him and myself. I was really out to please him, because he never knew I could do that many characters, and accurately. Of course, when I say accurately it was them during those days. They changed during the latter part of their careers. People forget that. When you do a caricature of anybody like that—like Hirschfeld, the Line King, you know, he drew pictures of people in the theater who aren't recognizable in their last days on Earth. They've changed. So you're apt to be criticized for the fact that it looks like them but many years later.

GROTH When you started off at *Mad*, your first four stories were crime satires. They were "Ganefs!," "Mole!," "Dragged Net!," and "Shadow!" [*Mad* #1-4]

ELDER Well, it's like the old Hollywood days. They'd come out with films that were pretty much all alike. Westerns for a time dominated the screen. Everybody loved them until the darn things wore off. Gangster movies were very, very famous, very popular in the later '20s and the early '30s. You had Cagney and Bogart, Edward G. Robinson. Then you had the romantic comedies with Cary Grant and Katherine Hepburn and that sort of thing. So it changed with the audience and the times.

GROTH Right. Then you did a couple of horror satires: "Outer Sanctum!" and "Ping Pong!" [*Mad* #5 and 6]

ELDER Well, you have to try something new.

GROTH Then you started to do character satires like "Shermlock Shomes." [*Mad* #7] One of the things that I liked most in your stories was, for example in the Holmes satire, suddenly toward the end bubbles are coming out of his pipe and Dr. Watson is holding up an umbrella. Would that sort of invention have just been a spontaneous decision on your part?

ELDER Probably so, because it had nothing to do with the story.

GROTH It had nothing to do with the story or the dialogue. It just pops up out of nowhere.

ELDER Harvey, when we went on these conventions, would answer questions from the audience and from the fans in general, and would tell them that he never knew what I was going to come up with. He laughed at everything, Harvey. If you laugh at something, you're more or less forgiving them.

GROTH I think the fact that it simply pops up for no reason makes it even funnier.

ELDER Yeah. It's like the Marx Brothers. They would do something anti-social out of nowhere.

GROTH Like a series of non sequiturs.

ELDER It's also battering the social divides to hell, such as people who are very rich and very mannered as opposed to those who are starving to work for a buck. Harvey would say, everybody will be reading Will's sight gags and not even read my stories. Everyone laughed and I expected them to laugh because the whole thing was ludicrous.

GROTH Do you, among the strips you did for *Mad* and *Panic*, have any favorite genres that you worked in or any types of strips that you preferred?

ELDER In *Mad* I liked the newspaper-comics and radio parodies. Those were the things I knew the best and I had always made fun of them when I was in school, so it came very naturally to me. Harvey knew that. I would have to say that the radio—"Dragged Net!" and "Outer Sanctum!"—and, of course, the newspaper funnies—"Poopeye!" [*Mad* #21], "Mickey Rodent!" [*Mad* #19], "Tick Dracy!" [*Panic* #5]—jeez, that list just goes on and on. It's hard for me to pick one; I like them all. There are things I like about all of them, but I can't say I have a favorite. It's like asking a parent which child is his favorite; you just can't do it…out loud!

Will and Harvey's Process

GROTH In the explanatory text in one of the *Mad* collections, there's a question posed to Kurtzman: "How closely did the artist follow the tissue overlay?" And

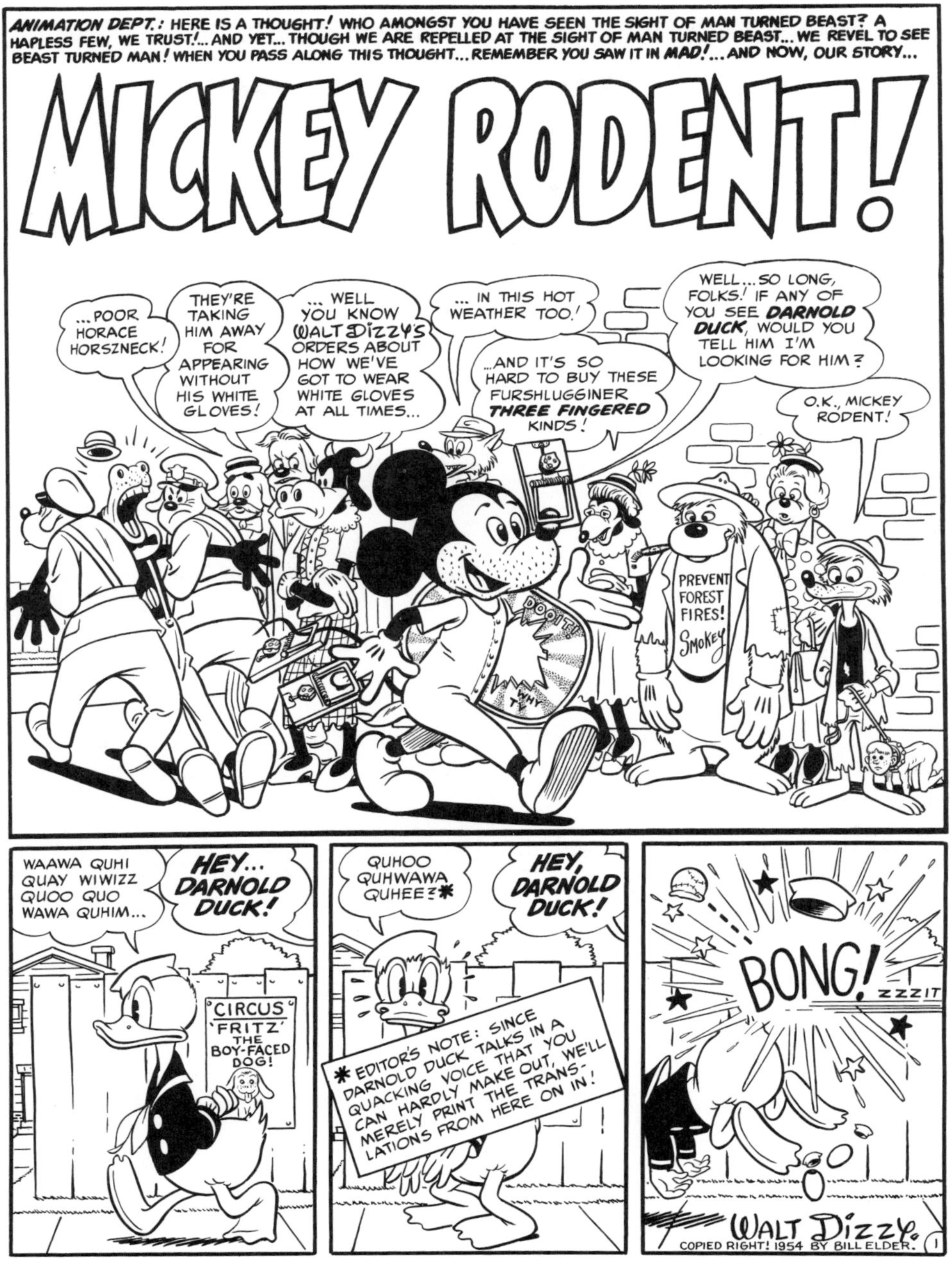
ANIMATION DEPT.: HERE IS A THOUGHT! WHO AMONGST YOU HAVE SEEN THE SIGHT OF MAN TURNED BEAST? A HAPLESS FEW, WE TRUST!... AND YET... THOUGH WE ARE REPELLED AT THE SIGHT OF MAN TURNED BEAST... WE REVEL TO SEE BEAST TURNED MAN! WHEN YOU PASS ALONG THIS THOUGHT... REMEMBER YOU SAW IT IN MAD!... AND NOW, OUR STORY...
MICKEY RODENT!
...POOR HORACE HORSZNECK!
THEY'RE TAKING HIM AWAY FOR APPEARING WITHOUT HIS WHITE GLOVES!
... WELL YOU KNOW WALT DIZZY'S ORDERS ABOUT HOW WE'VE GOT TO WEAR WHITE GLOVES AT ALL TIMES...
... IN THIS HOT WEATHER TOO!
...AND IT'S SO HARD TO BUY THESE FURSHLUGGINER THREE FINGERED KINDS!
WELL... SO LONG, FOLKS! IF ANY OF YOU SEE DARNOLD DUCK, WOULD YOU TELL HIM I'M LOOKING FOR HIM?
O.K., MICKEY RODENT!
DOOIT!
WHY TV
PREVENT FOREST FIRES! SMOKEY
WAAWA QUHI QUAY WIWIZZ QUOO QUO WAWA QUHIM...
HEY... DARNOLD DUCK!
CIRCUS 'FRITZ' THE BOY-FACED DOG!
QUHOO QUHWAWA QUHEE?*
HEY, DARNOLD DUCK!
* EDITOR'S NOTE: SINCE DARNOLD DUCK TALKS IN A QUACKING VOICE THAT YOU CAN HARDLY MAKE OUT, WE'LL MERELY PRINT THE TRANSLATIONS FROM HERE ON IN!
BONG!
ZZZIT
WALT DIZZY.
COPIED RIGHT! 1954 BY BILL ELDER.
1

Kurtzman replies, "They resented it at first, but we had thrashed that out in the war books."

ELDER Excuse you for a minute. Except that didn't work for me. He gave me full rein. He knew how wacky I could be, so Kurtzman was very kind to me. He said, "Will, get funny like you usually do. Get funny." And I'd try to.

GROTH What were these tissue overlays that they refer to? I understand that he laid out the strip, right?

ELDER Yes. The tissue overlays actually saved a step in the process of doing these satires.

GROTH Can you explain how that worked?

ELDER Well, it would be translated from the tracing paper with a drawing on it in pencil onto the illustration board. But what Harv used to do was to pencil on the illustration board and then lift it off with tracing paper. He would rather work on the tracing paper at first and then from the tracing paper onto the illustration board. Do you follow me or am I—

GROTH Yeah. Now these would be Harvey's drawings on the tracing paper?

ELDER Harvey's very rough layouts. In other words, he showed us the exact thing that was going on in each panel. What was happening. In other words, basically there was a story behind all of the garbage.

GROTH And then those rough layouts would be transferred onto the board?

ELDER Right. Illustration board. I would take a piece of a very thin, ordinary stationery paper and I would

blacken one side of it with a very soft pencil. I would slip that between the tracing paper and the illustration board, go over the tracing paper again as to where to put Harvey's layouts on the illustration paper. We would use the blackened page like carbon paper. Now, I don't use the real carbon paper because it has a wax finish and wax and ink do not mix. What I use is a pencil reproduction or drawing on the illustration board because you can always erase it. Wax you can't erase. It will smear, that wax carbon paper. If I'm getting complicated, let me know.

GROTH I'd be interested to know how much you changed or altered Harvey's layouts.

ELDER Harvey would be the first one to tell you that, if you think that I'm trying to grab credit from Harvey, on the contrary, we worked as a team and we worked very well. Harvey would be the first to tell you that my gags and my layouts and my rendering made that strip very plausible.

GROTH Let me ask you if you can remember some specifics. On page five in the first three panels of "Shermlock Shomes!" you had Holmes and Watson en route to another location. In the first panel they're in a soapbox-derby car. In the second panel they're on a camel and the third panel...

ELDER Oh, the modes of transportation.

GROTH That's right. What did Harvey give you to work with and how much did you add to that?

ELDER If Harvey were here he would tell you just exactly what I would say, and that is that I did most of the gags. In fact, I did almost all of them. Harvey would leave the funny ideas on paper, and I would embellish whatever was there with my own ideas.

GROTH So with that example, he would have drawn what in those panels?

ELDER He would draw very rough or very crude placement in each panels. In other words, figures he thinks should have been in an area of the panel, that's what he did. He handed me a sheet of paper the size of a comic-book page, but in this case one and a half to two times up so I could work a lot easier on the details by working on a much larger scale. When I finished the sketches, I would send it to Harvey or meet him. He thought they actually saved the strip, because he said, "I run out of ideas and come to my rescue if you can." I don't want to take all of the credit, but there was a section of my work in almost every panel. Harvey knew that I would handle it. After all, it reflects on all of us if we do good work.

GROTH The lettering was put in after you penciled it. Were the balloons blocked in before you penciled it?

ELDER I think so. They were real professionals, and they put the lettering in really tight at times and very well executed. We didn't have to worry about that.

GROTH In what form did you get the script from Harvey? Was the actual writing on the board you drew on?

ELDER He would write on there and he would segue with a balloon, so I knew right away it was dialogue.

GROTH How organic was the collaboration? Did Harvey change things based upon gags you would put in?

ELDER I would change things. I have a film that we've made. Have you seen it?

GROTH Well, I've seen one video with you and Harvey in it.

ELDER We were on the back porch one summer.

GROTH Where you're both sitting in chairs?

ELDER Well, I was sitting in one of those sling chairs, yes. Harvey was in a lounge chair or something.

We'd discuss ideas for humor takeoffs and things of that sort. I'd come up with a few ideas and he'd say OK and write it down very crudely as if it were a note. But when it came to that page of that particular panel, I would have to expect from Harvey a layout of very crude figures, if there were figures involved. Or things of transportation. Are they going to pot...what's his name? The guy from that space program? Spock.

GROTH Oh, Mr. Spock.

ELDER Yeah. He roughed it in very, very quick and fast. What I did is I took it from there, looked at Spock in the pages I remember him appearing in, and did a whole thing over from scratch. But at least I was sure of where Harvey wanted the panel to be, or the figures in the panel to be.

GROTH That was in *Little Annie Fanny*.

ELDER That was *Little Annie Fanny*. Right. The same principle applied to everything I did.

GROTH How elastic was Harvey in terms of the writing? Did he change things after he saw your drawing?

ELDER Very rarely did he do that with me. I must brag about that. I'm very proud of it. The fact is, he let me work alone. He knew that I was a nut if I kept quiet and stuck to myself and did my own work without anybody supervising me. Because usually he accepted it when he finally got it.

GROTH Did you fiddle with the writing at all?

ELDER Hardly. Very, very rarely did I do that. Hardly.

GROTH Do you remember if Harvey ever changed the writing after you did a drawing to accommodate your drawing and your gags?

ELDER He might have. I wasn't aware of it. What I was aware of was turning in the work on my behalf with an illustration.

GROTH I know you might not remember all of this stuff because they're very, very...I'm getting into some minutiae...

ELDER Over 50 years ago...

GROTH In the Holmes story, for example, you have a panel where Sherlock is playing the violin with the mop. One side of the mop is going into Watson's mouth and the other side is splattering against—

ELDER I vaguely remember that. Yeah.

GROTH Would Harvey have just drawn Sherlock Holmes with a violin instrument and you created the mop?

ELDER I don't know. I'm not too sure

about that, but I think, as I said earlier, he made the stories less lengthy by the fact he threw it my way and we would meet deadlines. The trick was to get all of the stuff ready for reproduction. He wanted everything to be orderly. Harvey was very meticulous. He wanted everything to be orderly. The fact that we went to Music and Art High School together, he was like my kid brother or vice versa. He figured he'd leave me alone. He would never bother with me.

If you notice, there're about four stories in every comic book of *Mad*. And one of those stories he would keep open for me. Because I would be working on an illustration—for example, an ad parody I did. It was wash and tone. It wasn't exactly black and white or line work. It was a washed advertised fiction of a guy going...Harry Chester was the model in this case. The guy going to the electric chair. Well, there's this young guy with this jockey suit on, I guess you would call it. A young midget. Walking around the lobby of the hotel yelling. But in this case, he was witness to an execution. We had a priest in the background, someone uncuffing Harry Chester, and you see a hand sticking out from the side of the illustration with one of those long matches giving the criminal a chance to have his last smoke. And the chair is in the immediate half-distance. That took time because I wanted to make it look real. By looking real it becomes more convincing as a gag. If I made it crudely, it would look like a gag right from the very get-go. So I would make it almost exactly like the advertisement but a different subject. Nothing like Madison Avenue would put out. We weren't knocking the products, we were knocking the people who were advertising the products.

GROTH The "Mickey Rodent" strip that you did, I was curious as to which artist you based the Mickey Mouse and Donald Duck renderings on? Would that have been Floyd Gottfredson's newspaper strip?

ELDER I had a lot of things laid out before me on the floor of my studio. I saw things that look typically Disney, whoever handled that particular part of it. But I would lay out and I'd say, "If I can get this style, the original style of Mickey with the sharp looking body." I didn't have a crude body like "Steamboat Willie." Do you remember that first one?

GROTH Yes.

ELDER That was far from "Steamboat Willie." I would use the best Mickey Mouse figure I could find.

GROTH Were you aware of the Donald Duck comics, and Carl Barks' work at the time?

ELDER No. I didn't know Carl Barks at all. I heard of him later after he had left or was retired. Yes, I did use his figures. They were very recognizable, and my gag wouldn't be any good if they weren't recognizable.

GROTH I thought a real stroke of inspiration in the strip was when Darnold Duck was pointing to your signature and saying, "Look at that signature! It's not Walt Dizzy's style!" And then there were references to the differences in line work between your Donald Duck and the original.

ELDER That was a lot of my doing, I must say. But Harvey wrote the general theme of the story, the basics. The idea, the general idea, he came up with it. He'd talk to me and say, "Will, I have an idea for Mickey Rodent, Disney's bread and butter. I want to give it the works. See what you can do." He comes back and he says, "I want the story to exemplify the Disney characters. And suddenly this Duck rebels against whatever Disney has done to the fowls of America, the ducks," and then he says, "I have a surprise ending. I'd like to end with a real duck." That was Harvey. What I did in between, like people in the woods or in the beginning splash page, you have people watching one of their friends being dragged off to the police station, handled by police that look like animals—horses, cows, whatever. One of the victims, one of the people who are watching this going on has a little leash. And at the end of the leash there is a little naked man. That was a crazy idea I thought of.

GROTH —I'm curious to know what you think is the most purely Elder-esque strip you did during that period.

ELDER That's very hard because there was so much involved in every story and I want to…it's like asking which was my favorite. I guess the ones that were most me were the ones where I had the most freedom. Harvey gave me that freedom on every strip, he gave me a good layout to follow and then just let me go and I liked that. There were almost no changes and I just got to be me on every story. I think all the ones I did with Harvey allowed me to shine through because I didn't have to work on the layout also, I could just start in with the jokes, the gags, all my funnies. With Al [Feldstein, editor of *Panic*] I had to do a lot of extra work because I had to first tighten up the layouts before I could start to do my stuff, so it was different and also a very long time ago. I liked doing the Marx Brothers, "The Night at the Castle," where Groucho is walking toward the beautiful maid [from *Humbug*]. That was a lot of hard work, but I enjoyed it. Because especially if I do the Marx Brothers it's because of the fact that Bill Gaines always thought I was the Marx Brothers in cartoon form. Maybe I was, maybe I wasn't. But I certainly enjoyed them. You could get away with murder portraying the Marx Brothers. Everything they did was acceptable, because they were loony to begin with.

GROTH Speaking of the Marx Brothers, were you aware of how much sexuality was in your strips, which was unusual for the time? I mean, there was an undercurrent of sexuality throughout a lot of your satiric work.

ELDER Well, the same thing applied to the Marx Brothers. You always found Harpo chasing the women.

GROTH That's why it occurred to me.

ELDER In fact, that one picture they made, *Monkey Business*, they're on board a ship and he chases this woman up and down the stairs. And he continues to chase her all over the place.

GROTH And then when he got distracted with another woman, he just turned from the first woman he was chasing and started chasing the second...

ELDER And then there's a very buxom, sexy gal. He brings her some ice and stuff out of college, in the football team. He brings in the ice and they all jump on this girl and hug the hell out of her. Chico, Harpo and Groucho—they all jump on this girl. And they start ogling her every time they see her. Or make an innuendo type of gag.

GROTH You had to draw these sexy girls, and we're talking about the 1950s. Were you aware that this sort of content was a little outré by the standards of comics at the time?

ELDER Yes, I was. In fact, I figured out, what makes for humor? At least, American humor, because if you took this to China, they wouldn't know what you were talking about. Humor depends on the neighborhood it's born in. It was typically American to ogle these women because of the Hollywood movies. There was always a sense of sexuality or sensuality in all of the movies I've seen. But then you have all of these beautiful movie queens. Marilyn Monroe is the first one I think of. I was wild about her, too. She had something that no other sweetheart had. I used to call them sweethearts. Betty Grable, Claudette Colbert, Jean Harlow. You always had these sex queens.

GROTH You were there at the end of Kurtzman's run on *Mad*. At that point you were pretty close with Harvey, I assume?

ELDER Yeah. We were good friends to begin with besides being collaborators.

GROTH My understanding is that Harvey was getting frustrated working for Gaines and that he demanded 51 percent of *Mad*.

ELDER Yeah. I thought that was kind of strange.

GROTH And Gaines refused to give it to him but he did offer to give him some percentage, I think it was 10 percent.

ELDER Oh, yeah.

GROTH And Harvey refused it. I'm wondering how much in the loop you were about these negotiations and if you conferred with Harvey, if Harvey sought your advice.

ELDER Well, what I'm about to tell you, you're the second guy I've spoken about this with. That's the wrong way to put it, but anyway. I spoke to someone else about that, and I thought I made a mistake, but I don't think that I did make a mistake. I know he's not here to defend himself, so I don't have to be as careful. I'm not trying to be cowardly about it or be a first-class villain, but the fact remains I was involved indirectly, not directly. I figured he was leaving because something happened. I didn't know why he was leaving. If there was a gap in our means of working together, I'd like to know about it and be prepared about it. But I thought he moved too fast.

GROTH Harvey?

ELDER He might have moved a little better a couple of years from that particular period. But he moved too fast and he wanted too much. I think that was a mistake. Harvey deserved a lot of credit, but that's no way to seek it.

Gary Groth co-founded Fantagraphics Books, Inc. in 1976 to publish *The Comics Journal*, the premier magazine of comics journalism and criticism, to which Groth has contributed over the years. Guided by Groth and Kim Thompson, Fantagraphics Books went on to publish the first wave of "alternative comics" and has continued to champion and release literary comics that are acclaimed worldwide.

Gary Groth

"My Strategy Was To Create The Opposite": An Interview With Yoshihiro Tatsumi

Yoshihiro Tatsumi is a pivotal figure in the history of manga. Like American comic books of the same period, manga in the '40s and '50s was dominated by a juvenile idiom. There was good work done within the parameters of this idiom, but to an artist with serious aesthetic ambition, it was confining, indeed stifling. At about the same time that a handful of cartoonists in the U.S.—Kurtzman, Eisner, Krigstein—were bucking the trend and trying to create work that was more literate and graphically sophisticated than the editors and publishers wanted, the aesthetically restless Tatsumi broke from the industry norm in Japan and started making comics of an intensely personal kind. In 1957, he began writing and drawing comics that he called *gekiga* (literally "dramatic pictures"), which exorcised his own private demons and reflected his intensely subjective perception of the world around him. He still had to make a living by drawing commercial comics (and even became a commercial comics publisher himself) but continued to draw his own comics when he had the time and an outlet.

The first (authorized) English translation of his work came out in 2005: *Push Man and Other Stories*, edited by Adrian Tomine and published by Drawn & Quarterly. In late spring of '06, D&Q's publicist called and asked me if I'd be interested in interviewing

Tatsumi at Comic-Con: International in San Diego in August. I got back to her after I'd looked through—but not read—*Push Man* and agreed to interview him. Cursory research indicated Tatsumi was a fascinating historical figure, and the work looked meaty and interesting. We set up a time and a place and secured a translator.

In the interests of full disclosure and critical honesty, I should say that after I'd read *Push Man*, I had misgivings over his work, which were not allayed by reading the subsequent volume, *Abandon the Old in Tokyo*, which seemed to me largely supererogatory. The cartoonist Greg Stump has pointed out how relentlessly, uncompromisingly bleak Tatsumi's stories are. And indeed they are, but this isn't by itself a recommendation any more than a happy ending is reason to condemn a story. Although there have been exceptions, I usually only interview artists whose work I like, and I didn't feel entirely comfortable interviewing Tatsumi. I was troubled by a number of tics that comprised the backbone of Tatsumi's aesthetic: the narrowness, aridity and sameness of the vision; the dramatic implausibility and jerry-rigged mechanics of many of the stories; characters who are either stereotypes or ciphers (albeit purposeful ciphers); and a tendency toward heavy-handed, literal-minded metaphors (the rat in "My Hitler," the piranhas in "Piranha").

That said, the work was clearly a sincere expression of Tatsumi's convictions, and his artistic choices, whatever my reservations, took courage and tenacity; I thought I could do a good job and looked forward to interviewing him. Tatsumi's schedule was booked solidly throughout the convention; the interview was supposed to take place Saturday afternoon between public appearances at the con. I hadn't quite reckoned with how cumbersome and time-consuming the translation process is; I would ask a question, which would be translated into Japanese; Tatsumi would answer in Japanese, and the translator would translate it for me into English. The interview therefore yielded less than half the conversation of an interview where both parties speak the same language. When we had finished lunch, I asked him if he'd be willing to continue the interview in the early evening after his last convention panel (and before dinner), to which he agreed. We clocked in over five hours of taping altogether.

Physically, Tatsumi is a compact man with a gracious manner (and obviously patient); his conversation is straightforward, and his sense of humor was, well, given his work, surprising. I'd like to think we got along well. I would especially like to praise our translator, Taro Nettleton, whose translation reflected the talk's colloquial nature, and who navigated the ebbs and flows and back-and-forth of the conversation expertly. I hope this interview serves as both an introduction and deepening explication of Tatsumi's life and work.

Gary Groth You started *gekiga* in 1957. There's a missing six years between 1957 and 1963 when you started publishing. What did you do in that time?

Yoshihiro Tatsumi I was creating works primarily for the rental-books industry, in those six years. And I was publishing through this one publisher called Henomaru Publisher, and the president of this publishing company had aspirations to move to Tokyo. Masumi Kuoda brought the idea of publishing a collection of shorter works up to me, and so the publisher thought maybe this could lead to something else, primarily publishing a magazine, a monthly magazine in Tokyo. So he took this idea, and he started to run this collection of shorter works, which was then this book entitled *Shadow*, and this went on for about a decade. And it was really this format of the collection that became wildly popular at the time. And while I and my colleagues believed that *gekiga* was most suited to book-length works, and I certainly created book-length works at the time, it was these collections that were the most popular. And that's really what spread *gekiga* style. These collected volumes were about 128 pages long, and they would come out each month, and at the height of their popularity there were hundreds of these collections coming out each month.

GROTH And what inspired you to change direction from more commercial work, to work of a more intense and personal nature?

TATSUMI I had seven colleagues, with whom I moved to Tokyo from Osaka. And we had a discussion about how we could promote our work, and at this time I was the only person doing this *gekiga*, and so one of my colleagues asked, "Could we all use this term *gekiga*, to kind of label our works? And that way we could promote and sell our work better when we go to Tokyo." And so that was the decision to use the phrase. Actually, in terms of content, even before they started using this phrase *gekiga*, they were already working in that direction. And the name basically was adopted or used, because there was a need to distinguish the comics that I and my colleagues were working on from those comics that were meant for children. It created a category that helped guide how to shelve them in these rental bookstores. Although my own works were not that violent, some of my colleagues' works were quite violent. So people started to feel that they shouldn't be shelved with other comics that are for kids.

GROTH What year did you move to Tokyo?

TATSUMI Nineteen-fifty-seven.

GROTH Was there a point at which you recognized that the medium was a serious medium of expression? Or was it an evolutionary part of your thought process?

TATSUMI Two years prior to starting to do this *gekiga*, as an experiment, I created a longer piece that was drawn very roughly. And I was sure that the editors would turn it down, so I went, luckily, on a day when the editor wasn't there, and I was sure that later on, I would hear that they couldn't publish it. But, to my surprise, it went straight through, and it was published, and in fact it did quite well. I even heard from my colleagues that they really liked the piece, and that they felt that it expressed something new. It was at that point that I felt confident in this kind of new direction I was taking, as a more expressive kind of form.

GROTH Was the content of this longer piece substantially different from what you had done previously?

TATSUMI It wasn't entirely different from my previous work. The previous genre I was working in was mainly detective stories, thrillers, that kind of thing. And with this experimental book-length work, I was dealing with everyday events, very familiar events, kind of everyday occurrences. Maybe, you know, a child would suddenly be involved in some sort of incident. But they were everyday occurrences. And since no one else was doing that kind of work at the time, I was sure that it would fail, but...

GROTH Am I correct in inferring that comics were dominated by essentially children's fare at the time?

TATSUMI Yes.

GROTH So this would be a radical departure from that?

TATSUMI Well, yes, it was very different from the kind of mainstream comics. And the kind of content that my colleagues and I were creating was only possible in the rental-comics genre. And yes, the main difference was that we were addressing an audience of our own age. But I found out later that many of our readers were laborers, workers who had recently moved to Tokyo from more rural areas, and found whatever jobs they could find. And also I heard—we couldn't really research who were reading our works—but afterwards I found out that there were also a lot of prostitutes reading our works. *[Laughs.]*

GROTH Was that a big market?

TATSUMI Not yet. I would get some feedback when the distributors came to pick up the books from the publishers. They would tell them what kind of people were renting out the books. So I did have some indication of the fact that the readership was increasing in age.

It was in October of 1955 that I published my first self-conscious *gekiga* work, which was called "The Black Blizzard."

GROTH Now, between '57, when you were in Tokyo, and 1969, when, I understand, that the stories in *The Push Man* originally appeared—

TATSUMI That's correct, yeah.

GROTH Were you doing longer stories, between '57 and '69? And then you had to start doing shorter stories, which appeared in a magazine called *Gekiga Young*, which was a young men's magazine? Is that correct? I just want to make sure I get my facts straight.

TATSUMI What was the name of it?

GROTH *Gekiga Young.*

TATSUMI Yes, almost all the works in *The Push Man* were published first in *Gekiga Young*. And I started to write these shorter pieces for magazines. Basically the rental-book business collapsed. And then, I had to start writing for monthly and weekly magazines. That meant that I had to write these shorter pieces like the ones that are in *Push Man*. The ones that I wrote for this *Gekiga Young*, the pay was pretty poor, and the conditions were not that good. But, it was the first time that I found an editor that I could work with at the magazine. And so I would talk with him about what kind of themes I wanted to explore. And it was the first time I was engaged in that kind of a situation where I could discuss the work I was doing with an editor, and to have that be published.

GROTH Your stories are so personal, they're such personal expressions, that I can't imagine an editor could do much to mold them one way or the other. I'd like to ask you why your vision is so despairing of humanity, which seems a constant in the two books that Drawn & Quarterly has published so far. Could you elaborate upon your perception of humanity as shown through the prism of your artistic sensibility?

TATSUMI Uh, yes, definitely. The works are completely a reflection of the kind of anger and the pain, the desire to escape that I felt at the time. And for me personally, to try to express that within eight pages, which is quite short, was quite a struggle for me.

GROTH Did you feel constrained by the requirements of eight pages?

TATSUMI Yes, I found it quite claustrophobic. I think I touched on this before, but, when Tezuka moved to Tokyo and started working for magazines, I felt that his work had become really cluttered and

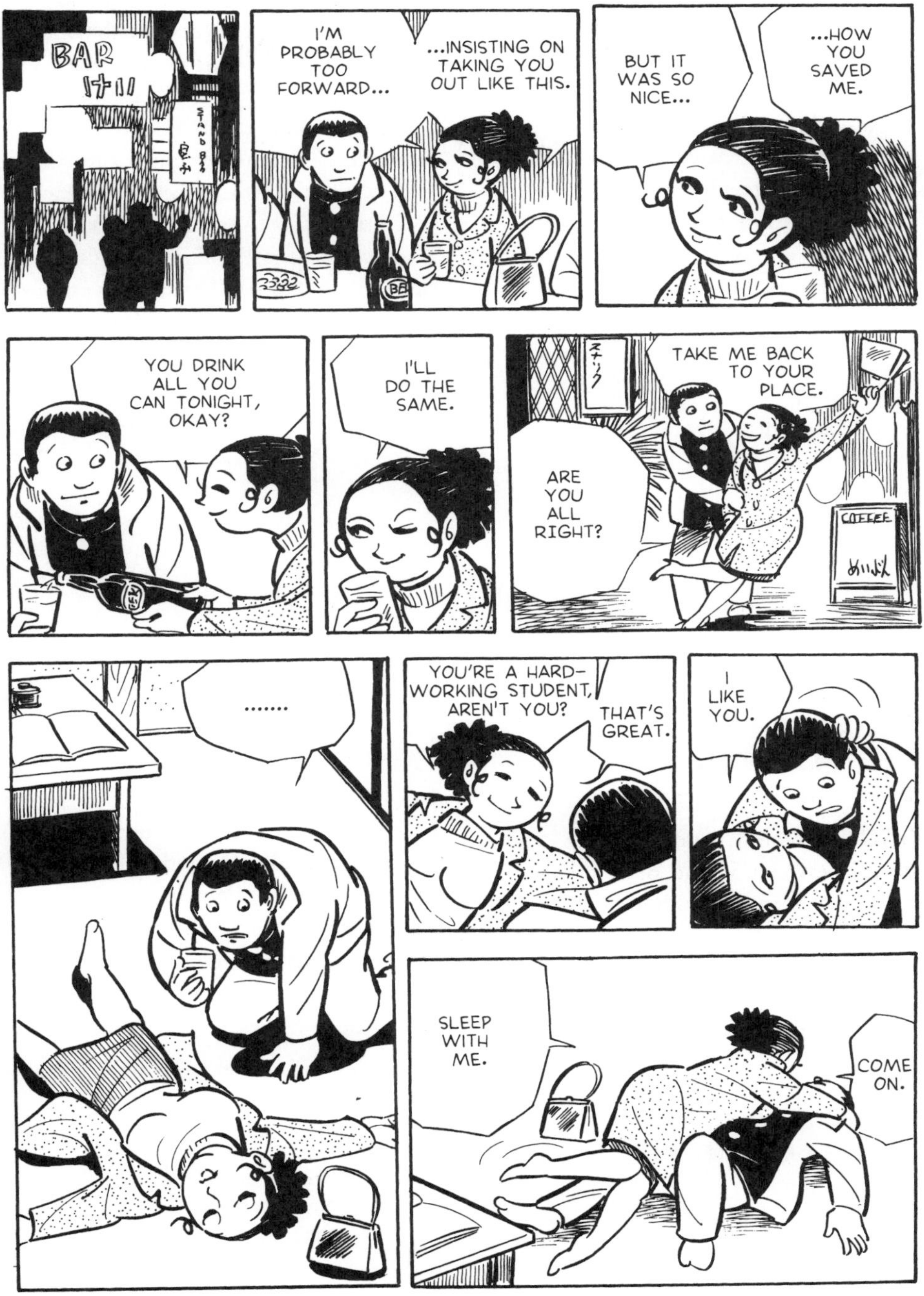
BAR
I'M PROBABLY TOO FORWARD...
...INSISTING ON TAKING YOU OUT LIKE THIS.
BUT IT WAS SO NICE...
...HOW YOU SAVED ME.
YOU DRINK ALL YOU CAN TONIGHT, OKAY?
I'LL DO THE SAME.
TAKE ME BACK TO YOUR PLACE.
ARE YOU ALL RIGHT?
COFFEE
....
YOU'RE A HARD-WORKING STUDENT, AREN'T YOU?
THAT'S GREAT.
I LIKE YOU.
SLEEP WITH ME.
COME ON.

claustrophobic. And I realized that I was going through the same process, and it was then that I understood what Tezuka was going through. That meant that there had to be more panels on a page, so it was very claustrophobic. But even beyond that, with Tezuka's work, I just started to feel bored by them, even beyond or before this sort of technical analysis, I just found it boring. And so I was very conscious that the short-story format was very easy to become boring, to become stale, unless you composed the short story really, really well.

GROTH One of your consistent techniques is for the men in your stories to be passive, to rarely speak. They drift silently through your stories, whereas the women are veritable chatterboxes. I'd like to know why you use that technique as consistently as you do. What are the aesthetic reasons behind that?

TATSUMI In part it was strategic, because *Gekiga Young* was an adult magazine, with erotic themes, sexual themes. All of the other stories in the magazine, and especially the ones toward the front of the magazine, were longer pieces—the authors got 24 pages that were relatively easier to work with. They were all sexual content, and so my strategy was to create the opposite of what was being depicted in those works. In those works, it was always the men who were the aggressors, the women were passive, and the men would dominate over the women. So to do the opposite, I thought, would create interest in the readership. At the same time, the narratives that were depicted in these other people's stories, didn't ring true to me.

I thought that men are not always stronger than women, and men can be weak and vulnerable and passive. But in terms of the men being silent, I think that that is a very perceptive point that you make. I'm really glad that you noticed that, because actually, the way that happened, in these discussions with this editor that I liked, at the time, I was still making works where I was relying on the speech balloon to explain the situation in the stories. Because the pieces were already short and cluttered, my editor suggested that I take out most of the speech bubbles, and that getting rid of those would not take away from the story in any way. That way you could see the image more clearly, and he thought that would be a more effective way for me to work. That was how I got to the silent character, by getting rid of the speech balloons.

GROTH Now, was the magazine essentially pornography?

TATSUMI Yeah.

GROTH So in a way you were writing and drawing these stories as an antidote?

TATSUMI Right.

GROTH The women in the stories are almost always depicted as opportunists or parasites, and I was wondering why you made that decision, or if you even agree with my description. *[Laughs.]*

TATSUMI Really? Are the women parasites? *[Laughter.]* *[Looking at his wife.]* No, it's partly to do with my personal experience that I can't really express right now. *[Laughter.]*

GROTH *[Turning to her]* Mrs. Tatsumi, it might be time to interview you. *[Laughter.]*

TATSUMI Umm, it's hard for me to speak in general terms, about, you know, the way I depict women. Because *Push Man* collects about 20 stories, and I've written about a thousand…And I think that I have depicted strong men in other works, but certainly during that period, I think I did have some anxiety and fear of women.

This is a little bit off the topic and I apologize. But, my works obviously didn't fit in very well within this magazine that was essentially a pornographic comics magazine.

GROTH Right, that was my next question.

TATSUMI So at a certain point, the editor was…well, the magazine wanted to stop publishing my series within the magazine. And so the editor was told about this decision, and this editor, who I liked a lot, said "The only reason that I work at this magazine, which I find boring, essentially, is because Tatsumi's work is printed in it." And so actually, when my work was dropped from the magazine, the editor quit the company, and moved back home to Nagoya.

GROTH In protest.

TATSUMI The works that are collected in *The Push Man* essentially killed this editor's career. Unfortunately. *[Laughs.]*

GROTH Was the editor a man or a woman?

TATSUMI He's a man. He was quite young at the time, and when *The Push Man* came out through D&Q, I tried to find him, because I thought he would be really excited about it, but I haven't been able to find him.

GROTH When the editor quit in protest, did the magazine relent and continue to publish your work or were you out?

TATSUMI When the editor was told that they were dropping me, the editor said that well then, I really have serious doubts about the conscience of this magazine, and I'm quitting. And he quit, and the serial was dropped. Or the serial was dropped and he quit. That was that.

GROTH It's my experience that people buy pornography to read fantasy. And the last thing in the world they want to read are grim existential protests against modern life. So why in the world did

THE MORE PEOPLE FLOCK TOGETHER, THE MORE ALIENATED THEY BECOME.

they let you do that in the first place?

TATSUMI I don't think that the publishers would have felt that opposed to it, because I was quite conscious about the kind of magazine that it was. And so, I was very aware of what I could get away with, and to stay within those boundaries. I do include sex scenes, for example, in my works, to sort of appease the [publishers].

GROTH Would you have done even harsher stories if you didn't have these restrictions?

TATSUMI I'm really not sure.

GROTH That'd be brutal.

TATSUMI It's hard to say, it's hard to speculate, because if they were any more tragic or devastating, they wouldn't have been published. I was very aware that I was walking a really fine line. It would have certainly been much easier for me to create erotic stories. I mean, I would have had more pages to work with, as well. But I wasn't really interested in making that kind of work.

GROTH One of the motifs, or at least, one of the recurring symbols I noticed in your work is the individual within a crowd. And both stories "The Push Man" and "The Burden," as well as the story that you showed me earlier in this book, that was drawn in 1972, I think, end with the individual within a crowd. Does that image or the idea behind it have a special significance to you? In "Beloved Monkey," the person in the very end of the story says, "The more people flock together, the more alienated they become." Could you elaborate on that and talk about the significance of the individual in the crowd?

TATSUMI Well, you know, that's a basic fact, that you're much lonelier. If you're just with one other person, it's fine if you don't know them. But when you're with 10 other people that you don't know, you feel that much lonelier. It's the condition of urban living. When you move to the metropolis, and you don't know where you are, and you don't have any work, I think that that can be a very alienating experience. Furthermore, I think that, when you're living in those conditions, you start to envy other people that are around you, you start to imagine that everyone around you is living a better life than you are. I think that that's a basic condition of living in the city. And when you're with just one other person, and you envy them, you can just not see them. That's fine. But that becomes very difficult when you are living in the city.

GROTH Is this a condition of modern life that you deplore, or that you accept simply as a part of life?

TATSUMI No, I accept it as an inevitable part of life. I think that a crowd, a mass of strangers, is essentially frightening. When you're walking down the street and a mass of people that you don't recognize or don't know come toward you, I think that's a frightening experience. I think that the last scene of the "Beloved Monkey" story is when the traffic light changes, and you're waiting for this mass of people to come walking towards you. I think that's a scary experience.

GROTH Do you see your stories as a criticism of alienation, or as simply a depiction of what is?

TATSUMI It's like half and half, really. I think it's part reality and part criticism. I think, with *gekiga*, it's still manga or comics, and really, criticism is an essential part of comics. I think if I just depicted reality, it would be boring. You can't really just do one or the other.

GROTH Do you think criticism is an essential part of art? That art is intrinsically critical of the status quo, or of life?

TATSUMI Yes.

Gary Groth

"It's Gotta Be Real To Me, Somehow":
An Interview With Kim Deitch

Kim Deitch has had a long and storied cartooning career, beginning in 1967 when he drew comic strips for the *East Village Other*, an underground paper published in New York. Deitch went on to move to San Francisco, then the hub of the underground comics movement, where he began writing and drawing stories for anthologies (such as *Hydrogen Bomb Funnies* and *Up from The Deep*) before he published his own solo comics (three issues of *Corn Fed*) and helped found a publishing co-op (Cartoonist Co-Op Press). He then contributed to the highly regarded *Arcade* and the not-so-highly-regarded *Comix Book*, and has, to date, amassed a substantial body of work available in over a half-dozen book compilations. Deitch has been drawing comics for over 40 years, and he's done his best work in the last 10 of those 40 years. The same cannot be said about the careers of most cartoonists, or of many artists generally. There is often a slackening of creative powers after so many years of hard-at-it work, but Deitch seems to just be hitting his stride. His work is characterized by an obsession with the history of American popular art, especially animation and vaudeville, and often features multi-generational sagas populated by both the animated characters themselves and their oddball, off-kilter creators. (Deitch grew up in a fecund creative environment; His father,

Gene Deitch, was the creator of Tom Terrific, among other characters, an animator at UPA in the 1950s.) Kim Deitch creates a world with one foot in the fantasy of cartoon characters and one foot firmly rooted in reality, unified by a rich, idiosyncratic, unique visual style that brings both worlds to vibrant life. At 60+, he is one of the most vital cartoonists working today.

Gary Groth You did *A Shroud for Waldo* for the *L.A. Weekly*. Can you tell me how that came about?

Kim Deitch How it came about it was, when I took a trip to L.A., spiraling out the 1982 San Diego convention, I met Carol Lay. She told me that she had a buddy of hers who wanted to meet me, and that was Matt Groening. And I guess I went over to the L.A. *Reader* office to meet him, so I got to know the people at the L.A. *Reader* office.

GROTH Did Matt work there? What was his involvement with the *L.A. Reader*?

DEITCH He was a staff artist, although he seemed to have a little more sway than that. He might have had some editorial position as well. The strip he's doing now *[Liteig Hell]* he was doing

then, and never really stopped doing it through all of this. So I met him, and through him I met James Vowell, the publisher at the *L.A. Weekly*, a really good guy, too. I had it in my mind I wanted to do a story about Los Angeles, and even featuring Larry Farrel. I was already working on that when I was still in Berkeley. It hadn't really gelled, but I spent a year in North Carolina, when I was on salary from Brian Yuzna, so when I finally got to L.A., I had a bunch of money. Between that and managing to talk the L.A. *Reader* into taking the strip, they gave me like $50 a week, and then I had all this money saved. That's what bankrolled *Hollywoodland*.

It's weird. I couldn't sell it to another paper, and believe me, I canvassed all over the country. I got a mailing list, I sent it to everybody. But, a continued story, nobody wants that in an independent-distributed comic strip. I was really delighted when I saw *The Shutterbug Follies* by Jason Little in the *New York Press*. I thought, "Ah! Here's somebody doing it!" And I was cutting it out and saving it. But they dropped it before he even finished the story.

That, to me, was my hope that maybe people would go along with a serialized story in an alternative comic strip, but really, that's not what's wanted. It's the same thing that goes on in regular comics: It's got to be, get in, get your fast little gag, and get out again, usually drawn in some sort of minimalistic style. And, to me, and this is just a matter of a taste [that's] totally boring and uninteresting. I don't follow any of those things. It is just probably personal taste, because I know there are some really good ones out there. My wife is really big on *Mutts*, and whenever I take the time to look at it, I can see that *Mutts* indeed is a fine strip.

But then, I've never been any good for whimsicality anyway. *Krazy Kat* is lost on me, and I know that's heresy *[Groth laughs]*. It looks nice and all, but really. We've got piles of it in the house, because Pam reads it, but every now an then, she'll show me one and I'll go, "Yeah, that is good," but mostly, I'm not interested.

GROTH You want meaty stories.

DEITCH Yeah. *Krazy Kat* is just old pothead humor. That doesn't interest me.

GROTH *A Shroud for Waldo* is the origin of Waldo. It's almost impossible to summarize. It was the beginning of a trend for you, in that you started doing these really complicated, intricately woven, labyrinthine stories.

DEITCH I think that one could almost stand being revisited and drawn and plotted a little better than it is. When I tried to read it not long ago, it seemed flawed to me, although I think the basic ideas are cool: the big Waldo backstory. I did 100 percent better on that one serializing it in the papers. That time, I had two papers. That basically came out of an offer the *L.A. Weekly* made me to do a strip. Then I managed to sell it to a paper here in town as well. But it wasn't exactly a rip-roaring success. What it essentially did was it subsidized my drawing it, and ultimately it made it into book form. But it's a little jagged-y. I can't read that one without wincing a little bit now, not because of the storyline, but because it doesn't hang together as good as it could.

Again, I was traveling all over the place when I did it. I drew a lot of that in Philadelphia; I drew a lot at my mother's house in Connecticut; a bunch of it in Virginia and probably several other places that are escaping me right now. Even though I was based in Virginia, I was really still living out of a suitcase in those days, until the suitcase finally fell apart.

One of these days, if I live long enough, maybe I'll go back and try to do something with it, try to redraw it. It's sort of fun, and the backstory itself, I'm tickled by it. The fact that he's not really a cat anyway, but a demon from Hell makes a lot more sense. I got all this weird apocryphal Christianity rolling through it, too, which to me is entertaining.

GROTH Where did the idea of throwing Jesus into the mix come from?

DEITCH Oh, I don't know. I like Jesus. That is great story: the story of Jesus Christ is really something else. It's got all the drama you could ever want, and human interest. So, it's also this archetypal cornerstone of Western culture and a whole lot more besides.

GROTH One thing that occurs to me about Waldo is that he's a pretty nihilistic character, but he's also completely self-satisfied.

DEITCH Yeah, he's weirdly at peace with himself.

GROTH And you've done at least two stories where they end with him reveling in his own joy of life: *A Shroud for Waldo* and the shorter story that appeared in *Raw*, "Hell to Pay."

DEITCH In some ways, he knows how to live, I guess *[Groth laughs]*, although I don't really like him.

GROTH Is that right?

DEITCH No. What's to like? He's a schmuck. He's entertaining—but a nice guy? No. I have friends that aren't nice guys. I probably have a few friends I don't really like, too. I know that sounds contradictory, but nonetheless, it's probably true.

GROTH The characters you don't like probably make the most fascinating characters, too.

DEITCH Well, that's the thing. Interesting people aren't necessarily all going to be swell guys and gals.

GROTH Your next huge book is *The Boulevard of Broken Dreams*, which

appeared in…

DEITCH Started in *Raw*.

GROTH OK, started in *Raw*…

DEITCH …finished with you guys.

GROTH Finished with three comics that we published.

DEITCH Three or four, yeah. You republished the *Raw* as a comic, and then there were three behind it.

GROTH I wasn't really aware that you collaborated with Simon on that, so I'd like to know how that broke down.

DEITCH While I was still in Virginia, me and Simon were still pretty close, and I made several visits to see him. On one of the visits—it was just when VCRs were starting to get big—all he wanted to do on my visit was show me all the cartoons he'd taped off TV. Some of them good, and since we grew up with cartoons, it wasn't uninteresting.

And I guess he put my head in the frame of mind, because one evening, we were both smoking weed and being recreationally creative, we essentially came up with the opening sequence of *The Boulevard of Broken Dreams*, which is that Winsor Newton thing. It's based on an event that both me and Simon were aware of that in 1927 in some speakeasy, Max Fleischer threw a testimonial dinner for Winsor McCay. It basically went down just like the beginning of *The Boulevard of Broken Dreams*, where Winsor McCay got up, and started to make this lofty speech about where animation has been, and where the future might take it, and he hadn't gotten too far before he looked around and realized that he was losing his audience. What Winsor McCay said [is] "Goddamnit! You guys have taken the art I've created, and turned it into shit. Bad luck to you," *[Groth laughs]*, and he sat down in a huff.

I'm a little surprised I didn't keep that "bad luck to you" line, somehow it escaped when we were working it out. But we basically worked out this fictitious sequence based on that testimonial dinner. I remember Simon came up with changing Winsor McCay's name to Winsor Newton, and I remember me insisting that, when we created this delusional character, that the delusional character had to be Waldo. We worked it out, and I don't believe we had it on paper. We just worked it out talking. I don't know where it would have gone, because at that time I was working one the skein of stories that became *Shadowland*, which was what I was working on when I first met you.

I came over to Art Spiegelman's house maybe two or three days after that session with Simon. We were just sitting around talking trash. In the midst of talking trash, I started running this send-up or adaptation of the Max Fleischer/McCay testimonial dinner to Art, and while Art was listening to it, it was really surprising, I could see the expression on his face changing while telling him, and he's just looking at me, and at a certain point he goes, "Kim, Kim. If you ever want to stop clowning around and do a story that might make you some real money. I think this might be one."

I said, "Really? You think so?" Shortly after that, I went back and I told that to Simon.

The other thing that Art had said, even before that, is that, at some point he was on a rant about something, and he said, "You know, I'd use a 40-page story in *Raw*, but it had better fucking well be one hell of a 40-page story."

So I had that in my brain, too.

GROTH *[Laughs.]* A challenge.

DEITCH So then I went to Simon and I said, "Simon, I ran the thing down to Art, and he thought it really had possibilities."

Simon said, "Yeah, yeah."

So basically, what happened then is I went back to Art and I said, "Art, I'm going to take your advice. We want to do the animation story, and what's more, we want to do it in *your* magazine."

Art went, "Oh yeah, huh?" *[Groth laughs.]* Somehow I managed to talk him into it. At the end, he even gave us, more or less, a 40-page slot. At a certain point, he gave me this choice: "Well, you can either have it one of two ways. You can either have 40 pages even, and we'll let you do a sequence of it in color, or all black and white, and we'll give you 42 pages." *[Groth laughs.]*

I definitely took the 42. So that is how the first episode of that is exactly 42 pages. I just felt that I wanted that little wiggle room to make it good. Color's nice, but it's beside the point, as far as I'm concerned, on that story.

GROTH So how did you and Simon collaborate on this? What did Simon do?

DEITCH It was like the way that Ben Hecht and Charles MacArthur collaborated. Basically, I was doing most of the hands-on putting it down

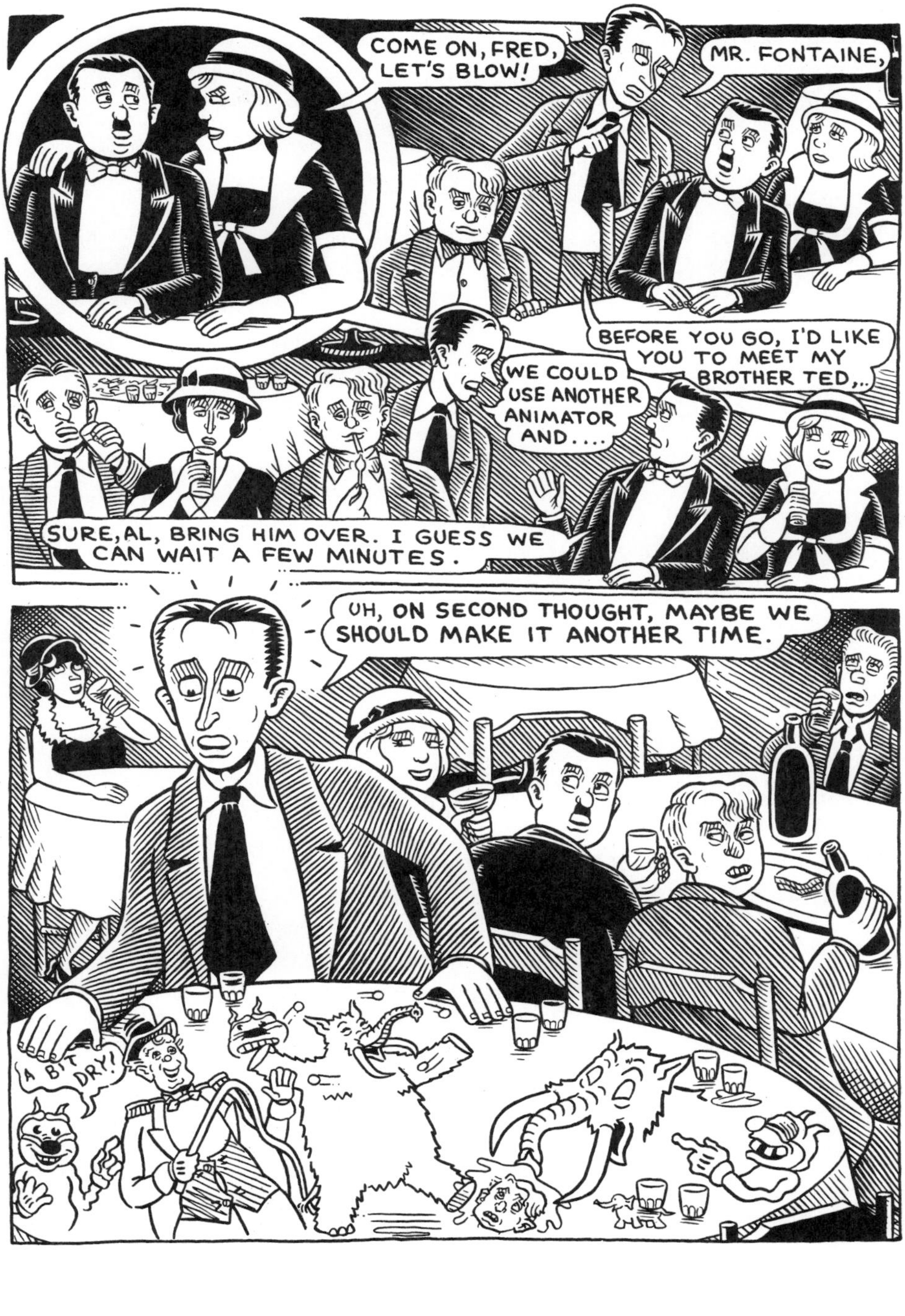

COME ON, FRED, LET'S BLOW!
MR. FONTAINE,
BEFORE YOU GO, I'D LIKE YOU TO MEET MY BROTHER TED,..
WE COULD USE ANOTHER ANIMATOR AND....
SURE, AL, BRING HIM OVER. I GUESS WE CAN WAIT A FEW MINUTES.
UH, ON SECOND THOUGHT, MAYBE WE SHOULD MAKE IT ANOTHER TIME.
A BIT DRY!

on paper, and Simon was talking and brainstorming with me. At some points, he designed things, I can specifically remember that that character the Sandman that was in the Fontaine Fables, that's a straight-ahead Simon Deitch design. He came up with the name Winsor Newton and he was right in there with me on it. Basically, the way I sold it to Simon was: "Look. You've been backseat-driving on stories that I've done for years." Occasionally, you can find an old *EVO* strip that's signed by both of us. I said, "Here's an opportunity for [us], why don't we make it a *real* partnership. I mean, there's the Hernandez Brothers. Why couldn't there be the Deitch Brothers? The beauty of it too is, you can enter on a fairly high tier, because here we be in *Raw* magazine. I'll tell you, Simon, I've been to those signings for *Raw*, and man, those books just march out of the store like they had legs on them."

That's how I sold that idea to Simon. Of course, nothing ever runs that way. We got episode #1 done, and immediately Art decides to stop doing *Raw*. I pleaded with him. I said, "Let me edit it." Oh, no way was he gonna do that. So we did the best we could with it later and Art basically made it up to me down the road, 'cause he definitely was instrumental in helping me sell that book to Pantheon all those years later.

GROTH The crux of the book is the relationships among the animators and that seems very Kim Deitchian to me.

DEITCH Here's my father's big trip about the book. "All the dysfunctionality you have among the animators," he says. "That's hogwash. I've been in that business and I can think of 'here's a guy who maybe drank himself to death, and here's a guy who didn't do so well,' but it's nothing like what you've been showing, and for you to say, 'This is like how it really was,' is bullshit."

And I thought about it, and said "Well, he's got a point. He's got a point." But a lot of it's true. Like that Jack Schick character, there's a book that influenced a lot of what went into *Boulevard of Broken Dreams* by an animator named Seamus Culhane who wrote a book, a really good book called *Talking Animals and Other People*, and he had a chapter in there on a situation that took place at Van Beuren Studios, where Burt Gillette (Schick/Gillette, get it?), who had directed "The Three Little Pigs" for Walt Disney, they imported him over to Van Beuren to upgrade the Van Beuren line, but he was basically completely insane. Ultimately, I think he ended his days in a nuthouse. So Burt Gillette became Jack Schick.

There was a girl animator named Lillian Friedman: Was she like our character, Lillian Freer? Probably not, I really didn't know that much about her, but that's where the name Lillian came from, and she was probably one of the earliest credited female animators that I know of, having worked at Max Fleisher sometime in the '30s. Lillian Friedman, she might even still be alive, but I doubt it.

GROTH They all seemed plausible.

DEITCH Yeah, that's the thing. I projected a lot of the kind of really get-down raucousness of my background in underground comics onto that animation situation.

GROTH Bert Simon struck me as a stand-in for your father.

DEITCH Yeah, there is a character that is absolutely based on my father.

GROTH The guy who comes in and wants to crank up the quality.

DEITCH Yeah, that's it. Yeah, so a lot of that's based on my father's take on walking into Terrytoons, where he was hired to take over by CBS. That's definitely based on my old man.

GROTH Is the Winsor Newton live-action performance based on historical precedent with Winsor McCay?

DEITCH Absolutely: haven't you ever heard of "Gertie the Dinosaur?"

GROTH Well, sure. I wasn't aware he did it as a live—

DEITCH Absolutely: The best version of it I ever saw was the one Walt Disney put together on the old *Disneyland* show, where they got this Fleischer animator, Dick Huemer, to make himself up as Winsor McCay, and do the "Gertie the Dinosaur" vaudeville act as he remembered Winsor McCay doing it back in the early teens. They might still be recycling that sequence on the Disney Channel, I don't know. I remember it vividly from my childhood. The old Disneyland show was often pretty classy and Disney did some pretty interesting episodes about the history of animation, where he actually did credit others than Walt Disney. Most notably, and admirably, wonderfully, the salute to Winsor McCay where he's doing it as the vaudeville act. The one you see on film, they re-jiggered it a little bit to make it a one-reeler.

He used to come out on the vaudeville stage: he was already a practiced vaudevillian before he ever did that. A famous early Winsor McCay act was like a chalk-talk act where he drew the seven ages of man as elucidated in *As You Like It,* the famous soliloquy, right on stage, just drawing it from baby to doddering old man, and everything in between. So he was already doing vaudeville before he even started doing animation in vaudeville; and *Little Nemo* must have been part of an early vaudeville act, too, the Little Nemo cartoon.

I mean, yeah, McCay was an interesting renaissance man of the early 20th century. It was all killed by Hearst, who took care of him, but at a certain point decided, "I want this guy on my editorial page." Then he just became, oh, I forget, Hearst's big editorial guy…

GROTH Arthur Brisbane.

DEITCH Yeah, he became Arthur Brisbane's creature. He was there 20 years until he died.

GROTH Doing those elaborate drawings for his editorials.

DEITCH I wonder if he ran into young Samuel Fuller at that time, who was also Arthur Brisbane's copy boy.

GROTH *[Laughs.]* I see another story there.

DEITCH Yeah, that would make a good one. Strange encounter with Winsor McCay and Samuel Fuller, who seemed to have some cartoonist chops, himself.

GROTH Fuller did?

DEITCH Yeah. There's a good

documentary about him where he goes all over this stuff that I saw on one of the independent movie channels. It was quite good. He had a pretty credible cartoon of himself as Brisbane's copy boy that was really just this side of professional. And also during WWII, his little diaries are full of in-depth cartoons.

GROTH *Boulevard of Broken Dreams* was this great conflation between invention and historical fact. Now, your father, who is Bert Simon in the story, also knew an old-time animator named Ted who had a nephew named Nathan.

DEITCH That's pure bullshit. I made that story up. I asked him, "You don't mind if I take a little license for the sake of a good yarn?" That's hogwash. Although I was thinking of the animator Jim Tyer at Terrytoons, who wasn't any kind of dysfunctional but this kind of wild-ass animator. You look at old Terrytoons from before my father, and some of them are "ho hum, ho hum," and then all of a sudden there'll be this wild, cartoony action sequence animated by Tyer that's not even sticking to the model sheets. It's just wild and wonderful. When my father discovered him at Terrytoons, he just prized him, and used him every conceivable way he could think of. That guy lived long enough to do some of the animation in *Fritz the Cat*, although I've never seen *Fritz the Cat*.

GROTH So that entire preface you wrote about you and your father going to visit this guy, and the mother putting the moves on your father and so forth, and which you said your father never remembered. That's all bullshit?

DEITCH That's all bullshit. *[Groth laughs.]* I remember once being with my father at the George Eastman house in the late '50s and we were at some cocktail party. My mother wasn't along, and I remember some woman putting the moves on him, even while I stood there. I might have been thinking about that a little bit. But he was not responding.

GROTH Well, we're going to get more deeply into bullshit with *Alias the Cat*, but *Boulevard of Broken Dreams* is broken down into three chapters. The second chapter is Ted Mishkin's story, and of course, it includes your usual sanitarium, as so many of your stories do…

DEITCH Yeah, well, I had experience there. Not that I've ever used much of it in any really accurate way.

GROTH Waldo is very much a delusional obsession with Ted.

DEITCH Yeah, I had already pioneered that with an early *Arcade* strip called "Mishkin's Folly," which I guess is supposed to be the nephew as an older guy, delusional.

GROTH I thought Doctor Reinman narrating the story was a great touch.

DEITCH His physical characteristics are based on the guy who ran New York Hospital, the one who saw me capture the escaping nut.

GROTH Is that right?

DEITCH Mister Mirback, yes.

GROTH Part Three is probably the most intricate: He goes into flashbacks and flash-forwards. Then you bring the story up to date. How carefully worked out was it when you started the first story for *Raw*? Did you have the second two chapters laid out in your head?

DEITCH No. Each one was carefully constructed before the work began, but I had no idea while I was working on the first section what the next section was gonna be like except maybe a general idea. I was drawing on a lot of different things. One inspiration that I got for some of the stuff in that last part was: When I was in L.A. doing *Hollywoodland*, one of the people I met was the widow of the experimental abstract animator Oskar Fischinger, and so at one point when Lillian is getting involved in all of her leftist stuff, I think she has a fling with some guy who's doing abstract animation, and it was based on Oskar Fischinger. His house was like—he'd been dead for a while—but it was almost like he was still there. All his paintings and whatnot were all around.

GROTH One of the fascinating things about your stuff is that it's all so organic. You can create these stories separately, but they all come together, because you're revisiting the same characters, and you have this Rashômon-like approach to the same material, where they overlap each other.

DEITCH It's because I want it to be real: at least, somehow plausibly real anyway. So I'm really believing it, so people reading it are gonna really believe it. I must be doing something fairly right, because I'm astonished at how much people read of mine that I made up that people are taking for true.

GROTH Because it does have the kind of historical plausibility to it.

DEITCH Some of it, yeah.

GROTH The tapestry is so dense that, not withstanding the visual stylization, there's a realism to it.

DEITCH I hope so.

GROTH Maybe a psychological realism?

DEITCH Yeah, something like that. It's gotta be real to me, somehow. I've gotta be really living it. The cornerstone of almost all good writing is that somehow it's got to be a plausible personal fantasy that's working for the person who's making it up.

GROTH As well as social or political realism. You even include the intimations of the blacklisting of the '50s.

DEITCH Yeah, I'd heard a ton about that. I wanted the thing to have a certain dramatic ring of truth. All that Hollywood stuff—my father didn't work for Disney when the '42 strike happened, but my best friend Tony Eastman's father and mother worked there. So I'd heard many, many, many stories about the Disney strike from veteran strikers involved in the thing. That was this pivotal moment in animation, and that's how the left-wing politics of Hollywood manifested itself in the animation industry. I mean, it was manifesting itself all over the place. You read that book, *Dutch*, the Ronald Reagan biography. You know, *he* almost joined the Communist Party himself. Covered it up later on. He wanted to, but they wouldn't let him. They just didn't think he was Commie material.

GROTH There's a social texture to

your work that gives it this incredible plausibility.

DEITCH The social thing has been seeping in since some time [in the] '90s: *Boulevard of Broken Dreams.* The other turning point is that's probably the beginning of where I started following the old writing saw "write what you know," whereas before I was going by the other writing saw, which I would define as "go where no man has gone before." Maybe now, what I'm doing, it's a little bit of a blend of both. ★

"I Could Relate Very Closely To Your Isolation":

A Conversation Between Daniel Clowes and Jonathan Lethem

Jonathan Lethem Hi. Thanks for coming. I'm quite excited to be in this unusual role for me, interviewing Dan, who I'm barely going to introduce, because I think everyone already knows who he is. I stumbled across a quote recently where Chris Ware said that Dan is easily the best cartoonist in America. I thought that stood very well for my own feelings. I was telling Dan downstairs about how much his work has come to mean for me personally, how it often feels like a kind of x-ray of what I'm feeling. I named a recent collection of short stories *Men and Cartoons* partly because I was thinking about Dan's work. I want to get to a few of these egg-heady questions I've written up…

This conversation with Daniel Clowes and Jonathan Lethem took place at the 4th annual MoCCA Art Festival, June 12, 2005. It was transcribed by Kent Worcester and published with the permission of the Museum of Comic and Cartoon Art (MoCCA).

Daniel Clowes Let's start with some softballs here.

LETHEM First I want to reminisce for a moment. Dan and I used to both live a few blocks from one another in Berkeley, without knowing each other.

CLOWES When did you leave?

LETHEM Over eight years ago. Actually, you and I were introduced to one another once in Berkeley. It was just before I left. It was at a party held by a collector type, very much like the subject of Dan's work and some of my short stories. Dan recognized the vanity license plates on my car. My car had a license plate that said, "Squalor." Dan said, "Oh yeah, I've seen your car around town."

I've been saving this story for you: After I left California eight years ago, I gave the car to my sister. She drove it for a couple of years, and it grew more and more true to its license plate. When she left she gave it away to a friend of hers who didn't have a car, which in California says a lot about the state of your self-existence and probably your self-esteem. Within a few months of my sister joining me in New York, she learned that Squalor had been used in an armed robbery of a fast food restaurant. Of course, the police found the car.

CLOWES Pretty easy to identify. Do you ever see the old hippie in Berkeley who had the license plate, "Rubber Saul"?

LETHEM Well, speaking of hippies, I wanted to ask you, while we were still keeping things anecdotal, why Berkeley? You've really made it your home. I lived

there for ten years and I always felt that I was in a love-hate relationship.

CLOWES I moved to Berkeley for the same reason that every cartoonist lives where they do, it's because my wife lived there. I had no real say in it. I couldn't say, "I need to be in Kansas, because that is where my cartooning muse lives." I liked Berkeley. I was living in Chicago at the time, and had a hideous marriage there and wanted to get out. That's the farthest point in the U.S., either Florida or Berkeley, and I opted for a "blue state."

I lived in New York for six years in the late Seventies–early Eighties. My life in Oakland is…I see, like, two people a day walking down the street. My wife is like, "did you see that guy walking down the street? Who is he? He doesn't belong around here." Today I walked out of my hotel in New York and there were more people in five seconds than I'd see in a decade back home. There were like legless transsexuals; gangs of people in thongs; endless amounts of crazy stuff. It was total sensory overload.

LETHEM You always mention Chicago, where you are from. I wonder though, looking at *Ice Storm*, and looking back at some of the other…

CLOWES *[Sarcastic]:* That's great promotion.

LETHEM I'm sorry, *Ice Harvest*…

CLOWES *Haven.*

LETHEM Maybe I can tell you about *Ice Harvest* if you like.

CLOWES My dad actually called me and said, "I read *Ice House*—it's great!"

LETHEM Looking at the nature of

encounters on the street, talking about people in thongs, and the number of people you run into in Oakland as opposed to New York. I wondered where Chicago fits. What was it like on the street when you were growing up?

CLOWES That's what my comics are, is my vision of that. It's interesting reading your books where you are setting things in Brooklyn and you have this Brooklyn world that is teeming with that 1970s Brooklyn life. As a kid growing up in Chicago I felt deeply jealous of New York. Chicago really is a second-tier, b-list city in many ways, and so, as a defense, I developed an affinity for stuff like *Cracked* magazine and the Monkees rather than the Beatles. But I always knew that one day, the moment I turned eighteen I was going to be in New York. It was the home of *Mad* magazine, comic books, and all the stuff I loved as a kid.

LETHEM And of course when you did move to New York you moved to Brooklyn, which is like the *Cracked* magazine of the City.

CLOWES I was from the South Side of Chicago, which is very much the Brooklyn of Chicago. It's not the Upper East Side. And Oakland is very much like that. I can't seem to get to the A-level.

LETHEM What strikes me looking at your work is an incredible poignancy in the grasping for senses of community and connection between your characters. There is some sort of curse, a logistical, architectural, infrastructural curse, placed on your characters by their environment that keeps them from

moving out of their private, fetishistic little orbits into some vision of community. It's ironic since California, especially Northern California, is predicated on being a place where you can realize a kind of utopia. I wonder if you, in your own life, you were reaching for some sort of community or whether you were always an observer of this fallen world.

CLOWES I've never felt comfortable. I never wanted to be in a community of people like me. As a kid I was a big baseball fan, but for a long time I never went to a game. I just listened on the radio. I would spend hours a day in my bedroom, listening to the radio. I finally went to a game and it was a bunch of drunk, fat guys. I felt such a sense of loss. I had such a horrible time. I read your essay about going to see *The Searchers*, and yelling at the audience for laughing at the film, and I could relate very closely to your alienation.

LETHEM This is one of the paradoxes that draws me to your work. You seem fascinated by the private appreciation of things that are meant for a mass audience. Your characters have developed a keen sense that they are the only ones who adequately and honestly appreciate these items. They have a private relationship with public artifacts.

CLOWES I have no response to that. *[audience laughs]* Yeah, I tend to focus on the personal minutiae in my room. I don't know if you have heard of the prose poet Russell Edson who published poems in the late 1960s, early 1970s. He wrote these interesting little prose poems. He's actually the son of a cartoonist named Gus Edson. His poems are about things like chairs and tables fighting with each other—the table is a hideous father figure who imposes his will on the poor chair. He plays out these little family dramas using inanimate objects. That's the kind of thing I relate to.

LETHEM I wondered if you were a fan of Steven Milhouser's novels?

CLOWES They have been recommended to me so many times, and I've never read him. They're hard to find.

LETHEM You'd dig him. He's attentive to the nature of childhood friendship—the bizarre intensity of childhood friendship where your best friend is also a kind of enemy, because they know too much about you. That's what his first two novels center on, and they're close to your own work in some ways.

CLOWES They are somewhat obscure, I'm guessing...

LETHEM Yes. He won a Pulitzer prize many years later, but that didn't help sell his early novels. But I wanted to talk to you about childhood and friendship. The lost utopia of childhood is such an intense subject in your work. Do you find that you make friendships of the same intensity as you used to? Do you?

CLOWES No, not at all. Do you?

LETHEM No. Have you kept your childhood friends?

CLOWES My childhood best friend might be in this room. He was at the Festival earlier. I looked at him and thought, "Who is that horrible looking old man?" He could say the same thing about me, obviously.

LETHEM The work that comes to mind of course is *Ghost World*. I've heard you say that you put some of your thoughts in the mouths of girls instead of boys because you thought the dialogue would be more palatable.

CLOWES It wasn't intentional. At first I was just working with the two characters, and then I found that I felt a lot more freedom to speak through these teenage girls than I would through my typical male stand-in character.

LETHEM I wanted to talk about the difference between comics and film, which you're in a privileged position to discuss. Your work began with film and television influences—not only the iconography but also the underlying storytelling modes. What limits do you encounter as you try to transfer modes or strategies from one medium to another?

CLOWES It is a very intuitive process. I've written a couple of scripts that have not been turned into movies, and I've thought, maybe I should turn these stories into comics. But then I realized that it would take as much work to adapt a screenplay into a comic book as it would to start from the beginning. It's a very different thing. I was going to ask you about the comic book you're writing for Marvel [Omega the Unknown]. I feel that your experience would be very useful for me to steal ideas from, in terms of how to navigate that leap from one medium to another.

LETHEM Well, I drew comic books as a teenager. I wanted to be a cartoonist. I had a character called Fig-Leaf Man. But I worked without any sense of form. Now that I'm writing a script for Marvel, I'm forced to be conscious of the differences between a novel and a comic. I'm trying to minimize the language, to place greater emphasis on the images.

CLOWES So much of writing a novel is in the descriptions—the narrator's complex view of the world. How do you capture that interior world in a comic book?

LETHEM There's no way I could ever verbally twist the artist into producing exactly what I see in my mind's eye. I have to accept that I'm working in a collaborative enterprise. And I'm in the artist's hands. The words are subsidiary. That's something you don't have to consider in creating your own comics.

CLOWES That is something I have to consider in writing these screenplays. I've worked on two films with Terry Zwigoff, and he is a very close friend and I know that he understands the visual language I'm describing. But when we worked on *Art School Confidential*, Terry had never been to art school so he was relying on me to a

certain extent to fill in the visual details. Certain things on the set would be just perfect, and other things were absolutely wrong. "What are you doing, you fools?" It's very easy to let these things get out of your control.

LETHEM For me, it comes up against the limits of how much visualization I can do. Even when I try to write visual language I can't account for every detail on the page. Every person who reads even the most verbal description of a scene by a novelist will come up with a completely different image in their minds eye.

CLOWES What would be your feeling if the artist came up with a page that seemed totally wrong?

LETHEM I'll cross that bridge when I come to it. I'm actually waiting for the first pages. I expect there's going to be a feedback process where I'll get to have some input.

CLOWES In Hollywood they would slam the door in your face.

LETHEM This reminds me of another thing I wanted to ask you about. You continue to produce works in installments, a little like Charles Dickens, which is no longer common for novelists. I'm curious about how much a project changes according to responses you get from readers once you've published an issue or two.

CLOWES Well, *Ice Haven* was produced as a single comic book. I had been reading a lot of Sunday comic sections from like 1950, and I loved how very different strips like *Blondie, Mutt and Jeff* and *Prince Valiant* would appear next to each other but would seem

interrelated because they were rooted in a specific comic strip language and printed on the same four-color press. I liked the idea of taking divergent styles and fitting them together. That was my initial impetus, but when it came back from the printer it didn't feel right as a comic "pamphlet." That's when I had the idea of redoing it as a book, and adding to it a little bit. I wanted it to have the feel of those old *Peanuts* or *Dennis the Menace* collections.

LETHEM One of the nicest things they've done with the *Peanuts* reissues is to retain that horizontal canvas.

CLOWES There is a stability to those horizontal pages.

LETHEM One of things I liked so much in *Ice Haven* is the way you sought to simultaneously break down the story into different comic book styles, but then pull it together into a single master narrative. Every one of the elements feeds into the larger story. It's like an anthology.

CLOWES It would be hard to do that in a novel.

LETHEM The only person who comes to mind is Italo Calvino, who wrote an entire novel made up of first chapters.

CLOWES Or *Ulysses*. But somehow the comfort of being able to flip through

a comic makes it easier to ground yourself in the story.

LETHEM One of the things I fastened onto in *Ice Haven* was the Rocky the Cave Man from 100,000 BC.

CLOWES My Fred Flintstone.

LETHEM And Rocky had this moment where he looks with enormous displeasure at a waterfall. The sound of it was so irritating. It seems to me a passing joke, but one that also disclosed something very specific about your themes. That's to say, one of the things you seem fascinated by is the way in which the natural world is decanted into artificiality by media and culture. But also the reverse: that our sentiment for the environment is a completely conjured, acculturated thing. It reminded me of this great story about the first European to see the Grand Canyon, who wrote back to his friends that he had seen something extraordinary but that he suspected he would be the last person ever to bother to travel all that way to see it. He had no way to guess that the Grand Canyon would be posited as something heartwarming and alluring, that would draw families from all over the globe to visit.

CLOWES Right. The idea that every German tourist will go to the Grand Canyon. Well, I wish I could take credit for that. Really, it was just a leitmotif throughout the story—all of these characters who are irritated by outside pressures and noises. The detective who holds the gun on the guy who plays music too loud in the motel room next door; the poet who is endlessly irritated by the children in the rock band next door. And Rocky is one of them. So I thought, what noise could irritate him? A rushing waterfall.

LETHEM What I like is that your explanation is empathetic—that in the space of that one page you really tried to get inside his emotions.

CLOWES Rocky is actually based on a pathetic tin-toy Flintstone knock-off I've had for years. I thought, "this poor guy deserves a comic."

LETHEM One thing I've thought about in this argument cultural meanings and natural ones, or the pursuit of natural ones, is the motif of pornography that runs through your work. A lot of your male characters are quite disconcerted by their responsiveness to porn, and unnerved by it. Your female characters are quite often delightfully agreeable. There's that lovely woman in *David Boring*, I'm forgetting her name…

CLOWES Wanda?

LETHEM She's pretty sweet and charming. Enid in *Ghost World* appropriates that fetish mask, that bondage trinket from the sex shop. And again there's this question of what's natural and what's cultural. On the level of sexuality you seem to be worrying over this question. Whether you can ever get back to some sort of pure natural state of your own sexual being.

CLOWES As a teenager I did not have a lot of sexual experience. It was certainly glamorized and glorified. I thought of women as being much more demure about the whole thing. Then going to art school I met art chicks

who turned my head around on that. To me, it's less exciting to depict sex as a free-for-all orgy, something that's healthy and abundantly available and not such a big deal. It's more interesting to have it seem fraught with tension and embarrassment. But that's just me, I guess.

LETHEM To stay on the same topic, but to make it a bit more general: I'm really interested in the emphasis you've given to mannerism and style. It's something that is there from the very beginning, with *Lloyd Lewellyn*, where you offer an extremely loving mockery of beatnik poseurdom. You seem to be drawn to articulate the innumerable ways that style reveals character. Random Wilder is another great example. He's cloaked himself in the mantle of the observer, the poet on the margins, yet very upstanding.

CLOWES The town eccentric.

LETHEM Again and again you seize on this place where people dress themselves up and deciding that, "Gee, 1957 is my year," or whatever year or style or them they embrace. And the observer characters like Enid seem to me to share your ambivalence. They mock human beings for this propensity but they're also drawn to it. Enid at one point says that she wishes find a way to dress that would be her own permanent solution. She could wear those clothes forever and her problems would be solved. It's as if she herself wants to become one of your beatnik poseurs.

CLOWES I certainly went through that as a kid. My parents were very much opposed to any kind of system,

whether it was a religious system or anything else. They didn't really impose any way of thinking on me. So I was always looking for some kind of system or crowd. Especially moving to New York. You have this feeling that you walk around any corner and there would be the coolest store in the world that sells, you know, rare Japanese comics from 1931. And then at a certain point I realized that a lot of cool things don't actually exist, and I realized that a lot of the comics that I liked, I didn't really like *them*, I liked what they promised or suggested. When I first saw EC comics I thought they were the greatest comics I had ever seen. And having read all of them, they're not great comics. They are wordy, poorly-written pulp stories that were often beautifully illustrated but don't necessarily work as comics. They are more like illustrated prose. But instead of being about idealized superheroes or funny animals or things like that, they were about bald men who wanted to stick their wives down the garbage disposal. Stories kids would not be able to relate to at all. And I thought, "This is the area I want to explore." But this may be completely tangential to your question.

LETHEM No; I love those remarks. I've always had this feeling that even if you finally get an issue of the *Fantastic Four* that you'd been hunting for for years it wouldn't satisfy. All it would do is imply some vast story that was going to be so satisfying only you could get all the issues and read them straight through. But you never quite did that.

CLOWES And even if you did, it never ended.

LETHEM And even if you did, it wasn't there. It was like something that existed between you and the author.

CLOWES The old bait and switch. We were constantly being encouraged to buy one more issue.

LETHEM But this isn't completely different from the way you can feel enormously stirred by a book on your shelf that you tell yourself you're going to read. You can spend ten years imagining the contents of, say, *Ulysses*. Sometimes that's much more inspiring than encountering the real book itself.

CLOWES It's a little like seeing *The Searchers* where you've already decided it will be a great movie.

LETHEM I want to go at this question of the role of comics in your imaginative life. I'm really stirred by the use of superheroes in your recent work, for example in the *Yellow Streak*, and the way the characters are obviously daring themselves to take this plunge to become vigilantes or superheroes, yet are unsure which way to go. How long can you work in this vocabulary? Would you go to Marvel or DC and invent a superhero?

CLOWES Up until the age of sixteen that would have been my ideal career path. Up until twenty-three I would have done it for the money. "Well, okay, I'll draw *Iron Fist*." After I started doing my own comics, I realized that drawing superheroes would be the ultimate drudgery. I would truly rather work in a jewelry shop or something. The thing that stuck with me about superheroes was not what happened in a specific issue of *The Inhumans* or anything, but remembering how I felt when I first saw single panels; single images. To me, all of superherodom is summed up

in those black light posters they made from blown-up Jack Kirby panels in the '60s. They were much stronger than any actual Marvel comics and they were embedded into some deep synapse in my brain. That's where all that came from. With *The Death Ray*, I wanted to take the idea of that kind of pop art image that has such strength to it and actually make a story that delivered on the promise of the image.

LETHEM There's a visual move that you make that I particularly love, where in individual panels the image looms so large that the word balloons are pushed away or cut short. It reminds me of a Walter Mosley project where he has persuaded Marvel to let him to republish early issues of the *Fantastic Four* in enormous blow-ups. The panels have a power to stir you as individual artworks. Of course, after Roy Lichtenstein this shouldn't come as a terrible surprise.

CLOWES I have the same feeling about certain film stills. I don't know if you had that experience of looking through old *Famous Monsters of Filmlands* as a kid. You would see a picture from an old vampire movie and think, "Good lord!" There's something so visceral about it. But when you see the movie you can see the image from the still in full motion and it has nothing. The power is gone.

LETHEM When you read books on early film history you can see stills from lost films. There's a single frame from an early version of *Frankenstein*…

CLOWES The Thomas Edison one?

LETHEM Yes, the Edison

Frankenstein. The most incredible image, and it creates this sense of a vast lost edifice, if only you could glimpse it. This again leads down to the path of fetishization, where the best song on any Dylan album is the one that didn't make it, and even better is the one that he played in the studio but didn't record.

CLOWES I think that's why I'm so slow to produce comics, because I feel that it has to be perfect. When I write screenplays I can start writing and I don't feel that it has to be perfect. But when I draw three panels I feel that they are etched in stone and I don't want to dissipate all that creative energy on something I'm going to have to change.

LETHEM Writing a few good paragraphs or pages in fiction locks you in a way similar to what you've described. I'm going to guess that it's easier for you to stay relaxed when you work on screenplays because, finally, movies are not a verbal product. It's a blueprint.

CLOWES It's a template. I actually try to write my screenplays as finished pieces because that's the only way I know how to work. But I have such tremendous leeway with the knowledge that I can change a character's name at the press of a button. I was curious about this. When you write your novels—there is such a density of detail in your descriptions. Is that a first draft thing, or you adding detail as you go along, or are you editing out detail as you go along?

LETHEM I've actually arrived at a method that I don't recommend to anyone. Quite seriously, I never describe

this process to my students when I teach writing. I feel very much like a cartoonist drawing panels now. I work very slowly and very permanently. I like to get everything…

CLOWES And in sequence?

LETHEM Right. And in sequence. Sequence is for me religious, because I want to write the book the way it will be read.

CLOWES And do you know what is going to happen when you start?

LETHEM I always have a sense. Not an outline, but images. I have a few key destinations. I have to get "there." I have to invent or improves everything to get to that point on the horizon.

CLOWES Walter Murch's book on film editing [*In the Blink of an Eye*] often talks about when they are having trouble with a stretch of a film they get rid of a big scene, and often all the little scenes that surround the larger scene are more effective because the big scene is implied rather than shown.

LETHEM I love that book.

CLOWES It's a great book.

LETHEM In a couple of minutes we'll turn to the audience for questions, but I wondered if there are any questions you wanted to ask me.

CLOWES I don't have a question, but I do have a general sense that we have crossed paths in our lives. We've lived on both coasts, and you've written about seeing *2001* at the Thalia, and I thought, "Oh yes, I recall seeing *2001* at the Thalia." I was reading your essay about the Hoyt-Schermerhorn subway station and when I went to art school at Pratt we had to change at Hoyt-Schermerhorn station. And that was such an exotic locale for a kid from the south side of Chicago. *Schermerhorn.* So I feel an affinity with your work, but I don't have a specific question about it.

LETHEM I've enjoyed the same feeling about the resonances in your work. I flatter myself thinking you're the comic book artist I would have turned out to be if I'd stayed with it.

CLOWES Just take the Famous Cartoonists correspondence course.

LETHEM Let's leave it there: a mutual admiration society. Let's see where the audience takes us.

Audience member 1 Last night we had a discussion about how you reveal the inner motivations of your characters without a lot of dialogue.

CLOWES In my own case the writing process is absolutely immediate and intuitive. If I think about it too much it becomes stagey and actorly. I tend to write off the top of my head. Then it's a process of editing it.

LETHEM Dan took the words out of my mouth. I always think of method acting as having a relationship to what I do. That's not to say that I can act. But when things are going well I'm thinking and feeling what these characters are thinking and feeling. If you had a candid camera at my desk you'd see me twitching and moving along with my characters.

CLOWES I dress up as my characters.

LETHEM The dreadful thing in dialogue is when it's used to convey information that everyone knows. That is when it falls dead to the ground.

CLOWES That's always the last resort; when you have a character say, "My mother the mayor, who died in 1984…"

Audience member 2 You talked about the fetishization of unrealized art, that the Dylan song you never hear is always the best. I assume that the relationship between the unrealized stories and ideas in your head and the stories you write is a complex one. Do you feel that the media you both work in present particular barriers to that?

CLOWES That was your question.

LETHEM Language is extremely artificial. One thing that I've come to realize is that I have to embrace the fact that I'm working with an absolute concoction. It's very strange to put words in sequence on a page. I'm not as close to the natural world, perhaps, as a musician, or a sculpture, or a painter. What I'm doing is embedded in many degrees of artificiality. And I've decided that's OK. That this is the magic of literature—that it's made of something kind of rarified. If you overheard insects twittering, that's what we're doing—twittering at each other. It is basic to the medium. I have felt an enormous satisfaction with each book I've completed, but also a terrifying sense of failure. Publication is like sweeping your workshop clean.

CLOWES That sounds good to me.

Audience member 3 When, how, and why do you stop, as a creator and as a collector?

CLOWES I have to consciously reject the impulse to have everything by everyone that I like. I have literally six feet of books by Robert Crumb, eighty percent of which reprint the same stories. Now I can go to the store and see a new collection of Crumb's work and think to myself that I don't need to buy this because I already have the stories at home. It's like being an alcoholic: "No, I won't have that first sip." It's in my nature to have it all.

LETHEM The rise of the Internet has sort of exploded the need to own the object.

CLOWES I find it so distressing, actually. I don't understand the idea of downloading rather than owning the object. There are a few things I've had to download because they were not available in any other format, and I've wound up making my own CD covers and pretending they're some rare limited release.

Audience member 4 I was wondering if I could turn the tables on you guys, and ask what it is like to be on the panel now and still doing art and writing that is so consciously pulling on what we think of as outsider media and genres.

CLOWES I don't particularly enjoy being up here, but you are good people and I love you all. It's hard not to be just self-deprecating and flippant. You look like an asshole saying, "Yes, what I do is one of the most important things anyone could possibly be doing." It's much easier to be an obnoxious creep on these things, but Mr. Lethem was so kind to come out on a horrible sweltering New York Sunday afternoon that I thought I had to try my best to answer his actual questions.

LETHEM I'm going to answer the other part of what you said. I usually dodge these questions of inside versus outside and the exalting of pop forms, the gentrification of pop forms, as opposed to the old resistance. One of the things I've tried to get comfortable with is understanding that though we are here all pretty much not dressed like Vulcans and we're having a conversation that dares to imagine that what we do is a serious kind of art, the resistance against that view is still quite strong. The reaction is tangible. You read hostile dissections of—I hate to use the word—postmodern culture, but that's what we're all indulging in here, and you can almost always discern some reactionary discomfort with the whole freight of enlightment culture, the egalitarian implications contained therein. In fact, attacks on postmodernism are attacks on modernism itself—on any appropriation of vernacular modes in high art, or, ultimately, on the mixing of different classes. So, I'd like to assert that we're doing something quite dangerous and important by caring about this stuff seriously. It's not just an embarrassing game but a kind of contest that's very alive right now and matters to me, anyway, tremendously.

CLOWES Very nice. That was beautiful. ★

Jonathan Lethem is the author of *Chronic City* and seven other novels.

Sammy Harkham & Dan Nadel

New Art Comics Panel

Tom Spurgeon I'm your host today, Tom Spurgeon from the site *The Comics Reporter*. Just looking at the title of the panel *[pause]*: You know it's been about 30 years, since *Raw, Love and Rockets*, the first wave of what we call modern arts and culture in comics. Do you guys object to there being a label of "new," or a label of difference? That you guys feel that there is something "new" about the comics you do, as opposed to comics of that era?

Dan Nadel Do I object to it being called "new?" Well, yeah, a little bit. There are two things. One: It's been going on a long time, but it's really a function of distribution and awareness. I could argue that aesthetically, what I publish is much closer to the traditional comics as they were invented commercially in America at the turn of the century, more than anything published by Marvel or DC. You could argue that Marvel and DC are these

This New Art Comics HeroesCon panel discussion took place June 21, 2008. It was moderated by Tom Spurgeon. The participants are Sammy Harkham, editor and publisher of *Kramer's Ergot*, Dan Nadel, owner/publisher of PictureBox: transcribed by Brittany Kusa.

anomalies and what we are doing is highly traditional.

Sammy Harkham It's true, actually, yeah.

SPURGEON Comics from back then—how do you feel a kinship with them?

NADEL Oh, well, take somebody like Johnny Ryan. He's a classic, chaotic gagman. It's like looking at Milt Gross from the '20s or something—well, with a lot of cocks. *[Laughter.]* And vaginas, but, that's a function of the underground. The underground came out of being traditional. I mean, Crumb's a traditionalist, if nothing else. I think a lot of the artists I publish feel a kinship with both the first part of the 20th century, and stuff like Moebius or Gary Panter and all those guys are also linked to traditional illustration forms.

HARKHAM Or storytelling.

NADEL Yeah, and storytelling.

HARKHAM I can't even read most Marvel or DC comics.

NADEL I can't either.

HARKHAM I don't know how to read them, I can't follow them, you know? Whereas I feel most of the cartoonists we work with, or enjoy, are very straightforward in most ways.

NADEL Very straightforward. I mean, I think of someone like Kevin Huizenga as being as straightforward as Frank King. Or as straightforward as Harry Tuthill. And I thought my book, *Art Out of Time*, illustrated this. There was tons of this semi-popular stuff; it was much weirder than anything either of us will ever publish.

It almost got weirder because it was under commercial constraints, because of the limitations. It's like having an anvil and it crushes something and it forms a new shape.

SPURGEON *Art Out of Time* is a book that Dan edited and compiled about several artists who worked in the mainstream of American comics, at a time in which there was no underground, there was no kind of outsider printing or press. So, there were people that were a little stranger than some of the artists we might remember better [who] worked in mainstream comics, to often very odd results. Well, and that book was a very popular book. It just shows how little we know of those traditions and how what you guys do connects.

NADEL And it skewed our vision of comics history, just by virtue of the handful of people who wrote it, and were guided by—rightfully so—their own interests in primarily straight-ahead genre material. So I think we have been hugely affected by the tastes, the personal tastes of Blackbeard, Goulart, Marschall, Spiegelman, who else is there?

HARKHAM *[Laughs.]* I can't think of anyone else.

NADEL I mean, without their personal tastes we would have an entirely different vision, version, of comic's history. For better or for worse, but we do owe them a huge debt for paving the way.

SPURGEON Let me back up a minute. I was wondering if maybe it would be helpful if we talked a little bit about how you got into publishing, the actual act of publishing other people's work, and maybe that would give us an insight as to how your story might be different than those guys from 30 years back. I mean, Sammy, how did you end up publishing?

HARKHAM I got into publishing because I really wanted to start releasing my comics and I didn't think there would be interest. I just didn't even think of sending them to Fantagraphics or Drawn & Quarterly or anything like that.

Basically, what it comes down to is that you have certain modes that are already in place within alternative comics, right? I would say that for the couple of years leading up to that, DQ (Drawn & Quarterly) and Fanta (Fantagraphics) were very much not looking at outside work. They were publishing great cartoonists who draw narrative comics, right, and they're amazing craftsmen, in a very clear way. Like, you can show a Seth drawing, a Seth page, or a Joe Matt page—or you know, any of that stuff, to someone, and they love it. And there started to be this weird thing emerging in the early aughts, 2000, 2001. Gaston (Dominguez-Letelier) at Meltdown Comics in L.A. gave me a Matt Brinkman mini. And it was the most bizarre thing, because it sort of reminded me of *Frank*, the Jim Woodring comic, but it was drawn so rough. But the guy clearly could draw. It just didn't look like anything I had seen before. And all of this stuff started to appear, not work that was promising, but work that was clearly there. You know, the work was clearly there, and

Fantagraphics didn't seem to be looking at it. They weren't publishing anybody new. They were canceling stuff. A couple of years before that, in '98, they canceled *Poot, Trailer Trash*, I know a third one, but I can't remember.

NADEL *Grit Bath.*

HARKHAM *Grit Bath.* And it just didn't feel like those guys were opening their eyes, at all, to a lot of interesting work. That maybe on the surface, looked a little weirder, but at the end, was very, very traditional. And that's where *Kramers* was like "I gotta do this." As a fan, *Kramers Ergot*—this anthology that I do—is totally like a fanzine. You know, it totally is. It's like I love it, I want other people to see it, and that's where it comes from, you know? I want to present it in a way that's exciting, in a good way. Because even *Blab!*, not to dis *Blab!*, but *Blab!* was already drifting into an area that aesthetically wasn't that interesting to me. Even though it was publishing artists that I liked. I just wanted to do something that was straightforward. I felt like nothing was just giving me the work, as far as professionally produced comics. So that is why I got into it. And it's interesting, after 2004, no, 2003, when *Kramers* 4 came out, I published Marc Bell. I published Brinkman. Both of those guys already had things going on with Highwater. Both those things came out that summer. And then, pretty soon after that, a lot of the artists I started working with, like Lauren (Weinstein) got a book with Alternative and Christopher (CF) started getting a lot more stuff. *MOME* started coming together, all these things started happening. So that when I wanted to do issue 5, cause I liked the way 4 turned out, it was almost like, there's no need to do it, because… when you're obviously… it wasn't *Kramers Ergot* that did it, it was a push. Like all that stuff was emerging, and it sort of needed to crack. *[To Nadel]* What were you going to say? Sorry.

NADEL Oh, no, no. I was just going to say it's interesting. I mean there are two things. One: that Fantagraphics emerged out of fandom and out of a love of really traditional comics, basically. So they found their tastes as they went and found their footing. Whereas we've been very lucky to essentially, both with *The Comics Journal* and through reading all this stuff, to arrive having found our feet very young. Not our full footing, but enough of a basis. In other words, the territory has been mapped out for us. We can be, like, here is Chester Brown—he takes one path. Chris Ware takes another path. Jim Woodring takes this path. That stuff didn't exist when Fanta (started)—I mean all that existed was Crumb and the underground, essentially. But, it wasn't that diverse a movement. Whereas the 20 years from 1980 to 2000, or whatever, have been insanely fertile and diverse, so it's interesting. But what's even more funny about that, despite the diversity, when Mat Brinkman and Brian Chippendale and Christopher Forgues and Paper Rad started to emerge, it was I think, very much, almost a reaction to feeling like things had calcified into this literary-fiction genre model.

HARKHAM And, it's not a dis.

NADEL No, it's not a dis. And I think what happened is that these guys kind of emerged with another set of concerns entirely separate from the kind of concerns that even the most diverse of the '80s and '90s artists all share. Totally separate from what, you know, Clowes, Ware, Woodring, the Hernandez Brothers—these guys that I love.

HARKHAM You know what it is also—it was amazing to read comics that had a lot of these weird genre elements, but not presented ironically, at all.

Whereas one of the things that always felt like, almost, a given, if you drew a comic in the mid-'90s, was that it had to be ironic that you were drawing a comic, and that you knew you were working in a lowbrow [medium]. That's what I always find so ironic about it. People are always like, "It's so obscure," when actually, its like, they're not actually the ones that are obscure. It's the guy doing the photo-reference Captain America that's actually way more obscure and out of touch. *[Laughter.]* These guys are fully in touch with mainline contemporary modernist art trends. It's kind of funny. Graphic design and everything else. They're way more in touch with the world than the Captain America guy. Trust me.

SPURGEON And Dan, is there any story about how you kind of ramped up your operation? Because you have a fairly sizeable concern now, which doesn't seem like—you were around—but it doesn't seem like you were publishing as much as you do now.

NADEL Yeah. I started *The Ganzfeld* with Tim Hodler and Patrick Smith in 2000. Well, the first issue was published in 2000, we started in '99. I had interned for Spiegelman and Françoise Mouly for almost a year.

HARKHAM What were they working on at that time?

NADEL The first *Little Lit* volume. I did a lot of production work on it. I packed boxes for them. I must say—I've never learned as much about anything in a shorter period of time, as I did working for them. Just by watching them move around and the things they were talking about, I learned almost my entire foundation of publishing knowledge just by watching them and listening. Eavesdropping.

SPURGEON Who were some of the other people that had that similar gig? Did James Sturm?

NADEL Sturm, Paul Karasik. Various people. There are others that I am forgetting right now. Bob Sikoryak was sort of my boss, like my supervisor. But, anyway, I did that. I published a couple of issues of *Ganzfeld*—three of them—up to '03. I got really interested in bookmaking in general and started a little packaging business with a guy and did a couple books. Three books for Abrams. The idea was that I really was just interested in visual books in general. *The Ganzfeld* was a representation of my interests in a broad spectrum. The first book I published, aside from *The Ganzfeld*, was a book called *The Wilco Book*, the rock band Wilco, and that really took off and sold a ton.

HARKHAM Was that a PictureBox? A solo PictureBox?

NADEL That was a solo PictureBox.

HARKHAM Oh, whoa, I didn't know that.

NADEL Well, we pitched it around as a packaging deal. We had a number of publishers. None of who offered us enough money to make it worthwhile. They all lowballed it, and we sold three or four times as much as anybody expected. So we did that, and then the idea for PictureBox was that it was going to be a visual book publishing concern on the model of old 1960s Abrams, just a wide variety of books. Visual books on art, graphics, music and then I throw in the comics as well, and bring that in. The first four books where representative of that. It was the Wilco Book, a book with the band the Black Dice, a book with the painter Trenton Doyle Hancock that I did for a gallery, and the Paper Rad book. Then, over the next year, because a bunch of editorial projects lagged, comics stuff kind of crested a little bit over, but now, that's calming down and it's going to be much more even. It's going to be much more just a third art, a third graphics, and a third comics. I'm trying to minimize the comics, actually, just because I live with comics all of the time in my head, and I want to work on things that are not comics. *[Laughter.]*

HARKHAM But, is that economically, or just for your brain?

NADEL It's financially and for my brain, and I'm really in some ways, as interested in contemporary art as I am in comics, or as interested in graphics as I am in comics. Comics is just some weird insane obsession that keeps killing me and dragging me down. *[Laughter.]* No, not really. I love it. But it does feel like a constant distraction sometimes in my brain. But, no, PictureBox right now is doing a lot of books for galleries, some for museums, and then some self-interest—like I'm doing a book on John Kricfalusi, I'm doing a book on Syd Mead, who's a great production designer. A major catalog for a biennial coming up in New Orleans called *Prospect. 1*, and so on.

HARKHAM And it helps your comics, as well.

NADEL It helps everything. It also creates a larger…Sammy has a good point, I mean, the reason that I'm doing what I'm doing right now is that it creates a larger context. I want the comics to live inside the larger context of visual art. There's no point for me to have comics over here, and everything else over there, because that isn't how I think about it. Most of the artists I publish are as engaged in other activities as they are in comics. Brian Chippendale is at least half, maybe 60 percent of the time, really a drummer, and 40 percent of the time a cartoonist. Same with Ben (Jones) and Christopher, all these guys.

BUENAVENTURA They're all drummers. *[Laughter.]*

NADEL They're all drumming. It's like a drum circle.

HARKHAM It's like a wild drum circle. *[Laughter.]*

NADEL They're all naked. Except for black socks.

HARKHAM And they all take breaks for hackey-sack and comics.

NADEL Well there's some hackey-sack and then some paddleball.

HARKHAM Dude, it's a dark circle.

SPURGEON I guess the natural follow-up question—I don't want to spend a ton of time on this—there's the obvious business question. How you keep these things viable concerns in a business sense, or how you don't lose so much money that you can't do it anymore? Or, how you make money, even? I wonder if all of you could give me a sense of what its like right now in terms of, who's buying the books, where are you able to sell them? What is specifically difficult about right now? Maybe not this weekend… *[Laughter.]*

NADEL The rampant indifference is hard.

HARKHAM I understand it. By the way—this is aside—I get it. I don't begrudge superhero fans for not even looking at the work. It's not their world. It's like music, or something. You don't expect someone who's into jazz music to automatically like your drum circle CD-R. *[Laughter.]*

NADEL I know. Drum circles are tough to get into. ★

Sammy Harkham was born in 1980 in Los Angeles. He is the editor of *Kramers Ergot*, the latest volume of which was published by Buenaventura Press. Most recently he guest-edited *The Simpsons' Treehouse of Horror* #15, published by Bongo Comics, and is working on his solo comic book, *Crickets* #3.

Acknowledgements

Well, here it is, just in time to save the publishing industry: *The Best American Comics Criticism* anthology. Since I wrote so little of what comprises this book, I'm more indebted than most "acknowledgers." Bear with me on this long list of notable folks who contributed their time and effort and material.

First, my thanks to all of our contributors for allowing me to reprint, and in a few cases, debut their work. Most of the material herein comes from a number of publications, interviews, conventions, blogs and websites. Rarely do any of those venues provide good compensation, so what one will find is a collection of artists and writers inspired by a love of comics: many thanks to them for sharing that inspiration, a gift itself above and beyond the work.

One can check the table of contents to see the list of people to whom I am indebted. What it

won't show is the time many of them spent revising, re-editing, rereading new transcripts, asking publishers to release us from licensing and reprint fees (!), choosing artwork, and sending me so many spot-on recommendations for other excellent writers. Mssrs Ware, Parille, Seth, and Harvey updated their pieces for publication here. Clowes, Lethem, Harkham, and Nadel too, I mention, for allowing their improvised remarks to be published, but also for proofing them. Jeet Heer, for some of the above reasons, but I am especially thankful for his graceful contributor bio on behalf of John Updike, who is no longer with us.

For the original piece that appears as our cover, I'd like to thank Drew Friedman, an inspiring talent for me since the 1980s. I merely suggested to Drew that he render what the comic-book critics of America might look like, and the result is front and center. Any and all complaints from comics critics can be directed to the publisher. Apologies, of course, are offered to Charles Burns and the earnest staffers of *The Believer* for the appropriation of their iconic covers. Their complaints are taken for granted.

I'd like to thank my publishers at Fantagraphics – Gary Groth, Kim Thompson, and Eric Reynolds for backing me in putting this collection together. They more than anyone know the importance of what's going on in the lit-comics era, but that doesn't mean they're obligated to put out a book about it. Alexa Koenings, thank you for your elegant design! I also want to thank *Comics Journal* editor Kristy Valenti and Kim Thompson (2x!) for their copy-editing and formatting of so much material from so many sources into a single cohesive volume, and Jessica Lona and Ian Burns for their proofreading. Kim's patience in particular comes to mind in continually correcting the missing "s" in my spellings of Rorschach's name, or my adding the extra "e" in "Wimbledon Green." My endless series of incorrect titles and mistaken dates must have made him wonder how I managed to get myself the job of "editor" on this book more than once.

One job in journalism that never gets fun is transcribing: an excellent comics critic, Kent Worcester, is owed a great debt for transcribing the Lethem and Clowes conversation. My thanks for Adam Hayes and Jonathan Ross of Hot Sauce TV in the UK for not only allowing the Alan Moore transcript to be used, but providing the text – saving many hours of work for Fanta staffers. At Fanta, Brittany Kusa transcribed the New Art Comics panel, and Jessica Lona for checked the transcript of the Steve Ditko documentary against what was edited and aired. It literally saved this editor days of work when I had no days. Thanks!

Thanks too to the publishers, editors, bloggers, and executives who gave permission to use material or helped facilitate that: Tom Spurgeon of *The Comics Reporter*, Lloyd Wise at *Bookforum*, Robert Goodin at Robot Publishing, Mike Richardson andAmy Huey at Dark Horse, Rebecca Rosen and Peggy Burns at Drawn & Quarterly, Patrick Hederman at *The New York Review of Books*, Shakira Hodges at *The New York Times*, Ken Schneider and Jennifer Rowley at Random House, Victoria Fox and Melissa Brandt at Farrar, Straus, and Giroux, Alex Segura at DC Comics, Denis Kitchen at the

Eisner Studios, Adam Hayes and Jonathan Ross at Hot Sauce TV (UK). Denis has been helpful to me on a number of stories dating back to my college days in the 1980s, and as always, my stuff looks better for his help.

On a personal note: I'd like to thank my wife Bridie Macdonald, for her endless patience and support for five years. Honestly, you wouldn't have this book without her. For years of help and support on any number of projects and endless favors, I add Drew Friedman, Kathy Bidus, Kaz, Linda Marotta, Daniel and Erika Clowes, Todd Hignite, Harry Ralston, Glenn Bray and Lena Zwalve, Robert Nedelkoff, FX Feeney, and my coffee-house table partner Brian Doherty. Brian and I are kind of like junior-high lab partners, with comics as our frog. In Los Angeles, I cite Gaston Dominguez-Letelier and the staffs of Meltdown Comics, Skylight Books, and especially the House of Pies. The House of Pies has gotten used to me, sitting in a booth for hours on end with my laptop, taking advantage of their policy of endless refills of Diet Coke and iced tea. I add this book to the many other literary works rumored to have been devised on the premises.

And one disacknowledgement: I offer it to a guy at *The New York Times*, who shall remain nameless, and hereafter be known as the Slouch, so that Gray Lady's libel lawyers need not be consulted. The Slouch blew off this project to such an extent that I was not able to use a piece of my own from the paper of record. When all the numbers finally came together, we didn't have the money for it, and went with some of the excellent *New York Times* pieces you'll find herein. In fact, the Slouch actually quit his job at one point and my requests went unanswered and unfulfilled for months until his very helpful replacement took over. I don't know where this fellow's career in the newspaper racket will take him, but no doubt he'll go right to the top of the ladder in charge of hiring comics critics. I offer a big "no thank you" to you, sir. ★

Art Credits

Comics Tragedy:
Is the Superhero Invulnerable?

Page 24: panel from *Jimmy Corrigan: The Smartest Kid on Earth*. [©2000 F. C. Ware]

Page 27: sequence from *Understanding Comics*. [©2000 Scott McCloud]

Page 29: panel from *Jimmy Corrigan: The Smartest Kid on Earth*. [©2000 F. C. Ware]

Graphic Novels:
Can You Hear The Trucks?

Page 34: panel from *The Book of Genesis Illustrated by R. Crumb*. [©2009 Robert Crumb]

9/11 Comics

Page 37: page from *9-11: Artists Respond* Vol. 1. [©2002 Frank Miller]

Page 42: Rick Veitch wrote and Sergio Aragonés drew this page from "I Never Thought of Myself as a Hero…" in *9-11: The World's Finest Comic Book Writers & Artists Tell Stories to Remember* (Vol. 2). [©2002 DC Comics]

Page 44: sequence from "War of the Worlds" in *World War 3 Illustrated* #32. [©2001 Peter Kuper]

Page 45: splash page, by Randy Queen with Sarah Oates and Brett Evans, from *A Moment of Silence*. [©2001 Marvel Characters, Inc.]

Pages 48-49: sequence from *In the Shadow of No Towers*. [©2004 Art Spiegelman]

American Boys
(excerpt from *Men of Tomorrow*)

Page 52: this panel, drawn by Bob

Kane, is from "The Bat-Man: The Case of the Chemical Syndicate" in *Detective Comics* #27 (May 1939). [©1939 DC Comics]

Page 57: sequence from *To the Heart of the Storm*. [©1991 Will Eisner]

Page 63: Jerry Siegel wrote and Joe Shuster drew this panel from *Action Comics* #5 (October 1938). [©1938 DC Comics]

"Then Let Us Commit Them"
(excerpt from *The Ten-Cent Plague*)

Page 69: this panel, artist and writer uncredited, is from "No Body's Dummy" in *Pep Comics* #64 (November 1947). [™©1947 Archie Comics Publications]

Pages 72-73: sequence from Chester Gould's Oct. 24, 1943 *Dick Tracy* strip. [©2009 Tribune Media Services, Inc.]

Page 74: Charles Moulton wrote and Harry G. Peter drew this page from *Sensation Comics* #31 (July 1944). [©1944 DC Comics]

High Standards
(excerpt from *Wimbledon Green*)

These pages are excerpted from *Wimbledon Green*. [©2005 Seth]

The Walk Through the Rain:
Will Eisner and Frank Miller in conversation (excerpt from *Eisner/Miller*)

Page 86: splash page from *300*. [©1999 Frank Miller, Inc.]
Page 88: splash page from *Sin City: Family Values*. [©1997 Frank Miller]
Page 89: panel from *Fagin the Jew*. [©2003 Will Eisner]
Page 90: splash page from the Jan. 4, 1948 *Spirit* strip. [©1948 Will Eisner]

Will Eisner and Frank Miller:
The Raconteurs (excerpt from *Reading Comics*)

Page 93: art from *A Contract with God and Other Tenement Stories*. [©1996 Will Eisner]
Page 97: Frank Miller penciled and Klaus Janson inked this cover. [©1982 Marvel Comics Group]
Page 100: Frank Miller wrote and penciled this page from *Batman: The Dark Knight Returns*. Klaus Janson inked it. [©1986 DC Comics]
Page 102: From Miller's *Batman: The Dark Knight Strikes Again* (*DK2*). [©2002 DC Comics]

"A Great Bamboozler":
Howard Chaykin on Will Eisner

Page 104: Will Eisner and Bob Powell wrote, and Chuck Cuidera drew, "The Origin of Blackhawk" in *Military Comics* #1 (August 1941). [©1941 DC Comics]
Page 105: Cover to *Blackhawk Book Two: Red Hawk* drawn by Chaykin. [©1988 DC Comics]
Page 109: Howard Chaykin drew this *American Flagg!* #11 cover (August 1984). [©1984 Howard Chaykin, Inc.]

"There is White and There is Black and There is Nothing In Between"
(excerpt from *In Search of Steve Ditko*)

Page 114: this sequence, which Stan Lee wrote and Steve Ditko drew, is from "The Pincers of Power!" in *Strange Tales* #140 (January 1966). [©1966 Marvel Characters, Inc.]

Spider-Man Sucks

Page 117: this panel, which Stan Lee wrote and Steve Ditko drew, is from "Spider-Man goes Mad!" in *The Amazing Spider-Man* #24 (May 1965). [©1965 Marvel Characters, Inc.]
Page 119: Stan Lee wrote, John Romita penciled, and Mike Esposito inked this sequence from *Amazing Spider-Man* #50 (July 1967). [©1967 Marvel Characters, Inc.]

Letter of the Law:
Ditko's Mr. A Period

Page 122: Steve Ditko wrote and drew this Mr. A page. [©1972 Steve Ditko]
Page 124: sequence from Ditko's "Masquerade." [©1973 Steve Ditko]
Page 126: panel from Ditko's "Mr. A: Money." [©1968 Steve Ditko]
Page 127: this undated splash page is by Steve Ditko. [©Steve Ditko]

Like a Prairie Fire, Even Hotter:
Harold Gray, Politics, and the Not-So-Funny Funnies

Page 129: panel from Harold Gray's March 12, 1926 *Little Orphan Annie* strip. [©2009 Tribune Media Services, Inc.]

Drawn from Life

Page 133: this panel is from a Frank King *Gasoline Alley* strip reprinted in *Drawn & Quarterly* #4. [©1922, 1923, 1924, 1925 Tribune Media Services]
Page 138: the Jan. 15, 1921 *Gasoline Alley* strip. [©1921 Tribune Media Services]
Page 139: the April 13, 1921 *Gasoline Alley* strip. [©1921 Tribune Media Services]
Page 143: the April, 1926 *Gasoline Alley* strip. [©1926 Tribune Media Services]

George Herriman:
The Cat in the Hat

Page 144: George Herriman's Oct. 2, 1932 *Krazy Kat* strip. [©1932 King Features Syndicate, Inc.]
Page 146: the May 23, 1926 *Krazy Kat* strip. [©1926 King Features Syndicate,

Inc.]
Page 150: the Oct. 6, 1935 *Krazy Kat* strip. [©1935 King Features Syndicate, Inc.]

Thurber's Art
(excerpt from Introduction to *Is Sex Necessary?*)

Pages 154-155: panels from *Thurber: Writings and Drawings* (1996). [©1996 James Thurber Estate]

John Stanley's Teen Trilogy

Page 157: John Stanley panel from *Thirteen Going on Eighteen*.
Page 158: from *Dunc and Loo* #8.
Page 163: sequence from *Dunc and Loo*.
Page 164-165: sequence from *Dunc and Loo*.
Page 167: from *Kookie*.
Page 168-169: from *Thirteen Going on Eighteen*, written by John Stanley and drawn by an uncredited artist.
Page 170: from *Thirteen Going on Eighteen*.
Page 173: from *Thirteen Going on Eighteen*.
Page 174: Judy Jr. in *Thirteen Going on Eighteen*.

Schulz's Gifts

Page 176: Charles Schulz's Feb. 16, 1958 *Peanuts* strip. [©1958 United Features Syndicate, Inc.]
Page 177: the Aug. 12, 1957 strip. [©1958 United Features Syndicate, Inc.]

"A Mozart of Zaniness"

Page 179: Will Elder drew and Harvey Kurtzman wrote this panel from "L'L Ab'R," which ran in *Trump* #1 (January 1957). [©1957 Playboy]

"What's This One About?"
A Re-Reader's Guide to Daniel Clowes
David Boring

Pages 182-202: images in this chapter are from *David Boring*. [©2000 Daniel Clowes]

A Child's Garden of Detritus:
The Cartoon Chronicles of Lynda Barry

Page 203: Maybonne in "Choreography" in *Come Over, Come Over*. [©1990 Lynda Barry]
Page 204: sequence from *Big Ideas*. [©1993 Lynda Barry]
Page 208: sequence from *The Greatest*

of Marlys. [©1999 Lynda Barry]

Diary of a Teenage Rake:
An Appreciation of Phoebe Gloeckner's Masterpiece

Page 210: Minnie and Tabitha in *Diary of a Teenage Girl.* [©2002 Phoebe Gloeckner]
Page 211: sequence from *Diary of a Teenage Girl.* [©2002 Phoebe Gloeckner]
Page 214: Minnie and Kimmie in *Diary of a Teenage Girl.* [©2002 Phoebe Gloeckner]

What Went Wrong With the Masters Show

Page 216: cover to *Masters of American Comics*: image [©2005 The Estate of George Herriman], designed by Lorraine Wilde with Victoria Lam and Stuart Smith/Green Dragon Office, Los Angeles.
Page 217: Milton Caniff's April 12, 1944 *Terry and the Pirates* strip. [©1944 Tribune Media Services, Inc.]
Page 220: panel from *Jimbo in Purgatory.* [©2001 Gary Panter]

Töpffer in English

Page 224: sequence from Töpffer's "M. Jabot" in David Kunzle's *Rodolphe Töpffer: The Complete Comic Strips.* [©2007 University Press of Mississippi]
Page 227: sequence from Töpffer's "Monsieur Pencil Paris" in David Kunzle's *Rodolphe Töpffer: The Complete Comic Strips.* [©2007 University Press of Mississippi]

Epileptic:
Disorder in the House

Page 231-233: images from David B.'s *Epileptic.* [©2005 L'Association]

Fun Home:
Literary Cartooning in a Graphic Novel

Pages 234-241: All images in this chapter are from *Fun Home.* [©2006 Alison Bechdel]

Epics
(Kirby's Fourth World Omnibus; Kirby: King of Comics; Age of Bronze; Y: The Last Man)

Page 242: sequence is from "The Omega Effect!!" in *The Forever People* #6 (January 1972), written and penciled by Jack Kirby and inked by Mike Royer. [©1972 DC Comics]
Page 247: sequence from *Age of Bronze: Sacrifice.* [©2004 Eric Shanower]
Page 248: sequence from *Y: The Last Man* Vol. 10: *Whys and Wherefores,* which was written by Brian K. Vaughan, penciled by Pia Guerra and inked by José Marzán, Jr. [©2008 DC Comics]
Page 249: sequence from "The Hunger Dogs!" in *DC Graphic Novel* #4 (March 1985), which was written and penciled by Jack Kirby and inked by D. Bruce Berry, Mike Royer and Greg Theakston. [©1985 DC Comics]

Was this Review Helpful to You?:
Joe Matt's *Spent*

Pages 250-255 All images in this chapter are from Joe Matt's *Spent.* [©2007 Joe Matt]

C. Spinoza's *Pacho Clokey*

Pages 257-273 C. Spinoza's *Pacho Clokey* is by Nate Gruenwald. [©2000 Pachoclo Inc.]

Persian Miniatures:
Marjane Satrapi

Page 276: panel from Marjane Satrapi's *The Complete Persepolis.* [©2003 L'Association]
Page 277: panel from Carl Barks' "Ancient Persia" in *Donald Duck Four Color* #275 (May 1950). [©1950 The Walt Disney Company]
Page 278: from *The Complete Persepolis.* [©2003 L'Association]

"It Keeps Ending Up Looking Like It Was Drawn By Me"
An Interview With Chester Brown

Pages 285-298: all images in this chapter are from *Louis Riel.* [©2003 Chester Brown]

"I Feel My Zaniness Is Based on Truth"
An Interview With Will Elder

Page 297: this panel from "The Artist" (September 1963), which Harvey Kurtzman wrote and Will Elder drew, is from *Playboy's Little Annie Fanny* Vol. 1: 1962-1970. [©1963 Playboy]
Page 301: [©2009 The Estate of Will Elder]
Page 305: a page from "Mickey

Rodent" in *Mad* #19 (January 1955). [©1955 EC Publications, Inc.]

"My Strategy Was to Create the Opposite"
An Interview With Yoshihiro Tatsumi

Page 312: panel from "Occupied" in *Abandon the Old in Tokyo.* [©2006 Yoshihiro Tatsumi]
Page 317: page from the titular story in *The Push Man.* [©2005 Yoshihiro Tatsumi]
Page 319: panel from "Beloved Monkey" in *Abandon the Old in Tokyo.* [©2006 Yoshihiro Tatsumi]

"It Gotta Be Real to Me, Somehow"
An Interview With Kim Deitch

Page 322: Deitch with his signature characters. [©1989 Kim Deitch]
Page 327: page from *Boulevard of Broken Dreams.* [©2002 Kim Deitch]

"I Could Relate Very Closely To Your Alienation"
A Conversation Between Daniel Clowes and Jonathan Lethem

Page 333: panel from *Ice Haven.* [©2005 Daniel G. Clowes]
Page 338: panel from *Omega the Unknown* #7 (June 2008) written by Jonathan Lethem and Karl Rusnak and drawn by Gary Panter. [©2008 Marvel Characters, Inc.]
Page 340: panel from *Ice Haven.* [©2005 Daniel G. Clowes]
Page 342: sequence from *Eightball* #23: *The Death Ray.* [©2004 Daniel G. Clowes]

New Art Comics Panel
Sammy Harkham and Dan Nadel

Page 347: panel from "Fuck You" by Paper Rad in *Kramers Ergot* Vol. 6. [©2006 Paper Rad]

Index

B

C

D

W

X

Y

Z